The
BEST POSSIBLE
IMMIGRANTS

POLITICS AND CULTURE IN MODERN AMERICA

Series Editors:
Margot Canaday, Glenda Gilmore,
Michael Kazin, Stephen Pitti, Thomas J. Sugrue

Volumes in the series narrate and analyze political and social change in the broadest dimensions from 1865 to the present, including ideas about the ways people have sought and wielded power in the public sphere and the language and institutions of politics at all levels—local, national, and transnational. The series is motivated by a desire to reverse the fragmentation of modern U.S. history and to encourage synthetic perspectives on social movements and the state, on gender, race, and labor, and on intellectual history and popular culture.

The
BEST POSSIBLE
IMMIGRANTS

INTERNATIONAL ADOPTION
and the
AMERICAN FAMILY

Rachel Rains Winslow

PENN

UNIVERSITY OF PENNSYLVANIA PRESS

PHILADELPHIA

Published by
University of Pennsylvania Press
Philadelphia, Pennsylvania 19104-4112
www.upenn.edu/pennpress

Printed in the United States of America
on acid-free paper

1 3 5 7 9 10 8 6 4 2

Library of Congress Cataloging-in-Publication Data
ISBN 978-0-8122-4910-1

Amy, Erin, Kerry, Mesha, Andria, Kimberly, Jennifer, Stacy, Kari, and Val.
Without you, this project would have never existed.

CONTENTS

ABBREVIATIONS

AHEPA	American Hellenic Educational Progressive Association
CCAC	Citizens' Committee on Adoption of Children in California
CORDS	Civil Operations and Revolutionary Development Support
CWLA	Child Welfare League of America
FAP	Family Assistance Plan
FCVN	Friends of Children of Vietnam
FFAC	Friends for All Children
GVN	Government of South Vietnam
HAP	Holt Adoption Program
INS	Immigration and Naturalization Services
ISS	International Social Service-American Branch
IVAC	Interagency Vietnam Adoption Committee
MAC-V	Military Assistance Command-Vietnam
NAACP	National Foundation for the Advancement of Colored People
NABSW	National Association of Black Social Workers
NCAPO	National Council of Adoptive Parents Organizations
NCSW	National Conference of Social Work
NGO	Nongovernmental organization
NVA	North Vietnamese army
RRA	Refugee Review Act
SCA	Bureau of Security and Consular Affairs
UNRRA	UN Relief and Rehabilitation Administration
USAID	U.S. Agency for International Development
USCB	U.S. Children's Bureau
USCOM	U.S. Committee for the Care of European Children
WAIF	World Adoption International Fund

The Interest of Many

The Foundations of International Adoption

I N TWENTY-FIRST-CENTURY AMERICA, international adoption has become an integral and invisible part of the nation's social and cultural fabric. From popular icons like Madonna to the family down the street, adoptive parents have come to populate the front covers of magazines as well as middle-class neighborhoods. Indeed, the numbers reinforce its ubiquity and importance. International adoptions doubled in the 1990s and by 2014 reached an all-time high of 22,991. These realities have led some to label the United States an "adoption nation."[1]

Yet, according to more recent statistics, America's status as an "adoption nation" appears insecure. In 2013, U.S. citizens adopted only 7,092 children from other nations—a 69 percent decline since 2004. When the State Department released these figures, all the major news organizations heralded the institution's "steep" and "drastic" decline. The foremost question was unsurprising: what was the cause? Were stricter international regulations from the Hague Convention to blame? Did agencies provide too little oversight, leading countries like Russia to question U.S. procedure and curb their overseas programs? Was it because of foreign corruption, which left children's paperwork in administrative limbo? Or did increased demand from the evangelical Christian adoption movement prompt heightened scrutiny from foreign governments? Following the news storm, a few members of Congress issued press releases that assured constituents they were committed to maintaining robust international adoption programs. Proposed legislation included the Children in Families First Act. The bill, still under debate, aims to ensure a family for every child through more favorable international adoption laws and stricter control on foreign aid earmarked for adoption services. In other words, a handful of legislators wanted to ensure that international adoption remained a viable option for U.S. families.[2]

Declines in foreign adoptions are not new. Neither are the conflicts between sending and receiving nations, nor the internecine squabbles between public and private adoption interests. What no one suggested was that these recent events were part of a much longer story. A host of competing perspectives have long governed the formation and success of an international adoption tradition in the United States. The factions and processes partly responsible for current conditions are a messy, complicated negotiation that spans from the early Cold War to the U.S. withdrawal from Vietnam. While not an easily distillable story, it's an illuminating one that involves the influence of private institutions, adoptive parents' power as constituents, and Americans' captivation with foreign orphans.

From 1947 to 1975, U.S. citizens adopted an estimated 35,000 children from overseas. Although only a small percentage of the nonrelative adoptions that occurred in this period, these adoptions were widely publicized and highly visible.[3] Over this period, children came from a wide variety of nations in Europe, Asia, South America, and the Caribbean, with most adoptees arriving from South Korea, South Vietnam, Germany, Greece, and Italy. Wars in Europe and Asia had left thousands of children orphaned, many the offspring of American soldiers. Fearful that communist powers would frame the crisis as a failure of democracy, policymakers relaxed immigration laws for these largely nonwhite orphans and allowed them into the United States as refugees.[4] War orphans and "GI babies"—the offspring of U.S. soldiers and foreign women—received the most press in the United States. Yet from the onset American couples were eager to adopt all types of foreign children, regardless whether they had surviving parents or connections to the military. Expectant couples, especially mothers, bombarded social welfare agencies and political leaders with appeals.

Focusing on adoptions to the United States from Greece, South Korea, and South Vietnam, this book examines how the adoption of foreign children evolved beyond an episodic response to crises in the 1940s to become an enduring and embedded American institution by the 1970s. In an era when racial categories seemed fixed, families appeared homogeneous, and adoption remained hidden, what drove the expansion and institutionalization of a system that brought foreign, often nonwhite children into the homes of predominantly white, middle-class citizens? In fact, international

adoption succeeded as a long-term solution to child welfare not because it
was in the interest of one group, but rather because it was in the interest of
many. The system came about through the work of governments (national,
state, and foreign); social welfare professionals; volunteers (social entrepreneurs, religious humanitarians, and NGOs); national and local media;
adoptive parents; and prospective adoptive parents. These combined efforts
contributed to the making of a system that would embrace adoption as a
response to a host of overseas social welfare emergencies. It was, in short, a
wide-ranging social, cultural, and political project.

What united this disparate and, at times, unlikely coalition was its focus.
Destitute young children—whether neglected European war orphans,
ostracized Korean GI babies, or toddlers in squalid Vietnamese orphanages
—pricked the collective conscience of post-World War II America. The
narratives of these orphans as told by legislators, adoptive parents, social
workers, humanitarians, and the media circulated culturally, legitimizing
foreign children's place in American families and justifying expansive policies in support of foreign adoptees. In the view of many legislators, orphans
made ideal immigrants and citizens because "of their youth, flexibility, and
lack of ties to any other cultures." Such traits bolstered officials' conviction
that children could be transplanted with great public success, since "a child
in need does not know or care about national boundaries," as one social
welfare official commented. Christened "the best possible immigrants" by
the Senate Subcommittee on Immigration, international adoptees were so
highly desired by American families that U.S. immigration law would
broaden the definition of orphan in 1953 to include children with two living
parents.[5]

Despite the shared aim, however, such a diverse assembly of interests
signaled the intense conflicts that shaped international adoption's formative
decades and shed light on the nature of the U.S. social welfare system. In
the post-World War II era, both U.S. child welfare and international relief
programs relied heavily on private agencies and volunteers to serve the
public good. This public-private collaboration was mutually beneficial: private agencies gained access to public funding, and state projects used the
altruistic perception of voluntarism to burnish their image. From the New
Deal to the Great Society, as the state's role expanded in some ways and
contracted in others, this public-private infrastructure proved adaptable. It
fostered an environment where NGOs and volunteers catered to the interests of individual clients, minimized bureaucracy, and avoided regulations.[6]

Certainly, the state had a long history of relying on the private sector to supply social relief. In the late nineteenth and early twentieth centuries, Progressive reformers joined with local and state governments to regulate public health, punish criminals, and protect children, blurring the lines between public and private power. Public officials, for instance, empowered anticruelty crusaders to act as arms of the state by arresting alleged child abusers and bringing them before magistrates. Even as the state began to provide some direct aid at the insistence of maternalist advocates, such as through mother's pensions, the system upheld philanthropies and mutual aid societies as the best mechanisms to determine those "worthy" of relief. In some narratives, this private influence diminished under an expanded New Deal state. But historians have shown how the U.S. welfare system sustained a multifaceted configuration of public and private interests that corporations, labor, citizens-based movements, and the state maintained were essential to economic security. Indeed, as the case of employee benefits clearly illustrates, even with more expansive federal programs such as social security, the public system continued by design to require private supplementation.[7]

International adoption drew attention to this public-private collaboration. Nonstate actors and social entrepreneurs responded nimbly to crises, developing informal and improvisational policies to provide immediate child welfare solutions. Indeed, voluntary leadership was extremely popular with prospective adoptive parents, a group largely composed of middle-class women who voted with their dollars by choosing the services of private adoption agencies.[8] Legislators thus enacted few policies that limited either the power or the on-the-ground policymaking of volunteers. By offering legitimacy and funding to an array of private interests, all with competing visions of child saving, the state unwittingly perpetuated a series of conflicts among these private interests: those who viewed international adoption as under the jurisdiction of professional social work; those who viewed international adoption as an act of humanitarianism, religious faith, and/or relief; and those who viewed international adoption as a solution to the domestic demand for "adoptable" babies.

Over time, these discrete approaches to child saving hardened into models, or paradigms, that governed the adoption process. There were four paradigms of child saving that persisted from the mid-1940s to the mid-1970s—the consumer paradigm, the child welfare paradigm, the humanitarian paradigm, and the development paradigm. Since paradigms waxed and waned, overlapped, and could be used by different actors in varied ways, they reflected the improvisational nature of voluntarism and the unevenness of professionalization in the second half of the twentieth century. The classic narrative—that professional social workers controlled the development of adoption policy and practice by the mid-twentieth century—downplays the influence of volunteers and private adoption work. Not only does this narrative discount the reality that independent and humanitarian-brokered foreign adoptions *far exceeded* those arranged by professional social workers, but it also misses the opportunity to uncover voluntarism's centrality in the larger welfare state. This perspective obscures a system that functioned with a broader range of child saving paradigms.[9] Not a simple turf war, competing paradigms of child saving offered ideological and practical challenges to child welfare professionals' emphasis on social scientific principles of child placement, especially when adoption became one aspect of "emergency" international relief.

The four postwar paradigms illuminate how the institution of international adoption relied on a variety of child saving solutions to address state interests. The *consumer paradigm* was a fundamental part of early and mid-twentieth-century domestic adoption, but also surfaced in Greece in the early 1950s. Social entrepreneurs, well-meaning doctors, and for-profit organizations approached child saving with the view that any well-connected individual or group could successfully place children for adoption. With no need to rely on expert knowledge to assess family suitability, consumer-driven placements put more control in the hands of prospective adoptive parents. In effect, this applied market solutions to social problems. With demand for adoption high and the supply of "adoptable" babies low, independent services flourished in the mid-twentieth century. According to some estimates, non-experts conducted over half of all adoptions at the time. Social workers, leery of the potential harm caused by layperson adoption, often referred to these types of practitioners as operating on the "black market" or "gray market."

The *child welfare paradigm*, on the other hand, prioritized the "best interests of the child" through social scientific practice and careful casework. It was the hallmark of social workers and professional social welfare agencies, although some humanitarian agencies also followed professional child welfare standards, especially in Vietnam. During the infancy of international adoption, social workers—working for the U.S. Children's Bureau, public state agencies, and federal nonsectarian organizations—sought to handle international adoption much as they handled domestic adoption: as a scientific, expert-run enterprise. Schooled in Progressive Era ideas of child protection, these experts relied on social scientific studies of child placement and principles of social psychology to determine a child's "fit" with an adoptive family.

The *humanitarian paradigm*—a relief-based strategy—surfaced during World War II and continued through Operation Babylift in 1975. Religious humanitarians, popular media, some politicians, and secular NGOs drew on the humanitarian paradigm in Greece, South Korea, and South Vietnam, as well as in domestic transracial adoptions. Perhaps the most familiar model, humanitarian-driven adoption became synonymous with the rescue of children. While rescue was a loaded term for many childless couples and social workers—neither of whom saw the adoption process as a rescue mission—for religious humanitarians and other do-gooders this was precisely how they understood their work. Far from a utilitarian pairing of a needy child with a family, humanitarians imbued adoption with moral, and sometimes spiritual, significance. The U.S. media celebrated these child savers, popularizing and legitimizing altruistic adoptions.

By the mid-1960s, the U.S. government and some international relief organizations shifted from the humanitarian paradigm they had used in Greece and Korea to a *development paradigm*—one that encouraged "self-help" and "modernization" in the developing world. Rather than providing temporary relief by permanently placing children abroad, the development model prioritized the rehabilitation of indigenous social welfare infrastructures so that foreign systems could meet their own child welfare needs in the long term. While development efforts in foreign relief were nothing new, only in the case of Vietnam were they systematically applied to international adoption. Social welfare professionals, from both public and private agencies, also drew on the development model and employed it, at times, alongside the child welfare paradigm.

As these paradigms reveal, volunteers were essential in shaping international adoption. But they could never have done it alone. The efforts of private organizations and individuals succeeded because at every stage Congress and federal agencies made decisions to facilitate international adoption. Federal actions included liberalizing immigration policies, limiting the regulation of adoption markets, and perpetuating both public and private authority in the realm of policymaking.[10] It was the absence of a well-developed body of laws governing both international and domestic adoptions that encouraged the growth and influence of voluntarism. Since emergency actions frequently necessitated policy exceptions that circumvented existing strictures, attempts to regulate international adoptions produced limited results. Over time, these initial postwar emergency policies gave way to permanent avenues of family formation available almost exclusively to American families.[11]

If volunteers provided the impetus for crafting and maintaining an international adoption system, then immigration law was the mechanism that made it all possible. Until 1961, in a telling and strategic move, U.S. immigration law categorized foreign orphans as refugees. At a time when the "traditional" refugee was a European anticommunist, fleeing from political and religious persecution, officials remapped the definition of refugee so that foreign orphans from "friendly" countries such as Ireland, West Germany, and South Korea qualified. That federal policymakers used refugee law was no accident. Refugee policies resonate with political and diplomatic prerogatives.[12] Through more expansive refugee policies, sympathetic lawmakers could circumvent the existing race-based quota system, which remained under the 1952 McCarran-Walter Act. Indeed, one year later, and twelve years before the Hart-Celler Act would end "national origins" quotas, the 1953 Refugee Relief Act permitted 4,000 international adoptees to enter the United States regardless of origin country. If funneled through the immigration quota system, the number of South Korean adoptees would have been limited to one hundred—a number far below the demand from U.S. families.

But adoptees did not remain refugees. Once international adoption had received widespread acclaim and support, in 1961 it became a permanent part of immigration law, and foreign adoptees were reclassified as immigrants: albeit, immigrants subject to no quotas or ceilings. Since Hart-Celler maintained a global quota system of 20,000 immigrants per country and a 290,000 total ceiling, no other migrants enjoyed such privilege. In effect, through this law, the United States declared that it would welcome as many foreign orphans as U.S. couples wanted to adopt. Although international adoptees are rarely considered in immigration histories, their presence remaps refugee law and offers an alternative narrative of immigration reform.[13]

To best highlight the four competing paradigms that shaped the growth of international adoption, this project examines a period during which the United States established long-term adoption programs in Greece, South

Korea, and South Vietnam. International adoption began formally during World War II with displaced European children, especially relatives from Poland, Czechoslovakia, and Hungary. The first GI babies also came out of the Second World War—the offspring of American soldiers stationed in Germany and Japan. By starting in 1945, when Europe and the United States struggled with the resettlement of millions of displaced persons, *The Best Possible Immigrants* situates the roots of international adoption in Europe. This framing is essential, since it sheds light on the consumer-based foundations for adoption services (already existing in U.S. domestic adoption) and the initial market for war orphans, which drove later policies in Asia.[14] Unlike Germany, Japan, and other parts of Europe, however, the nations of Greece, South Korea, and South Vietnam each sustained international adoption programs that lasted for more than a decade. This allowed international and U.S.-based aid organizations to establish in-country adoption networks where policies and influence can be traced over a longer period. While this era witnessed other adoption campaigns—for instance, the resettlement of British children during World War II, and the airlifts of Hungarian orphans in 1957 and Cuban youth in 1961—these efforts never produced lasting adoption programs.

This study ends in 1976 as appellate justices finalized their opinion in *Nguyen Da Yen v. Kissinger*—the case against the U.S. government for its role in the airlift of thousands of children out of South Vietnam in 1975. This end point is significant for two reasons. First, it signals the growing distrust of humanitarianism as a motivation for child saving in light of U.S. actions during the Vietnam War. Second, it demonstrates the power of volunteer efforts in the evacuation of children from the orphanages of Saigon. This chronologically expansive, multi-sited framework captures a holistic view of international adoption as an institution.[15] As such, it exposes patterns in the social welfare state, immigration law, and U.S. foreign policy over time.

But this is not simply a story of social policy contests. Child saving paradigms also highlight the shifting ideologies of family and race in the post-World War II era, underscoring the important cultural work at the center of policy efforts. It was no accident that international adoption originated and grew at a time when there was widespread public support for international relief, the relaxing of racial exclusivity, and the baby boom. The popular media's obsession with adoption coverage further reveals how captivating such family-making was in pro-natalist postwar America.

Indeed, this book emphasizes how the work of religious organizations and adoptive parents heightened voluntarism's success in shaping international adoption. In the mid-twentieth-century United States, both family life and religious faith were deemed private realms—institutions ostensibly free from government interference that according to Cold War politicians, distinguished American society from "godless communism." Government policies intended to regulate middle-class families or religious groups were thus seen as suspect. Such thinking offered volunteers a significant advantage in international adoption. Even though NGOs, including faith-based organizations, often drew on state resources and collaborated with public agencies, they were nonetheless seen as private entities, distinct from public bureaucracy and "red tape"—a perception that offered them extensive improvisational opportunities. By accelerating adoptive placements, these methods served the interests of prospective adoptive parents, who became crucial boosters for private agencies. Through political lobbying, community organizing, and strategic promotion, adoptive parents reinforced the idea that the government should ease international adoptions, not hamper them with increased regulations. Such activism proved effective, in part, because of the Cold War context—an era in which appearing to keep family and religion in the private sphere held significant political sway despite a tradition of state involvement in reproduction and families. The popular media and key policymakers championed adoptive families and faith-based adoption agencies as ideal civic institutions, upholding liberal postwar values of colorblindness, democratic altruism, and consumer choice.

International adoption also ushered in, to borrow historian Mae Ngai's language, "the invention of new categories of identity."[16] The GI baby, the war orphan, and the foreign adoptee were neologisms that expressed a new social order. By bringing nonwhite children into their families, white adoptive parents ostensibly signaled a more racially tolerant America that, at the very least, protected and, at the most, championed multiracial families as early as the mid-1950s. Before colorblindness became the political strategy of the conservative movement in the late 1960s, these families offered evidence to the world that the United States had embraced a universal colorblind brotherhood.[17] Multiracial families with white parents and Asian children dovetailed with U.S. foreign policy efforts to woo Chinese, Japanese, Korean, and Vietnamese political support. Relatedly, white Americans grew increasingly tolerant of the Asian-American community who moved from "alien neighbors" in the 1930s, as historian Charlotte Brooks identifies, to "foreign friends" in the 1950s.[18]

At the same time, older categories of identity, namely the "hard-to-place" African American orphan, persisted. Even as the language of color-blindness made the proponents of international adoption seem racially progressive, until the mid-1960s volunteers, NGOs, policymakers, and adoptive parents operated in—and reinforced—a rigid black-white racial binary in U.S. society. While most adoption agencies placed GI babies with white fathers and full Korean or Vietnamese children in white homes, they placed orphans with African American fathers predominantly in black families. But by the late 1960s, domestic racial politics had shifted again. White families in metropolitan areas, less convinced of a racially bleak future for black children in light of the civil rights movement, were increasingly willing to adopt black children domestically and black-Vietnamese children from abroad. As these youths became less "hard-to-place," however, African American social workers became concerned about the erosion of black identity. By the 1970s, these professionals were the ones now insisting that black-Vietnamese children be placed in black homes, albeit for substantially different reasons from those proffered by white social workers in the 1950s.

Tracing these shifts over a thirty-year period reveals not only the constant remapping of children's racial identities, but also the ways racial discourses in the United States shaped policies abroad. Starting in connection with Greece, ethnic and racialized language seeped into policymaking, demonstrating how the United States still wrestled with ethnic whiteness in the 1940s. Korean and Vietnamese GI babies' ambiguous racial identification, and U.S. policymakers' particular concern over black-Vietnamese children, also reinforced how American notions of race served intentional, historically bounded purposes.[19] For instance, even as immigration law still prohibited most Asian immigration, and bigotry toward Koreans and Vietnamese was still commonplace, Americans largely claimed colorblindness and inclusivity in the case of mixed-race or full Asian orphans. Moreover, throughout the postwar era, it was undeniable that whiteness was part of, not apart from, the racial dialogue. White adoptive families seemingly embraced colorblindness as a way of making the world equal. Not many understood that by wanting their adopted children to be "just American" or "the same as everyone else," they were reinforcing white privilege while denying the realities of racism.[20] The exoticism bound up in adopting a foreign child heightened the appeal of international adoption without motivating adoptive parents to consider their own racial identity.[21]

Cold War rhetoric that championed U.S. humanitarian intervention overseas undoubtedly contributed to the narratives of colorblindness and racial liberalism that made foreign adoption possible.[22] Relief organizations and private citizens first considered the international adoption of French and Belgian orphans to the United States during and after World War I, but restrictive immigration laws and isolationist foreign policies quickly stymied such efforts.[23] Unlike policies during World War I, Cold War foreign policy enforced a domestic cultural mandate to embrace other nations, especially those vulnerable to communist takeovers like Greece, Korea, and Vietnam. Along these lines, scholars have also argued that the Cold War was one of the key reasons that white American families were suddenly willing to adopt across racial lines.[24] America had a well-documented global image problem because of its racist policies, something the Cold War brought to the fore. Linking adoption to the Cold War's language of rescue offered the required societal justification for otherwise untraditional adoptions, and served as a humanitarian smokescreen in nations suffering from U.S. political, economic, and military involvement.[25] By opening the immigration doors wider than ever before to needy, and often nonwhite, children, these race-blind policies draped the U.S. government and adoptive families in a cloak of colorblind humanitarianism, distracting international onlookers from the realities underneath.[26] In addition to the influence on U.S. foreign policy, this book emphasizes how Cold War rhetoric also influenced domestic adoptions. First, foreign adoptions led to the erosion of racial matching domestically. Second, the language of constant threats and emergencies justified the extension of private, voluntary power in social welfare by making it seem temporary.

But the Cold War alone does not provide sufficient explanation for the development of international adoption. U.S. child welfare agencies were scrambling to meet the demand for adoptable children before the Cold War began. In the early twentieth century, the press regularly reported on domestic "baby shortages." Even legislators in congressional hearings frequently referenced U.S. couples' astounding interest in adoption. These pressures accounted for the influence that childless couples had as prominent middle-class constituents, their frustration with and resistance to social welfare bureaucracy, and the long history of adoptions occurring outside the formal system. Without a wider lens, it would be easy to dismiss international adoption in its infancy as a particular Cold War response to civil rights pressures and the large number of American-fathered children. But this raises a series of questions. If the Cold War was the chief factor driving U.S. families to embrace children across racial and national boundaries, why did American soldiers begin adopting GI children from Germany and Japan during and immediately after World War II?[27] If the Cold War made Americans feel guilty for the children left by U.S. soldiers, how did that explain the large number of non-GI children adopted during the same period? And if the Cold War was chiefly responsible for international adoption programs, why has America's international adoption system only become more expansive since 1989? Ultimately, the institution of international adoption relied on a range of complex international and domestic processes, systems, and events, including, but not limited to, the Cold War.

Most important in this regard, it is impossible to understand the development of international adoption without examining both policy and culture. Policies are cultural, social, economic, and political products. On one hand, war orphans and adoptees provoked political discourses and practices that led to the revision of immigration and social welfare laws. Congressional records, hearings, federal immigration and child protection policies, state-based social welfare records, and NGO and agency accounts bring this policymaking to light. On the other hand, foreign orphans also prompted a cultural conversation that surfaced in films, comics, adoptive parent memoirs, media publications, and television—a reality which this book's primary source selection reflects. How these discourses informed one another and reflected idealizations of family, race, and citizenship in America resituates policy narratives in their cultural context.[28] Both fictional and factual accounts are equally instructive for the ways that they convince, compel, and create truth about orphans and families. Where policy documents fail to acknowledge voices outside the dominant racial, national, and gender constructions, these narratives can help bring to light overlooked perspectives.

One of my chief methodological concerns in using sources from those holding political or social power has been to access the accounts of "outsiders" like foreign birth mothers. Necessarily, this project requires examining what policymakers, religious humanitarians, adoptive parents, and legislators actually said and did regarding birth parents as well as what they left unsaid or only alluded to.[29] Greek, Korean, and Vietnamese birth mothers' stories resonate in agency relinquishment accounts, adoptive parent memoirs, and cultural texts, something I stress as an important counternarrative to the story of the state. When possible I do draw from children's accounts, particularly in the examination of Operation Babylift. Prior to the Vietnam War era, however, few sources exist from children's perspectives. Those that do are less helpful at tracing the development of international adoption as an institution. Minimizing sources from children is not intended to strip them of agency or suggest that they are unimportant players. In this vein, I am grateful for the many scholars, memoirists, and writers who have done an excellent job situating adoptees within the larger narratives of rescue, exclusion, and othering.[30]

A Note on Terminology

The meanings of key terms to describe players in adoption, racial belonging, and kinship have changed over time. Unless I have found it discursively useful to consider the older term, I generally have chosen words with contemporary resonance to minimize distraction from key points. Instead of natural mother, I use birth or biological mother; instead of negro, I use black or African American; instead of illegitimate, I use unmarried or single; instead of Oriental, I use Asian. While most people referred to foreign adoptions as intercountry adoptions until the 1980s, I use international, transnational, and intercountry interchangeably. I also use both mixed-race and multiracial, since each term is still commonly used in the historical, sociological, and anthropological literature.

One of the most problematic terms throughout is the word orphan. It is a delicate business determining how to refer to a child that either policy or culture has rendered an orphan but who has two living biological parents. The children whom officials deemed moldable, inherently "free" of national affiliation or familial complication, were rarely, if ever, "free."[31] Most "orphans" had surviving families. All orphans had national or ethnic identities they brought with them to the United States. Just as race, gender, and class are socially and historically constructed categories that can be used to reinforce power hierarchies, the term orphan has also changed to reflect different standards in racialized citizenship, social policy, and attitudes toward poor parents over the course of the twentieth century.[32]

Although I attempt to distinguish between cultural orphans, political orphans, and those who are orphans because social policies have rendered them adoptable, the trickiness of these categories means that there will be oversights. This process has reminded me how, at times, the assigning of identity and kinship is fraught more with politics than with sentiment.

CHAPTER 1

"Babyselling Rings,"
"Adoption Mills,"
and "Baby Rackets"

Formalizing Policies
and Manufacturing Markets

O N FEBRUARY 4, 1944, First Lady Eleanor Roosevelt featured the popular Cradle Society adoption agency and its director Florence Walrath in her syndicated column "My Day." In her column, which ran six days a week from 1935 to 1962, Roosevelt commended the adoption maven for her agency's cutting edge practices and the elimination of infection in her baby nurseries.[1] Walrath, wife of a prominent attorney, founded the agency in 1923 after successfully placing a child with her sister in the Chicago area, and became a well-known adoption destination for many celebrity clients, including Bob Hope and George Burns. Yet, social welfare officials were less impressed with the agency's lauded clientele. Starting in the 1930s, the Children's Bureau amassed a large file on the Cradle's practices, recording how its staff charged clients as much as $1,000 for an adoption in 1940 (equating to nearly $17,000 in 2014), refused to employ trained social workers, and placed children without a trial period. The agency's board also opposed efforts by child welfare experts to pass legislation in Illinois that would have made such trial periods mandatory. After receiving many "critical letters" in response to her column, Roosevelt contacted the Children's Bureau, asking if Walrath did a "good job." In her reply to the First Lady, Chief Katharine Lenroot concluded that the agency's history was mixed: "I am told that a number of Cradle adoptions have been eminently successful. However, I believe that on the whole this type of organization should not be encouraged."[2]

The Cradle's "type of organization" was one founded on the principle that any caring, well-connected individual could successfully place children for adoption. This was a notion that professional social workers worked passionately to invalidate throughout the first half of the twentieth century. As maternalist theories of family preservation and eugenicist perceptions of hereditary dysfunction began to lose credibility in the 1920s, adoption became less stigmatized. Social workers, therefore, increasingly relied on permanent, in-home placements as the best alternative for children who had been legally relinquished or abandoned.

Professional social workers, however, were latecomers. In the late nineteenth century, as progressive reformers started viewing all childhoods as worthy of protection from the adult world, the value of "useless" but "precious" adoptable babies rose markedly. Social entrepreneurs, well-meaning doctors, and for-profit enterprises capitalized on adoption's rising popularity to provide adoption services, predominantly to childless couples. Some philanthropic operations, like the Cradle, charged only fees for services. Others made considerable profits from adoption placements. Regardless of fee schedules or motivations, these entities existed in response to the high demand for independent adoption services. As a result, these firms developed client-driven services, functioning under what I call the *consumer paradigm*. This paradigm permitted prospective adoptive parents far more control over the process of child selection and timing.

The *child welfare paradigm*, conversely, was less influenced by adoptive parent demand and more by a child's "best interest." Professional agencies, such as the U.S. Children's Bureau and the Child Welfare League of America, believed that great harm came to children and families united by non-experts. To wrest control from these consumer enterprises, child welfare authorities developed a strategy that promoted their carefully trained personnel and scientifically based methods of child placement as necessary for risk-free adoptions. Thus, starting in the mid- to late 1940s, social welfare experts increasingly associated those operating under the consumer paradigm with the illegal "black market" and immoral "gray market," often erroneously, in order to turn public and legislative sentiment against them. By invoking the language of markets, experts subtly asserted that these independent adoption agencies violated notions of the "sacralized" child.

Despite such tactics, non-expert adoptions continued to thrive. Adoptive parent demand, jurisdictional conflicts, and the lack of uniform regulations perpetuated a two-tiered adoption system, where privileged clients could pay to guarantee faster and less invasive "market" services and the less affluent relied on the slower, more exacting, professional child welfare system. This domestic history laid the groundwork for the crucial role that U.S. social welfare policymaking played in the extension of adoption overseas. Indeed, these domestic origins reveal how volunteers' many challenges to the professional child welfare system were not a new phenomenon, but a pattern in the history of adoption.

Adoption and the State, 1851–1945

Modern, child-centered adoption law is a fairly recent trend in the United States. Although Massachusetts enacted the first comprehensive adoption law in 1851, it only guarded a child from economic exploitation and provided a legal avenue for changing an adoptive child's name. The statute did mandate that adoptive parents have "sufficient ability" to nurture and educate the child, but this prescription was similar to earlier acts that protected indentured or apprenticed children. The Massachusetts law, in fact, contained no clause considering an adoptive child's "best interests."[3] Legal scholars point to the 1855 Pennsylvania adoption statute as the first to explicitly endorse "the welfare of the child." Other states lagged behind, not incorporating specific provisions on assessing the "appropriateness of the adoption" until the late nineteenth and early twentieth centuries.[4] Yet, even with an increase in state adoption laws at the turn of the century, most families wanted neither the publicity nor the increased costs of legalizing existing relationships, making formal adoptions a decided minority. While many families treated adopted children as "their own," without a formal order of adoption, adoptees rarely enjoyed inheritance rights or equal status to biological kin. Regardless, few adoptive families saw a reason to legalize kinship ties before the 1935 Social Security Act provided survivorship benefits.[5]

During the Progressive Era, reformers increasingly advocated for an extension of government regulations to address a myriad of social problems, including adoptions. Through the labors of activists Florence Kelley and Lillian Wald, Congress established the Children's Bureau in 1912 to coordinate efforts to reduce infant mortality, target aid for poor children, and introduce laws restricting child labor. Advancing a broad reform agenda aimed at all children, not just the poor, the bureau leadership believed that the federal government had a duty to protect children's rights. Since municipalities and volunteers still maintained control of child welfare programs, the Children's Bureau used social scientific studies and statistical surveys of child care, delinquency, and nutrition to bolster its authority.[6] In 1919, the Children's Bureau held the first national conference that focused on child welfare standards, including a resolution that addressed adoption. The conference proceedings concluded that conscientious child placements under professional supervision, whether temporary or permanent, positively affected a child's long-term health and well-being. Conferences like these articulated the reigning professional position on adoption and began the process of standardizing child welfare services across regions.[7]

From the inception of progressive child welfare and adoption reform, private agencies worked alongside public entities to conduct studies, produce standards, and protect the "right to childhood." One of the best examples of this public-private collaboration was the Child Welfare League of America. Founded in 1915 by an association of fourteen public and private agencies, the private, nonsectarian Child Welfare League received funding from the Commonwealth Fund and Russell Sage Foundation. The league's primary mission was to lobby for standardization, arguing that it was the reform most likely to "enhance child welfare." To develop this commission, the league collaborated extensively with the Children's Bureau, sharing personnel, a commitment to establishing minimum placement standards, and a plan to make child placement investigations the purview of professionals. By 1921, the league served nearly seventy member agencies.[8] This alliance showed how the struggle for professional and expert status led both private and public agencies to pay social workers' salaries, complicating later efforts to delegitimize the non-expert services offered by private agencies.

Because of advocacy from Children's Bureau and Child Welfare League officials, the process of standardization slowly started to gain momentum in state laws across the country. In 1917, Minnesota was the first state to require an investigation of prospective adoptive parents and adoptable children before finalizing an adoption. Four years later, Ohio passed the first law mandating that licensed child welfare agencies conduct adoption investigations. Yet, by the early 1940s, only twenty other states had joined Ohio, signifying the extremely gradual pace of standardization.[9] While by 1950 most states did require adoption agencies to be licensed, the licensing conditions varied significantly by state. Furthermore, agencies processing international adoptions could skirt around licensing requirements, as Holt Adoption Program did in Korean adoptions from 1956 to 1961. The agency placed children nationwide without an Oregon social welfare license until federal immigration law stipulated in 1961 that international adoption agencies must be licensed in their home states.[10]

In part, this sluggish pace of reform came from social welfare professionals themselves. Before the 1930s, few social workers supported permanent adoptive placements. On one hand, they believed that children born to unmarried mothers were genetically suspect. Drawing on pseudo-scientific ideas of genetic theory, these experts argued that since nature trumped nurture, lower-class children could not thrive in wealthier, more educated adoptive homes and would prove a liability for adoptive couples. Thus it was less risky for such children to remain with their biological families.[11] On the other hand, maternalist reformers in the 1910s and 1920s thought that forcing women to care for their "illegitimate" children would give them necessary moral responsibility, as demonstrated by campaigns for mothers' pensions.[12] Social workers' views started changing in the 1920s, as child development theories began to prioritize environment over heredity and innovations in psychoanalysis influenced social welfare practitioners. Through careful and professional casework based on the principles of social psychology, social workers argued, a birth mother could be properly diagnosed and her child could be successfully placed with a thoroughly scrutinized married couple.[13] Social welfare experts also employed these scientific and psychological techniques to evaluate children. Establishing a new paradigm of "kinship by design," historian Ellen Herman has asserted that social workers "guaranteed" their professional placements by ensuring adoptive parents that their children were intellectually and psychologically superior.[14]

One way they accomplished this was by physically, religiously, and socially "matching" a child to her new parents so that the adoptive family modeled a biological one. A specifically American construct, matching was intended to make the social construction of families less risky through a type of social engineering, similar to eugenics.[15] Applying principles of professional casework and scientific matching made adoptions "safer" for both the child and the adoptive parents, so that more social workers prioritized it as a child welfare solution. The 1938 Child Welfare League standards reflected this new confidence in adoption by issuing different standards for adoptive or permanent placements than for temporary or foster care placements, for the first time. From the late 1930s to the late 1950s, the league strived to legislate every aspect of permanent child placement so that those conducting adoptions would be forced to conform to "sound," professional practices that safeguarded children's interests.[16]

Still, in 1948, Child Welfare League members admitted that "adoption as a professional service is still very young," highlighting the still malleable nature of adoption strictures and regulations in the postwar era.[17] Even with the increase in scientific casework and standardized regulations, conference surveys from the 1940s showed how professional child welfare policies varied significantly from state to state and from agency to agency. For example, in a survey of seventy-five agencies at the 1948 Child Welfare League Conference on Adoption, thirty-nine employed age limits in determining the adoptability of a child, whereas thirty-six reported that age was not a factor. Social workers justified the unevenness of these guidelines through the language of professional discretion, which gave them the responsibility to assess each particular adoptive placement on its context and merits. These "case-by-case" standards left an incredible amount of control in the hands of the individual social worker and further compromised efforts at standardization.[18]

"From Useful to Useless": Valuing Childhoods and Remaking Adoption

As the history of adoption legislation suggests, policies and regulations directed at child welfare and adoption integrally depended on shifting notions of childhood. Beginning in the 1840s, white, urban, middle- and upper-middle-class families increasingly idealized childhood as a period of innocence and prolonged dependency freed from the responsibilities of adult labor. This was possible because the market revolution had removed business from the home and children's work was no longer necessary for survival in middle-class families. Working-class, farm, immigrant, and black children, however, whose labor was still pivotal to the household economy, did not experience such protected childhoods.[19] During the antebellum era, temporary indenture and apprenticing were the most common types of "adoption," since families who cared for nonrelated children expected them to contribute to the family economy. Many Protestant reformers promoted these types of placements as superior alternatives to orphanages, believing that families offered children more stability. Based on this logic, Charles Loring Brace, head of the Children's Aid Society in New York City, created the placing out movement. Popularized by the orphan trains that sent over 200,000 children from cities on the Eastern Seaboard to Midwestern farms between the 1850s and the 1920s, reformers placed children in white, Protestant, "American" families as a way to assimilate poor Irish and Italian immigrant children. Interestingly, most of the placements were neither in the West nor permanent and few of the children placed were actually parentless orphans. As historians have shown, most working-class families used the placing out system as a temporary safety net in times of economic hardship or to expose their children to apprenticing opportunities. In fact, finding birth mothers willing to surrender their children permanently was rare.[20]

Both notions of children's value and adoption norms underwent significant, albeit gradual, changes starting in the 1890s. Middle-class reformers had long been uncomfortable with working-class and immigrant families' reliance on child labor, contending that "if children were useful and produced money, they were not being properly loved." Such convictions animated efforts to pass laws that prohibited child labor, established mandatory schooling, and differentiated between legitimate and illegitimate childhood work.[21] Extending the promise of a sheltered childhood to working-class children influenced the slow transition in adoption norms as well. In 1900, older children were still more likely to be adopted than infants, but this was starting to shift. In the mid- to late nineteenth century, adoptive parents viewed infants as an economic "liability." Unmarried, widowed, or deserted mothers without other options had to pay someone to take their young children. For women who could afford to pay the fee, one alternative was to board their infants in baby farms. Run by middle-aged women, baby farms often served as "legitimate," formal childcare services for "illegitimate" babies. With mortality rates reaching as high as 90 percent, however, progressive reformers pointed to the disease-ridden operations as evidence that financial profit and child care were incompatible.[22]

As parents turned from "searching for child labor to child love," in Viviana Zelizer's words, formal adoption became an increasingly popular way for childless, middle-class couples to form families. While it was not unusual for both sentiment and household economics to guide adoptions through the 1920s, by the 1930s childless couples paid increasingly more to guarantee a child who physically and intellectually "matched" them. Furthermore, as children started fulfilling primarily emotional rather than economic needs, they became "worth more" to adoptive families. Indeed, the currency of sentimentality became synonymous with adopting a female, blonde-haired, blue-eyed toddler.[23] Provided that the supply of these desirable assets remained available, childless couples could construct their own companionate, child-centered adoptive families.[24] Yet, there were never enough of these sentimentally valuable children to satisfy the demand of prospective adoptive parents, energizing for-profit adoptions and the consumer paradigm. The earliest "commercial adoptions," as historian Ellen Herman calls them, began in maternity homes and lying-in hospitals. Linked to baby farms, these institutions often served as baby dispensaries with doctors and midwives placing the children in adoptive homes for a hefty fee. In the early twentieth century, entrepreneurs placed newspaper advertisements and recruited birth mothers as a way of meeting adoptive parent demand. As early as 1910, the media publicized infant shortages, reporting that there were "not enough babies to go around."[25]

As commercial adoption interests expanded in the first twenty years of the twentieth century, so too did a philanthropic adoption sector. Unlike commercial practitioners, volunteer non-experts seldom profited from the placements, but were motivated instead by wanting to do moral good by placing needy children with families instead of in institutions. The first agencies that specialized in adoption were run by upper-class women like Florence Walrath, Clara Spence, Alice Chapin, and Louise Waterman Wise in the urban centers of New York City and Chicago. Herman contends that these women, serving as "adoption pioneers," combined "benevolence and civic duty with self-interest and class interest," often locating adoptable children for their friends. While most maternalist reformers campaigned for family preservation, these advocates saw adoption's potential to ensure upward mobility for adopted children of unwed mothers—a rare pro-adoption position in a eugenic age. Yet, even as Walrath and others threw off genetic constraints, they also conformed to them. When finding babies for elite families, the Spence Alumni Society would only place children of the highest quality, insinuating that "blood," in fact, mattered.[26]

Social workers perceived all unprofessional adoptions as risky. As Ellen Herman has aptly argued, the Children's Bureau and Child Welfare League

were principally concerned with making adoptions safe while also minimizing their risk. Both organizations asserted that adoptions based on sentiment or profit offered children no protection and endangered families.
Passing standards and regulations that outlawed these methods, or at the
minimum curtailed their extent, would ensure that only trained and
licensed professionals assumed such precious responsibility.

Beginning in the 1930s, social workers recognized that to truly marshal
the adoption system, they needed to delegitimize those volunteer non-
experts and commercial interests operating under the consumer paradigm
who had presided over permanent placements since the mid-nineteenth
century. The classic narrative of adoption history explains that as adoptions
became increasingly popular and more standardized, earlier adoption practices and practitioners faded away while professionals gradually asserted
their authority during the 1930s, finally consolidating their influence in the
post-World War II era. Yet even at mid-century, when social workers commanded more institutional clout than ever before, statistics revealed that
independent non-experts still conducted at least half of domestic adoptive
placements.[27] Although recent histories have grappled more fully with independent actors' resistance to the social welfare community, scholars still
have framed these events within the trajectory of child welfare professionalization.[28] Social workers' efforts to end volunteer and commercial
adoptions, however, reveal that the consumer paradigm commanded a significant degree of authority over adoptions for much longer than traditional histories suggest. To gain the trust and approval of adoptive families,
legislators, and the American public, and discredit the unlicensed, independent adoption operations that controlled the field in the 1930s and 1940s,
social workers characterized these enterprises as "black" and "gray markets"
that mercenarily or immorally violated sacred childhood. They hoped that
this strategy would further solidify their professional credibility and unique
responsibility to form families.[29]

Manufacturing Markets: Social Workers' Rhetorical Fight for Legitimacy

Starting in 1945, the Children's Bureau began referring to all commercial
adoptions as part of an illegal "black market" in children. In legal and

economic terms, black markets are sites of exchange that violate government regulations or laws. During the Second World War, these illicit markets allowed consumers to circumvent government rationing or restrictive
price controls on particular goods or services. Black markets have also provided access to illegal services or goods, such as alcohol during Prohibition
or abortions before *Roe v. Wade.* Using market language to refer to adoptions was certainly not a new phenomenon. Since 1910, the popular media
had drawn on market terminology to describe adoptive parents' frenzy over
blue-eyed, blonde-haired infants, what *Cosmopolitan* called a "desultory
and elusive traffic."[30] A 1939 *Collier's* article referred to this desperation as
responsible for the "traffic in babies," which the author insisted caused
babies to be "bootlegged," conjuring images of Prohibition era lawlessness
and greed.[31] The first widespread media reference explicitly labeling for-
profit adoptions as the "black market" was in a 1944 *Woman's Home Companion* article.[32] Not long after the article's release, social welfare leaders
regularly referred to cross-border adoptions between the United States and
Canada—especially adoptions from the Ideal Maternity Home in Nova
Scotia—as a "black market."[33] Social workers attempted to make all commercial placements—regardless of their actual legality or illegality—
synonymous with "black market" adoptions, intentionally emphasizing
how for-profit adoptions commodified the "priceless" child.[34] Black market
language was one way to express "moral outrage" with what social workers
likened to human trafficking. This further implied that adoptive parents
who opted for professional adoptions fulfilled their civic responsibility.[35]

Although Children's Bureau and Child Welfare League officials began
using the term "black market" as early as 1945, the organizations failed to
define what they meant by it for nearly a decade. Since at mid-century no
federal laws, and few state statutes, prohibited the sale of children, or even
banned charging excessive fees in adoptive placements, defining the exact
nature of the black market was tricky. When Children's Bureau leaders
finally settled on a definition of black marketers in 1955—"unauthorized
middle men who offer babies for a price unrelated to legitimate services
rendered natural and adopting parents"—it was artfully imprecise. As
Karen Balcom has correctly observed, this description provoked more questions than answers. "What was a legitimate service? A legitimate fee?" And,
who determined if a middleman was unauthorized?[36] At its core, the adoption "black market" became what Balcom has called "culturally loaded
shorthand" for social workers to differentiate their professional services,

and fees, from those of "babysellers."[37] Even if no state laws explicitly banned excessive adoption fees or cursory social investigations, social workers argued that commercial operations had no redeeming value because they performed adoptions just to satisfy childless couples, emphasizing consumerism over science. Equally troubling, in social welfare professionals' view, commercial adoptions encouraged unmarried women to have more babies. According to Children's Bureau Chief Maud Morlock, unmarried mothers were unfit parents from "broken homes," unaware "of the meaning of their behavior or of the influence of their life experiences."[38] Since social workers largely diagnosed unwed mothers as neurotic and lacking in self-awareness, professionals considered this trend disturbing.

But commercial adoptions were not social workers' only target. In a 1945 article on "black market" adoptions, Chief Morlock called all independent adoptions "dangerous," even when conducted by "well-meaning baby placers."[39] To differentiate these independent services from the black market, social workers, beginning in the late 1940s, increasingly referred to these placements as the "gray market." This language not only distanced professional placements from the perceived carelessness of sentimental operators but also marked the child welfare system's growing anxiety over independent adoptions. Attorneys first used the term "gray market" in 1946 as a reference to the importation of automotive parts manufactured overseas that had identical U.S. trademarks without consent of the trademark owner. Alternately called a "parallel market," this gray market drew opposition from critics who complained that federal agencies and courts needed to reform policies so that these types of trademark infringements would end.[40] Its first written use pertaining to adoption came in June 1949 from a *Woman's Home Companion* article, in which gray "marketers" were called "well meaning but fatally bungling amateurs." By 1950, it was a widely circulated term in both the media and social welfare communication.[41] Gray markets were construed as "semi-legal" avenues for adoption, even though in many states it was perfectly legal for an individual or organization to place a child and charge a fee to do so, as long as a judge approved the adoption in court. Although not "cradle-snatching for profit," in the words of Children's Bureau Director Martha Eliot, their services were still client driven. As with others operating under the consumer paradigm, these agencies relied on inexperienced volunteers and humanitarians who prioritized speedy and permanent placements over intensive social studies and waiting periods.[42]

Social workers used slippery language like black and gray markets to set licensed agencies apart as purveyors of scientific, methodical child placements.[43] Embracing terminology like "gray markets" signified social welfare professionals' resistance to any kind of "parallel adoption market," whether commercially driven or not. Even as social workers crusaded to remove child placement from the commercial and philanthropic spheres, they embraced economic language to differentiate authorized, professional child welfare services from the untrained, albeit, well-meaning volunteers. In doing this, they reinforced notions of childhood as "a separate noncommercial place" that the consumer paradigm violated.[44]

This market-based language ultimately proved ineffective at mobilizing public policies, however, partly because client-driven enterprises were more in sync with the postwar frenzy over consumer choice. During World War II, moral outrage against black markets had mobilized hundreds of thousands of volunteer groups, consumer activists, and labor organizations to collaborate in enforcing price controls and rationing regulations. Such collaborations made the "free-market entrepreneurs" who attempted to profit by "price gouging" seem undemocratic and hostile to aims of economic citizenship.[45] By the late 1940s, however, outrage against black markets had become harder to mobilize as Americans became more invested in preserving the freedom of consumer choice. Despite social workers' efforts, public demand and legislative inadequacies preserved several "competing" adoption markets throughout the 1970s. Indeed, only two states ever prohibited all independent placements: Delaware in 1952 and Connecticut in 1957. Since the federal government never made interstate adoptions illegal, however, these laws made little difference.[46] This perpetuated the consumer paradigm, which catered to the existing marketplace mentality when selecting child placement services. "Gray markets" then became an elite route for those who could pay to avoid the wait and restrictions of authorized agencies—a type of middle- and upper-class entitlement.

When Dr. Martha Eliot became head of the Children's Bureau in September 1951, she vowed to work at "wiping out" both black and gray markets. One of her strategies was to use the press to "muster public support," taking advantage of media-worthy black market adoptions to get her message to a national audience.[47] "Black market" actions, whether truly illegal or not, made for sensational media stories in part because they violated children's "pricelessness."[48] As reports of "baby selling rings," "adoption mills," and "baby rackets" escalated in the early 1950s, headlines exaggerated the already dramatic events.[49] One 1951 *Saturday Evening Post* article explained how "shysters and criminals . . . unscrupulous attorneys and other racketeers" in the "vicious" and "widespread black market" took advantage of desperate parents. The authors warned readers that black-market children were more likely to be "diseased," "fatally ill," or "feeble-minded." Although the average price for a black-market infant was estimated at $1,500 to $2,500, some attorneys charged as much as $10,000 (nearly $90,000 in today's dollars). These astronomical costs confirmed social workers' fears that allowing the free market to determine a child's "price" was perilous.[50] In the words of bureau staff, the media's "lively interest" presented a "golden opportunity" for policymakers to act, even though officials simultaneously admitted that the issue would not grow "cold" anytime soon.[51]

What concerned Dr. Eliot the most, however, were the "well-intentioned" gray market placements made by doctors and lawyers that lacked the social and legal protections of an agency placement.[52] Yet, the boundary between black and gray markets was hard to plot because gray-market operators accepted fees to cover professional costs. As a Children's Bureau progress report admitted in 1955, "no one has found a way to draw a line between the excessive fees charged by some doctors and lawyers and actual black marketing."[53] This signaled that both for-profit enterprises and philanthropic do-gooders catered to consumer interests.

This designation became even more convoluted when trying to distinguish between public and private agencies. The only public child welfare agencies were state Departments of Public Welfare and the U.S. Children's Bureau. While state agencies conducted child placements in addition to regulating state adoption laws, the Children's Bureau functioned only in an advisory capacity and did not process adoptions. Starting in the 1940s, the chief organization responsible for tracking international adoptions was a private, nonsectarian entity—International Social Service (ISS). Unlike the Child Welfare League and Children's Bureau, ISS conducted adoptive placements, although this was only a small part of the services the agency provided. The social welfare state relied on private agencies like ISS and the Child Welfare League to collaborate on standards, support public agencies, and lobby for regulations.

Although there were a handful of private adoption agencies that hired professional social workers and adhered to the child welfare standards and practices advanced by the Children's Bureau and Child Welfare League, the majority were run by volunteer, and sometimes untrained, staff, what social workers and adoption professionals called "independent.[54] This arrangement revealed how the federal government left significant authority unofficially in the hands of the voluntary sector, whether professionally trained or not. Furthermore, this framework, in part, made it difficult to discern between privately funded "legitimate" social workers—those subscribing to the child welfare paradigm—and "illegitimate" non-experts—operating under the consumer paradigm. Such confusion gave a wide range of independent adoption organizations and individuals regulatory and cultural legitimacy in the eyes of legislators and the public.

Adoption jurisdiction further contributed to the gray market's ambiguity. Depending on state law, gray market adoptions were often legal, which made shutting them down a matter of state regulation and support. Both commercial and humanitarian enterprises specialized in placing children across state lines because they could slip between jurisdictions to take advantage of state laws with fewer restrictions.[55] At the 1951 Conference on Interstate and International Placement, officials acknowledged that this practice existed for two reasons: a "lack of information on the part of state departments of social welfare concerning the movement of children," and a "lack of uniformity, legal and administrative, between states as to their responsibility for over-all setting of standards."[56]

A particular nuisance for social welfare officials, interstate placements enabled adoption practitioners to avoid restrictive state laws that required home investigations and post-placement oversight from social workers in order to expedite adoptions. Agencies like the Cradle in Illinois and the Tennessee Children's Home became associated with these interstate placements, which sometimes led to high-profile mishaps. The Tennessee Children's Home, run by influential child welfare attorney Georgia Tann, placed 1,000 children over state lines from the 1930s to 1950, 90 percent going to California and New York. Officials discovered that Tann not only boarded infants in unsanitary conditions but also profited from adoptions, violating Tennessee adoption law. As U.S. district attorney John Brown, part of the three-person committee appointed by Tennessee governor Gordon Browning to investigate charges against Tann, exclaimed, "There is no question that Miss Tann made money with the adoption of babies by out of state foster parents. . . . If we had known it, we would have fired her." While Tann died in 1950, the courts found her posthumously guilty and put a lien on her estate for $100,000.[57]

Social welfare agencies' concerns about the consumer paradigm certainly had merit. One Yale University study of Connecticut adoptions, conducted in 1949, compared one hundred agency placements with the same number of independent placements. They found that only forty-six of the independent placements were "good"—meaning healthy, "fit" children placed with stable, "suitable" families—while social workers deemed seventy-six of the agency placements "good." The study deemed twenty-eight of the independent placements "bad" and categorized only eight placements by social agencies as bad, leading the report to conclude that even trained social workers were subject to "human error." Although good agency results far exceeded good independent placements, Dr. Catherine Amatruda, assistant professor of pediatrics at Yale, contended that independent placements still had an edge, even if they were "barbaric."[58] She reflected, "agency placements are well done, on the whole, but they do not place enough babies, they do not satisfy enough adopting parents, and they work too slowly."[59] Amatruda's analysis revealed why the consumer paradigm persisted despite the efforts of social workers to discredit it. Indeed, independent adoptions commanded a significant share of the market. Twenty-two states reported in 1949 that 5,556 of 10,565 placements, or over half, were independently arranged.[60]

Agency officials did recognize their partial culpability in the viability and longevity of the consumer paradigm. Few professional social welfare agencies placed newborn babies, most would not accept applications from parents over age thirty-five, many strictly followed principles of religious matching, and some refused to place children in military families that moved frequently. While officials did encourage state agencies to examine their restrictions on age, religion, military families, and newborn placements, they had no regulatory power to enforce these changes in state law. Chief Eliot argued that "independent placements can be eliminated only when there is public understanding of the value of agency services," suggesting that both adoptive parents and birth parents had little regard for what social agencies contributed to the process.[61] Joseph Reid, director of the Child Welfare League, also observed "a direct relationship between agency practices and the gray market."[62] A doctor writing to the Children's Bureau put it another way: "The very fact that adoptions are performed outside of established agencies, to me at least signifies that perhaps the very heart of the case lies with these agencies."[63] In an emotional 1954 letter to Eliot, one adoptive mother confessed that she was one of the many who had bypassed agencies to obtain her son through gray-market channels. Now that he was seventeen, and the well-meaning individuals safe from harmful publicity, she could publicize that social welfare "agencies are responsible, 100%" for the "adoption racket."[64]

Pearl Buck attributed the success of black and gray markets to the lack of unity and leadership within the social welfare community. In 1955 the famous author and adoption advocate published an article in *Woman's Home Companion* accusing social workers of keeping children available for adoption needlessly in orphanages. She argued that adoption agencies' regional isolation and lack of cooperation contributed to the mismanagement of domestic adoption cases. Buck warned, "if the professional social agencies do not take leadership in setting the orphans free for adoption, the black markets can never be suppressed, for they exist always where supply does not meet demand."[65] In addition to "black markets," Buck also determined that "gray-market" adoptions would increase due to a lack of professional leadership. Commissioner of Social Security Charles Schottland and Joseph Reid of the Child Welfare League both responded to the magazine's editors, objecting that Buck had erroneously labeled all children in institutions "orphans" whose parents had released them for adoption. Schottland and Reid explained that most of the children in Buck's survey were not, in fact, legally available for adoption, rendering her calculations of "adoptable" children inaccurate. Still, neither agency refuted nor addressed Buck's assertion of a leadership vacuum and its role in sustaining the consumer paradigm.[66]

Some policymakers urged the Children's Bureau to support a uniform federal adoption law that would make it possible to enforce consistent policies across state lines. But the bureau explicitly objected to this path, arguing that a national law would be difficult to craft and "impractical" to police, given the diverse interests and needs of state governments.[67] This argument was a familiar one for mid-century audiences since it drew on the state sovereignty defense so popular with Southern Democrats who objected to national control over social benefit disbursements, in particular.[68] Instead, the agency worked at strengthening existing state laws to mandate juvenile court hearings, preserve confidentiality during the process, and establish a period of residence before finalizing the adoption. Yet without a standardized interstate policy framework, state legislatures still had the freedom to design and maintain laws without oversight. As Children's Bureau chief Katharine Lenroot observed, only one-quarter of states in 1948 had adequate laws that banned for-profit adoptions, mandated home investigations before and after the placements, and upheld rigorous licensing requirements.[69] Even after an intense publicity campaign, the figures in 1955 were not much better. The Children's Bureau's black-market study concluded that "the wide variation in State laws makes possible one dominant characteristic of the black market—the interstate movement of unwed mothers and adoptive couples. This wide variation not only invites black market operators to evade State regulations but it makes it difficult for a given State to control activities within its borders."[70] These jurisdictional gaps gave social workers little regulatory power to crack down on independent operations for bypassing professionals.

Social workers' unwillingness to use legislation to completely eradicate independent placements, however, made the "gray market" seem benign and sent a mixed message about its harm. This came in part from social workers' anxiety about aligning themselves against practices with large measures of community support. Helen Witmer, director of the Research Division for the Children's Bureau, expressed her concern over using the term "gray market" since it suggested "a disapproval of that kind of placement. While the Bureau is on record, of course, in favoring placement through social agencies," Witmer continued, "I think it would be very unwise to go out on a campaign against well-meaning doctors and lawyers at the same time that we are trying to do away with the wholly illegal black market operations."[71] Joseph Reid agreed, arguing that the social welfare agencies had been criticized for grouping doctors and lawyers together with black market operators. In Reid's view, the "dramatic publicity" of gray-market adoptions had done "more damage than good."[72]

As much as social workers strived to keep child placement separate from market forces that commodified children, changes in adoption standards revealed the power of consumer demand in shaping "best practices." Perhaps unsurprisingly, since domestic and international gray-market operators had more incentives to meet prospective adoptive parent demand, they led the way on eventual adoption "reforms." Decades before social workers abandoned the practice of religious matching, for instance, independent practitioners had already discontinued this "best practice," largely because they could never find enough eligible children for Jewish couples who comprised a significant portion of waiting families.[73] Pearl Buck, along with a few other independent child placers in the 1950s, also challenged racial matching of Asian or mixed-race children a decade before the social welfare profession revised their standards to minimize racial sameness.[74]

Another gray-market "reform" was the age of child placement. In the 1940s and 1950s, the Children's Bureau advised that children not be placed directly into an adoptive family from the hospital since this did not allow authorities enough time to assess potential mental and physical deficiencies that could indicate a child's future fitness. More "progressive" agencies and independent operators, however, frequently placed children before three months of age, violating the window that would "guarantee" professional results, but one that satisfied adoptive couples. Earlier placements became preferable once guarding against risk and ranking children's intellectual potential fell out of vogue. Moreover, mid-century studies on child attachment revealed the positive long-term outcomes of infant bonding, reinforcing the merit of earlier placements.[75] These types of negotiations not only underscored the flexibility of "scientific" thinking about child welfare, but also how independent and volunteer reformers asserted a somewhat progressive influence on adoption policies.

Conclusion

As the manufacturing of black and gray markets suggests, consumer demand and a limited supply of desirable children were only part of the reason that a consumer paradigm in adoption flourished. It was also rooted in the variations in state adoption policies and lack of federal statutes. Unlike the movement to prohibit child labor, where reform efforts started at the state level and then culminated in the federally mandated 1938 Fair Labor Standards Act, there was no effort to pass federal adoption laws. Indeed, the social welfare profession shied away from advocating for a uniform adoption statute that would standardize the norms and fees of permanent child placement, protesting that states' interests were too diverse. Instead, they launched a rhetorical campaign against social entrepreneurs, volunteer philanthropists, doctors, lawyers, and for-profit enterprises. Drawing on the dual notions of early-twentieth-century white childhood as both priceless and sacred, social welfare experts tried to damage commercial and philanthropic agencies by associating them with illicit "black markets" and immoral "gray markets." Yet, despite the social welfare profession's quest to legitimize its role as the only provider of adoption services, they were only slightly effective; independent agencies and individuals continued to perform at least half of adoptive placements into the late 1950s. When

Children's Bureau staff called the Cradle's Florence Walrath "a thorn in the flesh" of Chicago social welfare experts, they acknowledged not only the authority and presence of the consumer paradigm, but also its staying power.[76]

These domestic policy tensions provided the context into which international adoption was born. From its inception, international adoption services relied heavily on private organizations and citizens. These players not only took the lead in child placement, but also monopolized the media spotlight. While the success of private entities relied on the existing public-private collaboration in child welfare and the importance of voluntarism to state interests, it also depended upon the U.S. mission to rebuild post-World War II Europe. As the next chapter shows, the cultural mandate to help Europe's needy accelerated throughout the early Cold War, influencing immigration policies and shaping U.S. perceptions of orphans. The war orphan became a tangible symbol of European desperation at the same time as the U.S. government extended immigration laws to permit the entry of thousands of displaced European orphans as a democratic and capitalist bulwark against the Soviet Union. But it was the three-year Greek civil war that presented an opportunity for the consumer paradigm to emerge overseas. In the wake of Greece's devastated social welfare infrastructure, private humanitarian organizations and commercial operators began bringing Greek children to the United States. This foray into foreign adoption satisfied U.S. Cold War objectives and laid the political, cultural, and procedural groundwork for an ongoing international adoption system in the second half of the twentieth century.

CHAPTER 2

"An International Baby Hunt"

The "Gray Market" in Greece

ERNEST MITLER WAS AN INTIMIDATING FIGURE. With dark slicked-back hair and a serious expression, the Ivy League-educated attorney commanded attention. As New York City Assistant District Attorney in the early 1950s, Mitler conducted significant undercover work in black market baby operations, often posing as a prospective adoptive father. In the mid-1950s, he served as Special Counsel for the Senate Subcommittee on Juvenile Delinquency, and hunted down baby sellers from California to New Jersey. By 1957, his focus had shifted to international adoptions. Consulting for the New York State Joint Legislative Committee on Matrimonial and Family Law, he tracked down attorneys performing what officials feared were unauthorized adoptions in Greece. Such adoptions violated the sound standards of established social welfare professionals by propositioning mothers, accepting steep payments from prospective adoptive couples, and circumventing home investigations. In Mitler's view, these types of placements exacted a steep toll on U.S. credibility abroad. He warned, "with the increases in the number of children coming from the villages in Greece it is beginning to appear that we are engaging in an international baby hunt to accommodate the wants of American couples many of whom have been rejcted [sic] by American social agencies."[1]

Mitler was most concerned with operators like Leo Lamberson, an Indiana-based attorney who found American homes for Greek orphans. Painting him as a petty criminal who had served jail time for larceny and bootlegging, Mitler accused Lamberson of placing children haphazardly, often with different adoptive couples from those originally approved by the

Greek courts.[2] Mitler attributed the "insidious practice" of independent adoptions like those Lamberson performed to three principal factors: the dearth of national oversight by the U.S. Children's Bureau, the lack of international adoption law to check the role of "private individuals," and the desperate poverty of many Greek families that forced them to give up their children.[3] While Mitler accurately depicted the problem's scope, he failed to consider that the system not only permitted private interests in child welfare, but often prioritized those interests. Lamberson was a good example of this. The attorney got his start in international adoption work as a leader of the Greek fraternal organization the American Hellenic Educational Progressive Association (AHEPA), an approved volunteer organization first under the Displaced Persons Commission and later under the Refugee Relief Committee. Both the Displaced Persons Act and the Refugee Relief Act commissioned AHEPA to place Greek orphans in American families. While Lamberson did eventually cross into the realm of commercial adoptions, where his past refugee work gave his often illicit activities a legitimate air. Despite Mitler's first-rate detective work, public and congressional support of independent adoptions made obtaining prosecutions extremely difficult, even in states with stringent regulations like New York. Indeed, Lamberson was neither indicted nor disbarred for babyselling, nor did it affect his career; the Indiana attorney served as St. Joseph County's special public defender until he retired in the late 1960s.[4]

International adoption from Greece to the United States created a venue for volunteer adoptions to thrive. This was not just because there was a lack of federal legislation, as Mitler contended. It was also because private agencies and individuals already had significant influence in crafting and implementing U.S. child welfare policies. As Chapter 1 highlighted, social workers labeled independent placements by well-meaning individuals "gray-market" adoptions, designating them as "outside the system." Yet the skyrocketing popularity of independent adoptions led policymakers to protect these technically "unauthorized" placements. Officials allowed the consumer paradigm to thrive because social agencies served as gatekeepers for too few children and offered uneven services to birth mothers. Policymakers' tolerance of the consumer paradigm perpetuated an international adoption institution that valued voluntary organizations over professional child welfare agencies.

As the term "gray market" implies, there was tension in child welfare policies and practices between protecting the best interests of the child—as prioritized in the *child welfare paradigm*—and providing services to prospective adoptive parent clients—as emphasized in the *consumer paradigm.* Adoptive parents saw themselves as customers who, by selecting the adoption services they preferred, voted with their dollars rather than subjecting themselves to a publicly mandated system with strict regulations. In effect, this perpetuated a tiered system based on adoptive parents' ability to pay and sustained a fuzzy boundary between selling adoptive services and selling babies, a trend still seen in international adoption markets today.[5] Using emergency provisions as the basis for long-term social welfare solutions cultivated a policy environment receptive to the consumer paradigm with cursory oversight from licensed child welfare practitioners.

The Cold War also offered an ideological justification to extend and legislatively protect independent adoptions abroad, delaying the uniform professionalization of international adoption.[6] Just as demand for adoptable children rose considerably during the second half of the 1940s, Europe faced a seemingly insurmountable crisis as national leaders struggled to feed and house millions of displaced people during and after World War II.[7] U.S. media publicized the refugees' fate with a particular emphasis on children, imploring Americans to assist where they could. The cultural mandate to help Europe's needy accelerated throughout the early Cold War, influencing immigration policies and shaping U.S. perceptions of orphans. A symbol of European desperation, the war orphan was soon a rallying cry for American intervention, and U.S. families rushed to foster and adopt foreign children. While most war orphans were never adopted and would never become permanent members of American families, their popularity marked an important moment when the United States began to identify raising "abandoned" foreign children as part of its collective national responsibility.[8] War orphans also opened the legislative door to other foreign children, leading lawmakers to establish policies and systems that lasted long after European resettlement.

Constructing the War Orphan

By publicizing the plight of the war orphan, the mass media humanized the European crisis and raised awareness about the need for international adoption. The war orphan was first popularized as a casualty of World War II and later as part of the global fight against communism. Through newspaper photographs, magazine articles, and popular films, the American public learned of these "abandoned" children and many felt moved to act. Letters poured into the Children's Bureau, Congress, and the White House as citizens asked how they could help to alleviate Europe's burden by sending relief supplies, participating in child sponsorship, or helping refugee families, especially in England, Germany, France, and Belgium. One prominent theme overshadowed the others, however: American couples expressed a resounding interest in adopting these children and giving them permanent homes in the United States. As early as 1945, letters specifically requested information on adopting "war orphans" of British, Greek, and Irish descent.[9] One family who had grown attached to the five-year-old Belgian boy they were sponsoring under the national Foster Parents' Plan for War Children wanted information on pursuing a legal adoption.[10] Sometimes legislators even sent appeals to the Children's Bureau on behalf of their constituents.[11] Most striking was the frequency with which standard adoption inquiry letters from childless couples mentioned "war babies," displaced persons, or European orphans as alternatives to the backlogged domestic adoption system, which by 1951 averaged one available child for every ten prospective adoptive couples.[12]

International adoption formally began in the United States during World War II as one way to assist European allies. The U.S. Committee for the Care of European Children (USCOM), a private nonprofit organization commissioned by the State Department in July 1940, directed both the temporary and the permanent orphan migration programs until the early 1950s. The organization's board of directors brought together prominent businessmen like Marshall Field and philanthropists like First Lady Eleanor Roosevelt to first tackle temporary relocation for British children in 1940 and then mostly German-Jewish children until 1945. Those children permanently adopted before 1946 went to relatives living in the United States and the remaining children stayed in foster families until it was safe to return to their home countries. From 1946 to 1948, USCOM brought 1,387 children to the United States, most going to relatives, in response to President Truman's December 22, 1945, directive giving displaced orphans "preferential treatment in the granting of visas"[13] (see Appendix). In the late 1940s, U.S. volunteer organizations also brought French and Belgian children temporarily to the United States to help with the rebuilding of Western European institutions. While few of these children were available for "stranger adoption," this migration put another spotlight on European orphans.

During these refugee waves, the adoption of a foreign child was still subject to the national quotas established in the Immigration Act of 1924, better known as the National Origins Act. Once a country had exhausted its annual quota, applicants had to wait until the following year to reapply for visas. The post-World War II surfeit of displaced people, many of whom were trying to get to the United States, caused most national quotas to be almost immediately oversubscribed. Quota spots were especially difficult to secure for migrants from Eastern and Southern European nations with "less desirable" immigrant populations in the minds of 1920s legislators. For instance, Greece's annual quota permitted only 304 migrants in comparison with Germany's 25,957 and Great Britain's 65,721.[14] Therefore, less than eighteen months after President Truman's directive, only England, Germany, and Ireland still had quota spots remaining. Since no waiver existed for adoptive children, even in military families, it made international adoption from a country other than Germany almost impossible. Even Germany had complications since no U.S. consulate existed in the British, French, and Russian occupied zones, making a visa application for a foreign child living there technically infeasible.[15]

Despite these legislative hurdles, U.S. emergency relief in Europe contributed powerfully to Americans' conflation of displaced peoples with orphans and justified U.S. intervention. When addressing the nation about extending visas to displaced refugees, President Truman linked relief measures to European orphans, saying, "I desire that special attention be devoted to orphaned children to whom it is hoped the majority of visas will be issued."[16] In the 1947 Senate Judiciary Committee hearings on the Displaced Persons Act (DPA), Ben Brown of the State Department insisted that children in the occupied areas were a U.S. "responsibility" and "a problem that this Government must solve."[17] Child sponsorship programs through organizations like Save the Children and Foster Parents Plan for War Children also emphasized war orphans' needs and how these needs required an American response.[18] A Save the Children advertisement showed a smiling, seemingly healthy preschooler named Christina with short dark hair and a white dress. Yet the picture belied Christina's reality of hunger and hardship. Even though Christina's family had survived, their poverty made everyday life bleak and fraught with peril. According to the text that accompanied the photograph, the "lively, pretty" child had "experienced more of human misery than most of us see in a lifetime" and faced a future without hope.[19] Rather than shock American families with grotesque images of starving, diseased waifs, as organizations like the Christian Children's Fund did in Asia during the 1950s, Save the Children's promotional materials made European children relatable.[20] This advertisement was remarkable because of its ordinariness: Christina could have been mistaken for any American child. A logical marketing move, efforts like these helped to make U.S. couples feel responsible for the fate of Europe's needy children—orphans or not. As one prospective adoptive parent explained to the Children's Bureau, adopting war orphans "who may never become normal adults because of the effect of war, hunger and neglect" would "bring together people in this country who want children with children everywhere who desperately need love and a home."[21]

Media reports also cast displaced children as helpless without U.S. assistance. One *Life* article showed two Jewish orphans in a New York department store smiling happily as they clutched stuffed animals, surrounded by new clothes, the beneficiaries of American largesse and material wealth. The text revealed, however, that these orphans were just visiting from a French orphanage, part of a program organized by a Jewish women's group.[22] Reports like these convinced the American public that only U.S. intervention could solve the problems plaguing Europe. When one group of refugees arrived, reporters depicted their deprivation as so extreme that they didn't even recognize bread, let alone oranges or meat. In one news story, a "little 6-year-old blonde began to cry when she was given a plate of pot roast. She said she didn't know what it was." By coming to the United States, displaced children could expect abundant food, daily baths, new clothes, and trips to the circus—all marks of a sheltered, middle-class American childhood.[23]

These "dazzled but happy" refugees captured the hearts of Americans, who could not fathom "blonde" children without enough to eat. Since U.S. adoptive families had considered blondeness an especially desirable feature in an adopted child since the early twentieth century, descriptions like these heightened the orphans' desirability.[24] This outpouring led one *Collier's* article to resoundingly proclaim, "Uncle! Uncle! Hearts of America's Soldiers Go Out to Britain's War Orphans." "In typical soldier fashion," the reporter raved, U.S. GIs spent their hard-earned money to sponsor "blitz kids," fatherless, motherless, or parentless children often from London's "slums" who survived Germany's 1940 attack on England. Through the Stars and Stripes Orphan's Fund, soldiers became "uncles" to thousands of British children. Sponsors could even bring children on excursions to the

United States, which meant that, in the reporter's opinion, "the youngster [went] home with a massive stomach-ache and a lasting conviction that all Americans are millionaires, wildly generous, affectionate—and slightly screwy."[25] Spoiling "forlorn" children, even temporarily, cast Americans as altruistic allies and the United States as a land of consumer abundance.

Mainstream films further cemented popular constructions of the war orphan, reinforcing children's need, their availability, and the imperative of providing American assistance. The most famous of these was *Woman of the Year*, a 1942 film that boasted both box office and critical success.[26] Katherine Hepburn starred as the cosmopolitan and well-connected political columnist Tess Harding, whose career commitments led her to chronically neglect her husband, sports writer Sam Craig, played by Spencer Tracy. To fulfill her responsibility as chair of the Greek Child Refugee Committee, Tess agreed to foster Chris, a Greek war orphan who appeared to be about six years old (played by George Kezas). When her husband discovered she had acted without his knowledge in offering to host the orphan, Tess defended herself by emoting, "I want to help," insisting it was a "humanitarian idea," befitting her commitment to international causes. A reviewer for the *Portland Oregonian* had a more cynical take, observing that Tess, in her role as diplomat, had to "set a good example for America."[27]

After showing Chris his new room, Tess intended to leave the boy home alone as she, her housekeeper, and Sam attended an award banquet where Tess would accept the title as "Outstanding Woman of the Year."[28] By underestimating the supervision a young child required, the filmmakers made Tess seem preoccupied and selfish, ultimately leaving Chris "unmothered and unloved," in the words of a *New York Times* review.[29] Furthermore, against the backdrop of the awards ceremony, Tess's negligence as both wife and mother made her designation as an "outstanding woman" suspect. Conversely, Sam, the stalwart and steady father, was depicted as the key to the family's psychological stability. Rather than leave Chris unattended, Sam missed the award ceremony to watch the boy, temporarily assuming the "mother" role to compensate for his wife's rejection of her "true" gender role.[30]

While Tess accepted her award, Sam returned the boy to the Greek Children's Home. In the script, the screenwriters noted that the poster displayed near the entrance needed to be "a star-spangled affair showing a smiling American couple, with the husband holding a happy Greek child.

The message reads, 'America has a heart. Help Greek children. Greek Child Refugee Committee'."[31] When Sam brought Chris inside, the orphanage director commented on the "long waiting list" for families who wanted to adopt war orphans. These messages reinforced that Americans had embraced their national responsibility to help needy foreign children. When Tess discovered what Sam had done, she raced to retrieve Chris. But even when she tried to bring Chris back, she was more concerned about ruining her public, do-gooder image than with being a nurturing parent. So when the youngster refused to go with her, content to wait with his peers at the children's home until a more suitable mother came along, Tess received her "comeuppance." The filmmaker showed that Tess, the ambitious and distracted mother, was not deserving of such a precious resource.

The film's final scene also emphasized how crucial gendered marital roles were to a happily functioning household. Trying to win back Sam's affection after he left her because of the orphan "incident," Tess attempted to make his favorite breakfast from a cookbook annotated by Sam's mother. Although she failed miserably at first—at one point the coffeepot exploded on the stove—Tess redeemed herself by demonstrating her desire to please her husband through homemaking. As the New York Times reviewer tellingly summarized, not until "the good old American sports writer stands up on his hind feet," by sending Chris back and moving out, does "Mrs. Outstanding Woman discover what a wife should really be."[32] Perhaps because of its timeliness, the Motion Picture Academy awarded writers Ring Lardner, Jr., and Michael Kanin with an Oscar for the Best Original Screenplay.

Other 1940s films also depicted war orphans as parentless, but longing for a nuclear family, which typically meant leaving the wasteland of Europe for the promise of the United States. Four years after Woman of the Year's release, a U.S. army sergeant reached out to a Czech orphan in The Return of Rusty (1946), bringing the child home as a stowaway. Through several misadventures, the boy eventually found a home with a family in small-town America—a story line reminiscent of the Dondi strips that would appear almost a decade later. In a similar tale of an orphan's ingenuity, The Vicious Years (1950) showed how Mario, an Italian orphan, struggled to find a permanent adoptive family. Once he found loving parents, Mario's desperation to be accepted was so great that he concealed knowledge of a murder perpetrated by their son, Luca. When Luca tried to kill Mario because he was jealous of the attention the orphan had received, Luca's father discovered his crimes, turned him over to the authorities, and adopted Mario permanently. In this suspension of reality, the adoptive son was a more ideal relation than the biological child. *The Vicious Years* revealed how adoption could trump biological ties, satisfying the needs of both the parentless child and the childless parents. Between 1946 and 1952, a spate of classics featuring European orphans in transition or crisis were also made into films, including *Great Expectations* (1946), *Oliver Twist* (1948), *The Secret Garden* (1949), and *Les Misérables* (1952).[33] While not about war orphans in particular, these movies further contributed to notions of orphans as initially misunderstood but ultimately desirable family members and upstanding citizens.

Such popular constructions of the refugee and the war orphan affected more than just individual attitudes toward needy children. They also specifically influenced the formation of international adoption policy. As American couples increasingly expressed an interest in adopting foreign children, the clamor for a larger legislative initiative rose to a crescendo. Since no official international or national law existed to govern these adoptions, the U.S. Committee for the Care of European Children used corporate affidavits for unspecified children as the legal means for their immigration. These blanket assurances certified that the children would be the responsibility of individual families under "the supervision of social welfare agencies that met the standards set up by the Children's Bureau" and have a bond issued as a "safeguard against future contingencies."[34] Yet, the corporate affidavit model offered the most cursory type of protection—a "weak type of evidence" in judicial proceedings—that emphasized expediency over deliberation. Its primary purpose was to guarantee to U.S. authorities that the child would not become a state ward and thus a public financial burden.[35]

Another stopgap solution used by hundreds of families was to have a legislator propose an individual bill on their behalf. But the individual affidavit method was labor intensive for Senate committees responsible for compiling the reams of supporting paperwork necessary to demonstrate a prospective adoptive parent's record of stellar citizenship. Noting the deficiencies in the current system, the Children's Bureau became more proactive about working with the American Red Cross and the State Department to find a solution to the bottleneck, particularly for military families.[36]

Displaced Persons Act

The combination of agency initiative, constituent demand, and cumbersome independent bills led both houses of Congress to pass the Displaced Persons Act in 1948, providing an unprecedented 3,000 nonquota visas to orphaned children—a move that signaled U.S. policymakers' commitment to caring for foreign orphans. Offering 205,000 visas for displaced persons, this legislation was the first to provide relief because of persecution. But it was the orphan provisions that seemed the most permissive. According to an official legal report from the Displaced Persons Commission, attorneys argued that "the Congress by its legislative treatment of orphans has given very clear evidence that it was the intent of Congress to be as liberal as possible as far as this group was and is concerned."[37]

Prompted by a wealthy constituent's desire to adopt an identified orphan from Poland, Senator Irving M. Ives (R-N.Y.) introduced the orphan provision of the bill to help the "innocent victims of war." Ives stipulated that "this is not an immigration bill but an expression of the great heart of the United States which always went out to children" and should be kept "separate and distinct from the overall problem of the refugee, the persecuted, and the displaced person, or the immigrant."[38] He also urged the committee not to discriminate on the basis of race or nationality since this bill was intended as humanitarian relief. Yet Ives did not realize his desire for an orphan law that transcended national and racial boundaries, which representatives from both the State Department and the Department of Justice argued would prove extremely difficult to accomplish in light of current immigration law.[39] The DPA's final version provided three thousand orphan visas apart from standard immigration quotas. It defined orphans as under the age of sixteen, from Italy or the British, French, or American sectors of Germany and Austria, who were missing both parents—strikingly omitting Japan.[40] Ives's advocacy, however, had opened the legislative door to orphaned children and brought to the Senate's attention the plight of children outside Europe.

In the DPA hearings, legislators considered orphan provisions in light of U.S. parents' demand for adoptable children. Committee members specifically asked, "do you think there will be a sufficient number of citizens . . . who will qualify in order to adopt a reasonable percentage of these orphans who may desire to come to the United States?"[41] Without the reassurance from the State Department representative, Ben Brown, that their office believed both parents and organizations could care for these orphans, senators were hesitant to bring additional children into the country. This exchange illustrates that the DPA's orphan provisions partially rested on the existence of a U.S. market for orphans.

U.S. legislators framed the Displaced Persons Act as a beacon of U.S. benevolent intervention, reinforcing the connection between war orphans and national interests. As Rep. Frank Chelf (D-Ky.) gushed, "It is a pleasure indeed to see the law we passed last year is operating and is helping to bring these youngsters into the United States, where we can mold strong, good, substantial, God-fearing, God-loving American citizens of tomorrow from the little, tired, lonely, friendless orphans of today."[42] Spoken during a period of severe immigration restrictions, Chelf's comment, reminiscent of Emma Lazarus's "tired, poor, and huddled masses," signaled the privileged status of orphans and some refugees.[43] Lawmakers extended the popular DPA in 1950 and again in 1951. While the original DPA did not recognize Greek children as displaced persons, Congress modified the 1950 Act to include children up to sixteen years old from Greece, and up to ten from European countries not under Soviet control. A significant policy shift, this not only enabled U.S. couples to adopt Greek children but also secured the immigration mechanism for a long-term program in Greece, where orphan estimates were especially high.[44]

The amendment did much more than just extend the provisions governing the age and origin of permitted children. It also crucially redefined the term "orphan" to include children with surviving parents, making it arguably the most significant building block in international adoption. In the original DPA, and all prior temporary measures, orphans were strictly defined as children whose parents had both died or disappeared. The revised law added that a child would also be considered an orphan if he had "been abandoned, or deserted by, or separated or lost from both parents, or who has only one parent due to the death or disappearance of his other parent and the remaining parent is incapable of providing care for such orphan and agrees to release him for emigration and adoption or guardianship."[45] When considering lawmakers' intent behind words like "abandonment" and "separation," State Department General Counsel James McTigue argued against employing a strict construction of such categories. He contended, "The statutory use of the almost synonymous terms of 'abandonment,' 'desertion,' 'separation,' 'loss,' and 'disappearance' is evidence of the fact that the Congress was seeking to cover as many situations respecting the availability of orphans as it possibly could." In McTigue's view, the DPA overwhelmingly provided "no statutory distinction" between "abandonment in law" and "abandonment in fact." He concluded by stressing that the State Department was "fortunate in being able to lean upon such a clear and liberal congressional history which is not always found in statutory interpretation."[46] To powerful effect, this interpretation made the international definition of orphan compatible with the domestic one, which also allowed children with two living parents to qualify as orphans.

In addition to expanding the legal definition of orphan, the DPA also laid the framework for a laissez-faire approach to federal adoption policy grounded in emergency response. Since the DPA's original purpose was to alleviate a temporary refugee crisis by circumventing the stringent U.S. quota system, the law emphasized adaptability and variability over rigidity. Therefore, the act did not institute a permanent set of regulations that governed the adoption process nor specify procedures and standards for how to determine a child's orphan status and approve an adoptive home. Instead, the legislation only gave cursory parameters for visa qualification purpose. Because of its temporary nature, it provided no explicit safeguards for protecting children by requiring a licensed agency to supervise the process or complete a mandatory home study. In effect, the DPA was an immigration mechanism that granted U.S. citizens access to orphans. Policymakers allowed the U.S. Committee for the Care of European Children to continue its supervision over adoptive placements through the corporate affidavit method, extending a large amount of control to private agencies.

The DPA also provided the U.S. Committee for the Care of European Children with considerable flexibility to work through whatever organization had the funding and resources to process orphans for adoption. In Germany and Austria, for instance, the committee first worked with the United Nations Relief and Rehabilitation Administration (UNRRA), an international refugee resettlement alliance that took responsibility for locating orphaned children and housing them in camps until relatives could be traced or paperwork put in order for international placement. In 1946, the UN General Assembly formed the International Refugee Organization to handle UNRRA's previous work in Germany, Austria, and the remaining eligible European countries with the exception of Greece. Both these organizations had trained social welfare staff and broad-based international support, prioritizing family reunification over other goals.

In the case of Greece, the U.S. Committee for the Care of European Children designated the American Hellenic Educational Progressive Association as responsible for identifying and processing orphans. Known as AHEPA, the U.S.-based Greek fraternal society included 75,000 members nationwide. While experienced in helping Greek immigrants assimilate and obtain U.S. citizenship, AHEPA had no background in child welfare. Its membership also had clear loyalty to U.S. objectives over international ones. Yet under the Displaced Persons Act, AHEPA was considered just as legitimate an organization as UNRRA or the International Refugee Organization, groups with significant experience in child welfare. Thus, in situations deemed emergencies, the committee sanctioned a wide "variety of procedures and agencies."[47] Furthermore, since the DPA's original purpose was a temporary refugee measure, it logically, and for the most part accurately, categorized orphans as refugees. But as lawmakers extended the DPA in 1950 and 1951, fewer of the acknowledged orphans actually qualified as refugees. This sleight of hand transformed all international orphans into refugees for legislative purposes—a move with significant consequences for later legislation, which the next chapter explores in more detail.

Regardless of intent, the DPA's emphasis on flexibility opened the door for the consumer paradigm to take root in international adoption because of the significant demand for war orphans. The Children's Bureau and State Departments of Welfare fielded constant inquiries from prospective adoptive parents and legislators about adopting European war orphans, especially babies or younger children from Western European countries.[48] Overwhelmed by public pressure and inadequate centralized information about the foreign adoption process, the Children's Bureau compiled a report in July 1948 that revealed how few of these types of children actually existed. Of the 1,275 displaced children brought to the United States by March 1948, nearly 1,100 were Eastern European—largely from Poland, Czechoslovakia, and Hungary—and they were almost entirely between fourteen and eighteen. The report discovered that hardly any young children who were separated from their parents survived the war, making the young war orphan a rare occurrence.[49]

The few orphans who did come to the United States as adopted children were almost entirely adopted by relatives. While 127 German children had been adopted by 1948, these were mostly through Military Government Law No. 10, which authorized members of the U.S. armed forces to adopt German or mixed-race children through German courts as of December 1,

1947.[50] As the Children's Bureau repeatedly explained to prospective adoptive parents, European countries were "anxious to keep their children," even those born and raised in displaced persons' camps.[51] By mid-1951 the supply of adoptable European children had become so low that the Displaced Persons Commission stopped taking requests for unnamed children unless the family was open to adopting a "negro or Greek child."[52] The high degree of demand for foreign children who simply were not available for adoption influenced more creative—and potentially more exploitative—avenues for generating a supply of adoptable children. All this became possible because of the DPA's overly broad directive.

Despite such discouraging statistics, some Americans successfully adopted European children, through either individual bills or the DPA. In turn, media outlets shifted their focus from images of displaced war orphans in the 1940s to European orphans as adopted children beginning in the early 1950s. Articles and photographs featured adoptive parents overcoming obstacles to bring home neglected children in need of families. When asked why she chose to adopt an Italian war orphan, Martha Gellhorn pointed to a humanitarian mandate, "Most of the world has forgotten its hurt and homeless children or prefers to be blind."[53]

One story that received coverage in several newspapers involved a seventeen-month-old Greek orphan adopted by Korean War veteran and navy fighter pilot, Lt. Norman Donahoe and his wife Helen. Tired of waiting for a child in their home state of Texas, the childless couple located the Greek orphan, named Roni Marie, through friends in Athens. A winsome toddler with chubby cheeks and striking deep brown eyes, Roni Marie clung devotedly to her adoptive father as she posed for *New York Times* and *New York Herald Tribune* photographers. Donahoe had traveled from Korea directly to Greece to pick her up and then created a media sensation by trying to "hitch" a ride back to the States via military transport—with his wife eagerly awaiting them at a friend's house in Brooklyn.

The Donahoes's adoption would have been a hopeful sign to many prospective adoptive couples. Here was a childless family who had extinguished its options domestically but found a child through international channels. There was no discussion in the news reports of trying waiting periods, unsympathetic social workers, or dead ends. Instead, it required only the simple inquiry of a friend and an international flight, resulting in an undeniably charming infant.[54] For adoptive parents, social welfare bureaucracy seemed like the enemy—an insensitive impediment to the real needs of "war orphans" and their future families. Independent operators, like the nameless individuals responsible for Roni Marie's adoption, were part superhero and part stork, capable of scaling barriers to deliver babies to deserving couples. As one subtitle summarized, "A distinguished American writer's own story of her search through the orphanages of Italy for a child to adopt—and how after all the lacerating red tape, dire predictions and doubts, she and her small son have come happily home."[55]

The war orphan was a crucial, if confusing, symbol of the institutionalization of international adoption. Ultimately, few orphans from World War II became permanent members of American families—and most of those children were adopted by relatives. But their image left an indelible imprint on American culture, marking the moment when the United States began to identify raising "abandoned" foreign children as part of a collective national responsibility. Equally important, war orphans wedged open the door to other foreign children, as lawmakers established guidelines, systems, and policies in their name that endured long past European resettlement. Indeed, through ostensibly emergency legislation, the definition of foreign orphans was permanently expanded to include children with two living parents. Using emergency provisions as the basis for long-term policy structures helped to produce a climate receptive to the consumer paradigm with only spotty oversight from licensed child welfare practitioners—one that by the late 1950s would provoke Ernest Mitler to shift his gaze from domestic markets to those in Greece.

Paving the Way for an International Adoption Program in Greece

When Mitler's investigation began in the late 1950s, Greece had been a sending nation for adoptable children for nearly a decade. Although U.S. families also adopted internationally in the same era from Germany, Italy, and Ireland, the Greek program became the most robust. More than any other European nation, Greece suffered from political and economic turmoil long after World War II, mostly rooted in the three-year civil war from 1946 to 1949 that devastated the country. Although tensions had been building between Greek nationalists and the Greek Communist Party (KKE) throughout World War II, 1945 was a watershed year. Increasing violence toward communists and the failure of elites to institute moderate centrist politics eventually led to a takeover by the royalist Right in March 1946. These anticommunist forces, especially in local municipalities, imposed what one historian described as a "reign of terror," rendering the central government ineffective at reining in the provinces. Refusing to acknowledge the debatable plebiscite in September 1946 that returned the king to power, the KKE stationed their forces in the mountains of northern Greece and used guerilla tactics to leverage their 22,000 soldiers against the 120,000-man Greek National Army.[56] Britain, still recovering from World War II, sent resources to the National Army, but its ability to offer more significant aid was limited, leading the Greek government to request additional help from the United States.

On May 22, 1947, President Truman allocated $300 million to the Greek government, "to support free peoples who are resisting attempted subjugation by armed minorities or by outside pressures," famously known as the Truman Doctrine. Truman also sent a delegation of U.S. military advisors to Greece. At the end of 1947, the Joint Chiefs of Staff established the Joint United States Military Advisory and Planning Group expressly to assist the Greek Armed Forces in bringing national stability. These consultants worked with the Embassy, delegates from the government, and civilians to "defend their native" land "without the need of a single American rifleman."[57] As the Greek military gained U.S. resources and support, it succeeded in blockading the guerrillas and turning the war into one governed by more conventional military tactics. Coupled with the loss of Tito's crucial support in 1948 because of a split with Stalin, the KKE could not afford to keep fighting and surrendered in 1949. While Greece allegedly enjoyed peace after the war ended, as historian Mark Mazower argues, "it was a strange, strained peace, guarded by what was formally a democratic order but held in place by repression, persecution of the Left, and armed violence on the fringes of society."[58]

Displacement, separation, and exile characterized the war years and the lives of Greek civilians. The orphan crisis was especially acute. Since 12 percent of Greek children had lost one or both parents during World War II, the nearly 340,000 children orphaned over the course of the civil war overwhelmed the already shaky social welfare system.[59] Relatives who might have continued to care for orphaned children in better times often could not afford to do so. As child welfare officers stationed in Athens observed, "the poverty in the villages is unbelievable."[60] Since neither the nationalist government nor the communist resistance had the resources to meet all

Greek children's needs, they developed ways to care for orphans that reinforced their respective ideologies. The Greek nationalists sent children
to *paidopoleis* or child-towns for state education while the communists
evacuated groups of children behind the Iron Curtain to Yugoslavia in
what became known as the *paidomazoma* (meaning literally, "gathering
of the children")—a term coined by Greek anticommunists. *Paidomazoma* was a historical reference to the forcible conversion and conscrip-
tion of Greek Orthodox children under the Ottoman *devshirme* system
and one highly sensitive in the Greek national memory. Because most
families could not offer their children the same degree of protection as
before, the state began to assert itself as the ultimate protector of Greece's
children.[61] Once the nationalist side triumphed, this meant that the government would use children to symbolize its commitment to anticommunism.[62] This state "ownership" of children formed the philosophical
and logistical impetus for supporting an international adoption program
to the United States.

Unlike most other European nations, which staunchly objected to foreign adoption to the United States as a solution to their orphan woes, the
Greek nationalist state welcomed the relief. Officials wanted to protect
Greek children from further communist influence while also offering them
increased economic opportunities. Of the 120,000 orphaned children in
need of state support, welfare institutions and benevolent agencies had the
resources to support only 42,500, leading the Greek government to ask the
United States directly for assistance. In an informal note from the Hellenic
Ministry of Social Welfare to the U.S. Embassy in Athens, the Greek foreign
minister insisted, "we hardly need to emphasize how deeply grateful we feel
to the U.S. government and to Congress for the opportunity generously
granted to some of those unfortunate children to emigrate to the United
States for adoption." The Greek government did qualify, however, that it
expected the majority of these children to be placed in first and second-
generation Greek families that adhered to the Orthodox faith. This was
probably because 95 percent of the Greek children available for adoption
from 1950 to 1952 were older children with Greek American relatives interested in adopting them. U.S. foreign ministers emphasized this requirement
and stressed that social welfare agencies needed to comply with officials'
intent.[63] One year later, in 1951, the Displaced Persons Commission issued
a report assessing government "attitudes" toward international adoption.
The report found that Greek officials "expressed considerable interest" in

placing children in the United States with plans to use the entire quota.[64] At the same time as officials pursued an international adoption program with the United States, the Greek state was demanding that Yugoslavia return the children removed during the *paidomazoma*, illustrating how keenly national, anticommunist interests governed the migration of Greek children.[65]

The Greek state's need for orphan relief dovetailed with U.S. economic, social, and political objectives in Europe. The Truman Doctrine's influx of relief money tied the United States to Greece, a relationship that only became more intimate as the Cold War escalated, first with the Berlin Airlift from 1948 to 1949 and then with the Korean War from 1950 to 1953. One article published in *Senior Scholastic*, a magazine aimed at high school students, even used the adoptive family as a metaphor for U.S. political and economic interests in Greece. Titled "Orphan Greece: Shall Uncle Sam Adopt This Problem Child?," the article portrayed Greece as the child, the United States as the parent, and adoption as the only reasonable option for long-term self-sufficiency. Stressing U.S. authority and Greek dependency, President Truman argued, "If we falter in our leadership, we may endanger the peace of the world—and we shall surely endanger the welfare of our nation."[66]

Yet, this was a particular type of dependency meant to pull on American heartstrings and make the public emotionally invested in Greek's future. Further driving home Greek hardship, the *Senior Scholastic* article's sole photo showed a small peasant boy sitting in the front of the Parthenon amid piles of rubble while looking off into the distance. A decidedly mixed message, the child's distant, stony gaze symbolized Greece's uncertain future, but the scene of ancient ruins pointed to the nation's strong past as a glimmer of hope.[67] Focusing on a child also related to *Senior Scholastic*'s teenage readers and inspired them to adopt a more global outlook, subtly enlisting youth as junior cold warriors. Overall, text and photo both depicted Greece's child-like dependence on U.S. intervention, a concept reinforced in refugee hearings when one witness asserted, "Greece today exists wholly and solely because of American financial assistance. Without it, there would be no Greek nation. It couldn't feed itself, it couldn't clothe itself, it couldn't conduct the war it is conducting without American assistance."[68] As this quote implied, the Cold War linked together U.S. economic prosperity with foreign policy objectives, "yoking . . . free choice as consumers with political freedom" in the words of Lizabeth Cohen, and helped average U.S. citizens to invest in Greece's capitalist and democratic future by supporting foreign aid.[69]

International adoption achieved this relationship even more effectively since it brought American families and Greek orphans together, unifying international interests under both the symbolic and the literal U.S. family. As the State Department's General Counsel pleaded, "For those unfortunates who disappear behind the Iron Curtain there is little left except the slim hope that their children may start life anew in one of the democratic countries on the other side of the Iron Curtain. To say to them that we recognize the separation but not for the purposes of the Displaced Persons Act would be to slam the last door on their meager hopes and at the same time deny admission to an otherwise eligible orphan whose only fault is a technicality in the law."[70] Just like Greek officials, U.S. legislators depicted the Southern and Eastern European parents of Cold War orphans as unable to escape communist oppression—"absent" parents because they were lost to communism. But as long as immigration laws remained as liberal as possible, the United States could ensure that their children would still have a bright future in the "free West."[71]

Americans also wanted to help because of the growing cultural acceptance that Greeks were "white." In the early twentieth century, only those of Anglo-Saxon and Teutonic origin were viewed as fully "white," and immigration quotas reflected this racial hierarchy, granting the majority of spots to migrants from Northern and Western Europe. From the late 1920s until 1965, when legislators finally removed race-based quotas from immigration law, Matthew Frye Jacobson contends that Greeks and other Mediterranean peoples slowly and unevenly "became Caucasian."[72] Founded in 1922 by Greek immigrants, the Order of AHEPA (American Hellenic Educational Progressive Association), a fraternal organization, worked hard to cultivate "pure and undefiled Americanism," in the words of its mission statement. It did this by making English the organization's official language and extending membership to those without Greek descent, demonstrating the commitment of some Greek-Americans to assimilation and multiculturalism.[73] These "efforts" to assimilate also came across in popular media. AHEPA leaders admired one North Carolina newspaper editorial from the mid-1950s so much that they included the text in their organization's history:

> In days when it is politically expedient to exploit so-called "minorities" in this country, we don't see anybody shedding any crocodile tears over the plights of the Greeks in this country. The reason for

this is very plain: your average Greek-American is not in any "plight." He doesn't feel sorry for himself. He is not passing around the hat for sympathy and he is not trying to get on any unemployment dole. Because there is built into the Greek character those traits which make for self-sufficiency, thrift, the willingness to work, having sense of humor, self-respect and courage. The individual with these traits can look the world in the face. He never has to worry about being a minority, because he feels like a majority. And he is.[74]

AHEPA aligned its organization against civil rights reforms and adopted the rhetorical privileges of whiteness by implicitly denigrating blacks. Although Southern press reports like these painted Greeks in a positive ethnic light, they still reflected the prevalent sentiment that those from Greece constituted a minority, even if a "model" one. Nevertheless, others considered those from Mediterranean countries as less ideal immigrants. One prospective adoptive parent's specification for "homeless children from European countries: preferably those of Teutonic stock," while not the norm, indicated that Greeks had yet to be fully subsumed under the blanket of whiteness.[75]

Americans of Greek origin knew this and lobbied hard to convince legislators of their worthiness. During the deliberations over the 1947 Displaced Persons Act, AHEPA representatives asked that legislators extend 1,000 additional quota spaces to Greek migrants, many of whom had already come to the United States illegally. The AHEPA leaders suggested that rather than add to the total immigration numbers, these should be taken from Germany's generous and unused allotment. According to Mae Ngai, many Euro-American ethnics envisioned immigration reform as their "civil rights movement," an effort that would bring them the full benefits of citizenship.[76] In this vein, AHEPA representatives not only appealed on humanitarian grounds, arguing that Greece could not economically sustain its citizens' repatriation, but more important, on the "grounds of good sound business sense" since many Greek men were "self-supporting business people." The officers depicted those deserving of these additional quotas not as average workers, but as business owners, who had distinguished themselves by running "sound enterprises" that contributed to American economic vitality—an argument that also surfaced during later hearings.[77]

This positioned Greek Americans as staunch anticommunists. As one officer argued before the Senate Subcommittee, "there isn't one minority group in the country that has shown a greater aptitude for free enterprise," suggesting that Greek migrants were natural allies in advancing Cold War aims.[78] AHEPA leaders further contended, "if they [migrants] are forcibly returned to Greece, not only do they lose, but their business interests in America will suffer and in turn hurt other American business." This subtle line of attack drew on constructions of whiteness derived from migrants' economic contributions. Undesirable immigrants, and domestic nonwhites, extracted from the economy by relying on welfare services and becoming a "burden on the American taxpayer."[79] By highlighting Greek migrants' economic leadership and anticommunism, AHEPA officers inferred that Greeks had "earned" their status as white citizens and the quota numbers should reflect this. Taking 1,000 quota spaces from Germany would further seal Greece's white heritage.[80]

In addition to advocating for refugees, American-Greek organizations started targeting relief to help children and maintain social welfare support programs in Greece. The Greek War Relief Association, headquartered in New York City, launched its orphan support project in August 1946, with the mission of finding foster and permanent homes for orphaned children as well as rigorous social welfare training in Greece. This partnership with the Greek government and the United Nations had no foreign adoption program, instead focusing purely on domestic placements.[81] Yet, the Greek War Relief Association was soon overshadowed by the larger and more prominent Order of AHEPA. In addition to running a civic education program that prepared new immigrants for U.S. citizenship, AHEPA devoted itself to patriotic and philanthropic work, including selling war bonds, collaborating with Red Cross relief, and raising money for hospitals and orphanages.[82] Initially AHEPA began its outreach as a partner of the Greek War Relief Association, working together to build hospitals, but the fraternal order eventually gained official government status in its own right.[83]

AHEPA also embraced U.S. Cold War policies in Greece, adding political weight to its philanthropic work. In the order's internally commissioned history, the author highlighted AHEPA's commitment to the Truman Doctrine, U.S. policies in Europe, and its anticommunist allegiances, referring to the Greek communists as "terrorists" and "guerrillas." Presenting before the Senate Subcommittee on Displaced Persons, AHEPA blamed the current upheaval in Greece on "the Communist-inspired civil war and the present Communist-inspired aggression and insurrection against the recognized Government of Greece." Rather than seeing the civil war as an internal action, AHEPA officers considered it "a deliberate attempt on the part of Communist-controlled countries to the north of Greece to destroy Greece as a democracy," an assessment with which the subcommittee agreed.[84] The AHEPA leadership also expressed solidarity with Greek nationalists, especially over the *paidomazoma*, which AHEPA called "abductions."[85] In his 1952 message to AHEPA's thirtieth national convention, President Truman—an honorary order member himself—affirmed the special friendship between Greece and the United States, stating, "I doubt if this friendship has ever been at a higher level than it is today."[86] But it was Truman's evidence for this friendship, "Greek and American soldiers . . . fighting side by side [in Korea] in defense of the highest principles of justice and freedom," that tied it resolutely to Cold War interests.[87] Fittingly, in 1963, AHEPA erected a statue of Truman in Athens to commemorate the Truman Doctrine and his leadership in "saving" Greece from communist control.[88]

This loyalty to U.S. and Greek nationalist interests made AHEPA a favorite of the State Department, who designated the order as "an arm of the government of the United States in administering the resettlement of 10,000 Greek refugees." Much of AHEPA's lobbying work embraced the anticommunist language so popular during the early Cold War. When presenting an appeal for the 1953 Refugee Relief Act, AHEPA argued that Greek migrants made outstanding citizens, because "all of them, having lived through and having witnessed a lot of the evils of communism, have an intensified appreciation of democracy and constitute one of our most vital forces in combating subversive doctrines."[89] The administration also linked AHEPA's work to the preservation of democracy because of American democracy's roots in ancient Greece. This magnified AHEPA's relief work in a war-torn country as a larger Cold War fight for representative government and free-market capitalism. This idea—that those from the outside could be the most influential insiders in protecting the United States—appealed to State Department officials.[90] It also marked AHEPA's foray into international adoption as an explicitly anticommunist endeavor.

Shaping Greek Adoptions Through Private Interests

Its national loyalty, along with the large number of Greek children going to U.S. relatives, gave AHEPA an early foothold in Greek adoption.[91] AHEPA officials, including a Minnesota state representative, lobbied heavily for the 1950 amendment to the DPA, arguing that the "Greek-American community of the United States would see that these displaced persons and orphans would be properly taken care of" in order "to make democracy live."[92] In late 1950, AHEPA became a voluntary agency accredited by the Department of State's Voluntary Foreign Aid Committee based on its partnership with USCOM, an umbrella agency with existing accreditation. This meant that AHEPA could officially place children for adoption in U.S. homes based on USCOM's record. Through this arrangement, families contributed $100 to the agencies on a voluntary basis to support administrative costs, which were fairly low because AHEPA's staff was not paid.[93]

AHEPA's role as an adoption intermediary, and the significant role of the U.S. Committee for the Care of European Children (USCOM), signaled the influence of voluntarism on the structure of international adoption. USCOM, a private association, licensed AHEPA, another private agency, to work on placing Greek orphans in U.S. homes.[94] AHEPA had no background in child welfare work, no trained social workers on staff, and no professional accreditations or associations with other child welfare agencies. The fraternal order's representatives revealed this inexperience in their initial proposal to the Advisory Committee on Voluntary Aid. When suggesting how to process files for named orphans—those children intended for relatives or specific sponsors—AHEPA volunteers assumed that "in these cases there would be little or no need for screening by our organization unless your Committee or the other official bodies deem that it is necessary."[95] Since officials mandated the routine screening of named children to confirm their identities, verify their social histories, and assure that their parents or guardians had properly relinquished them, comments like these highlighted AHEPA's limited exposure to child welfare standards. This inattention to screening children suggested that AHEPA leaders were principally concerned with expedient resettlement of Greek children into Greek American families.

On the surface, it seemed curious that officials knowingly approved AHEPA since the European program functioned under child welfare paradigm practices. Evelyn Rausch, director of the Displaced Persons Orphan Program, assured Elliott Shirk, the director of resettlement, that those responsible for child placement were required to make comprehensive home studies, maintain compliance with state Departments of Welfare, and conduct thorough background checks on orphans. Rausch even recruited

U.S. adoption specialists to staff the commission's European headquarters in Frankfurt to ensure that the agency handled all cases meticulously.[96] Yet, three months after Rausch's letter, the two DPC social workers stationed in Greece, Lena Cochran and Helen McKay, informed Robert Corkery, European coordinator for the DPC, that matters looked rather different in Greece. Because of insufficient transportation, no local authority with extant records, overwhelmed staff, and inexperienced volunteers, children were routinely sent to the States without completed social histories.

Working in a country with deplorable conditions and few resources certainly caused some of the mishaps, but other difficulties came from AHEPA's direct management of cases. While the original arrangement intended that Cochran and McKay should supervise all of the casework, there were too many children to make this feasible. This not only meant that hundreds of orphans arrived in U.S. ports without being screened, but also meant that the operations in Greece were slipshod and rudimentary. This inattention to proper casework infuriated the two professional social workers in command. Both Cochran and McKay insisted, "In many people's minds we are identified more with AHEPA at this point than the D.P. Commission. We question seriously whether this is a desirable position for a government agency to be placed in," particularly since "we are . . . in the position of defending the AHEPA-U.S. Committee plan when in fact we disagree in many cases."[97] Cochran and McKay were not the only naysayers; the U.S. Consul in Athens and Greek travel agents responsible for arranging children's transportation also complained about AHEPA's inflated fees and unprofessional services.[98]

Once these concerns came to light, officials tried to remove the fraternal order from the program. Less than a year after accrediting AHEPA, USCOM director Ingeborg Olsen questioned her agency's decision to approve AHEPA and took her concerns to a higher authority. In a meeting with State Department officials from the Voluntary Foreign Aid division under the Bureau of Economic Affairs, Olsen explained that while her relations with AHEPA's leadership were cordial, she was dissatisfied with their lack of training. Her efforts, for instance, "to convince Ahepa [*sic*] of the fact that named children going to relatives or friends sometimes need special care when their placements were unsuccessful," went nowhere. When Olsen suggested that AHEPA fund a USCOM child welfare worker in Greece, the organization refused, instead focusing their resources on setting up a new orphan program.[99] Three weeks later, Voluntary Foreign Aid staff reported additional AHEPA problems to the Office of Greek, Turkish, and Iranian Affairs, another State Department agency.

Despite officials' attempts to have AHEPA work collaboratively with a child welfare agency knowledgeable in immigration and resettlement, the organization insisted on handling orphan services themselves. AHEPA leaders' persistence in processing adoptions colored the organization's actions as inherently political. Indeed, after "considerable criticism," Chairman of the AHEPA DP Committee George Polos flew to Greece to try to improve the program himself, insinuating that AHEPA's mismanagement compromised its national reputation as a bulwark against communism.[100] Polos's visit did little good and USCOM proceeded with the derecognition of AHEPA in early 1952.

In their efforts to limit AHEPA's influence, social welfare experts butted up against the same barriers they faced when trying to regulate domestic "gray market" adoptions. Once the Children's Bureau heard that USCOM planned to derecognize the fraternal order, Director Mildred Arnold sent a memo to her staff, informing them that AHEPA was no longer considered a voluntary organization accredited by the State Department to conduct adoptions and that they should notify all state Departments of Welfare at once. This was especially urgent, in Arnold's opinion, because it appeared that AHEPA planned to continue placing children without consulting professional child welfare agencies.[101] But there was little that Arnold could do besides inform state officials since many state laws allowed independent operations like AHEPA to place children. Although Children's Bureau representatives labored to convince State Department officials that "state departments of public welfare feel obliged to work only with accredited agencies," the federal government could do little. The state-based system was set up to legally permit both public and private, both accredited and unaccredited.

DPC officials also considered how they might force AHEPA to become accredited separate from USCOM. The Orphan Section Supervisor explained in a letter to her superior that state laws would offer the best way to convince the order that it needed to be licensed since it violated state law to process adoptions without a proper license.[102] This was not completely accurate, however. It was not illegal for unlicensed entities to process adoptions unless a state explicitly prohibited it. Some states, Minnesota and New York for example, had laws prohibiting the interstate transfer of children without the approval of a licensed agency. But just as many states didn't.

This seemed more like a case of wishful thinking on behalf of Children's Bureau officials who immediately recognized the danger in a well-respected, and politically well-connected, organization like AHEPA being permitted to make placements without professional ties.

Just as with doctors and attorneys who placed children domestically, AHEPA's philanthropy and community service accolades gave it an unblemished public record and credibility with legislators. When the famed juvenile delinquency hearings held one of their sessions in Pittsburgh, the subcommittee requested testimony from Louis Manesiotis, a Pennsylvania businessman who was also serving as the supreme governor of AHEPA. The order's facilitation of numerous youth programs and coordination with other local organizations—Kiwanis, American Legion, and Knights of Columbus—to protect against juvenile delinquency brought it praise from Senator Estes Kefauver.[103] Congress also recognized AHEPA as the leading Greek refugee organization with at least six invitations to appear before various committees. As Senator William Langer (R-N.D.) effused during a RRA hearing, AHEPA "has done a marvelous job," and is considered "one of the finest organizations in America. We have a great many members in our State, some of the finest citizens," all of whom "have a marvelous record."[104] Many prominent politicians numbered themselves among AHEPA's ranks, including Spiro Agnew, representative William Cramer (R-Fl.), Senator Samuel Ervin (D-N.C.), and California governor Goodwin Knight. In fact, Langer himself was also a member.[105]

Probably because of the fraternal order's political connections, alongside an unanticipated surge in Greek cases in late 1951, AHEPA gained new accreditation in early 1952 to operate separately from USCOM and continue placing orphans.[106] Even with this seeming affirmation of their commission, AHEPA staff continued to frustrate the DPC social workers by their administrative oversights, including failing to provide appropriate travel escorts and under-dressing orphans for their Atlantic voyage. But with a still unmanageable number of cases, DPC staff needed the extra hands. As cases continued pouring into the Greek office, social workers worried that the Displaced Persons Act's June 30 expiration would come before most of the children could be placed.[107] AHEPA staff remained in the country, working alongside DPC staff. In fact, even with the program expiring, AHEPA received 250 new orphan cases in mid-March that would keep AHEPA in Greece well into August, weeks after the other staff.[108] But AHEPA's perseverance failed to redeem its relationship with USCOM. When the agency was dissolved one year later, it transferred the over 200 cases left under the DPA to International Social Service, giving the refugee resettlement organization its inaugural international adoption caseload and ostensibly signaling the end of AHEPA's adoption work.[109] Yet, less than nine months later, a new law would grant another 4,000 nonquota visas to children under ten years old from Europe, Asia, and Palestine and allow AHEPA another chance at orphan placement.

"Going Rogue": AHEPA and Commercial Adoptions in Greece

In some ways, the Refugee Relief Act of 1953 (RRA) seemed like the DPA redux. Like its predecessor, it also provided nonquota visas for eligible orphans and gave approved voluntary agencies chief responsibility. Although AHEPA sought and received new accreditation under the RRA as a refugee service organization, it was not officially recognized as part of the orphan program.[110] This did not stop the order from pursuing another international adoption program independently from approved volunteer agencies like International Social Service (ISS). With the RRA in place, AHEPA began advertising its adoption services in the Greek press, announcing that they planned to facilitate the adoption of 250–300 Greek orphans to U.S. Greek-American homes, a reasonable assessment since Refugee Relief officials identified at least 600 children in foundling homes available for adoption.[111] The order's Supreme President Harrison Bouras visited Greece in 1954 to meet with local authorities and locate a Greek-based staff director. Bouras hired attorney and Greek Department of the Interior employee Michael Tsaparis, who became AHEPA's long-term liaison.[112] ISS, the self-appointed watchdog for intercountry adoption placements, found that AHEPA still had no "social welfare personnel on their staff" and did not "enlist the cooperation of local social agencies in making home investigations or supervising the child after the arrival," observations it passed along to the Children's Bureau.[113]

The ability for volunteers to influence the adoption process only increased under the RRA since for the first time the law permitted adoptions to be finalized in the foreign country.[114] This process, known as a proxy adoption, worked best for volunteers because it expedited placements, finalizing adoptions quickly for eager families. While independent operators in Korea used the proxy system to its greatest extent, a phenomenon the next chapter explores in detail, the earliest proxy adoptions were likely Greek children—a result of the country's already established relationship with organizations like AHEPA. As early as 1952, Greek orphanage patrons and officials had introduced the notion of proxy adoption as a preferable method for future Greek adoption since it guaranteed that the child would be placed in a permanent home.[115] For child welfare officials, the problem with these placements was that they required no social welfare investigation, allowing savvy adoptive parents to complete them without any professional assistance. While expedient in the short term, this led to some long-term complications. In one 1954 proxy placement through an attorney, a couple adopted two girls, nine and ten years old. Three years after the adoption was finalized in the United States, the adoptive parents drove the girls to a New York City airport and put them on a one-way flight to Greece. Since no social agency had paperwork related to the case, the ISS-Greek Branch director had no way to arrange for another placement. Technically, the girls were not protected under Greek law because they had been adopted by U.S. citizens. Since social workers could not determine whether the girls had been readopted in the United States, which would have made them permanent U.S. citizens, the now teenagers were in national limbo, without family or country.[116]

Social workers and government officials from the Refugee Relief Commission and State Department recognized that such adoptions could prove problematic and worked on commissioning professional private agencies like ISS to administer the RRA's orphan program.[117] Senator Estes Kefauver also worked from the congressional angle to end the interstate and intercountry traffic in adopted children. His Senate Subcommittee on Juvenile Delinquency interviewed hundreds of birth mothers, adoptive parents, and adoption professionals, developing legislation that would criminalize any commercial adoption transaction. The bill explicitly defined "interstate commerce" as including foreign nations, a point that professional intercountry adoption agencies greatly supported.[118] Even such ambitious legislation, however, did not touch independent placements by well-meaning doctors and lawyers, once again demonstrating an adoption system rife with ambiguities.[119] Yet, as the legislation failed to carry enough votes in the House, this suggested that legislators lacked the congressional support to federally restrict commercial baby operations since doing so would require reforming the state-based social welfare structure.[120] Peter Chumbris, professional staff member to the Senate Subcommittee on Juvenile Delinquency, concluded, "We cannot legislate everything. . . . We cannot

Figure 1. Langer, Kefauver, and Ernest Mitler photo at committee.
Senate Historical Office.

provide our legislation in such a way to take care of all the circumstances, and we do not want to make the law so rigid that . . . [it] will prevent children who could come into this country from coming into this country."[121]

Without these limitations in place, AHEPA continued to facilitate the adoption of Greek orphans using the proxy system. In July 1956, AHEPA captured the national spotlight through their airlift of twelve children with the promise to bring seventy more.[122] The largest group from Greece yet, the airlift, and its organizer Leo Lamberson, caught the attention of ISS officials and eventually of Ernest Mitler himself.

By the mid-1950s, the special counsel for the Subcommittee on Juvenile Delinquency had started investigating independent international adoptions, targeting commercial operators. Officially appointed by AHEPA officers, Lamberson initially operated in what those adhering to the child welfare paradigm called the "gray market"—part of the well-intentioned cadre of lawyers and humanitarians committed to helping adoptive parents find children. As an AHEPA representative and expert on refugee resettlement,

Lamberson was called to testify for the Senate hearings on extending the RRA. But committee members were also interested in his child placing expertise, asking for his opinion on proxy adoptions.[123] Even though groups like ISS clearly objected to AHEPA's practices, the organization never disguised its role in the orphan program. Indeed, Lamberson sent photos of his airlift directly to State Department staff.[124] Yet, according to Mitler, within a single year Lamberson went from a respected community leader and "expert" on child placement, albeit in the "gray market," to a rogue baby seller. How was that possible?

Lamberson, in fact, straddled both worlds, revealing that under the consumer paradigm of child placement blurry boundaries existed between public and private, authorized and unauthorized, and gray and black. Once AHEPA disbanded its Refugee Relief committee with the expiration of the first RRA, Mitler believed that Lamberson continued to collaborate with other AHEPA members to arrange adoptions, never officially disassociating his work from the popular fraternal order. According to Mitler, Lamberson began using letterhead with one initial changed (AHAPA) so that most Greek foundling home directors and social welfare staff would continue to provide him with privileged access, all without AHEPA's knowledge. Yet, since Lamberson maintained leadership roles within AHEPA throughout the 1950s and 60s, attended national conferences, and represented the organization in other venues, it was hard to believe that AHEPA knew nothing of Lamberson's activities. Even ISS Assistant Director Susan Pettiss believed that Lamberson was still operating under AHEPA's leadership in mid-1958.[125]

Additionally, Lamberson's fee structure varied dramatically depending on the client. One couple reported paying a total of $373—$165 to Lamberson and $208 to cover the Greek court fees and the child's transportation to New York.[126] Another Baltimore couple paid $900.[127] While $900 was significantly more than $373, and could have included a "donation" made to Lamberson, it was still less than half the $2,800 that New York Jewish families routinely paid.[128] These discrepancies suggested that Lamberson maintained his "gray market" adoption practice for U.S.-Greek couples, only covering his costs or asking for donations, while simultaneously extorting Jewish families. As historian Mark Mazower contends, anti-Semitism rose precipitously in Greece following the German occupation during World War II.[129] Since Lamberson spent considerable time in postwar Greece, these ideologies might have also informed his adoption practice. Nevertheless, the well-documented desperation of childless Jewish couples proved too profitable for the Indiana lawyer to resist.[130] Even though charging excessive adoption fees was illegal in New York, Mitler never succeeded at prosecuting Lamberson, underscoring independent operators' ability to distinguish between selling legitimate services to adoptive parents instead of illegally selling babies.

Prospective adoptive parents largely embraced the practice of purchasing intercountry adoption services, sustaining the expansion of the consumer paradigm abroad. Accustomed to increased levels of consumer choice in the postwar marketplace, adoptive parents enjoyed having options in adoption services as well. Most couples found that social agencies operating under the child welfare paradigm produced vexing delays and frequent rejections, making adopters "hostile" and "antagonistic" toward authorized agencies. Prospective adoptive parents voiced their objections with a "degree of bitterness" that even Ernest Mitler found "alarming." In his interviews of hundreds of adoptive parents, the special counsel discovered that adoptive parents' uniform distrust of agencies was the primary reason for a "black market."[131] As Mitler's data confirmed, few prospective adoptive parents opted for a social welfare agency adoption in Greece. Of the 558 Greek children brought to the United States from September 1957 to March 1959, Visa Office figures revealed that only 58, roughly 10 percent, came through traditional social agency channels. This led Mitler to exclaim: "the commercial operators [in Greece] have practically monopolized the field."[132]

Many adoptive parents appreciated that they could buy results. Since all agencies charged fees of some kind, prospective adoptive couples wanted to ensure that as "customers" they received the best service.[133] Child welfare agencies often promoted the quality of their services over volunteer practitioners to woo clients, citing dozens of instances of failed independent adoptions.[134] But speed, guaranteed approval, and the ability to adopt more than one child made independent routes more popular. Lamberson received mountains of letters from prospective adoptive parents, many of whom "made it plain that they were ready to spend any amount to secure a child."[135] In general, most prospective adoptive couples just failed to see the value in a social agency placement—an assumption reinforced by the Senate Subcommittee on Juvenile Delinquency. The subcommittee discovered that regardless of how a child was placed, "the net result [was] frequently a happy and good one," even if this was "a coincidence rather than a careful and intelligently worked out plan."[136] Findings like these demonstrated that adoptive parents acted as "purchaser consumers," those postwar individuals who "consumed in pursuit of private gain" rather than out of concern for the general good. By targeting adoptive parents's needs rather than the child's best interests, the consumer paradigm strove to provide more customer-friendly adoptions, practicing a type of market segmentation.[137]

The consumer paradigm philosophy influenced more than just adoptive parents, seeping into even professional organizations. Adoptive couples' ability to specify gender preferences was one example of this. When surveying the possibilities for a long-term adoption program in Greece, ISS conducted a survey of available sources for children, including gender ratios. Social workers discovered that both Greek and U.S. adoptive families preferred girls to boys in the one- to five-year-old age bracket. Based on this explicit consumer preference, social workers concluded, "demands for boys could fairly easily be met, while applications for girls could only be satisfied if the child were under 1 year old, with extremely rare exceptions for older ages."[138] The initial debate over the merits and limitations of proxy adoptions also reflected consumer influences. An attorney, on the board of directors for a Greek orphanage, suggested to Lena Cochran, one of the two DPC social workers based in Greece, that proxy adoptions would not only provide the Greek courts with assurance that the child would have a permanent placement but, more importantly, that orphanages would not have to assume care again if the child was sent back to Greece. Cochran worried that this system would give the adoptive parents "no freedom of choice whatsoever," language often associated with consumer selection and entitlement.[139] Finally, when considering taking actress Joan Fontaine as a client, ISS assistant director Susan Pettiss explicitly told the Greek Branch that she should have no special treatment. When Fontaine's representative visited Greece on her behalf to locate a child, the Greek Branch staff took him to several orphanages where he had the opportunity to assess dozens of children so that Fontaine "could choose one."[140] Incidents such as these prompted one prospective adoptive mother to write to Kefauver in frustration, "one is led to believe that one must be either a millionaire or movie star to be able to adopt a child without waiting. Why?"[141] Because of market consideration like these, the "best interest of the child" was often subjectively tied to the interests of the sending nation and adoptive parents.

Both Greek and American laws encouraged this child-shopping mentality. When U.S. couples visited Greece, it was "comparatively easy" for them to visit a foundling home, select a child, apply for a visa, and be home within a month. Neither the Greek adoption ruling nor the RRA required social agency approval, freeing the prospective adoptive couple from the longer waiting periods necessary to get a homestudy or conduct a social investigation of the child. This concerned the ISS Greek Branch staff since they recognized that "it will be a rare exception if such a prospective parent, who has come to Greece with the express purpose of adopting a child, will accept the advice to wait and to follow our more lengthy but safer procedure. So far, no client has accepted such advice."[142] Easing adoption guidelines made adopting a Greek child akin to purchasing a souvenir with little opportunity to consider the potential long-term complications. Since Greek law made it considerably harder for Greek parents to adopt an orphan domestically than for foreign parents to take the same child abroad, this emphasis on U.S. adoptive tourism seemed even more intentional.[143] Only after an extensive survey of Greek children placed with U.S. couples, and some negative international press coverage, did Greece finally revise its adoption law in 1966 to require that foreign couples use accredited international adoption agencies.[144]

Adoptive parents were not the only ones with preferences in choosing adoption services. During Mitler's 1959 investigation, he found that Greek orphanage directors viewed the lengthy process and long readoption period required by authorized U.S. agencies as an impediment to the child welfare agency process. When using independent attorneys like Lamberson, directors found they "acted much more rapidly than the social agencies." This impressed local officials because it decreased the community's responsibility for supporting the children, often in situations with severe overcrowding. Furthermore, agencies like ISS required a one- to two-year observation period under agency supervision to ensure that the child had adjusted well to her new family before issuing adoption paperwork and citizenship. Attorneys, however, used the proxy process, which gave the children immediate citizenship and security—an assurance that the orphanage directors preferred.[145]

Greece's economic devastation also produced conditions that propelled the independent system. The poverty of rural Greeks throughout the 1950s forced parents to use orphanages as temporary housing. Enterprising individuals saw an opportunity both to satisfy the U.S. demand for healthy, young children and to temporarily alleviate the financial strain many Greek households faced. U.S. and Greek attorneys offered families $200 to $500 for a child, which represented approximately a year's wages for a poor family.[146] When one Children's Bureau official worried that Greek children coming to the southern United States were "separated from their families purely because of financial reasons," another administrator countered that conditions in Greece were "bleak, providing a minimal subsistence with no foreseeable opportunity for these children to become a part of normal family and community life."[147] In this view, "normal families" looked strikingly similar to middle-class American families who prioritized consumer abundance.

Long after the immediate war orphan crisis, Greek families continued to use international adoption as one way to mitigate extreme poverty—a different phenomenon from Southern European immigration during the late nineteenth and early twentieth centuries when fathers and older sons migrated to the United States to find work. Since mothers and young children were rarely separated from one another in earlier immigration phases, this made foreign adoption a new and particularly risky kind of immigration strategy.[148] Yet, one mother who admitted that parting from her daughter would "break her heart," saw the opportunity as too great to pass up. As the mother "pinn[ed] her hopes on the future when one day Georgia will be financially independent," she joined many other families who saw their children's emigration as a distant stab at social mobility.[149]

These sacrifices made even more sense when contextualized within Greek adoption law. In Greek law, birth parents lost no rights when the court granted an adoption decree. Greek families thus viewed placing a child in the United States as a type of foster home and many did not understand that their parental rights had been terminated.[150] Some attorneys also found it in their best interest to allow parents to believe they would still have parental rights. In one 1956 independent placement case, an attorney assured a birth mother that her child was going to a family in Athens and she could visit whenever she wanted, when the child was in fact promised to a U.S. couple. Social workers came to the conclusion that the birth mother had been deceived since she "did not seem to realize the document she had signed was an official release for adoption."[151] Another attorney promised a Greek mother a fifty-dollar monthly pension and the opportunity to rejoin her child in the United States if she verbally relinquished her child. Just like most scams, the mother never heard from the attorney again.[152] Although independent adoptions also harmed U.S. adoptive couples, destitute Greek families bore the weight of a loosely policed and poorly regulated system, intended to benefit U.S. interests above all else.

Conclusion

In the conclusion of his 1959 report, Ernest Mitler called international adoption in the late 1940s a "salvage operation," suggesting that the use of volunteers was justifiable in light of the temporary orphan crisis. He argued, "since a post war crisis necessitating the quick transfer of children from . . . Greece to the United States no longer exists, there is no longer any justification for using unsound or careless techniques to rush these children to American homes."[153] What Mitler's analysis failed to consider was that relying on private, volunteer operators was not a momentary "salvage operation," but a pattern in the U.S. social welfare state of cultivating volunteer interests—a pattern that became increasingly legitimate under the Cold War mission of democratic humanitarianism. As organizations like AHEPA demonstrated, voluntarism, along with the consumer paradigm, was central to domestic and international social welfare policies and practices, no matter how much social welfare professionals claimed otherwise. Adoptive parents supported the growth of consumer-driven organizations because they provided an alternative to the child welfare paradigm's much stricter regulations. In effect, this perpetuated a tiered system based on adoptive parents' ability to pay, making it increasingly hard to distinguish between selling adoption services and selling adoptable babies. Mitler's investigative work ultimately led to few convictions and revealed legislators' hesitancy to rein in private adoption efforts. Strikingly, Kefauver was never able to pass legislation that made black market placements illegal, even though he and his allies reintroduced bills throughout the 1950s and 1960s banning commercial adoptions.[154] Even in the 1960s and 1970s, the coexisting images of needy war orphans and brave independent volunteers continued to shape policymakers' protection of an expansive definition of orphan and fewer regulations.

Nearly ten years after the Displaced Persons Act ended, most Americans continued to see foreign adoption as an emergency mission or "salvage operation." In part because of the piercing war orphan image, prospective adoptive parents increasingly looked abroad in the 1940s and 1950s to expand their families and sought out independent practitioners who treated them more like customers, especially in Greece. Cold War ideologies that stressed the key role that individual U.S. citizens played in containing the communist threat while embracing their global neighbors further legitimized the role of humanitarian intervention. Indeed, the combined influences of voluntarism and humanitarianism on international adoption policies would prove a substantial challenge to social workers trying to regulate Korean adoptions, starting in 1954. While independent groups relied on the proxy system in Greece, the number of proxy adoptions exploded in Korea where U.S. soldiers and notions of racial purity produced an abundance of so-called GI babies. The next chapter explores Harry and Bertha Holt's development of the humanitarian paradigm in Korean adoptions and the efforts of professional social workers to limit their authority.

CHAPTER 3

"The Great Heart of America"

Volunteer Humanitarians
and Korean Adoptions

T HE AIRCRAFT CRAWLED INTO THE GATE on January 31, 1958, after circling around the slick runway. With the help of several Holt Adoption agency staff, a weary, grizzled Harry Holt shepherded the expectant children off the plane to greet the welcoming party of reporters and adoptive parents. Tragically, this "babylift" from Seoul began with 101 Korean orphans but arrived at the San Francisco airport with only 99. One eight-month-old baby died from tuberculosis complications over the Pacific, and another was left behind in Honolulu to be treated for lung abscesses. Of the remaining children, 27 would be redirected to special hospitals in San Francisco, Los Angeles, and Denver for tuberculosis treatment before they could go to their permanent adoptive homes. Yet, in spite of these pressures, Holt walked off the plane singleminded and optimistic. He expressed remorse for the loss of a child but qualified to a reporter that "it came off pretty well, didn't it?" As the last children were led off the plane, a local reporter asked the Oregon farmer when his emergency mission to the GI children of Korea would end. Holt shrugged, "Gosh, who knows? I've got applications for some 2,000 more children on file."[1]

Harry and Bertha Holt, an evangelical couple from rural Oregon, drew national attention to intercountry adoption in 1955 by adopting eight Korean GI orphans through a special act of Congress. In the following year, hundreds of families bombarded the Holts with requests to help them adopt "GI babies" as well, leading the couple to open an adoption agency in 1956.[2] The Holts' airlifts were possible because of the 1953 Refugee Relief Act. Although often seen as inconsequential in immigration history, the act offered four thousand non-quota visas for overseas orphans *regardless* of origin country, distinguishing it from the earlier Displaced Persons Act intended for European orphans. Using a provision of the Refugee Relief Act that permitted Americans to adopt orphans by proxy—the same mechanism Leo Lamberson and AHEPA used in Greece—the Holts rapidly processed adoptions and sent planeloads of children to U.S. families. Although the proxy process was legal, social work organizations believed the Holts' interpretation of the law endangered children through risky placements.

The Oregon couple's use of the humanitarian paradigm shaped the nature of voluntarism in Korean adoptions. While reminiscent of independent, client-driven adoptions under the consumer paradigm, the humanitarian paradigm differentiated itself through the emotional language of love and rescue. By adopting eight Korean orphans and then launching an adoption program to assist other families, Harry and Bertha Holt modeled adoption as an altruistic act. This made the Holts popular with the Cold War public. Legislators and the press viewed mixed-race Korean adoptees—children of Korean mothers, and white or black U.S. GIs—as salient symbols of America's growing political interest in Asia. Furthermore, white adoptive parents and religious humanitarians welcomed mixed-race and Korean children into their families, employing the language of colorblindness and Cold War democracy to justify their actions. Significantly, lawmakers styled these race-blind adoptions as humanitarian acts and Asian orphans as "model minorities"—living emblems that appeared to solve America's "race problem."[3]

But humanitarian motives alone were not enough; the Holts' success also hinged on the state's reliance on private organizations to tackle social welfare crises. The absence of a permanent international adoption policy in the 1950s produced what I call a policy vacuum. This legislative void existed, in part, because lawmakers questioned the necessity of federal intervention when the government had relied historically on volunteers for humanitarian action. Indeed, private aid organizations had only recently managed the relocation of European displaced children with minimal state support. Additionally, conflicting state laws and a lack of federal adoption legislation had produced uneven standards across state lines, which further contributed to the persistence of the policy vacuum. These conditions cultivated what political scientist Michael Barnett has called a "codependent relationship" between the state

and humanitarian organizations, fostering an environment where voluntarism flourished.[4] Thus, using existing immigration law, the savvy Holts
crafted a type of ad hoc international adoption policy, which allowed them
to incorporate their own adoption philosophies and religious worldview.

The Holts were not the only ones, however, with a vested interest in
advocating for Korean orphans. For long-established private child welfare
agencies and professional social workers, the Holts' efforts seemed provin-
cial and dangerous. Advocates of the child welfare paradigm—including
International Social Service, the U.S. Children's Bureau, and the Child Welfare League of America—labored to align international adoption standards
with those expert-aided domestic adoptions. Recognizing that humanitarians were different opponents from for-profit adoption agencies, child welfare professionals used legislative action and public relations tactics to make
the Holts' process suspect without critiquing their motives. More important, social workers sought to fill the policy vacuum, insisting that private
organizations had successfully bypassed expert practices because of such
legislative "loopholes." But just as with the earlier consumer paradigm, the
language of loopholes misrepresented the reality that, one, legislators intentionally maintained such legislative "gaps" and, two, humanitarians like the
Holts were successful not because they were working outside the system
but because they were shaping it while still in its initial stages of negotiation.[5] Even once social workers closed "loopholes," the Holts' informal policymaking continued to influence the structure of international adoption
long past the 1950s, weaving voluntarism—and humanitarianism—into the
institution's very fabric.

A Shift Toward Humanitarianism: Korean Adoption
in Immigration Law and Popular Culture

International orphan legislation was born during a period of advances and
constraints in immigration law. The 1924 Johnson-Reed Act excluded Asian
immigrants on the basis of race while establishing European migrants' quotas on the basis of nationality rather than race or ethnicity. During World
War II, popular propaganda lauded the United States as a nation committed to racial, ethnic, and religious diversity. To underscore American commitment to ideals of cultural pluralism, the U.S. government initiated a
wave of reforms, beginning with the repeal of the Chinese Exclusion Acts

in 1943. Three years later, Congress lifted restrictions against Filipino and South Indian immigration and amended the War Brides Act in 1947, permitting Asian American servicemen to bring their Asian-born wives to the United States. This liberalization of immigration law culminated with the 1952 McCarran-Walter Act, which for the first time allowed Asian immigrants to become U.S. citizens, established immigrant quotas for Asians, and included a provision for family reunification.[6] Yet even in a legislative context that appeared to liberalize immigration laws, the 1952 act maintained a quota system that reified racial difference and privileged certain migrant groups.

Although ostensibly discrete, immigration and refugee policy shared similar functions and strictures during the postwar period. Government officials considered refugee law an emergency response to specific global problems, most notably conflicts linked to the growing influence of communist regimes. For the first time, in 1950, Congress designated foreign assistance not just for economic relief but for "mutual security of the free world," ensuring that Cold War military aims were inseparable from relief. In a 1953 letter to Congress, President Eisenhower linked humanitarian relief to immigration, urging representatives to pass refugee legislation because refugees "look to the free world for haven."[7] The humanitarian rhetoric persistent in refugee law did not, however, shorten the path to citizenship or alter the standards for admittance. This has led some to argue that refugee law, especially under the RRA, offered legislators a way to uphold immigration and citizenship screening while relaxing aspects of the rigid quota system, meeting persistent humanitarian needs.[8] As discussed in the previous chapter, beginning with the Displaced Persons Act of 1948 (DPA), legislators incorporated orphan provisions into refugee legislation, even though the creators of the bill specified from the outset that orphans were not technically considered refugees. Under its provisions, from 1948 to 1953, U.S. citizens adopted 4,052 European children and 466 Asian children (mostly Japanese-American).[9] Most important, the DPA established that orphans could be considered refugees for the purposes of immigration law. Yet legislators intended the DPA to relocate only European orphans, upholding the restrictive quota system already in place. Few Japanese American orphans qualified for the existing visas, and those who did were adopted by military families.

Subsequent laws after the DPA demonstrated how orphan provisions evolved into a more racially inclusive refugee law. In 1950, congressional legislation extended citizenship to the foreign wives and children of American military forces, regardless of race. Although this act did not directly affect orphans, it did establish a precedent for exceptions to race-based immigration quotas, revising Section 13(c) of the 1924 Immigration Act.[10] Also tangentially related to future orphan provisions was the landmark McCarran-Walter Act in 1952, which made all races eligible for naturalization and gave internationally adopted children the blanket of citizenship.[11] Finally, one month before the passage of the RRA, the House ratified a joint resolution that permitted the admission of five hundred orphans adopted abroad by military families.[12] Unlike the DPA, this resolution provided orphans with non-quota visas safe from racial restrictions. The House set two significant procedural standards through this resolution: it initiated adoptions from abroad—or by proxy—while also giving the State Department and Congress, perhaps unwittingly, the authority to approve adoptive families, effectively bypassing a home study by social welfare agencies. Lawmakers argued that it would increase efficiency to approve five hundred non-quota visas at once, rather than reviewing hundreds of individual requests from military personnel.[13] This practical policy decision set a precedent that reverberated throughout the subsequent RRA and decisively shaped 1950s intercountry adoption.

As the last chapter showed, the RRA signaled a new direction in orphan provisions. Although still considered an emergency, and therefore temporary, provision, the RRA lasted for over three years and permitted children to be adopted by proxy regardless of race, nationality, or ethnicity. Because of the sheer number of available visas without race-based restrictions, the RRA made mass adoption from Asian countries possible.[14] While lawmakers established a committee of voluntary professional social welfare agencies and state welfare departments to oversee legislative implementation, this role brokered no real power since states legislated adoption policy.[15] Regardless of the RRA's original intentions, throughout the 1950s the Subcommittee on Refugees and Escapees—the lawmakers responsible for administering the RRA—used the classification of orphans as refugees to accomplish not only foreign objectives but also domestic ones. Coinciding with the U.S. baby boom and an increased social pressure to have children, the RRA became an efficient route to provide orphans with families and American couples with kin. According to calculations in the RRA's final report, even though the number of adoptable children increased in the postwar era, prospective adoptive parents still exceeded available children ten to one. The report further claimed that adoptions increased 80 percent over the same period.[16] In fact, the subcommittee concluded that the growing "popularity" of adoptions had led to a "supply and demand" crisis that the RRA sought to rectify.[17]

Many families were driven to adopt South Korean orphans because they wanted to reach out to those "less fortunate" while also taking responsibility for children who were considered partially American. After watching the *Loretta Young Show*'s rendition of Harry and Bertha Holt's story, a California family expressed that "our children have so much, we ought to do something to share what we have."[18] A congregation in Lakewood, California, ceremonially adopted the two children placed with the Trumbull family because they were "proud" of the family's beneficence in adopting these needy "Korean War waifs."[19] Although humanitarianism certainly prompted some to adopt GI babies, many parents just wanted a child and could not obtain one easily in the United States. This demand from American families drove the subcommittee and State Department to push for numerous extensions of the RRA. For instance, when an article about GI orphans ran in the March 1955 edition of *JET* magazine, the RRA administrator Scott McLeod informed Representative Adam Clayton Powell that "letters are still coming in, after topping the 500 mark."[20] In the 1956 report that would lead to an extension of refugee visas that year, the subcommittee drew a direct link between the demand for children and the continuation of orphan provisions. It stated that "based on the hundreds of letters from reputable United States citizens wanting to adopt foreign orphans . . . it may be concluded that it would be to the advantage of this country, as well as the orphan, to increase the number of orphan visas permissible." From January 1954 to July 1957, ISS alone received over 12,000 inquiries into international adoption from prospective adoptive parents.[21]

Yet the plentiful supply of nonwhite U.S. orphans indicates that other factors, besides an increased demand for children, made Korean orphans "adoptable." Media reports frequently stressed the racial persecution that these part-American orphans faced by remaining in Korea. *Look* magazine described Korean GI orphans as "the least wanted children on earth today," because "a Korean baby with Eurasian features bears an unmistakable brand" that makes him or her unacceptable to Koreans who value racial purity.[22] Other accounts noted how mothers abandoned their GI children in irrigation ditches where mobs of Korean children would try to kill them, highlighting their helplessness and need for U.S. intervention.[23] In one news article, an adoptive parent commented that, since these were the children of American servicemen, "the responsibility of caring for and raising these children belongs to the American people."[24] The Sieber family of Nevada rejected the notion that they were performing an act of charity by adopting GI babies; instead, they believed it was a duty. "Americans fathered many of the children who now live a near-starvation existence in Korea," the family maintained, and "Americans have an obligation toward them."[25]

The term "GI baby" itself revealed U.S. responsibility for these Korean children. First coined during the post-World War II period to describe children in Europe and Japan fathered by American soldiers, the media popularized the term during the Korean War to label the thousands of children with white fathers and Korean mothers. Orphanage officials vainly attempted to call the biracial children "U.N. orphans," which more accurately identified them as the offspring of British and French soldiers as well. But U.S. dominance in the region caused "GI babies" to stick. As Americans witnessed the ostracism of not only "innocent" children, but also children abandoned by U.S. military fathers, certain families blurred previously rigid racial boundaries, identified Korean GI orphans as "American," and thus began to chip away at the definition of the "adoptable" child.

Officials also capitalized on the report's findings that international adoption gave citizens an opportunity to express their distinctly American altruism.[26] In the words of one report, the "admission of 4,000 orphans brought happiness to many American homes, and an awareness of the part citizens can play in helping their Government carry out its foreign policy." This cast U.S. adoptive families as crucial political actors.[27] Authors of the RRA gushed, "Friendly international relations engendered by America's helping hand stretch[ed] out to these children were a forward step toward better international understanding and lasting peace in the world," concluding, "there could be no better basis for mutual understanding between nations than the love and concern for little children."[28] In legislative hearings, officials emphasized that "each dollar expended to help a refugee or an escapee helps to prove America's concern for the oppressed."[29] In this way, children were reduced to metaphorical olive branches—peace offerings for America to improve its international reputation. It also did not hurt that, in the words of the Subcommittee on Immigration, international orphans made the "best possible immigrants from the standpoint of their youth, flexibility, and lack of ties to any other cultures."[30] Since, according to officials, orphans' youth prohibited them from forming strong cultural ties to their home countries, the children assimilated easily into American culture and posed no threat to political institutions. These factors made them ideal foreign recipients of U.S. beneficence.[31]

Such themes also resounded far from the halls of government. On September 25, 1955, cartoonists Gus Edson and Irwin Hasen launched a syndicated comic strip about a school-age war orphan. Set in southern Europe near the end of World War II, the comic began with American GIs Ted Wills and Whitford (Whitey) McGowan discovering a young boy wandering amid rubble, crying out *donde*, the Spanish word for where. The soldiers cared for him until the war's end forced them to return to the United States and leave behind the boy they now called Dondi. Not easily deserted, Dondi stowed away on the military transport bringing the GIs home and charmed his way into staying with the soldiers permanently, eventually being adopted and becoming a U.S. citizen. Over the comic's course from 1955 to 1986, the chameleon-like orphan lived with four different families, changed ethnic origin three times, and became a legal immigrant through an act of Congress. Run in over one hundred dailies across the country, from the *Chicago Tribune* and *New York News* to the *Miami Herald* and *Los Angeles Times*, *Dondi* had a national presence. At its height in the 1950s and 1960s, the comic's readership was estimated in the millions, with syndication stretching to Canada, Trinidad, and Puerto Rico. Its popularity also led to the production of a 1961 feature film with Edson serving as writer and associate producer. Twice, Edson and Hasen won the National Cartoonists Society award for the best story strip of the year.[32]

Dondi was, in fact, a product of the Eisenhower administration's goodwill campaigns in Europe. Gus Edson, already a noted cartoonist, was inspired to create *Dondi* after the USO sponsored a National Cartoonist Society (NCS) trip to Europe in 1952 where he witnessed hordes of Italian street children, a group his collaborator Irwin Hasen later called, "the flotsam and jetsam of war." A noted "family man," according to local press coverage, Edson was also an active political volunteer, serving as chairman of the NCS Advisory Committee to the Treasury and providing entertainment for the armed forces. For his service, he was awarded commendations by the U.S. Treasury and Department of Defense in 1949 and 1954.[33]

Because of these roots, Edson's patriotism infused the strip, glorifying U.S. humanitarianism while downplaying its accompanying political and cultural power. For instance, while on vacation with his new family, Dondi disappears off the yacht and goes missing, leading Whitey to call himself a "thoughtless harum-scarum lug" for losing the boy. His fiancée Monique rejects this label, explaining, "Nonsense, Whitey—You've proved by your attachment to Dondi that your heart is as big as the world!"[34] By caring about those from other nations, Americans personified the expansiveness and generosity of U.S. intervention, characterized by "heart," not force. Indeed, the comic and film consistently rejected the one-sidedness of international adoption, depicting Dondi as a willing agent in his relocation. The GIs, those representative of U.S. military power, don't "kidnap" him; Dondi himself chooses to stowaway on the U.S.-bound ship. The movie's promotional poster described him as, "The War Orphan Who Makes His Own Break for the Land of the Free" and a newscaster in the film exclaimed that Dondi had, in fact, "adopted" America.[35] Dondi showed that when given the chance, foreign orphans would always choose to become Americans. Only because orphans like Dondi "adopted" the United States would Americans reciprocate by adopting them.

But even as many Americans welcomed the increasing stream of international adoptees, not everyone was willing to embrace such a broad extension of family and nationalism. Before Whitey and Monique died in an auto accident on their honeymoon, Dondi had frequent run-ins with Whitey's mother, the rich, bigoted and self-absorbed Mrs. McGowan. When the matriarch learns that Whitey has proposed to his girlfriend, Monique, so that they could adopt Dondi, she ridicules the decision, scoffing to Monique, "He's asking you to become a foster mother to a nobody . . . what kind of life can you and Whitford have with that sniveling little foreigner clinging to your necks?" As the strip's obvious villain, Mrs. McGowan symbolizes an older moment in U.S. history—one limited by nativism, biological privilege, and classism. In contrast, Dondi's new family—first symbolized by Whitey and Monique, later by another married couple—was open to new cultures and experiences, capable of resisting the old guard by throwing off class and national background. This expansive, and yet contained, family signaled a better America that offered hope beyond national borders.[36]

With the nuclear family as the ideal civic institution, government was simultaneously the problem and the solution for orphans trying to become Americans. Using strikingly similar language to Harry Holt's, the authors depicted immigration officials and the "Welfare Department" in both the strip and the film as obstacles to Dondi's citizenship and familial happiness. These forces, the authors suggested, stood in contrast to "the great heart of

America." When the authorities get ready to deport Dondi for being illegal, Whitey asks, "Now don't tell me there isn't one little loophole in the law that one little boy can't manage to squeeze through?" The immigration captain sneers, "Oh you're right, Mr. [McGowan]. There is. It's what you call an . . . 'Act of Congress.' "[37] Only through "loopholes," designed to "get around" government, could private citizens encourage legislators to act. It is also private citizens who distribute 100,000 "Save Dondi Wire Your Congressman" stickers. When one GI laments, "I don't know my Congressman's name!" Another GI responds, "That's okay, Pal. I'll lend you mine. We're all in this together."[38] Interactions like these suggested that the adoption of foreign orphans fostered national unity through inclusivity. Drawing on a mishmash of patriotic and Cold War rhetoric, the film's newscaster emphasized how such humanitarianism was uniquely American.

> This boy thinks America is a place where everybody is a "swell guy." Who are we, gentlemen, to tell Dondi he is wrong? At a time when the attitudes of so many peoples in this world are tinged with envy and suspicion shall we tell Dondi all America is NOT his buddy? Shall we shatter the bright hope, the shining ideal this child of misfortune has been cherishing? Shall we say, "No, Dondi, this land of the free and home of the brave is *not* for you?" Have we no place for a little fellow brave enough to make his own break for new life in the New World? His is the spirit of all immigrants who have made this nation great! He is democracy itself![39]

The reality of immigration policy in the 1940s and 1950s differed significantly from this "shining ideal." In reality, the quota system continued to privilege Northern and Western Europeans while excluding "less desirable" immigrants based on skin color or racial prejudice. Immigration restrictions also constructed and perpetuated "illegal aliens," those Filipino, Mexican, Chinese, and Japanese migrants who became racialized "others" without rights or citizenship.[40] This classification even seeped into a scene from the film. When Dondi shows up in steerage, one GI tries to talk Whitey out of smuggling him into the country, protesting, "You ain't goin' to hide him again! He's a stowaway! He's a . . . a . . . 'Illegal alien.' " Yet another GI corrects him, clarifying, "He's a *kid*!"[41] This underscored how being a child and an illegal alien were incompatible identities. Since children were innocent and malleable, the "best possible immigrants," they were not in the same category as deviant and criminal "illegal aliens." For those advocating for the adoption of foreign children—even nonwhite children—immigration restrictions seemed unjust and begged to be broken or circumvented.

Regardless of the initial complications, U.S. families' adoption of foreign orphans ultimately relied on the support and backing of the federal government. During a 1961 interview, Hasen characterized the essence of Dondi's story as the "making of an American," one who might not have had the privilege of being born in the United States, but could be made "just as American" through an act of Congress—a process that, in real life, happened hundreds of times between 1945 and the early 1960s. When Congress voted Dondi a citizen in the cartoon strip, Edson received a letter from the Immigration Department, notifying him that it had decided to make Dondi an honorary citizen. Edson considered the cartoon character "twice blessed," in having both symbolic and literal citizenship.[42] It was striking that at an historical moment when U.S. immigration had locked the doors to so many, officials offered a fictional character citizenship, perpetuating the myth that America was still a place for the "huddled masses."

This frame of humanitarian exceptionalism made racial and national distinctions seem immaterial. Hasen and Edson drew Dondi to be racially ambiguous with dark hair, dark eyes, and a clear language barrier. In this way, his racial composition could shift as convenient to the story, as it did in the 1960s when the story made him a Korean War orphan and in the 1970s when there were allusions to his Vietnamese heritage. When asked in the early 1960s to pinpoint Dondi's ethnic background, the cartoonists demurred, more eager to identify the orphan as "a combination of dondis." To make this point, Hasen related a well-rehearsed story about his experience with ethnic restaurant owners in New York City's "melting pot." Once these owners discovered that their diner was Dondi's creator, they couldn't wait to guess the child's ethnic background. He joked, "at the Hungarian restaurant, they called Dondi the Hungarian boy, at the Italian restaurant, he was the Italian boy," underscoring that Dondi was a "symbol" who had "universality built into him," and was intentionally relatable to everyone. The interviewer agreed, emphasizing that it was immaterial whether Dondi's background was Korean or Eastern European, since "he can represent them all."[43]

Yet, even though leaders, officials, and adoptive parents appeared to dismiss foreign orphans' racial and national differences as unimportant, such distinctions critically informed adoption narratives. In a dizzying pastiche of cultural symbolism, the *New York Daily News* and Trans-World Airlines used Dondi's image in an oversized card intended for the National Orphans Home in Korea. Publicity photos revealed that the card was delivered to Korean officials in 1957 by Col. Dean Hess, whose popular autobiography featuring his work with Korean War orphans had just been adapted into a film titled *Battle Hymn*, starring Rock Hudson. With a movie photograph in the background, featuring Hudson and a beautiful, ostensibly Korean, woman clinging to his arm (the Welsh actress Anna Kashfi acting in the role as the teacher En Soon Yang), Hess handed the life-sized Dondi to the officials.

It was Dondi, the cartoon orphan representing the real Korean children already adopted by U.S. families, who brought these threads together. As the picture confirmed, the international cooperation between Korea and the United States was one characterized by benevolent white male leadership wrapped in corporate humanitarianism.[44] Yet, just as the fictional Korean teacher En Soon Yang appeared no more than an exotic decoration to Hess's bravado, foreign orphans were still marked as other, albeit in more subtle ways. For example, in the *Dondi* film, McGowan has to auction off his prized foreign souvenirs—including a bridal veil from the Sultan of Yemen's harem—to find room in his duffle to hide Dondi. Placed in context, this reduces Dondi to the best kind of exotic souvenir, worthy of replacing other trophies of Orientalist conquest. It also revealed how the anxiety over race had not disappeared: it had just been pushed below the surface, perpetuating the myth that race blindness was attainable.

As the *Dondi* narrative suggests, the permanent adoption of foreign orphans became saturated with humanitarianism in the 1950s. Earlier narratives of isolation and bigotry became less resonant as average Americans encountered orphans—even make-believe orphans like Dondi—over their morning coffee or on the evening news. These cultural works tilled the social and political soil for adoption advocacy in Cold War America. From this perspective, adoption was a humanitarian act, not a political one. Adoptive parents had "hearts as big as the world," like the GIs who rescued Dondi, and needed all the help U.S. social welfare structures could offer. When government officials and child welfare professionals eased the process so that needy children could be placed in U.S. families with little delay, they were popular heroes. When they upheld existing laws or required more stringent guidelines, they were villains. It was in this context that international adoption from Korea originated.

Figure 2. Col. Dean Hess presenting a *Dondi* card to Korean officials

Gus Edson papers, Special Collections Research Center, Syracuse University Libraries.

Although the story of Dondi was a fictional account, strains of its narrative would have seemed familiar to readers following the newsworthy Holt family and their efforts to launch a Korean adoption program. Nine months before Edson released the first *Dondi* strip from his home office in Connecticut, on the other side of the United States, Harry and Bertha Holt were first hearing of Korea's orphan crisis. Their response would pivotally shape the development and institution of international adoption. Informed by Cold War humanitarianism and their Christian faith, the Holts would use the Refugee Relief Act's provisions and the favorable social context to facilitate international adoptions on their own terms.

"Love Is the Key": The Humanitarian Paradigm

The evening of December 14, 1954, was a fateful one for the Holt family. At the invitation of a neighbor, they attended a film screening describing postwar South Korea. Dr. Bob Pierce, director of World Vision—an evangelical relief organization that provided international humanitarian services, built churches, and funded evangelism—hosted the event. The documentary film, titled *Other Sheep*, detailed the plight facing hundreds of "mixed-race" GI babies. Statistics were generally hard to gather, but the UN estimated that while there were over 100,000 GI children, only 1,500 needed homes.[45] Although most families would raise these children, others were influenced by cultural norms of racial purity. According to Dr. Pierce, GI children often suffered ostracism, beatings, and occasionally even death at the hands of their peers, leading some mothers to abandon them. The tableaux of blond-haired, blue-eyed Koreans living in garbage dumps, deserted and alone, moved the Holts. Along with the American public, their concern was decidedly linked to GI children's status as the offspring of U.S. military personnel. When they remarked that "we had never thought of such suffering and heartbreak . . . such poverty and despair . . . such wistful little faces searching for someone to care," their reaction was not directed toward any suffering child but specifically to children they considered partly American. Watching the children's desperate situation compelled the Holts to act. After the screening, they offered to sponsor twenty children. But they still felt deep unease. Later that night the Oregon couple lay in bed unable to sleep because, in Bertha Holt's words, "They haunted us—those forlorn, emaciated children who were crowded into institutions where they were starving for love as much as a lack of food."[46]

Thus, three months later, Harry Holt booked a flight to South Korea with the intention of adopting eight GI children, who would double their family's size. They owned a thirteen-room ranch-style home, referred to as the "pink mansion" in their small Oregon town, and had a plentiful income from their lumber mill and farm to support a large number of orphans. After four months in South Korea, Harry Holt received government approval to adopt all eight children.[47] During this first trip, Holt sought to bring home not only his own children but orphans for other families as well. In addition to the Holt eight, the Oregon entrepreneur ferried six other orphans: two adopted through state welfare departments, two adopted by proxy for another Oregon family, one adopted by a Texas family, and one named Lee Young Soni. Soni was the first black-Korean child to be adopted through the Michigan Department of Social Welfare, whose adoptive family was an African American couple living in Benton Harbor, Michigan. This first "babylift" demonstrated Holt's early commitment to facilitating adoptions for U.S. families.

The Refugee Relief Act made such actions logistically possible, but the law also had limitations. While the law provided visas for eligible orphans, it limited the number of visas to two per family, except in the case of siblings. Holt discovered this a month before he left for Korea but, in his haste to travel, decided to leave without the assurance that he would be able to return with the anticipated eight children. When a friend mentioned this inconsistency to him, Holt responded, "Yes I know, but this is the Lord's work. He will direct Congress."[48] Immediately, the couple sent a letter to Senator Richard Neuberger, an Oregon Democrat newly elected to the Senate in 1954, asking him to sponsor a bill that would allow them to adopt six more children given the desperate circumstances in South Korea. Neuberger agreed, believing the Holts' project embodied the "American spirit" of humanitarian goodness and moral purity.[49]

Although the senator thought it unlikely that the bill would pass before January, he introduced "A Bill for Relief of Certain Korean War Orphans" on June 24, 1955, while Holt was still in Korea.[50] Following Neuberger's advice, the Holts collected hundreds of letters from acquaintances that vouched for their character and ability to care for adoptive children. In a surprising turn of events for congressional legislation, the bill passed both houses and had presidential approval by August 12, 1955—a speed that

Figure 3. Holt children arrive in the United States, October 14, 1955.
Printed with permission, but not endorsement, from Holt International.

shocked representative Edith Green (D-Ore.): "Ordinarily it takes several months, sometimes years, after a private bill is introduced before it is passed."[51] In part, this speed relied on the persistence of both Neuberger and Green. Indeed, Neuberger pushed the bill through at 11:53 p.m., the last legislation of the session before Congress adjourned. While the legislators were astounded by the speed, Bertha Holt knew that "those tired, worn-out senators just had to sit there until they passed our bill. Even if they wanted to quit and go home, the Lord wouldn't let them until those children were taken care of."[52] Her theory notwithstanding, Neuberger's commitment to the Holts' mission likely contributed to their success with Congress, and the terms of the RRA complemented such advocacy. Letters submitted on the Holts' behalf emphasized the desperate situation that Korean orphans faced and painted the Oregon couple as altruists. Their efforts garnered national media coverage, giving them credibility with adoptive families and piquing the attention of professional social workers.

Holt's mission soon became about much more than just incorporating eight children into his family or sending money to sponsor other orphans he had visited in South Korea. When Harry Holt returned to Oregon on October 14, 1955, with his adopted children, he still "could not forget those tiny, outstretched arms he had left behind in Korea." In these first months, Holt continued to work under the auspices of World Vision and encouraged families to send donations directly to that organization. Once he returned to South Korea in April, however, he realized that the World Vision Reception Center was too small to house the hundred or more orphans Holt had in mind. He sent his wife a letter urging her to sell $10,000 worth of stock and open a bank account under the name Holt Adoption Program (HAP), so he could start building a larger orphanage.[53] Less than seven months after the first "stork flight" delivered Korean GI orphans to American soil, Holt had rededicated his life to what he considered a divinely appointed mission.

The Holt Adoption Program had a distinctive philosophy shaped by the Holts' experiences and worldview, rather than the social welfare standards of the time. For the Holts, protecting children meant removing them from the aftermath of war and sparing them from racial marginalization in South Korea. The tedious process of approving American homes did not concern them, as activists on a mission. Their more urgent task, the couple felt, was to save the lives—and souls—of GI children.[54] With great conviction, the Holts believed that orphans needed a chance to survive and, subsequently, to be placed into a "loving" evangelical household. The child welfare system, in their opinion, delayed such action by charging exorbitant fees and subjecting families to invasive inspections by social workers. As Bertha Holt wrote, "I think of all the love-hungry, emaciated little babies over there starving and dying for want of a home . . . and all these love-hungry couples over here just pining their hearts out for children to love [and] I am forced to conclude that the Welfare needs to incorporate common sense into its program."[55]

The Holts' conservative Christian theology guided their involvement with Korean orphans because it stressed the importance of child-saving and seeking conversions through missionary work. The burgeoning neo-evangelical movement led by cultural icons like Billy Graham in the late 1940s and early 1950s shaped the Holts' passion for world evangelization. Certainly, missionaries had worked in the Far East for centuries; however, "this new breed of evangelical missionary, eager to dispense material aid as well as the gospel," in historian Andrew Preston's words, "thrived in the Cold War," and fostered evangelistic leaders like Billy Graham.[56] In the 1940s, Graham's international outreach organization, Youth for Christ, developed church leaders in evangelism and missionary work. One such leader was Bob Pierce, who founded World Vision in 1952. By the 1980s World Vision's dual focus on evangelism and social justice would shape it into the largest relief organization in the world. Its mission in Asia was simple, according to Vice President Paul Rees. World Vision deemphasized planning and administration, responding instead "emergency by emergency, crisis by crisis" to "a summons from Christ to act, and act now."[57]

The Holts' close relationship with World Vision indicated that they shared a like-minded purpose for addressing emergencies where they could meet physical needs as well as spiritual ones. Through the Child Evangelism Club they ran out of their home, the Holts actively practiced evangelism in the States as they later would in Korea and with prospective adoptive families. Agency letters, sent to prospective adoptive families in 1955 and 1956, included extensive gospel messages and evangelistic tracts. Throughout the second half of the 1950s, the Holts also recorded their frequent evangelistic outreaches in Korea. And Bertha Holt's nightly prayer over the new family members once they arrived home further emphasized the significance of conversion as an integral part of their motivation to intercede in Korea. She prayed, "Father in heaven . . . I would pray for these children. . . . I commit them to Thee . . . asking that each one might come to know Christ as Savior and King."[58]

Perhaps because of their otherworldly focus, the Holts' adoption process downplayed rigorous screening procedures and challenged the secular principles of professional social work. Couples interested in adopting a child through the Holts would submit an application form with extensive information on their religious faith, yet with only cursory data about their residences and incomes. Then, the Holts used a California credit agency to conduct a criminal and credit background check on the applicants. Unlike public social welfare agencies, they never visited families' homes, interviewed couples, or mandated physical or mental health evaluations. The Holts required applicants to pay for the credit check, the child's airfare, and a small processing fee—a fraction of what the average social welfare adoption cost. Also, the average Holt adoption process lasted less than six months, while the standard professional placement took one to two years.[59] Even though 1950s social workers championed the Progressive-era notion of scientific matching, the Holts' ideology and practice decried the social welfare practice of racial matching. As Bertha Holt explained, "human nature is universal . . . not confined to any race or standard of living . . . [because] love is the key that unlocks a heart."[60]

Yet the Holts' claim that all people were "equal" in the eyes of God was misleading. Even though they espoused colorblind views, the couple did not embrace all cultures as equal. While in Korea, Holt struggled with the cultural differences, complaining frequently about the cuisine, the "incompetent" nurses, and the desolation of Korea. As soon as he returned to the States, the Oregon farmer asserted, "I will bring my eight up as Americans in America."[61] Since the Holts identified their adopted children as Americans rather than Korean-Americans, they celebrated American holidays, served American food, and dressed their children in American clothes. They did not encourage their children to be bilingual or practice Korean traditions because they did not consider these valuable. This Western notion of cultural supremacy had a long tradition in Protestant mission communities. As historian Richard Eves asserts, "the Christian vision of equality is only notional, for in practice it does not entail respect for the other, but rather antipathy to the other's difference, seeking to erase difference and subsume the other into the same."[62] The Holts demonstrated a marked ambivalence toward Korean culture and their children's Korean identity.

Also, the Holts' fundamental belief in the "power of love" to create families was unevenly practiced regarding race. While they scoffed at racial matching practices, they only permitted black-Korean children to be placed in African American homes.[63] Although they received many letters from prospective parents who were "willing to take the babies with oriental and negro blood," the couple hoped that "the negro people will open their hearts and homes to those children," since they felt "it would be so much kinder for the children to grow up in the society of the race their fathers belonged to."[64] The Holts believed that Korean orphans could "become white" and assimilate, but black-Korean children would always be marked by their racial difference. This practice belied Bertha Holt's adamant stance against the social welfare community's scientific matching practices.

To make their adoption program work, the Holts, and other independent agencies, relied on the Refugee Relief Act. Section 5 of the RRA permitted a foreign child to be adopted by an American couple sight unseen as long as the child qualified as an orphan under immigration policy. This effectively circumvented professional social workers' approval and state welfare departments' oversight, requiring only a U.S. State Department health test to get the child's visa. Before the Holts discovered that they could adopt GI children by proxy, they had started the adoption process through their local social welfare office. The Portland Department of Public Welfare rejected the Oregon couple's request to adopt eight children after it deemed their home unsuitable for such a large family.[65] Rather than allowing this rejection to signal the end of their hopes, the Holts used the existing RRA provisions and their relationships with legislators to forge another way. Bertha Holt wrote that while a social welfare "representative had voted against our adopting eight children, the Lord managed to legally bypass its roadblock" and allowed social workers "no authority over us."[66] Perhaps spurred by their own experience with welfare officials, the Holts included a card in their quarterly newsletter that accurately outlined the differences between the welfare method and their interpretation of the proxy process. Not surprisingly, the Holts stressed the negative aspects of an adoption through official welfare channels. They also boasted that they "saved" more children than those organizations encumbered by "bureaucratic red tape."[67] The proxy process gave Congress rather than social welfare agencies final authority in child placement, a necessary strategy for the Holts' program to work.

Even though the Holts never lost their initial passion for rescuing needy children, over time they, like those practitioners who operated under the consumer paradigm, began to prioritize the needs of prospective adoptive couples as well. The Holts gravitated to the proxy method because it was

fast and relatively inexpensive, and did not require time-consuming or invasive interference from social workers. Since the Holts felt their direction came
from God, they resented being "under the watchful eyes of the local welfare
[officer]" who placed limited value on the Holts' spiritual certainty.[68] Furthermore, it fulfilled the Holts' mission to process adoptions at a rapid pace. Not
only did the expedited time frame benefit adoptive parents, it also contributed to the Holts' mission. Since the initial provision of the RRA was set to
expire on December 31, 1956, the couple recognized that they needed to
"hurry to rescue as many as possible."[69] Their urgency necessitated a process
that could be completed in a couple of months. The proxy method allowed
adoptions to be processed expediently, accomplishing the goal to get the children to the United States before the legislation changed while also placating
anxious, would-be parents who were often tired of waiting.

Using the immigration system as a de facto international adoption program also undermined social workers' preferred placement timeline. After
home placement, the child welfare experts insisted upon a waiting period
before the adoption was finalized. Since social welfare professionals wanted
to avoid making adoptions permanent before a bond had been documented, they often recommended a two-year wait before finalizing adoption paperwork. But immigration specialists, lawyers, and legislators had
the opposite timeline for migrants, wanting to ensure that permanent connections were established before granting visas. During the Displaced Persons Act hearings in the House and Senate, immigration policymakers and
administration officials reinforced this principle as it applied to orphans.
Ugo Carusi, INS commissioner, recommended that the legislation include
provisions to guarantee that children would not become state wards. INS
suggested that adoptive parents "furnish a bond to insure that adoption
shall be effected, and that if for any reason the adoption should fail, that
the orphan admitted shall be adequately provided for and educated until
maturity at the expense of the citizen who proposed the adoption."[70] While
this language was not adopted into the final act, the DPA did specify that
orphans must have "satisfactory assurances" that they "will be cared for
properly," stressing the worthiness of immediate and permanent placements.[71] This system worked against the social welfare establishment and in
favor of humanitarians like the Holts, who stressed immediacy and finality
in placing GI children.

Another aspect of the proxy process that appealed to the Holts as well
as prospective parents was its affordability. To this point, international

adoption had been an option only for middle- or upper-class families because of its cost. Without the supervision of a social worker, families did not need to pay for professional consultation or parenting education, greatly reducing the cost of an adoption. The proxy method also enabled the Holts to adopt a large number of children simultaneously on behalf of their clients. Much of their publicity came from the dramatic "airlifts" when HAP staff would bring as many as ninety children from South Korea to the United States in one trip.[72] While this did not necessarily benefit the prospective parents, it fit within the Holt philosophy to rescue as many children as possible in a short period of time. Additionally, it set the Oregon couple apart from social welfare agencies that, at the most, transported only a dozen children at a time.[73]

Altogether, unconventional though they were, the Holts' tactics were extremely popular with adoptive parents, legislators, and the media. Although other independent agencies operating in South Korea also used the proxy process, Holt Adoption Program was the industry leader.[74] In 1956, the Holts' enterprise placed 179 of 320 total Korean children adopted into U.S. homes, far exceeding the numbers of both independent agencies and state programs. Of the 916 orphan visas issued to Korean adoptees during the 1957 fiscal year, 500 arrived through the Holts' agency.[75] Legislators also lauded the Holts' humanitarianism. Senator Neuberger, the Oregon Democrat who championed the Holts' cause, described the Holts' act of bringing children to a secure and prosperous America from the "ravaged and tormented country of [South] Korea" as "noble and unselfish," and Holt himself as a beacon of the "brotherhood of man." Like the media, Neuberger continued to conflate Christianity, nationalism, and humanism, stressing that "Harry Holt and his wife symbolize to me the Biblical Good Samaritan."[76]

And the media frenzy surrounding their every airlift undoubtedly generated significant publicity for their program. When Holt returned with his newly adopted octet on October 14, 1955, more than fifty U.S. reporters were in the crowd of one thousand that greeted the flight.[77] Over the next decade, whenever the Holts shuttled another airlift of babies, reporters waited expectantly, hoping to capture an image of the rescue campaign that would merit a spot on their newspaper's front page. Headlines proclaimed "Mr. Holt Moves the World," "International Santa Claus," and "'Stork' Plane Brings 12 Korean Foundlings," heralding the uniqueness of the Holts' program. Another journalist associated Holts' success with the triumph of individualism and an American determination to right wrongs. While the writer recognized that Holt had received help from organizations like World Vision, he effused that the "spark of initiative and flame of determination were Mr. Holts [sic]. . . . He has virtually given life to hundreds of children. Given his example, can anyone doubt the power of the individual?"[78] Perhaps an Oregon social worker best summarized the media portrayal of Harry Holt, commenting that "most of us feel that [Holt] is doing a wonderful job of remedying a great social injustice."[79] This national exposure propelled the Holts into the consciousness of the American public and adoptive families—many of whom felt alienated by the formality of the social welfare process but were inspired by the Holts' humanitarian rescue mission. Their program succeeded, in part, because the couple proved both persistent and entrepreneurial in exploiting the vacuum in immigrant and refugee policy, drawing praise and business from prospective adoptive parents. But it was their humanitarian credentials that caused legislators and the media to champion their cause and to christen them Cold War heroes.

"Best Interests of the Child": The Child Welfare Paradigm

For those agencies committed to the child welfare paradigm's rigorous professional standards, the Holts became a threat, and an intense rivalry formed between welfare officials and the Oregon couple. To combat the Holt Adoption Program's popularity and success, one organization forged a loose, decentralized public-private child welfare collaboration into a tight-knit network that relied on strength in numbers. In the nascent era of international adoption, International Social Service—American Branch (ISS), a nonsectarian refugee and family organization founded in 1921, collaborated with federal and state child welfare agencies to help families find adoptable children as well as to ensure that organizations upheld professional standards.[80] Working with the Child Welfare League, the Children's Bureau, and state Departments of Welfare, ISS primarily served as a facilitator between agencies, although it did also conduct international adoptions using Jane Russell's agency, World Adoption International Fund (WAIF), as an intermediary. ISS, like other professional social welfare agencies, incorporated standards for child placement that it considered "best practices" or scientifically verifiable methods for maximizing a successful bond between adoptive children and their new parents. In addition to the racial and religious matching of parents and child, these standards evaluated prospective adoptive parents using a range of benchmarks, including age, marital status, income, religion, health, and the presence of other children in the family.[81] Once a child was placed, a licensed social worker would monitor the relationship for a year before the adoption was finalized. The administrators of the RRA recognized ISS as a key service organization by designating it a member of the Intercountry Adoption Subcommittee.[82]

Yet, as the previous chapters briefly explored, regulatory organizations and the judiciary process continually challenged and revised "best practices." Starting in the mid-1950s, adoptive parents, acting through the courts, increasingly contested the practices of racial and religious matching. When a Presbyterian couple disputed the Adoption Act in Illinois, which prohibited them from adopting Roman Catholic twin girls, the state supreme court ruled that the law did not proscribe families from adopting children of different religions.[83] A Maryland couple was not as fortunate, however, when they challenged the welfare board's matching practices in state court. Invoking their constitutional rights of religious freedom and equal protection under the law, Mr. and Mrs. Frantum argued that as Lutherans they should be allowed to adopt a Roman Catholic boy. The Baltimore Welfare Department disagreed, not only advocating for the biological mother, who insisted her child be raised as a Catholic, but also admitting that they thought Mr. and Mrs. Frantum, ages fifty-four and forty-eight, were too old to parent a two-year-old. The court agreed, ruling in favor of the welfare department.[84] These disputes signified the willingness of prospective adoptive parents to contest policies that restricted their abilities to form families while simultaneously illustrating the significant policy variance between states.[85]

International adoption also poked holes in the practice of racial matching, further exposing the subjectivity of best practices. Starting in 1958, the Child Welfare League began publishing *Standard for Adoption Service*, a manual that offered member agencies more uniform standards of practice about criteria for adoptive parents as well as the placement of adoptive children. Although the manual's authors acknowledged that agencies should not allow racial background alone to determine placement, they reasoned that "at the present time, however, children placed in adoptive families with similar racial characteristics such as color, can become more easily integrated into the average family group and community," and further argued that "a child who appears to be predominantly white will ordinarily adjust best in a white family, and should therefore be placed with a family that can accept him, knowing his background."[86] The authors even suggested using geneticists and anthropologists to determine where a mixed-race child would best assimilate based on physical features. Yet, in the 1963 revision, the manual had removed all references to racial matching and deleted the section on interracial background, establishing that race should no longer factor into the placement of an adoptive child.[87] This shift in the practice of racial matching, predating the 1964 Civil Rights Act, suggests that the prevalence of interracial family placements had influenced social welfare standards.

The RRA accentuated the lack of unity within the social welfare community and highlighted professionals' inability to curtail the influence of volunteer humanitarians. Because the act placed international adoption policy supervision concurrently under the Departments of State and Justice, it failed to give social welfare agencies substantive authority. Thus the RRA created a jurisdictional nightmare that made professional intervention time-consuming and often fruitless. Exploiting this policy "Bermuda Triangle," the Holts used the decentralization to their advantage when creating their proxy adoption-based program. From social workers' point of view, proxy adoptions were deeply flawed for several reasons: they rushed a careful, calculated process, circumvented licensed social workers, allowed a child to be adopted "sight unseen," and eliminated a trial period, giving parents immediate legal custody.[88] As William Kirk, the executive director of ISS, wrote to one of his board members in 1958, proxy adoptions bound a family together legally before they had a chance to gauge compatibility by living together, "which has long been considered a necessity for the protection of children in domestic adoptions in the U.S."[89] While the social welfare community agreed that the situation in Korea was desperate, this did not alter the reality that it considered adoption an immutable placement. To ISS, the Holts' slipshod tactics and abuse of the proxy "loophole" violated key principles of modern social welfare practice and ultimately harmed the children they were trying to help. In response, ISS mounted an intense opposition to both proxy adoptions and the humanitarian paradigm—building an informal coalition in the second half of the 1950s that promoted the child welfare paradigm as the only legitimate adoption method.

"Strong Opposition": Paradigms in Conflict

In 1955, soon after Harry Holt arrived back in the United States with his adopted children, an ISS social worker convinced the embassy to stop issuing immigrant visas in Seoul for proxy adoptions, claiming they were illegal. After a concerted effort to leverage their congressional contacts and reopen the embassy for visa processing, the Holts succeeded in getting State Department support. The deputy administrator of the Refugee Relief Program informed Senator Neuberger's office that "proxy adoptions are permissible if legal in the adoptive country."[90] The first attempt by ISS to challenge the legality of proxy adoption had failed and Holt used this to his advantage. Writing to prospective clients, he claimed that "welfare groups are building up strong opposition against adoption by proxy" and in an effort to protect their interests "are going all out to influence Congress to turn it down. If they should win," he warned, "I cannot help you get a child."[91]

In early 1956, World Vision financed a West Coast trip for Susan Pettiss, the assistant executive director of ISS, hoping to ameliorate the growing tensions between the social welfare community and Holt Adoption Program. The meeting focused on common ground between ISS and the Holts—both sides agreed that the situation in Korea required attention from U.S. authorities. As one of the only U.S. advocates for orphaned children around the world, ISS's mission did not always enjoy support from state agencies. Pettiss believed that local agencies showed bias toward finding homes for U.S.-born children and struggled to "comprehend the desperate situation of the children in Korea and evaluate potential families in that light."[92] Besides agreeing on the general plight of Korean orphans, Pettiss and Holt concurred that the situation was particularly dire for black-Korean children since they were exceptionally hard to place. As a result of their brief acquaintance, Pettiss wrote, "I was impressed by Mr. Holt's real sincerity," describing him as "disarming, friendly, [and] unpretentious."[93]

This seemingly friendly encounter did not change Pettiss's mind about the Holts' methods, however. During her visit, Pettiss reaffirmed her distrust of proxy adoption and the implications of such placements. After discussing specific cases with social workers in California and Oregon, Pettiss reiterated that proxy adoptions were dangerous and expressed deep concern over HAP's plans to use a credit agency to conduct home studies.

She noted that Holt's defensiveness toward social welfare agencies prevented him from comprehending the long-term implications of his speedy placements. Even if she questioned the professional merit of rapid adoptions, Pettiss did recognize that they mattered to the general public. She lamented the agonizingly protracted processing time of professional social agencies, particularly since "Mr. Holt [was] breathing down their necks."[94] While Pettiss's visit created the appearance of cooperation between the two organizations, neither side made the concrete changes necessary to establish a lasting peace. By mid-1956, Pettiss perceived HAP not just as a nuisance but also as a serious threat to intercountry adoption.

One of the ways that social workers rhetorically combated proxy adoption law was to deem it a "flagrant loophole."[95] This language evolved when social welfare agencies made the explicit connection between proxy adoptions and the military act issued two months before, which first permitted adoptions to be completed abroad. Social workers suggested that legislators did not anticipate the creation of "a legal loophole that has made it possible for children to be adopted by proxy."[96] In a letter to Pettiss, Children's Bureau Director Martha Elliott classified all uses of proxy as "an effort to get around the intent of the Section 5 of the Refugee Relief Act," which seemed to undermine "the soundness of social planning for these . . . future citizens."[97]

Yet in 1956, 1957, and 1960—during the height of the disputes between the Holts and child welfare experts—the Subcommittee on Refugees and Escapees, chaired by Senator William Langer (R-N.D.) from 1953 until his death in 1959, continued to extend adoption provisions and modify requirements without ending the purportedly "unintended loophole."[98] As the Senate black-market adoption hearings throughout the 1950s revealed, lawmakers were reluctant to intervene in adoptions across state and national borders since states had jurisdiction over child welfare policy.[99] Federal agencies, such as the U.S. Children's Bureau, historically served state-run Departments of Public Welfare. While the bureau occasionally acted as a liaison between states and the federal government for international adoptions from Canada and Europe, this was not its primary role and meant that there was little existing social welfare oversight on a federal scale. Indeed, the 1957 Subcommittee on Refugees and Escapees report acknowledged that the RRA's proxy provision allowed for two competing policy systems: one under state jurisdiction and one under the oversight of foreign governments. Yet the subcommittee permitted this situation to continue, justifying the jurisdictional conflict by classifying all orphan provisions until 1961 as "emergency" legislation. They did this with the full awareness that professional agencies like ISS were troubled by the Holts' use of the proxy system, even mentioning the Oregon couple by name in the report.[100] Social workers' language of "loopholes" misrepresented certain legislators' intention to maintain the "emergency" proxy provision as long as necessary to achieve their policy goals.

Constituent pressure likely played a role in extending proxy adoption law, something the Children's Bureau conceded.[101] When the orphan provision neared its original expiration date of December 31, 1956, Chairman Langer received ninety-six letters from his North Dakota constituents interested in seeing the proxy proviso extended so they could adopt internationally.[102] During the much publicized 1959 extension hearings, adoptive parent groups and individuals bombarded the chair with telegrams and letters asking that he protect the ability to adopt by proxy.[103] When a geology professor from the University of Wisconsin and an adoptive father of five pled with Senator Langer to extend the law, he responded, "I agree with you 100% both to the enactment of S.1532 and to the continuance of proxy adoptions." Then the senator asked permission to forward the letter to Senator Neuberger and include it in the *Congressional Record*, suggesting that constituent appeals contributed to legislators' decision to maintain the proxy option.[104] From the perspective of legislators like Senator Neuberger, the Holts continued to be the most efficient at solving the humanitarian "problem" of GI children—pleasing both the general public and adoptive families. As Holt himself put it in a letter to USCB Director Arnold, "if any of your organizations can present figures that are half as good as ours, I will personally buy you a new hat."[105] Continued support from the South Korean government, which awarded Holt a humanitarian commendation in 1955, also mattered.[106]

Refugee Relief Act revisions in 1956 and 1957 further illustrated the subcommittee's desire to maintain proxy adoptions. Through Senator Neuberger's advocacy, prospective adoptive parents' demand, and officials' opinion that the original four thousand orphan visas would be "exhausted long before the expiration date of December 31, 1956," legislators extended the RRA for one year and increased the number of non-quota visas to nine thousand.[107] When this law expired on July 31, 1957, lawmakers could not reach an agreement in time on another extension. In the forty-day gap between laws, the Holts drew on their past experience with special legislation, encouraging one of their previous clients, Mr. and Mrs. Harold Kay, to appeal directly to Congress for their second child's adoption.[108] Even in situations without the usual umbrella of proxy, the Holts avoided professional agencies and had Congress perform social welfare screening instead.

The last revision of adoption law before ISS launched its legislative counterattack came in 1957, when Congress ended the RRA and placed adoption policy under the Immigration and Nationality Act, while still framing orphans as refugees. Titled the Refugee-Escapee Act, this provision established an unlimited number of non-quota visas for orphans under the age of fourteen and made two important revisions to the RRA. First, it mandated that adoptive parents meet any state preadoption requirements, increasing the authority of certain professional state agencies. Second, on the recommendation of President Eisenhower the Refugee-Escapee Act also permitted the immigration of orphans with tuberculosis; this would become an especially contested policy over the next year. Again, Congress reemphasized the temporary nature of these provisions, extending the law only until June 30, 1959.[109] While during the 1957 revision Pettiss wanted to propose legislation outlawing proxy adoptions, ISS felt that "it would not be strategic to push for that measure at that time as it was a controversial issue and might jeopardize" future legislation.[110] Before attacking proxy adoptions in Congress, ISS wanted to ensure that it would win.

Closing the "Flagrant Loophole"

Until ISS could build the political support necessary for adoption reform, Pettiss suggested that the organization focus on educating the public about the "risks and dangers" inherent in proxy adoptions. Swaying public opinion in favor of child welfare professionals, she hoped, would give them increased credibility with legislators. To start, ISS published a press release featuring a sample of headlines that warned about problems with proxy adoptions. These sensational titles included "Babies by Mail Often Racket Deal," "Adoption-by-Proxy Cases Frequently Mean Trouble," and "Heartbreak and Suffering Often Result from System."[111] The agency also scrutinized and responded to articles that ISS felt promoted the Holts' program. In late December 1957, *Time* magazine published a favorable article about the Holt family and their religiously centered adoption program, leading ISS executive director, William Kirk to complain. He argued, "this kind of favorable publicity greatly strengthens [Holt's] standing with Korean authorities," making it difficult for Holt "to understand some of the problems involved." For future articles, he urged the staff to "dig deeper" into the Holts' activities and contact ISS officials to have the perspective of "knowing and able professionals."[112]

In another attempt to sway media opinion, Kirk sent a letter to the managing editor of *Ebony* after the magazine published an article written by Pearl Buck. Buck, who ran her own domestic adoption agency called Welcome House, had included photographs and information about the Holt program. The *Ebony* article resulted from Buck's and ISS's efforts to address the need for African American families to adopt black-Korean GI orphans. In fact, the Holts also had difficulty placing these orphans and agreed with Susan Pettiss during her 1956 West Coast trip that something needed to be done about it. After ISS's contributions to resolve the shortage of black families, Kirk was frustrated to learn that the article contained only a cursory mention of his agency. Yet, he was even more upset that the article mentioned the Holts, writing, "we are extremely distressed that you have seemed to endorse the proxy adoption scheme of Mr. Harry Holt. . . . It seemed to us that Mr. Holt's operation had by this time been so thoroughly discredited that no responsible publication would even imply endorsement."[113] Although ISS hoped to see the Holts' agency censured, it lacked the appropriate "ammunition" to discredit a noteworthy American family and their lauded humanitarian crusade.

Starting in late 1957, however, ISS gained its first substantive leverage against the "rogue" agency. The Holts' transport of tubercular children into the United States provoked an intense reaction from the public health community. In 1955, President Eisenhower lobbied Congress for a reevaluation of immigration restrictions against tubercular migrants, arguing that "the [U.S.] no longer regard[s] tuberculosis with dread. Our treatment standards are high and modern treatment is increasingly effective."[114] The president believed that accepting these migrants would not negatively affect public health and convinced Congress of this by 1957. Legislators inserted a provision into the 1957 INA that allowed children with contagious diseases like tuberculosis to be admitted into the United States at both the Surgeon and Attorney Generals' discretion. The Holts, overwhelmed with sick children in their orphanage, brought children over immediately for care in American hospitals.[115] When they shuttled their first planeload of sick children into Oregon, a tremendous public uproar ensued, especially in states that admitted the orphans.[116] While the Holts did nothing illegal, ISS, along with the U.S. Department of Health, Education, and Welfare and the American Medical Association, used this conflict to strengthen the campaign against proxy adoptions. The organizations conflated the transport of unhealthy children with the Holts' overall "ill-considered and hasty placements."[117]

ISS also tried to discredit proxy adoptions by tracking cases of unsuitable parents through state welfare agencies, providing further "ammunition with Congressional leaders."[118] In one instance, ISS closely followed the case of Mr. and Mrs. Henry Butler, a HAP family who exemplified one of ISS's worst nightmares—an adoption that ended in disruption, requiring the child to be placed in a new family. Rejected by Indiana welfare officials, Mrs. Butler suffered from a history of mental illness and the couple lived in squalor. Under her care, the child endured physical and emotional abuse, including indelible bite marks all over her body.[119] Professional social workers used cases like these to show lawmakers the risks of volunteer placements. Building on these controversies, ISS joined together with the Child Welfare League to publish a study in August 1958 on proxy adoptions' effect on a child's development, health, and welfare. Compiled by social scientists Laurin and Virginia Hyde, the Hyde Report studied the proxy placements of ninety-seven children into seventy-seven families. After a thorough evaluation, the Hydes concluded that twenty-nine of the placements were either "not successful" or "in question" and that "adopting a child sight-unseen . . . has already produced many tragic consequences, including the death, beating and abandonment of children."[120]

With the completion of the Hyde Report, ISS crystallized its strategy for combating the general threat of proxy adoption and the specific threat of the Holts' successful agency. The report provided ISS with the expert-backed proof "to educate the public as to the hazards inherent in proxy adoptions," and ISS board members met regularly with their legislative and executive branch contacts to emphasize these points.[121] With the proxy provision set to expire in June 1959, ISS, the Child Welfare League, and the Children's Bureau sent their directors to testify before the Senate Immigration and Naturalization Subcommittee. Using the Hyde Report as evidence, they asked senators to close the jurisdictional gaps that allowed proxy adoptions. They argued that this would not only protect children from negligence and harm but also would make legislation for international orphans a permanent social policy.[122] At first, not wanting to dispute the motives of a popular family, Child Welfare League director Joseph Reid described the Holts as well-meaning but misguided humanitarians. But then, his rhetoric changed, and he accused the Oregon couple of bribing South Korean officials and securing a "monopoly" on Korean orphans, conflating consumer and humanitarian adoption paradigms.[123] As the only advocate for proxy adoptions at the hearing, Senator Neuberger acknowledged that problems had occurred with these placements, but he feared that eliminating them would limit the number of children who could be helped. He did encourage the committee to increase unspecified safeguards to prevent children's exploitation, offering a compromise between volunteers and child welfare professionals.[124]

Yet perhaps ISS's most effective strategy was one borrowed from civil rights activists. By 1959, ISS and the Children's Bureau contended that proxy adoptions damaged the U.S. image abroad, drawing on recent news coverage in communist nations.[125] In an internationally publicized statement, North Korean officials accused Syngman Rhee's government of releasing 1312 children to "American slave traders." Continuing the slavery metaphor, the Pyongyang broadcast stated that most of the orphans "were divided among American capitalists and plantation owners and many children died while they were being sold around like animals in the foreign land." Social welfare officials seized on this statement and its implications for fighting proxy adoptions. As Children's Bureau Director Arnold explained in a memo after the article's release, "the widespread abuses under the proxy method of adoption" have given the U.S. government little defense against these claims. "Now, however," Arnold continued, "the Department's legislative proposals can be pointed out as the means the Administration is taking of assuring itself that children are not unnecessarily separated from their families and homeland." While Arnold admitted that the indictment contained little truth, she did not hesitate to blame the Holt program, suggesting that it originated in the rumors of Holt "paying" the South Korean government eighty dollars per child.[126] By conflating proxy adoption with racist imperialism, social welfare officials forced legislators to consider whether the expansive policy did more harm than good.

Even with the increasingly effective social welfare lobby, it took two more years before legislators would ban proxy adoptions entirely. As Neuberger proposed, the Senate voted in 1959 to extend the current orphan law for another year. Legislators, however, added a rider mandating that INS officers also conduct home investigations to safeguard the welfare of the children. The Holts "rejoiced" when they heard the news that INS, instead of social welfare agencies, would be responsible for conducting home studies—unsurprising given their past hardships with social workers.[127] On July 14, 1960, Congress extended the 1959 act for another year to assess the INS home study's effectiveness before making legislation permanent. Under the 1959 amendment and 1960 extension, HAP adoptions increased annually. In 1959, HAP placed 389 Korean orphans with U.S. families—this number rose to 488 in 1960 and 659 in 1961.[128] Even with INS home studies, the agency continued to navigate the policy vacuum, remaining outside the jurisdiction of the social welfare system.

Yet the Holts' improvised policy solutions could not ultimately weather the counter campaign launched by ISS and its allies. The persistence of ISS in lobbying Congress finally succeeded; in 1961, legislators passed a bill requiring parents to meet their prospective child before the adoption could be finalized, effectively ending the proxy provision. Although the Holts waged a desperate fight to maintain their right to perform proxy adoptions, legislators validated some of child welfare experts' concerns. Still, the piecemeal changes afforded HAP and other independent agencies the opportunity to adapt slowly to the required legislation. For example, even though proxy adoptions were technically outlawed, families could still adopt children from overseas sight unseen, providing that their home state permitted readoption in the United States.[129] This concession placated social welfare agencies because it required that licensed social workers perform a thorough home investigation before the adoption was finalized.

HAP's adoptions dropped by over 60 percent in 1962 to only 199 placements, demonstrating the significance of proxy adoptions to their agency strategy.[130] Bertha Holt grieved for the former process. At the fifth annual HAP picnic in 1962, she reflected that "there were no babies younger than 18 months old [any more] from Korea. Legislation had prevented infants and parents from enjoying each other at the very time they needed each other most."[131] To conform to changing legislation, the Holts surrendered the control and autonomy to which they had grown accustomed. While HAP would not become an official, licensed adoption agency until after Harry Holt's death in 1964, this legislative triumph signified a reversal of fortune—if they wanted to continue practicing, they would have to conform to professional child welfare standards.

Perhaps most significantly, lawmakers incorporated the new orphan law into the 1961 INA, making the adoption of foreign orphans a permanent part of U.S. law.[132] President Eisenhower, who first advocated for a permanent adoption law in 1957, noted that "orphans admitted under earlier special legislation have successfully adjusted to American family life" and that many Americans were still "eager to adopt children from abroad."[133] Since the emergency facing South Korean GI orphans had passed, lawmakers could no longer justify "stopgap" provisions that excluded the role of licensed social workers. In addition, with the 1961 revision lawmakers no longer positioned orphans as refugees who required "emergency" legislation but as a permanent category of immigrants, a "milestone" in the words of Susan Pettiss.[134] Yet, unlike most immigrants, foreign children were not subject to quota restrictions, cementing their status as "desirable" migrants and possibly even as ambassadors for the imminent removal of the quota system in the 1965 INA. As President Eisenhower had predicted in 1957, the demand for foreign children by American couples persisted even as the baby boom began to ebb in the early 1960s.[135]

Conclusion

Independent adoption practitioners, religious humanitarians, legislators, and professional social workers vied for the authority to create international adoption policy in the postwar period, frequently using adoption law to further their own competing interests. This improvisational policymaking revealed the competing paradigms at work in child welfare throughout the 1950s. The humanitarian paradigm emerged at a point of intense Cold War anxiety and an increasing demand for "adoptable" babies. Legislators justified the maintenance of a seven-year policy vacuum as an act of beneficence and humanitarianism that furthered U.S. foreign policy goals and strengthened its mission abroad. Legislators and the media pointed to volunteers and adoptive parents alike as exemplars of the "great heart of America" because they were ensuring the fortunes of the "best possible immigrants." This climate permitted religious humanitarians, like Harry Holt, to fashion improvised policies that expedited adoptive placements. Exploiting a policy vacuum in the area of intercountry adoption—a vacuum created by conflicting state laws and a lack of federal adoption legislation—Holt's methods drew the attention, and ire, of child welfare experts. Their multi-year campaign to discredit the Holts achieved some success, and international adoption law became permanent in 1961.

While it seemed that the 1961 legislation signaled the death knell of the humanitarian paradigm, there was one important piece missing from the final law. Lawmakers gave the Children's Bureau no supervisory or regulatory authority over international adoptions, leaving it to the Attorney General and individual states. A sign of INS's hesitancy to release authority over immigration, this policy meant that during the next foreign emergency there was still no single child welfare agency responsible for controlling information, organizing a team of experienced social workers, and ensuring that "best practices" remained in operation. This "disappointment," in the words of Susan Pettiss, propped open the door for volunteers to continue to shape international adoption, especially in the wake of the Vietnam War.[136]

Notably, the humanitarian paradigm's continued clout throughout the 1950s and 60s signaled the growing influence of adoptive parents as a social movement. Through individual advocacy and affinity groups, adoptive parents and prospective adoptive parents, adopting both domestically and internationally, demonstrated that they were a powerful postwar constituency with considerable congressional influence. The next chapter will explore how adoptive parents styled their nonbiological and often transracial families as mainstream and normal, upsetting notions of the homogeneous 1950s family and marking adoptive families as humanitarian models. It was indeed the advocacy of adoptive parents that contributed to the success—and endurance—of international adoption's consumer and humanitarian paradigms.

CHAPTER 4

Coming Out of the Shadows

Adoptive Parents as Public Figures

IN 1948, Children's Bureau chief Katherine Lenroot received a letter from an especially passionate adoptive mother. Madelon Neuvirth, a Columbus, Ohio, resident and director of the Chosen Parents League, wrote to the chief expressly to advocate for adoptive families. In her multipage appeal, she insisted that adoption should not be considered "special," but a common way to form a family. This mainstream acceptance was necessary, she maintained, because "we want only to make our children, whom we did not bear, the happiest, most wanted, most loved and *most normal* children in the world."[1] In Neuvirth's mind, adoption was not to be relegated to the shadowy branches of a family tree, but prominently displayed for all to see. Neuvirth was not alone. Starting in the late 1940s and continuing through the 1960s, parents who adopted both domestically and internationally echoed her refrain.

As volunteers and child welfare advocates shaped and defined adoption policies in Europe and Asia, and as politicians and officials removed barriers to the immigration of foreign orphans, U.S. adoptive parents built a visible and influential social and political network centered on their identity as adopters. They did this through public policy—in citizens' committees, lobbying, and Senator Estes Kefauver's famed juvenile delinquency hearings—and through culture—in adoptive parent memoirs and expansive media coverage like the Hildy McCoy case. Although hardly conforming to idealized American families, adoptive couples of both foreign and domestic children advocated for their nonbiological and, at times, transracial and interreligious families to be considered natural and chosen. Their campaigns subverted long-held American paradigms of biology, while at the same time paradoxically reinforcing the importance of the nuclear family and "fit" parenting.[2] International adoption's positive humanitarian press also burnished the image of all adopters and pushed adoption to the fore of U.S. culture.[3] Adoptive parents then used their increased credibility and leverage to make the institutionalization of international adoption a long-term reality by advocating for a range of adoption-friendly policies. This community was instrumental to the success of international adoption.

Both domestic and international factors made adoptive parents' advocacy possible. Although records were increasingly shrouded in secrecy in the postwar era, denying adult adoptees access to their pasts, the act of adoption itself was losing its hiddenness. Achieving incremental acceptance in the early twentieth century, by the postwar period adoption had won "widespread cultural legitimacy," and became even "fashionable," in the words of one reporter.[4] The celebration of adoptive parenthood was possible, in part, because of an increasing faith in science and technology to control nature, which, beginning in the early twentieth century, minimized the necessity of biology and replaced it with sociocultural norms.[5] Deemphasizing motherhood as "natural," adoptive mothers joined with other mid-century middle-class mothers whose expert training and education made them exemplary caregivers.[6] Churches, government agencies, and the media also helped to promote adoption by stressing that good parenting was an essential civic duty. In turn, birth parents—often single mothers—were increasingly deemed "unfit," by professionals and the public, because of their perceived psychological instability and negligent parenting. Identifying "unfit" birth parents as "moron girls" while embracing "fit" adoptive parents as the "mothers of tomorrow," policymakers contended, would mitigate delinquency, crime, and other social ills.[7]

It was also no accident that adoptive parents found a voice in the post-World War II era. At a time when the United States strove to keep nonwhite nations within its sphere of influence, parents who adopted internationally were a too-good-to-be-true public relations story. It was, in fact, adoptive parents who bolstered the influence of volunteers like the Holts. Their support of the rescue campaigns in Greece, Korea, and other Cold War hotspots provided crucial backing for the humanitarian paradigm to flourish in the 1950s. They shone in the media as racially progressive humanitarians, offering a powerful counterpoint to the negative press accounts of Jim Crow segregation that appeared both at home and abroad.[8] Without a doubt, international and transracial families played a critical role in revising public assumptions about adoption and legitimizing adoptive parenting. Yet the race blindness couched in the supremacy of the middle-class, white family was a safe type of social subversion that pointed toward American exceptionalist narratives. Only by being assimilated into whiteness could nonwhite children emerge as "normal" Americans. Drawing on Cold War symbolism that imbued domestic family values with international significance, postwar adoptive families emerged from the shadows to become a central, and enduring, part of the American story.

A National Discourse on Parenting: Hildy and Estes

In early March 1951, Melvin and Frances Ellis brought home their ten-day-old adoptive daughter, whom they immediately named Hildy. Arranged privately through a physician, this adoption brought together the Ellises, a forty-something, childless Jewish couple from nearby Brookline, with Marjorie McCoy, an unwed Catholic birth mother studying to be a nurse.[9] Although it was unusual for a Catholic child to be placed with a Jewish family, Dr. Herman Sands, McCoy's physician, insisted he had informed her of the Ellises' faith. Yet, one month later, McCoy contacted the adoptive family, insisting that no one had informed her that the Ellises were Jewish. While McCoy did not want to keep Hildy herself, she wanted the girl placed with the Catholic Charitable Bureau until a suitable Catholic family could be located. When the Brookline couple refused to return Hildy, McCoy filed suit and took the battle to court.[10]

After a protracted contest, the Ellises ran out of appeals in 1955. On February 14, Justice Williams of the Massachusetts Supreme Judicial Court ruled in McCoy's favor based on the 1950 state law, which found that "petitions for adoption are bound to give controlling effect to identity of religious faith 'when practicable'."[11] In a last ditch effort to keep four-year-old Hildy, the Ellises promised to raise her as a Catholic. Rejecting this plea, the court ordered the Ellises to surrender Hildy to McCoy by June 30. Unwilling to give Hildy up, the Ellises fled Massachusetts and became fugitives. Over the course of the next year, the family moved six times to avoid detection, eventually settling in Miami, Florida. The Massachusetts court failed to locate the "fugitive family" until May 1957, a few months after

Hildy's sixth birthday. While the court requested that Melvin Ellis be immediately extradited to face kidnapping charges, Florida governor Leroy Collins refused, arguing that "it was the Ellises . . . who have given of themselves to Hildy, as only parents can understand."[12] In mid-July, Miami Circuit Court Judge John Prunty approved the Ellises' Florida adoption petition, ruling that the couple were "fit parents" and it would be in Hildy's "best interests" to remain with them. Marjorie McCoy stated her intent to keep fighting: "Some day [Hildy] will learn the facts about her mother's desire to protect her with the privacy that others are willing to destroy. Meanwhile . . . I entrust her to the loving protection of God. The rest is in the hands of my attorneys."[13] The ruling of the Miami judge remained final; the Ellises raised Hildy to adulthood.

Hildy's story garnered extensive media attention and, as *Time* reported, became "familiar to newspaper readers across the U.S."[14] Starting in 1955 with the Ellises' flight, Hildy's custody battle quickly became national news, captivating a large audience, including subscribers to religious newspapers and the primarily African American readership of the *Chicago Defender*. After reading articles in their local papers, citizens wrote letters to Mamie Eisenhower, begging her to intercede on the Ellises' behalf. Even a 1957 review of a newly released adoption handbook used the Hildy case as the article hook, using the story's familiarity to resonate with prospective adoptive parents.[15] Most press coverage focused on the Ellises, whose plight received sympathy from opinion makers. Since the Ellises were Jewish, such understanding partly reflected the decline in anti-Semitism after World War II. More than one-third of American Jews moved to the suburbs between 1945 and 1965, easing their assimilation into white, middle-class culture. This increased their neighbors' exposure to Judaism, making it one of America's "civic religions" along with Protestantism and Catholicism. Although discrimination did persist in corporate leadership and top universities, a 1952 *Look* magazine article emphasized U.S. Jews' loyalty to America, tolerant attitudes, and Judeo-Christian morals.[16] Indeed, reporters portrayed the couple as stable, middle-class small business owners who owned a "comfortable suburban home." According to journalists, the couple were also commendable parents, giving Hildy "solicitous attention" and watching over her "gently and lovingly."[17] Condemning the Massachusetts court ruling that returned Hildy to McCoy, one editorialist remarked: "As to the injury to be inflicted on a four-year-old by tearing her away from the parents she loved and the home she had always known, the judge said nothing."[18] When the Miami judge ultimately approved the Ellises' adoption petition, a *New York Times* photo captured the doting father beaming at his little girl as she threw her arms around him and smiled for the camera.[19] This image framed the judge's ruling as a happy ending, even though the Ellises were still fugitives under Massachusetts law.

The media also represented the Ellises as parents who would sacrifice anything for their daughter. Melvin Ellis informed one reporter: "I'm not a willing hero or martyr but I'll do anything to help the child. I am prepared to go to jail, if necessary, [in] protest against [this] law and its administration"—a striking statement, given that the Ellises' story at times appeared alongside civil rights movement coverage.[20] Evoking images of frequently jailed civil rights activists, Ellis sought to transform the criminal kidnapping charge into an act of civil disobedience. His challenge implied that adoptive parents could be aggressive advocates for their families, willing to take extra-legal steps to ensure that their interests were protected. During her testimony before Governor Collins, Frances Ellis pleaded, "I don't like to say it because it sounds dramatic but I don't think [Hildy] would survive [being separated from us]."[21] Even though Ellis did not have a bodily experience of birth, she insisted on her deep motherly attachment to Hildy. Indeed, the Ellises rejoiced at their opportunity to parent and embraced the new identity it offered them. As Frances Ellis expressed it, "I can't tell you how nice it is not to be able to go out except on Saturday nights like other parents."[22] Her sentiment demonstrates how much couples without children were excluded from the 1950s child-centered culture and, as Elaine Tyler May has written, "heightened the private anguish of infertility."[23]

But not all the media were the Ellises' fans. The Massachusetts Catholic community and the Catholic press generally supported McCoy, adhering to the valued tradition of religious matching and the preservation of culture from assimilation. Perhaps because of past abuses, American Catholics were especially insistent on maintaining authority in adoption placements. For instance, the Catholic New York Foundling Society's attempt to place Irish orphans with devout Catholic Mexican families in 1900 backfired when nominally religious whites in Arizona refused to allow white children to be raised in ethnic homes. In that case, the courts ruled against the foundling society.[24] Catholics won a more favorable ruling from the Massachusetts court in the McCoy case, but they still felt indicted by the national media blitz that followed. *The Pilot*, the Boston Archdiocese's official newspaper, accused the Ellises of "crass and contrived emotionalism" and the media of "incomprehensible" misinformation about McCoy's intentions, including a misreport that Hildy would be placed in an institution rather than with another family.[25] In the Catholic magazine *America*, one writer argued that the press misconstrued the case to be about religious difference when it actually concerned "the plea of a tormented mother [McCoy], the rights of a baby who could not speak for herself, and the majesty of the law by which society itself is governed."[26] Some Catholics, however, expressed ambivalence about Hildy being returned to McCoy, arguing that while officials had handled the case poorly from the beginning, this was now irrelevant. In a letter to *The Pilot*, Gloucester District Judge Edward Morley wrote, "What is the best thing for this four-year-old girl? Certainly she is not responsible for her plight. Is it a Christian thing to destroy the love and affection which have grown up between the child and the only ones she has known as father and mother?"[27]

Outside the legal system and the Catholic community, Marjorie McCoy had few supporters. In the court of public opinion, she actually became the defendant. Although she had some legal recourse as a birth mother—which was not available to biological parents outside the United States—most news reports downplayed her right to influence Hildy's religious upbringing and criticized her "game playing" with a little girl's life. This public reaction reflected shifting societal norms about the usefulness of religious matching, brought on by the increase in transracial and international adoptions. Furthermore, professionals and the public increasingly embraced adoption as the "best solution" to single mother pregnancies. Thus, even though McCoy had not broken the law, reporters blamed her for "the bitter custody battle" in which Hildy became a pawn.[28] One reporter concluded that "Gov. Leroy Collins put the love of [the Ellises] for their foster daughter Hildy, ahead of religious and legal obstacles today." McCoy was the "obstacle" to family formation and Hildy's emotional well being.[29]

Was such public sentiment justified? From all accounts, it seems that McCoy's intentions were sincere. Even though she would not raise Hildy herself, it mattered to her that her biological daughter was brought up by Catholics—one of the few aspects of Hildy's life still legally in her purview. McCoy contacted officials when Hildy was only five weeks old so it was still well within the adjustment timeframe of six months social workers recommended before finalizing an adoption. Nothing suggests that McCoy pursued her case cavalierly or out of spite, and the Massachusetts courts did rule in her favor. But this was a case where it appeared almost "natural" to side with the adoptive parents—and the media did. Perhaps accurately, the press contrasted the Ellises' parental devotion with McCoy's detachment. One article described the birth mother as "wan and tearless" when she relinquished Hildy, noting that she simply "turned her back and walked away." The Ellises, however, comforted their new daughter in "safe [and] protecting arms."[30] Florida Governor Collins also stressed the differences between McCoy and the Ellises. In his extradition refusal, he proclaimed that "the great and good God of all of us, regardless of faith, grants to every child . . . the right to be wanted and . . . loved. Hildy's mother denied both of these rights to her. It was the Ellises . . . who have been the persons through whom God has assured to Hildy these . . . rights as one of his children."[31] Through this lens of the nuclear family and civic religion—a compelling one for postwar Americans—family devotion trumped biology and religious matching.

This framing of Marjorie McCoy is especially significant when contextualized within the national anxiety over juvenile crime and "black market" adoption. Experts explained youth crime by blaming the "disorganized" or "lenient" family—those "broken homes" that were predominantly lower-class, immigrant, African American, and female-headed.[32] In 1955 Estes Kefauver, chair of the Senate subcommittee investigating juvenile delinquency and an adoptive father himself, conducted hearings on interstate adoption practices (often with the help of Ernest Mitler). Although baby selling and farming dated back to the early twentieth century, as the first chapter examined in detail, the interstate traffic of infants increased dramatically with the rise of adoptions in the 1950s. Social workers challenged both the consumer and the humanitarian paradigms, deeming such practitioners as "black" and "gray" marketers who were "operating on the fringe of the law." But establishing regulations that differentiated between these two methods of adoption while limiting their influence proved problematic. Further complicating matters, to avoid prosecution in any of the fifteen states that by 1955 had criminalized baby selling, for-profit operators often conducted their businesses across state lines.[33]

Kefauver articulated two explicit connections between interstate black market adoptions and juvenile crime. First, he highlighted how young girls became pregnant as a rebellious act. According to the New York assistant commissioner of youth services, "out-of-wedlock pregnanc[ies]," which he also termed "sex offenses," were a leading result of delinquent behavior perpetrated by "promiscuous" girls.[34] Kefauver argued that since 40 percent of unmarried mothers were under the age of twenty and few facilities offered them support, they became a "juvenile problem." Not only were these single women more vulnerable to delinquent influences and future criminal behavior, but they also were more likely to settle for black market representatives who offered to pay their hospital bills. As Senator Thye of Minnesota asserted, "A young girl confronted with such an unfortunate situation, bewildered as she would naturally be, becomes the prey of those who would seize the opportunity" to sell her child. Second, once a potentially delinquent mother relinquished her baby to black marketers, the chances of her child being raised by "unfit" parents increased. Black market placements that bypassed established expert procedures deeply concerned the subcommittee. In Kefauver's words, "poor placement of a child can produce maladjustments lead[ing] to abnormal and delinquent conduct."[35]

Key legislators and social welfare officials viewed some adoptive parents with great suspicion, but they also asserted that careful adoptive placement could "save" children from delinquency through skilled, intentional parenting. Kefauver contended that while "no child is born delinquent," many factors increased the likelihood of delinquency, especially "the profound influence" of parents and immediate family.[36] The Planned Parenthood Chapter in Chicago concurred, sending a support letter and its brochure titled, "The Roots of Delinquency," to Kefauver. Director Mary Louise Mitchell stressed that "wanted babies" became "well-balanced and emotionally stable" adults, pointing to her clinic's adult education program as one way to curb delinquency. In this way, adoptive parenthood was seen as a solution. As one adoptive mother wrote, "If God would grant me one great power of my choosing . . . I would prevail upon every childless couple who desire children to open their hearts and homes to them. Within our generation, I think we would all see a wonderful decrease in juvenile delinquency."[37] Officials agreed that bad parents produced future generations of bad parents. Judge Anna Kross, the New York City Commissioner of Corrections, emphasized the cyclical nature of delinquency: "Of course, the parents are to blame, but have you ever met the parents of the youths that are in trouble? They were also youths in trouble. And who prepared them for their role as parents? They just went on doing what comes naturally."[38] Kross's statement suggests why public skepticism mounted about the merits of "natural" parenting.

The Hildy case and Kefauver hearings illuminate many of the larger issues shaping postwar adoption. They both demonstrated how adoptive parents like the Ellises labored to create public identities that highlighted their normalness and commitment to dominant cultural values. Also, the media joined with adoptive parents in this campaign, depicting the Ellises not as outsiders with unusual, mixed-religious families, but as mainstream Americans. While Kefauver's committee could have demonized adoption and adoptive parents—echoing the progressive reformers' fears about genetic risk—it instead affirmed that adoption was a social good, one that protected children from delinquency when conducted correctly. This dovetailed with the popular emphasis starting in the 1920s that parenting was a skill rather than a biological endowment and gave adoptive parents increased political and social legitimacy in popular culture.[39]

While adoptive parents benefited from the postwar national discourse on parenting, birth mothers remained stigmatized. To be sure, birth mothers never had significant mainstream public support or extensive rights. Charles Loring Brace's orphan train movement, in an effort to "clean up" New York City, routinely placed immigrant children with adoptive families, often without their parents' knowledge.[40] Most early twentieth-century reformers viewed unwed mothers as in need of either salvation or sterilization but certainly not as ideal parents. By the 1940s, social welfare officials often considered adoption in the "best interest of the child" but made conscious choices to protect birth mothers from exploitation.[41] Despite such efforts, the Kefauver hearings reflected the cultural preoccupation with psychoanalysis that diagnosed white single mothers as mentally ill—at times victims, at other times sinners, but still reformable. As victims, they could be manipulated by shady black market operators who could deftly manipulate them; as sinners they could fall prey to other delinquents or their own questionable character. Either way, these characterizations painted mothers without husbands as easily influenced, mentally and emotionally unstable, and potentially amoral. Still, categorizing unwed mothers as either victims or sinners meant that delinquent girls were no longer "ruined" and could be reformed if married.[42] The Hildy case further emphasized how birth mothers could not be trusted to act as competent parents. Both the media and the Florida governor reinforced the image of McCoy as a woman who pursued her own happiness over Hildy's.

Finally, both the Ellises' story and the black market adoption hearings spoke to another reality: not enough "adoptable" babies existed through "official" routes to meet demand. The demand for healthy, white infants had outstripped supply throughout the twentieth century, but the baby

boom coupled with an increasingly positive public perception of adoptive
families created an adoption frenzy. In 1945, approximately 53,000 prospective parents applied to adopt. A decade later the number had nearly doubled, thanks in part to a growing supply of infants available for adoption.
Medical officials often pressured unmarried mothers to relinquish their
children in record numbers. Poking holes in the dogma of racial and religious matching also meant more children available to adopt than ever
before.[43] Even so, by 1956 there was only one child available for every twelve
prospective parents. For Jewish families like the Ellises, there was only one
child for every twenty-five couples since fewer unwed Jewish mothers surrendered their babies.[44] For Jewish agencies, which sometimes placed no
more than two babies per year, religious matching was not sustainable to
satisfy the demand from Jewish adoptive couples.[45] Under such circumstances it is not surprising that demand invigorated the consumer and
humanitarian paradigms of child placement, helped to broaden the definition of the adoptable child, and challenged laws that sanctioned religious
and racial matching. Indeed, the demand for babies had significant international implications, literally pushing adoptive parents to other parts of the
globe. In the Kefauver hearings, a committee member advised couples
weary of long waiting periods to turn their gaze abroad and adopt children
available in Europe under the provisions of the 1953 Refugee Relief Act.[46] In
addition to growing public clout, adoptive families benefited from geopolitical events that offered them an opportunity to adopt children and simultaneously fulfill humanitarian needs. Officials thus reinforced the symbiotic
relationship between international and domestic adoption policies.

Civic Parenthood—The California Citizens' Committee
and Adoptive Parent Advocacy

The conversation over parental "fitness" sustained by media coverage of
adoptive parents and congressional hearings gestured to the prestige of civic
parenthood in the post-World War II era. More than just providing individual fulfillment, middle-class parenting ostensibly protected the nation from
excesses and delinquency—marking parents as "responsible citizen[s]."[47]
For some adoptive parents, the emphasis on civic parenthood offered an
opportunity to advocate for policies and programs that affected their
families directly. Beginning in the late 1940s, adoptive parents lobbied for a

variety of adoption-related causes, including the extension of inheritance rights to adopted children, the protection of adoptive parent privacy, and the reform of adoptive services. Hardly a homogeneous bloc, however, there was no one adoptive parent agenda. They tended to support the interests—and paradigm—that had enabled their particular family formation, whether through independent channels under the consumer or humanitarian paradigm, or through child welfare paradigm agencies. Some adoptive parents lobbied for increased professional adoption services and stricter regulations against independent placements, while others advocated for legislation that maintained and encouraged the growth of volunteers. Since adoptive parents worked hard to cultivate an image of normalcy, their advocacy often did not seem revolutionary or even self-serving, but part of their democratic responsibility. Nevertheless, this advocacy reinforced adoptive parents' identity as average citizens committed to both preserving and reforming the institutions that made their kinship possible.

One type of adoptive parent advocacy began in 1949 as part of the Citizens' Committee on Adoption of Children in California (CCAC), a broad coalition of state residents committed to strengthening statewide adoption structures. Citizens' committees popped up across the country in the postwar era, protesting issues from the lack of comic book censoring and nuclear armament to protecting public spaces and public schools.[48] Comprised of prominent businesspeople, legislators, ministers, doctors, attorneys, social workers, and philanthropists—some of whom also were adoptive parents— CCAC sought to cultivate consensus among citizens before proposing state legislation with the intent to produce successful regulations with broad community support.[49] Explicitly "charitable" in objective and purpose, and supported by a two-year grant from the Columbia and Rosenberg Foundations, CCAC's mandate was to bring together citizens and professionals to address California's adoption laws and processes.[50]

Relying on county-based subcommittees to determine the issues facing specific communities, the state committee produced four separate studies on the adoptive child, the "natural" parents, adoption agencies, and independent adoptions.[51] The California committee primarily sought to understand adoptive parents' "criticisms" of social welfare agencies and the related popularity of independent adoptions. The founding members acknowledged that a community-based approach to rethinking the adoption system was "new and untried" and would require creativity and persistence in charting alternate routes. CCAC's work commanded national attention as a strategy for redirecting the huge demand for consumer-driven and humanitarian adoption services. The Children's Bureau publicized a report from the Los Angeles County subcommittee among the state Departments of Welfare, giving California's experiment nationwide exposure. Since the Golden State conducted 10 percent of all adoptions nationally, CCAC's results would inform other state governments of ways to involve citizens in regulating adoptions.[52]

CCAC prided itself on bringing together opposing points of view to reach a "constructive resolution." Los Angeles County supported the largest and most active local committee.[53] The licensed agencies there had an abysmally low record of placements, completing only 145 of 1519 adoptions. Since nearly 40 percent of California's adoptions were conducted in Los Angeles County, these numbers were particularly daunting for social welfare agencies. The 110-member CCAC in Los Angeles explicitly sought to bring together "friends and enemies," code for adoptive parents and social workers. One leader explained that both sides were "emotionally involved" because of recent conflicts between Los Angeles County child welfare departments and adoptive parent groups. The increasingly limited supply of adoptable children in the 1950s had provoked certain prospective adoptive parents to lobby to "secure more babies for adoption" and to question "certain basic adoption laws and their administration," a move that made social workers irritable and defensive. As social workers within CCAC voiced, it was an "uncontroverted" fact that "the inherent rights of children released for adoption, and of their natural parents, are constantly jeopardized by the desires of childless couples who are seeking children."[54] But while the committee's members were still sometimes "poles apart," leaders found that the two sides could have productive dialogues over their differences and even accomplish projects together, producing educational content about independent adoptions and hosting public informational meetings.[55]

Adoptive parent concerns about the lack of adoptable children surfaced during committee deliberations. At the August 1950 meeting, representatives concluded, "the Committee might well . . . offer childless couples as much help as possible." Members proposed offering fertility services and attempted to make the adoption of special needs children more appealing.[56] Working across perspectives, however, meant that adoptive parents' interests were not necessarily the priority. When committee members asked, "How does the adoption law safeguard adoptive parents prior to the completion of an independent adoption?" the response revealed the tensions and risks in adoptive kinship. As the report stated:

> It is difficult to understand what interest the petitioners [adoptive parents] have which should be safeguarded prior to the entry of a decree. . . . They have no proprietary interest in the child. They do have protection against whimsical withdrawal of the consent of the natural parents to the adoption, but they have acquired no right to anything prior to the decree, except the right to have their petition considered by the court.[57]

These stark terms underscored adoptive parents' legal inferiority to birth parents and potentially threatened their attempts to present adoption as better than biology.

Some adoptive parents believed that guaranteeing standards for birth parents offered their families the most protection and the strongest claims to normalcy. Adoptive parents working through authorized social agencies acknowledged that protecting birth parents' rights ultimately was in their best interest as well. As social workers often explained, if the conditions of surrender were ideal, it protected adoptive parents' identity from discovery and relieved them of future contact from their child's birth family—a phenomenon that historian Wayne Carp has shown was unique to the postwar era.[58] The CCAC publicized many cases where inadequate casework made placements more tenuous, demonstrating how adoptive parents benefited from better services to birth parents. In one case, a doctor trying to find a baby for his childless clients pressured an unmarried mother to release her child by explaining that she would have to pay the hospital bills to take the baby. While the judge eventually ruled in favor of the birth mother, the baby had already lived for several months with the adoptive parents, who were understandably crushed to surrender the child.[59] To avoid tragedies like these, CCAC's adoptive parents advocated for birth parents to receive proper relinquishment counseling and ample financial resources.[60]

CCAC also worked to provide decent housing, prenatal care, and adequate nutrition to unmarried mothers through the state-funded Aid to Needy Children program. To further help shift community opinion about possible adoption avenues, organizers in Los Angeles targeted volunteer and sectarian organizations that ran existing programs for unmarried mothers at the Salvation Army, St. Anne's Maternity Home, and the

Unmarried Mothers Auxiliary. CCAC's representatives hoped these partnerships would increase the community's awareness of the risks inherent in adoptions conducted outside licensed agencies.[61] In addition to supporting increased social worker presence in rural counties where independent adoptions were particularly pervasive, public agencies even considered a state-funded program that would provide mothers with living arrangements, medical services, and flexibility to make social agencies a viable alternative to consumer-paradigm adoptions.[62]

Organizers intended that these services and education campaigns would protect the unmarried mother from "community attitudes" that considered her "unfit, immoral, and looked down upon with scorn." Although CCAC seemed to be looking out for birth mothers' interests, the organization also regarded them as pitiful figures in need of paternalistic guidance. As one doctor reflected, this outreach gave adoptive parents the opportunity to act as "Good Samaritans" who correctly identified the unmarried mother as "a problem of society for which we must all accept a measure of responsibility" so that these "innocent victims" could be "rehabilitated." Such attitudes were also evident in CCAC's refusal to extend committee spots to birth mothers.[63] Even with ostensible unity, some committee members still wondered if the current process protected birth parents too much. One representative asked "whether a child of an unmarried mother of a low economic status would not be better off in a good adoptive home," assuming a correlation between economic security and good parenting. Even though other members clarified that the laws protected "the right of the natural parent without reference to economic or marital status," these questions exposed how adoptive parents had more privilege and bargaining power in helping to craft legal definitions of a child's best interests.[64]

This privilege became even more apparent a decade later with CCAC's second iteration. The first committee had to grapple with the steadily shrinking pool of adoptable children and the glut of willing adoptive parents. By the early 1960s, agencies were receiving fewer applications, which meant there were more children waiting for adoptive homes, especially in the foster care system. Since the pendulum had swung back toward recruiting adoptive parents, the committee catered more toward adoptive parent concerns and worked to "eliminate delays and complications."[65] Despite this changed focus, the 1963 committee still worked to resolve the complex tangle of perspectives and tensions underlying the adoption system. Indeed, in the grant request, organizers asked both, "To what extent are there children in ANC [Aid for Needy Children] families for whom adoption would offer a better life? On the other hand, are ANC parents put under compulsion to release their children for adoption without adequate justification?"[66] As the juxtaposition of these questions suggested, the diverse composition of CCAC meant that adoptive parents were only one voice of many, producing a balanced approach to adoption reform.

Another type of adoptive parent advocacy came from adoptive parent societies and affinity organizations, groups whose membership was solely comprised of adoptive parents or prospective adoptive parents. Sociologist David Kirk, in his 1964 book *Shared Fate*, intensively studied two such groups: the Adopted Children's Association of Los Angeles and the Whittier (California) Adopted Children's Association. He found that, on one hand, these groups served as "self-help organizations" for couples navigating the adoption process or transitioning to adoptive parenthood. But, on the other hand, these associations served as lobbying groups. The Los Angeles and Whittier organizations, for instance, worked to reform California adoption laws and serve as adoption boosters in their communities. An adoptive parent himself, Kirk likened adoptive parents' groups to civil rights organizations like the NAACP, both minority groups working through formal and informal channels to expand access to services.[67] Lacking the diverse constituency of Citizens' Committees, these groups often worked single-mindedly to protect adoptive parent interests.

Such advocacy was not limited to California. The earliest documented adoptive parent group was the Chosen Parents League, an organization founded in 1947 in Columbus, Ohio.[68] In a 1948 letter to Children's Bureau Chief Katherine Lenroot, the league's director Madelon Neuvirth described her group's mission as uniting needy children with adoptive parents. She observed that organizations like hers were forming across Ohio and throughout the United States, giving hope and encouragement to other adoptive parents tired of navigating the "endless red tape." In the 1950s, adoptive parent groups were started in New York, California, New Jersey, and Oregon.[69] Ohio's Chosen Parents League advocated for an earlier placement age, based on recent psychological attachment studies that revealed the benefits of children going to permanent homes as soon as possible. Neuvirth called the six months that most children waited in institutions before going to adoptive parents a "waste" and appealed to Lenroot to save babies from such insecurity. Neuvirth's group also promoted adoptive parents as ideal parents, even as she underscored their social vulnerability. As she exclaimed, "We who have adopted children don't have them because 'oh, well, we're going to have a baby—we'll have to make the best of it!'—we have them because we CHOOSE to. . . . we almost go begging for them."[70] Statements like Neuvirth's resonated with the postwar language of consumer choice.

Larger adoption advocacy groups emerged in the 1960s. By 1964, the Adoptive Parents Committee of New York founded the liaison group, the National Council of Adoptive Parents Organizations (NCAPO), to serve as a lobbying organization for local adoptive parent groups throughout the United States. Its mission was to "let every child eligible for adoption become available for adoption."[71] Its advisory board included a number of doctors, attorneys, and ministers, in addition to adoption advocate senator Maurine Neuberger (D-Ore.)—the widow of former senator and Holt ally Richard Neuberger—and noted adoptive parents Pearl Buck and David Kirk.[72] Its monthly newsletter, *National Adoptalk*, highlighted adoptive families' personal stories, reviewed books on adoption, publicized national magazine articles about adoption, and, most importantly, circulated opinions about adoption legislation.

National Adoptalk also criticized unflattering media representations of adoption and adoptive parents. The group immediately went on the defensive after CBS aired *Slattery's People*, a drama about a Korean adoption through a private agency that went terribly wrong. The group called the show a "slanderous thinly disguised story of the Holt Adoption Program." To keep the show from ever being rerun, NCAPO, Adoptive Parents Committees of New York and New Jersey, Nebraska Orphan Aid & Hope, Parents for Overseas Adoption, and Holtap of New Jersey deluged media organizations and government officials with letters of complaint. CBS, Bing Crosby Enterprises, and sponsors Philip Morris, Procter & Gamble, and Sterling Drug Co. all received letters. NCAPO also directed appeals to government officials in the Immigration Department, the Korean Embassy, and the New York Consulate.[73]

More importantly, adoptive parents organized to influence state and national adoption legislation. Adoptive parents' associations got their start in the 1950s and early 1960s advocating for extensions to proxy adoption provisions.[74] In 1963, California adoptive parent groups successfully lobbied the state legislature to pass a bill that made an additional report by the State Department of Public Welfare unnecessary in foreign adoptions, allowing the federal home investigation to be sufficient.[75] In Massachusetts, an adoptive parent successfully lobbied for a state law that granted adopted children the same inheritance rights as biological kin. A networker with hundreds of adoptive parent contacts, Marion MacLeod, called each couple personally to ask that they contact their state senator to request a vote in the bill's favor.[76] Several years later a reporter credited MacLeod with single-handedly "reshaping the world of adopted children in Massachusetts."[77] In another round of successful petitioning, the Adoptive Parents Committee of New York introduced and sponsored a bill that overturned a New York state law prohibiting residents from adopting more than two children from abroad. NCAPO credited Nita Savitz, the organization's legislative representative, with the bill's passage.[78] One hundred Massachusetts adoptive mothers also urged the legislature to pass a bill that would prohibit a child from inheriting from her biological parents. Laws like these helped to give adoptive families the appearance of being just like any other nuclear family. As one adoptive mother contended, "Emotional setbacks far outweigh the pittances left by illegitimate parents," highlighting some adoptive parents' insecurities about their socially constructed families.[79]

Defending so-called "private" adoptions became one of NCAPO's chief legislative aims. *National Adoptalk* sounded the alarm when legislators proposed Senate Bill 1541 in 1964 (later Senate Bill 624 or the Dodd bill), a law that would make black market adoptions illegal across state lines or from foreign countries. Informing readers that this would end adoptions through all private agencies, *National Adoptalk* argued that "the bill would . . . make any reasonable doctor or lawyer afraid of handling an adoption for fear of any payment being construed as nonlegal." The editors urged adoptive parents to write to their legislators on behalf of the children who "cannot write for themselves." NCAPO Executive Director Arthur Glickman objected to the bill in a letter that was printed in the *Congressional Record*, and remained unmoved by Senator Thomas Dodd's assurances that NCAPO misunderstood the bill's intention. While the adoptive parents' lobby failed to stop the bill from passing the Senate, the Dodd Bill died in the House when the American Bar Association protested harsher restrictions on independent adoptions.[80]

This advocacy came, in part, from adoptive parents' insecurity over their status with social welfare officials. Even though social workers generally believed that adoptions were the "best solution" to "out-of-wedlock" births, they still advocated for rigorous assessments of adoptive parents. In the lauded 1950 article "Moppets on the Market," the authors argued for tighter regulatory laws to "protect the child from separation from natural parents who might give him a good home if sufficient help were available to them, and from adoption by persons unfit to rear a child."[81] Conversely, legislators and the media rarely considered unfit adoptive parents a threat. They instead viewed single biological mothers as the less "natural" choice for children—a counternarrative that adoptive parents endeavored to promote.

Popularizing Adoptive Families: Ordinariness and Extraordinariness

Some adoptive parents voiced their political and social concerns in the postwar era by joining citizens' committees and forming adoptive parents' societies. While significant, these associations often happened within small communities without much publicity. But adoptive parents publicly bolstered their image as well—publishing memoirs and receiving positive exposure in local and national media. Throughout the 1950s and 1960s, a select group of adoptive parents, nine mothers and four fathers, published thirteen memoirs describing their personal experiences with adoption and child rearing and their intimate struggles over childlessness. Six of these books came from mainstream New York, Boston, and London presses, four went into multiple editions, and five garnered reviews in major newspapers such as the *New York Times* and *Chicago Tribune.* At a time of ostensible social conformity, nearly half the memoirs highlighted transracial or international adoption. This knit together domestic and international adopters into one adoptive community, reinforcing that adoption itself was the distinguishing mark.[82] Underscoring this relationship was an explosion of press coverage on waiting children, adoptions, and international child rescue. By familiarizing and humanizing adoption, the media reinforced adoptive families' conformity. Adoptive parents were featured regularly in prominent newspapers, magazines with a national readership, and women's magazines like *Ladies Home Journal* and *Good Housekeeping.* Just as importantly, small-town and regional newspapers covered adoptions that took place in their communities, marking them as newsworthy human interest stories that bestowed legitimacy and "prestige."[83]

Scholars have argued that the baby boom's emphasis on biological parenting popularized infertility treatments and made adoption seem "second best." Certainly, medical solutions to infertility became more effective after

1945, leading "unprecedented" numbers of couples to doctors to solve their childlessness.[84] Yet, at a time when medical technology offered more options than ever to have a biological family, the memoirs show that adoptive parents did not consider adoption inferior. Together, the genres of memoir and media refashioned adoptive parenthood as simultaneously ordinary—characterized by expert parenting, clearly marked gender divisions, and middle-class suburban lifestyles—and extraordinary—characterized by "choice," altruism, and racial colorblindness. Aided by positive press coverage, memoirs allowed adoptive couples to craft public identities that both reflected and reinforced the dominant cultural values of postwar America. Yet, contradictory narratives within the memoirs also revealed how adoptive parents struggled to define themselves. Memoirists rejected their popular image as "do-gooders" but simultaneously portrayed themselves as rescuers of children by juxtaposing their own comfortable homes and doting methods against biological parents' pathologies and negligence. They celebrated adoption as unique while also styling adoptive families as ordinary. Even as adoptive couples asserted more cultural clout, the memoirs show that they struggled to come to terms with what it meant to be an adoptive parent in both the public and private spheres.

In part, the increasing prominence of scientific motherhood, which emphasized maternal training and education, ushered adoptive mothers into the mainstream. Improved formula design and new norms of child feeding made it possible to separate components of child rearing from the body. While from 1900 to 1930 an estimated 85 to 90 percent of women breastfed their infants, later physicians and hospitals increasingly encouraged middle-class mothers to use more controllable and scientifically safe infant formula. Most doctors still considered breast milk the best option, but they cast doubt on a mother's ability to produce an adequate supply to keep her child healthy, designating her body as "unreliable."[85] Even Dr. Spock conceded in his 1957 edition of *Baby and Child Care* that bottle-fed babies were just as happy as breastfed ones.[86] According to Linda Blum, the bottle not only became "an emblem of modernity, progress, and enhanced autonomy for affluent women in their maternal bodies," it also offered adoptive mothers an opportunity to situate their "out of body" motherhood as more acceptable than biology, allowing for the possibility that a "bottle mother may still be a perfect mother." Furthermore, it differentiated middle-class motherhood from poorer, more "primitive" mothers who had no choice but to breastfeed.[87]

Despite the changing social milieu, most memoirists expressed disappointment with their inability to conceive a child. Still, this fact was used
more as a literary device to show eventual redemption than to denote social
difference. The postwar culture's glorification of motherhood and the
nuclear family meant that childlessness stigmatized women, excluding them
from a feminine identity and even true democratic citizenship. As one sociologist wrote in 1964, adoptive parents experienced "social deprivation"
because of their "minority group" status.[88] Certainly, some memoirs echoed
this theme. One writer mused, "every time I walked down the street and
saw a fulfilled mother strutting along the sidewalk behind a baby buggy, I
was possessed with violent jealousy, envy, and acute self-pity." Another
considered having a child "an inalienable right" and was "astonished and
indignant to find out otherwise." A woman who served as a temporary
foster parent before adopting admitted that she "was . . . tired of these
people who were blessed with children of their own but couldn't keep them
and care for them when the going got rough."[89] These sentiments exposed
the alienation women without children felt and helped explain how adoption transformed their lives from empty to full.

Since adoptive couples experienced parental fulfillment through adoption, they resisted altruistic labels, instead emphasizing how much they
received from the relationship. Many well-wishers considered adoptive parents morally superior for caring for those who were not their "own." As
memoirist Helen Doss recalled, one onlooker gushed, "what a wonderful
thing you and the Reverend are doing . . . to take in all these poor, neglected
little orphans that nobody wanted and give them food and shelter."[90] In
response to a similar sentiment, another mother qualified "that this was
not charity but love; that we were the indebted ones." Using less sentimental language, Harry Bell insisted that most people "probably think that we
are a couple of do-gooders, when actually we are two of the most selfish
people in the world. We adopted Barbara because we wanted her . . . not
because we thought we were doing her a favor." A review of Bell's book
echoed that refrain, insisting that adoptive parents just wanted to be parents
like everyone else.[91] Occasionally, memoirs revealed adoptive parents' own
struggles with perceiving themselves as "do-gooders." One couple admitted
that while they initially "felt some of the self-righteous glow about 'giving
a home' to some 'poor little waif'," they soon learned that the concept of
rescue was "unfortunately, at the bottom of some . . . popular superficial
thinking." Most parents would have agreed with a journalist who remarked,

"it would be hard to say who benefited more," the couples or the children. Given the postwar cultural climate, adopted children were just as responsible for the "rescue" of childless couples. In the words of one reviewer, adoption brought couples from "empty frustration" to "loving fulfillment."[92]

More than any other theme, adoptive parent memoirs stressed the ordinariness of daily child development and parenting of adoptive children. Memoirs often chronicled the classic moments of childhood: tantrums, sibling relationships, favorite toys, holidays, babysitters, haircuts, discipline, and bedtime routines. Stressing such ordinary family routines, childish foibles, and parenting wins and losses highlighted similarities over difference. Several memoir writers also referred to parenting manuals and experts to stress how they were average American parents. "Like most young parents today," one couple compared, "we owned a copy of Dr. Spock's pocketbook on childcare." Another mother mentioned that, in addition to relying on Dr. Spock for advice on how to raise her three adopted children, she subscribed to *Parents Magazine*.[93] One couple detailed how they learned from child-rearing experts not to overparent. In their estimation, this strategy worked, "because the children [became] more like normal, ordinary children."[94] Parents who adopted easily adaptable younger children characterized discipline issues as typical for toddlers. One father took comfort in Dr. Spock's encouragement that the terrible twos "happen[ed] to all normal youngsters who are growing up" and were a uniting thread of parenthood.[95]

Unlike parents of toddlers, however, couples who adopted older or troubled children often endured lengthy adjustment periods. Their stories instead underscored how good parenting could reform even incorrigible youngsters and mold them into normal children. One couple characterized their five-year-old daughter Martha as "our year's work." They described how their consistent nurturing changed her personality: "Care and kisses freed her from anxieties, so that her spirit could stretch, her eyes and hair and skin grow lovely. She had come to depend on us, and it was this, paradoxically, that made her independent and adventurous"—a transformation the *Chicago Tribune* called "vivid, warm, moving, and dramatic."[96] Frances Palmer—whose popular memoir went through four editions with excerpts featured in *McCall's* and *Reader's Digest*—adopted five- and eight-year-old siblings requiring constant supervision. Palmer took particular pride in how her careful parenting transformed her recalcitrant and initially unlovable children. Her daughter's good behavior in a fabric store prompted the clerk to compliment the adoptive mother, observing, " 'You must have started training her when she was a day old.' I just smiled. I didn't explain" that it had only been a year since "Ruth and I had met." One reviewer for Palmer's book agreed that discipline transformed children who had been "frighteningly warped" by a series of foster homes. Through the Palmers' hard work, the reviewer concluded, they have "rewarded the children and themselves, and also society, which has been saved from at least four potential delinquents."[97]

But even careful interventions did not guarantee success. The Hydes, an older Southern California couple, began fostering six Mexican-American siblings when the youngest was three and the oldest twelve. Hyde described Martha, the twelve-year-old, as "set in her ways" when she came to them. After four years with the family, Martha ran away from home, moving from the local juvenile hall to the LA Youth Authority, and finally to a boarding home in the San Fernando Valley. Hyde reflected that even though they gave it "a long, hard try . . . we didn't reach Marty in time to sell her our kind of life. If we had known her two years sooner, we could have won her," as they did with the other five children.[98] In this account, a young adolescent was considered no longer moldable, and thus was unaffected by even the most loving and intentional parenting. A story like Martha's served as an admonition—this was the fate of children raised without stability and discipline. Through such illustrations, adoptive parents joined with legislators and media to stress skillful parenting as the surest way to stem juvenile delinquency.

By highlighting adoptive parents' conformity to 1950s gender roles, memoirs and media portrayals depicted adoptive families as ordinary. Memoirists and reporters highlighted adoptive mothers' "natural aptitude" as parents, exemplars of "loving care" who found their true fulfillment in motherhood. In nearly all the memoirs, mothers were the primary parents, expected to devote themselves completely to the task of childraising. Media photographs too showed adoptive mothers posing for the cameras amid the daily chores of giving the children baths, feeding them, or managing household tasks.[99] When adoptive mothers did work outside the home, news coverage and women's magazines emphasized how such self-sacrifice enhanced, rather than detracted from, women's homekeeping. Bertha Holt's expanding role as an adoption spokeswoman offers a case in point. When her husband's heart trouble reduced his ability to travel, she took over Harry's role as media spokesperson. Local reporters contacted her for reactions to social welfare conflicts, a movie based on the Holts' story, and to discuss agency policy. In her husband's absence, Holt ran the agency finances and authored several books narrating her family's story.[100] Since women were often seen as most suitable to champion the domestic and international rights of children, their volunteer work was considered feminine and altruistic—a "safe" way for women to contribute and find meaning outside their households. Such thinking afforded one adoptive mother the opportunity to volunteer for the League of Women Voters, NAACP, Civil Liberties Union, and UNICEF.[101] Other adoptive mothers also wrote memoirs and lobbied for adoptive legislation—work that could be seen as an extension of motherhood and traditional social norms.

Beginning in the 1950s, adoptive mothers won social accolades previously reserved for biological mothers. After twenty-one years in existence, in 1956, the American Mothers Committee awarded adoptive mother of eleven, Jane Maxwell Pritchard, American Mother of the Year. Ten years later the committee honored Bertha Holt with the same title. Award winners exhibited six qualities: "successful mother[hood] as evidenced by the character and achievements of her individual children," religious membership, "motherly" traits—such as kindness, cheerfulness, and homemaking—Golden Rule adherence, public service credentials, and ambassadorship for the committee.[102] One commentator dubbed the award the "highest womanly honor in the world" and considered Holt "typical of the noble mothers who have worked so hard to make America a sanctuary for family life."[103] In the post–World War II era, a "sense of civic and international understanding" was an integral part of serving the public good and one that adoptive mothers like Pritchard and Holt exemplified.[104] Still, this narrowed the scope of "ideal motherhood," making it only accessible to those with the economic resources to volunteer, or adopt large numbers of children, while maintaining their primary role as homemakers.

But civic parenthood and conformity did not rest solely on adoptive mothers. Fathers in the 1950s were expected to contribute to their families as both breadwinners and playmates, protecting their families from too much mothering.[105] News coverage lauded Harry Holt's ability to provide for his large family, labeling him a millionaire and "well-to-do farmer." Articles detailed his real estate holdings, annual salary, and farming business.[106] One editorial even depicted Holt as an "International Santa Claus," the consummate father who provides "immeasurable dimensions and gifts." Like other adoptive parents who mortgaged homes and sold assets

Figure 4. Bertha Holt as Mother of the Year with Vice President Hubert Humphrey, 1966.
Printed with permission, but not endorsement, from Holt International.

to cover the costs of adoption, Holt dug "deeply into his own funds" to
finance the Korean adoption program, which one reporter estimated had
cost over $50,000 by the end of 1956.[107] Such coverage framed Holt as a
veritable breadwinner writ large who shouldered the financial responsibility for thousands of children abandoned by American soldiers. His example reaffirmed the place within the ranks of true fathers of all middle-
class adoptive men who financially provided for abandoned children. But
such breadwinning was not to be done from afar; fathers were also
encouraged to be their children's playmates. One of the most circulated
photographs of the Holt clan included Harry sprawled on an orphanage
floor with infants and toddlers clustered around him. Feeding one child
with a bottle while another climbed over him, Holt seemed the very picture of ease and playfulness—a man at home with his children. Masculine
influence, in 1950s thought, guarded against anxieties of overmothering,

Figure 5. Harry Holt on floor with children, 1955.
Printed with permission, but not endorsement, from Holt International.

Momism, and delinquency. It was a father's active role, in the words of one magazine article that made children more "self-reliant and resourceful."[108]

One memoirist and adoptive father emphasized how the unique process of adopting a child demanded that a father become more of a partner. Ernest Cady, a newspaperman from Columbus, Ohio, wrote his well-received memoir about his experience adopting three children. Cady believed that, unlike biological childbearing, the process of adoption required the enthusiasm of both parents. Calling it a "true partnership undertaking," he insisted, "unless both parties are deeply interested, sincere, and persistent, they won't even get a child." Thus, in Cady's view, the process acted as a sorting mechanism, ensuring that adoptive fathers were engaged fathers.[109] To his point, 30 percent of the thirteen memoirs written in this era came from fathers. Reviewers liked Cady's positive take on adoptive fatherhood and praised his book. A *Washington Post* writer applauded Cady for the lack of "gooeyness," which he complained, "often clogs books of this type." Comments like these reinforced notions of men's rationality and women's emotionalism, underscoring fatherhood's "unique" contribution to American family life.[110]

Another path of normalcy for adoptive families in the 1950s and 1960s was identifying with mainstream Christianity or "civic religion." In the postwar era, religious membership afforded an opportunity for an increasingly suburbanized society to forge a sense of community and belonging. Even though scholars contest the depth of spirituality during this period, they agree that religion remained an "American way of life." Across denominations, church attendance rose significantly throughout the era, with more families participating in church membership in 1957 than in the previous one hundred years of American history.[111] Adoptive families were no exception. Of the thirteen memoirists, nearly half incorporated Christian faith into their everyday lives, saying grace before meals, praying with their children before bed, baptizing adopted children, and relying on faith to help them with parenting challenges.[112] But for others, Christianity shaped every aspect of their private and public lives. Memoirist Edna Stride, who used Holt Adoption Program to adopt two Korean American girls, dismissed those who credited luck with the adoption of their daughters, insisting that God was responsible for their success. Families like the Holts and Strides viewed adoption as a gift from God who preordained these children for specific families.[113]

News coverage of adoption also did not shy away from religious language and imagery. In 1956, *Life* magazine devoted an entire issue to Christianity and featured the Holt family in an article titled, "The Lord is Their Sponsor." An *Oakland Tribune* writer observed that "Harry Holt epitomized the spirit of God." Reporters sometimes even quoted Bible passages in their articles without justification or explanation, signaling that they expected their readership to understand the references. One article concluded the Holts' story by printing verbatim Holt Adoption Program's foundational verse from Isaiah 43:5–7 about "the seed from the east." Another article quoted Bertha Holt's recitation of a passage from Psalm 118:23: "the Lord has done this, and it is marvelous in our eyes."[114] Finally, a Southern California newspaper covering the baptism of two GI orphans reported how the entire congregation committed to supporting the adoptive children, symbolically uniting the family together with the church body.[115]

Another gauge of normality was adoptive parents' ability to lead consumer-oriented middle-class lifestyles. The postwar period witnessed a precipitous rise in consumer spending as families released pent-up desires held in check by the Depression and rationing during World War II. Increasingly, the preservation of home life became equated with the purchase of household extras. For adoptive father Harry Bell, mass-market consumer goods were the symbols of a full childhood. His memoir referred to dozens of product names he introduced to his adoptive daughter, including Doctor Dentons, Kiddie Kars, Tinkertoys, Popsicles, Dixie Cups, Band-Aids, and Hopalong Cassidy guns. When Christmas arrived, Bell and his wife provided young Barbara with a lavish amount of gifts to ensure they "hadn't forgotten to buy everything [they] could think of to make her Christmas complete."[116] Mass-circulation magazines, aimed at female homemakers responsible for household purchases, emphasized these consumer sensibilities in their coverage of adoptive families too. The Dosses, the model "U.N. family" who had adopted 12 transracial children, won NBC's Christmas Family of the Year Award, which overwhelmed the family with a wide range of goods including appliances, bikes, furniture, and a giant play structure. *Life* sent an entire crew to the family's home for two days to capture their reactions to being surrounded by consumer bliss.[117] Such reports stressed the link between child rearing and the American marketplace, an association already deeply embedded in American culture by the early twentieth century. Even though scholars have acknowledged that in the 1950s discretionary spending was no longer restricted to middle-class families, the relationship between child rearing and consumerism continued to express middle-class sensibilities, as it had decades before.[118]

Magazines also identified this access to discretionary items as a uniquely American privilege, insinuating that the American way of life was superior to that of communist countries. As the famous "kitchen debate" between Richard Nixon and Nikita Khrushchev made clear, America's ability to win the ideological Cold War partly depended upon the glorification of the middle-class family who embraced technological achievements and an increased standard of living.[119] According to newscaster George Putnam, "shopping centers were concrete expressions of the practical idealism that built America . . . plenty of free parking for all those cars that we capitalists seem to acquire. Who can help but contrast [them] with what you'd find under communism?"[120] When a wealthy Los Angeles widow adopted a ten-year-old Korean orphan who was featured in a 1951 *Life* article about the Korean War, the magazine documented his transition to the United States by shadowing him during his first week in California at an amusement park, talking on the phone, and watching television. As the journalist summarized, this newly adopted child "was happily learning about life in the U.S."—a life shaped by American consumption.[121] Two years later, another

Life pictorial once again illustrated that orphans saw the United States as a place of abundant commodities. A four-year-old GI orphan adopted by a single U.S. navy officer personified American boyhood by sporting military regalia like his dad, eating ice cream, and dressing up as a cowboy with his pistols firing at the camera. After repeated queries from reporters about his new life, he made only one remark: now that he was in the United States, the home of the TV Western, he wanted to buy caps for his pistol.[122]

To further emphasize their ordinariness, memoirists writing about transracial or international adoption either minimized racial difference or treated it as a problem that careful, progressive parenting could solve. Helen Doss popularized transracial adoption in her 1952 bestselling memoir, *The Family Nobody Wanted*, which was adapted for a TV special in 1956. Starting in the mid-1940s, the Dosses adopted twelve children domestically, ten of whom came from multiracial Asian, Native American, and Latino backgrounds. Telling her story with "the friendly simplicity of a woman talking over the back fence," in the words of one reviewer, Doss devoted her memoir to the daily rhythm of sibling rivalry, imaginary play, and schoolyard conflicts, emphasizing how her racially different brood was just an average American family. Even though Doss considered herself racially progressive, she pragmatically acknowledged that "any American child of dark skin must learn to adjust to a 'white' society."[123]

Unlike Doss, the Strides, a couple from Orange County, California, just focused on their Korean daughter Karen's, quick assimilation. They bought her a "big blond-haired doll," emphasized her fair skin, and described Korea as the place where "full-blooded Koreans" had tried to stone her and slash her body with knives.[124] This attempt to "whiten" Karen relied on distancing her from her homeland. Another family who adopted both a Japanese-American war orphan and two German orphans effectively reduced racial difference to superficial cultural preferences, rather than larger identity issues. For example, when explaining ethnic identity to her children, the author relied on broad stereotypes, explaining that while Germans are good composers and love flowers, the Japanese are artistic. Since the couple wanted to deemphasize difference, they "didn't dwell on the subject of race and nationality. We figured that as the children grew and acquired more knowledge and understanding, this matter would right itself."[125] By making careful and colorblind parenting choices, the couple assumed they had "solved the problem" of racial difference.

The press interpreted adoptive parents' efforts to minimize racial differences as evidence of their progressiveness. When *Life* magazine covered the Dosses' adoption story, the reporter mentioned that children of "mixed-race" parentage were often "unadoptable," but praised the couple's tolerance in forming their own "model United Nations." In a follow-up article, the reporter also downplayed the importance of the children's race, only mentioning it in the article's subtitle.[126] In another example, this race-blind philosophy was more explicit. *Look* magazine reported that the Roberts family of Southern California adopted a mixed-race child named Kim accidentally. The parents failed to realize until she was six months old that she was "part-Negro." Since they were already attached to her, they decided to adopt two more biracial children—one part Japanese and one part Spanish—to make Kim feel less self-conscious and create what they described as an "international house." The article mentioned that Kim's parents helped her to fit in by telling Kim she just had "a better tan than most of us." Amazed by the support of their neighbors and relatives, the Roberts family concluded that "we want her to be proud of her race."[127] Being "proud of her race," however, depended on her racial difference disappearing as she blended into white society with "tanned" skin. While the media highlighted intense racial divisions in its coverage of civil rights struggles, their depiction of this Southern California family symbolized an environment that was purportedly more accepting of racial difference while committed to making it disappear.[128]

Indeed, the press praised transracial and international adoptions as evidence of American racial progress and adoptive parents as emissaries of international good will. At his death, one media report heralded Harry Holt as a "pioneer in race relations" for his facilitation of Korean adoption.[129] An even more stunning overstatement came when Holt visited thirty adoptive families in Southern California. Covering the meeting, the *Los Angeles Times* proclaimed: "The birthday of Abraham Lincoln had meaning in Los Angeles yesterday for more than 30 emancipated Korean American youngsters who held a reunion with their benefactor."[130] Such oversimplified connections exposed reporters' own biases. News reports portrayed Korea as a backward, racist society that shunned GI children. As one article stated, "the Korean people are intensely proud of their racial background, and they do not readily accept persons of Korean descent whose blood is mixed. A child born of a Korean mother and Caucasian or Japanese father is generally rejected socially and has little chance for a normal life."[131] A *Los Angeles*

Times reporter argued that "button-black eyes shining from tiny, brown, round faces might be resisted by destitute Koreans, but not by many Americans."[132] Indeed, the press frequently mentioned such intolerance as justification for the children's adoption into U.S. homes, implying that Americans had no such "race problem." An article in the Portland *Oregonian* mentioned that there were at least 1,000 American families who desired to provide homes for Korean orphans. One columnist rhapsodized about a Miami couple who adopted two children after reading about the "unwanted GI babies" by calling them the "city's humanitarian hero and heroine." He also mentioned that two other Korean orphans were "now in the tender care of [a] West Virginia couple who wanted the unwanted children."[133] Nevertheless, U.S. racial prejudice continued to shape adoption practice. The Holts' agency placed part-black children only with black families, for instance. And the Dosses' repeated attempts to adopt a German-black GI orphan failed because of intense social pressure from family and friends.[134] Even the "U.N. family" could not make room for an African American child—a fact never mentioned by the media.

The media's omission of race, except when noting racial progress, was influenced by complex social factors. As Stephanie Coontz contends, some of this can be attributed to "the media's denial of diversity" and their portrayal of even multiethnic families as "happy and homogeneous."[135] The attenuation of racial identity also stemmed from the political mandate to advance American exceptionalism as colorblind. According to Cold War architect Dean Acheson, American foreign relations objectives necessitated that social and cultural leaders express positive "attitudes" about American intervention in Asia: "if these attitudes are to be effective, they must become articulated through all the institutions of our national life . . . [including] the press."[136] When *Life* correspondent Dick Pollard tried to convince the reluctant Dosses to allow the magazine to photograph their family, he appealed to the international issues at stake. "I wish you could realize how a general knowledge of your 'United Nations' family could help our country," Pollard thundered. "Anti-American propaganda abroad emphasizes our intolerant side. If people in other countries could open a copy of *Life* and learned about your interracial family, they would see our better side, a glimpse of democracy in action."[137] Both government sanctioning of transracial families through immigration policy and Cold War public relations campaigns reinforced the message at home and abroad that Americans did not have a "race problem."

The media were not alone in depicting adoption, and adoptive parents, as extraordinary. In their quest to justify that their family model was not second-best, adoptive parents often unintentionally styled their families as special. Parents labeled adopted children "chosen," for instance, insinuating that adoption could be superior to biologically based families.[138] In one memoir preface, a psychologist commented that the author's two adopted children were "as their very own, with something added because they were 'selected'," suggesting that forming a family through adoption contained aspects preferable to biology.[139] An adoptive father also contended that "while natural children sometimes are unwelcome, every adopted child is a wanted child," a sentiment in broad sympathy with Planned Parenthood's famed slogan "every child a wanted child."[140] Memoirs also highlighted the special qualifications of adoptive parents. Since approximately twelve prospective couples existed for every available child, memoirs touted the thorough screening and vetted qualifications of adoptive parents. In an almost Darwinian fashion, the authors suggested that only the most deserving parents were able to adopt.[141]

Emphasizing that adoption was an ideal arrangement, comprised of wanted children and deserving parents, required ignoring or downplaying birth parents. While some adoptive parents would have preferred that court officials tell them at the adoption hearing that the "background [about the child] was so limited that [it's like] 'she dropped out of heaven and landed on [y]our doorstep,'" this was rarely the case.[142] In most domestic adoption cases, adoptive couples had some knowledge about or contact with the birth parents. The challenge to biological parenting, so well placed in the national spotlight by Hildy's saga, reverberated through the memoirs of adoptive parents, as they stressed the belief that bearing a child did not make a woman a mother. Memoirists highlighted that their parenthood was more fit because sentiment and training had perfected their vocation. Their books sought to show, in the words of one author, that parenthood was "compounded more of love than biology."[143] Further emphasizing this point, one adoptive father wrote, "Mothers are not all alike, sentimentalists to the contrary notwithstanding. Some can relinquish a baby or even an older child, put the matter resolutely out of their minds, and go on their way toward a new life."[144] At a 1956 adoptive parents workshop hosted by several child welfare agencies, a psychoanalyst legitimized adoptive parents' desire to downplay the birth mother's importance by telling the attendees they could even refer to her as "that other woman."[145] Adoptive parents concurred. In their how-to manuals on adoption, two memoirists, Helen Doss and Ernest Cady, encouraged adoptive parents to feign ignorance when children asked about their birth parents, even suggesting that it might be better for their children to believe their biological parents had died.[146]

Ironically, by denigrating birth mothers, adoptive parents unavoidably cast themselves as "do-gooders," a label many publicly eschewed. In one memoir, the author explained that before her adoption of a school-age boy became final, his birth mother wanted to see him. Since, according to the social worker, the mother was "simple" and "never seemed to inquire about or care anything for the boy," the social worker attributed the mother's sudden interest to an "instinct of pride."[147] This depiction cast the birth mother—whom the adoptive mother callously described as "a disarranged heap of skin and bones"—as a primitive animal with instincts rather than a human mother with enlightened emotions and careful training. To legitimize their own parenting, memoir writers often portrayed birth mothers as "unfit." One author painted a vivid picture of an emotional child relinquishment. As "fresh tears streaked her heavy make-up," the birth mother refused to relinquish her baby, admitting that "with you, my kid would have had a chance. But now that I seen her, I'm too selfish to give her up."[148] What the birth mother identified as "selfishness" was likely evidence of healthy parental attachment. Indeed, the social worker had previously warned the couple that if the mother saw the baby, typically she would choose to keep her child. But the author's inclusion of this quote implied her agreement with the birth mother's assessment. In similar language to the Ellises', another mother claimed that she was prepared to break laws to keep her adoptive daughter from her birth family. She and her husband had "made up our minds that if we didn't win, we'd take Martha and flee the country," and considered this a "badge of motherhood."[149] Adoptive parents marshaled this protective impulse as evidence of their worthiness to parent, subtly embracing the "do-gooder" label they ostensibly rejected.

But in some cases, the "do-gooder" label seemed merited, especially given that some children did suffer abuse and neglect under the care of their biological parents. One memoirist noted how her four-year-old son, Curtis, arrived poorly dressed, yet with instructions that his clothes be returned to his biological parents immediately. Curtis's upbringing had lacked "ordinary experiences," in the words of the author, because he had never owned shoes, owned toys, attended church, or visited a supermarket.

In addition, Curtis also "distrusted adults completely . . . he constantly feared that he would be left."[150] Adoptive children's fear of abandonment was a consistent theme in another memoir as well. Of the four school-age children Frances Palmer adopted, all of them had been left alone for days, often without food, by their biological parents.[151] Another author explained how the coloring books she initially gave her daughter Martha revealed an abusive past. She recollected that she "had those dreadful coloring-books still, tucked away in the attic, in case I needed reminding how, in that early time, all the skies in her pictures had been colored black and all the figures, animal or human, had had red spots 'where they been hit'." Unlike abusive and negligent biological parents, adoptive parents could offer, in the words of one writer, "growth that had been impossible in the disorderly, unreasonable, senseless past."[152]

With domestic adoption, couples risked interference from birth mothers—in some cases, even after the courts finalized the adoption. International adoption, on the other hand, afforded adoptive couples geographic, legal, and cultural distance. Since in the decades after World War II no international regulations or global social welfare procedures governed international adoptions, birth parents were left legally unprotected, without representation or recourse. U.S. officials' reclassification of orphans in the 1948 Displaced Persons Act, as discussed in detail in Chapter 2, further created a legislative environment that favored adoptive parents over birth mothers. Although many factors contributed to this shift, historian Rickie Solinger argues that by legally expanding the definitions of orphan and abandonment to ensure an easier process for U.S. adoptive parents, legislators erased international birth mothers from the adoption process.[153]

Unlike the vocal middle-class constituents who made up the majority of adoptive parents, foreign birth mothers lacked both cultural and legislative means to defend their parental rights. As the face of Korean adoption in the 1950s, Harry and Bertha Holt's actions toward birth mothers were especially significant. Overall, the Oregon couple believed that Korean birth mothers' lives would be improved by accepting the Christian faith and relinquishing their children. In a way similar to Kefauver's subcommittee on juvenile delinquency, the Holts rendered birth mothers, on one hand, as victims. In 1956, a Holt representative working in South Korea wrote: "Of course we don't urge [Korean mothers] to give [their children] to us, but they know the children will never fit into Korean society."[154] This staff member emphasized that, because of Korean racism, birth mothers must succumb to the inevitability of relinquishment. As women with no reasonable option to keep their children, birth mothers became pawns without individual will.

On the other hand, the Holts represented birth mothers as free agents who could "choose" to give up their children, both granting and denying agency as it suited their rhetorical purposes. In one particularly poignant letter, Harry described a young birth mother who "almost had hysterics in the office. She thought she could keep track of her baby after he had gone to America. I had to tell her it is a clean break and forever. Poor girl, her baby wasn't weaned yet and she cried and cried. Pray for these dear mothers who *choose* to give up their babies."[155] Even as this birth mother visibly struggled with the implications of surrendering her child and felt emotionally torn about her options, Holt represented her moment of anguish as a choice. In reality, this vignette exposes the different cultural ideas of adoption held by Koreans and how little recourse birth mothers had in the aftermath of war. Traditionally, Korea had a stronger extended family network where alternate custody arrangements such as adoption were often considered temporary. Since the war had impoverished many families and overwhelmed the South Korean social service system, many women did not have the resources or safety net to keep their children and considered surrendering their babies to American orphanages their only option.[156]

These stories of sobbing mothers, crying babies, and Western intervention contradicted and subverted agency stories of rescue and voluntary relinquishment. In one letter, Holt painted images "of the sobbing mothers who brought their Amerasian babies to the office to be adopted." He also recollected that "the children cried for their mothers, kicking and screaming when [our staff] took them off their backs." Rather than a picture of humanitarian rescue, this *mise en scène* had almost imperialist undertones, evoking images of white exploitation of native peoples.[157] Soft power was also evident in the Holts' proselytizing. Another young mother who brought her five-year-old son to the Holt agency's office fought the impulse to cry and was unable to speak. Holt wrote that he "could see the load on her heart so I told her of the One who gave His only begotten Son and told her I would pray for her that she might receive His gift."[158] These stories stood in bleak contrast to the media descriptions of GI babies as "the least wanted children on earth today," which never hinted at the mothers who were left behind. Such accounts suggested that other factors, including U.S. global prerogatives and Korean politics, contributed to GI children being framed as "unwanted."[159]

The Holt Adoption Program was not the only agency to downplay the needs of birth mothers. One interagency memo from International Social Service (ISS) is worth analyzing in detail because it reveals agency expectations and assumptions while giving a rare glimpse of birth mothers' advocacy for their own interests. Mr. Paek, an in-country representative working for ISS, requested that the U.S. office provide updated photos of five Korean children adopted by U.S. families because "these particular mothers have been quite insistent," needing "reassurance" that only "a picture [c]ould give."[160] The agency representative acknowledged that ISS had debated the "appropriateness of such requests," but felt that in this case it should be honored, especially because Mr. Paek had made a "special plea." Birth mothers were at the mercy of agency discretion when trying to maintain contact with their kin.

While Mr. Paek interceded on their behalf, how many other officials declined these requests, either to protect the adoptive parents' interests or for the mother's "own good"? ISS representatives determined that the most "desirable" photos to send were those "during the first quarter of the post-placement supervisory year, when it has the most meaning and effectiveness." In most cases, this meant that these photos would depict children aged only three to four months since the mother had last seen them. How did they determine that less recent pictures would be the most meaningful and effective? Did officials hesitate to share pictures because they worried about the birth mothers' ability to let go? In the end, ISS representatives decided that providing photographs was "not essential in all cases," since "some of the natural mothers have made a final and irrevocable break at the point of separation."[161] This memo revealed that some birth mothers were not ready to permanently end relationships with their children, even if they were unable to care for them. Moreover, it demonstrated how agencies assumed that some birth mothers had made "a final and irrevocable break," based solely on their disinterest in receiving photographs. It was more likely that some mothers felt disempowered, with no standing to advocate for a connection with their birth children. Others might have felt that a photo would reinforce their separation and increase their grief. Since these mothers no longer had any legal right to their children, they became spectral mothers; they mattered enough that adoption agencies worried about their contact with adoptive parents, but not enough to merit even a photographic update in most cases.

Conclusion

Although they were outsiders throughout much of the nineteenth and early twentieth centuries, in the post-World War II era adoptive couples made their families, and thereby the institution of adoption, a celebrated fixture of American life. By presenting themselves as competent middle-class parents and average Americans who epitomized "civic parenthood," adoptive couples reinforced dominant cultural values and made clear distinctions about who made good parents. They did this by relying on sociocultural definitions of parenthood, especially motherhood, rather than biological ones. In addition to their increasing cultural clout, adoptive parents also carved out a political voice. As seen in Kefauver's juvenile delinquency hearings, affinity groups, and state and federal lobbying efforts, adoptive parents used their increased legitimacy to shape the long-term presence of an international adoption system. Not a single bloc or movement, adoptive parents supported an array of adoption policies and providers. Nevertheless, it was their demand for adoptable babies, whether at home or abroad, that sustained American support for adoptive families. And that demand, in turn, energized the consumer and humanitarian paradigms of child placement, legitimizing the work of volunteer and commercial agencies.

The stories of adoptive couples, and their middle-class families, further inspired lawmakers and the American public to see average citizens as both domestic altruists and international humanitarians. Highlighting families like the Dosses and the Holts, the media linked transracial and international adoptions to Cold War humanitarianism and colorblindness, imbuing domestic family creation with international significance. But, as their memoirs demonstrated, adoptive parents straddled ordinariness and extraordinariness. Full of contradictions, they celebrated their families' unique qualities while also insisting that their families were natural. Though they rejected their popular image as "do-gooders," adoptive couples also portrayed themselves as rescuers of children from negligent, and sometimes abusive, birth parents. These tensions highlighted the intricate realities of adoptive kinship.

Ironically, even as adoptive parents embraced children not previously considered adoptable and formed interracial and interreligious families, their advocacy actually contributed to defining the American family in precise and narrow ways. Transracial and transnational adoptive families acted as too-good-to-be-true public relations victories amid Cold War propaganda contests. These families formed an ersatz civic institution that promised a "colorful" and "global" U.S. populace forged into one "fictive ethnicity."[162] Yet, this exposed the assumption that racial progress and colorblindness—or the ignoring of racial difference—were synonymous. Instead of progress, this empowered white, affluent parents to remake non-white adoptees as Americans—only "different" enough to prove U.S. exceptionalism and the extent of American democracy. Although African American children were generally excluded from this colorblind vision, starting in the mid-1960s the color line grew less impenetrable. As white families began to adopt African American children in large numbers for the first time, adoption's "color line" appeared to evaporate. But geopolitical changes would soon suggest otherwise. Indeed, in the rapidly destabilizing region of South Vietnam, intercountry adoption and the domestic adoption of African American children became intertwined concerns. Such concerns would reveal how domestic notions of racial difference persisted and evolved in the world of international relief.

CHAPTER 5

A New Kind of Racial Alchemy

International Development,
Transracial Adoption, and the Vietnam War

O N JUNE 25, 1973, the *Chicago Defender*, an African American paper
with national circulation, published an editorial criticizing the desertion of American-fathered black-Vietnamese children, as troops left in
droves after the Paris Peace Accords. Calling it one of the war's "most
gripping, tragic experiences," the editorialists explained that "these black
children" had been abandoned in "a society where their color accentuates
a traditional native hostility to racial mixture," governed by an "Oriental
mentality" with a "medieval concept of morality and ethnic purity."
Rejected by even "their own mothers," the children lived in orphanages
bereft of "maternal love and . . . affection." While "white tots" found homes
with "compassionate white families in America," the editors argued that
black children were destitute. The article mentioned *international* discrimination toward black children; yet the editorial's title, "Orphans of the
Storm," was taken from an influential 1972 book exposing the racism in
domestic child welfare services. The book, *Children of the Storm*, written by
two social workers, had fast become a crucial reference on the system's
biased roots.[1] Pulling together ostensibly discrete conversations, the newspaper article signaled the growing concern in the black community about
the fate of black children both domestically and internationally.

This editorial followed a particularly eventful year in domestic transracial adoption. As white families' adoptions of nonwhite children reached
their highest historic levels in the early seventies, the Children's Bureau

announced that agencies now faced an unprecedented shortage of black infants available for adoption. The National Association of Black Social Workers (NABSW), aware of this trend since the late 1960s, issued a provocative response in mid-1972, calling for white families' adoptions of black babies to cease. NABSW president Cenie J. Williams further shocked social welfare agencies and adoptive parents when he insisted, "black children should remain in foster homes and institutions rather than be placed in the homes of willing white families."[2] For much of the black community, the rise in transracial adoptions signified yet another attempt to undermine the black family, an argument bolstered by *Children of the Storm*'s findings.

At the same time that domestic tensions over transracial adoption escalated, child welfare concerns in South Vietnam were becoming more acute. For nearly a decade, military service members, aid workers, and government officials had worked to help those children temporarily or permanently orphaned as a result of the drawn-out war. Amid growing public concerns over the conflict, media exposés in the early 1970s drew U.S. attention to Vietnam's humanitarian crisis. While press reports and adoption agencies highlighted the fate of American-fathered children in general, the official response catalyzed around how to help part-black children in Vietnam, who, experts argued, would become future targets of discrimination. In response, the U.S. Agency for International Development (USAID) commissioned a coalition representative of both black and white social welfare communities to facilitate the adoption of part-black children into black U.S. homes. As the first explicitly interracial experiment in international adoption policymaking, the Interagency Vietnam Adoption Committee (IVAC) provided black social workers access to the world of international adoption, an area with little black representation, and promised to give professionals a way to preserve the black family both at home and abroad. As IVAC's formation and NABSW's statement reflected, the problem was not that black-Vietnamese children were unadoptable, as "Orphans of the Storm" had suggested. The problem, according to black social workers, was that the adopting families were almost exclusively white. In part, such challenges to transracial adoption led officials, for the first time, to question the merit of placing children outside their home countries.

In South Korea, U.S. officials had deemed international adoption the best relief strategy for GI children and nearly all Korean orphans. The State Department, which had supported a large-scale international adoption program in Korea through the Refugee Relief Act, charted a different course in

South Vietnam, however. Drawing on a range of experts, USAID instead cobbled together a new paradigm of child saving that generally discouraged international adoption as harmful to nation-building efforts. The *development paradigm* was a mishmash of ideologies and practices that reflected the lingering imprint of modernization campaigns, child welfare professionals' increasing efforts to maintain biological families, and black social workers' calls for self-determination. While development efforts in foreign relief were nothing new, only in the case of Vietnam were they systematically applied to international adoption. But as was the case for much of adoption history, the development paradigm did not function alone. For humanitarian entrepreneurs and volunteers in South Vietnam, the development paradigm and its adherents were anathema, creating useless bureaucracy that harmed rather than helped Vietnamese orphans. These advocates still viewed adoption as the best option for all children.

Both the development paradigm and the humanitarian paradigm brought race to the fore in ways that reinforced how efforts in Southeast Asia were "inseparable from a process of national self-definition" in the United States.[3] It was in this context that social welfare officials, USAID staff, black and white social workers, and international adoption agencies manufactured conflicting racial categories for American-fathered orphans that specified to whom black-Vietnamese children belonged. For USAID officials, along with some social welfare experts, children with black fathers were racially black and belonged in the United States with black families. In their quest for a certain kind of order in South Vietnam, these policymakers inscribed any vestige of "blackness" as a threat to the development of "traditional" societies. In contrast, international adoption advocates deemphasized the race of all Vietnamese children and marked them as adoptable by white U.S. families. This race-blind position subsumed multiracial children under whiteness while reconstituting a deliberate racial hierarchy in prospective adoptive parents. To make their respective cases, both sides drew on popular 1970s discourses of dependency, welfare, and absent fathers—evidence that the designation of American-fathered Vietnamese orphans as black or white was a politically and socially charged project that "echoed and amplified" domestic anxieties. Neither group believed that the children belonged in South Vietnam, despite evidence that they would thrive as Vietnamese. Only black social workers, in solidarity with global decolonization movements, could envision a future for black-Vietnamese children in South Vietnam. Ultimately, these positions reinforced the alchemical nature of race as a "complex of social meanings constantly being transformed."[4]

International Development and Vietnamese Adoptions

In the same year that President Kennedy first sent 400 Green Berets to instruct the South Vietnamese in counterinsurgency tactics, Congress overwhelmingly passed a sweeping humanitarian bill. The 1961 Foreign Assistance Act authorized the president to establish USAID with the intent to separate military and political objectives from Cold War humanitarian relief. Responsible for coordinating economic assistance programs, USAID worked closely with domestic and international groups such as CARE, Church World Service, UNICEF, and World Vision. The agency oversaw disbursement of loan monies and supervised corresponding development projects after they were studied by experts, vetted by regional specialists, and funded by congressional committees.[5] Even though USAID was a government agency, policymakers intended that the group would help to depoliticize humanitarian aid. Since USAID fell under the bureaucratic and ideological purview of the State Department, however, it could hardly remain impervious to presidential and executive branch authority.[6]

At the root of USAID's creation was a shift in the way the government envisioned foreign aid. What had been a relief-based effort spearheaded by a hodge-podge of private agencies would now be a government-directed development program, informed by modernization theory, and intent on remaking the Third World in the image of the West. Drawing on earlier patterns of manifest destiny and imperialism, and relying on significant government funds, social scientists such as Lucian Pye, Walt Whitman Rostow, and Daniel Lerner held that U.S. expertise was the only way "traditional" societies would transition to "modern" ones. A kind of "social engineering," modernization theory promised to transform not only economic and political structures, but also "systems of social values." To fully modernize, "undeveloped" societies required frequent exposure to both Western mores and funds. Above all, modernization made solving the "problem" of decolonization simple and scientific while appeasing liberals' anxieties about how to approach the new global order. Modernization theory also justified U.S. military intervention in Vietnam. Leading thinkers like Harvard University political scientist Samuel Huntington even argued that the military devastation of Vietnamese society would socially transform the "backward" country, accelerating urbanization and a desire for capitalist markets. This attempt to "bomb the [Vietnamese] into the future," in historian Michael Latham's words, created a child welfare crisis in South Vietnam.[7]

Starting in 1965, social workers and aid organizations conducted site visits, held conferences, and made recommendations to Congress and USAID about how to approach the increase in orphans and mixed-race children as a result of U.S. military action. Most believed that because the Vietnamese had a decidedly different understanding of orphans from that in Western cultures, intercountry adoption was not necessary. Extended families in South Vietnam were large, strong, and locally based. When single women had children, families offered support in most cases. If children were placed in orphanages, the majority stayed only temporarily as a way for families to cope with difficult economic circumstances or migration—much like U.S. orphanages during the nineteenth and early twentieth centuries. Even when children's biological parents had died, their extended families would often care for them. Social workers argued that unlike Korea, and in some ways Japan, Vietnam did not have a tradition of racial purity and on the whole was not likely to reject mixed-race children.[8] Additionally, focusing on the fifteen to twenty-five thousand who were "American-fathered," of whom only a thousand lived in orphanages, would neglect the hundreds of thousands of Vietnamese children in need of medical care, housing, food, and other kinds of relief.[9]

Relief evaluations took these factors into account when making proposals. Reporting to the Subcommittee on Refugees in 1965 after a visit to South Vietnam, ISS director Paul Cherney made three recommendations: first, restore children to homes and families in South Vietnam; second, train and support native social welfare workers; and third, use U.S. aid if necessary to help build a new social welfare infrastructure.[10] Not even a line item in his comprehensive plan, Cherney only considered intercountry adoption an alternative in select cases. In 1967, the subcommittee sent another study mission to Vietnam to make recommendations for Congress. The 1967 delegates also consistently urged the subcommittee and executive branch to see the issue of GI children as only a small part of the overall child welfare crisis. A 1971 international social welfare conference on the Special Needs of Vietnamese Children echoed these earlier assessments and recommended that orphans remain in South Vietnam.[11]

Despite discouragement from the child welfare community and the Vietnamese government, U.S. childless couples were eager to adopt Vietnamese children. Couples began contacting the Children's Bureau and ISS as early as 1963, requesting information on Vietnamese adoption. In the words of one prospective adoptive parent, "I can think of few things more pitiful than a filthy little child with no place to go, nothing to eat, and no one to even bandage his sores."[12] But even though the American people "flooded" legislators, voluntary agencies, and church groups with pleas to adopt Vietnamese children, demand from prospective adoptive parents never successfully spurred Congress or the administration to act. Some legislators did propose expanded orphan support and adoption legislation several times in the early 1970s. Without resounding support from the executive branch, however, legislators were unable to push their bills through.

While adoptions from Vietnam to the United States did occur, they were rare. The GVN's Social Ministry did not support American adoption of Vietnamese children except as a last resort.[13] Beginning formally in 1965, South Vietnam's government only authorized one agency, International Social Service (ISS), to place children abroad. Yet, the GVN's strict adoption laws— requiring prospective non-Vietnamese adoptive couples to be childless, married for a minimum of ten years, and older than thirty years of age—left only a small field of qualified prospective adoptive parents. In 1969, after reacting to some ill-advised adoption placements by Rosemary Taylor, an Australian aid worker who would later join with Friends for All Children (FFAC), the GVN issued a decree restricting any large-scale deportation of children for international adoption. Just three years later, faced with an increasing number of abandoned children because of inflation, an escalating refugee population, and the withdrawal of U.S. troops, the GVN relaxed its standards, contributing to a rise in adoptions to the United States: 682 in 1973, 1,362 in 1974, and 400 in the first three months of 1975.[14] Increasing numbers of children in state care also heightened the need for more voluntary agencies. In response, by the end of 1973, the Vietnamese Ministry of Social Welfare licensed Holt Adoption Program and FFAC to facilitate adoptions. By the end of 1974, four additional agencies brought the total number of organizations permitted to conduct adoptions to seven.

Yet, in contrast to the response after the Korean War, these private adoption efforts had less clout with the U.S. government. Experts' prominent positions in the 1960s executive branch, along with the 1961 reforms to immigration law, led USAID to rely more on professionals than on lay people. And based on their country-based research, commission members were reluctant to pursue intercountry adoption as the primary solution to South Vietnam's child welfare emergency. In the words of one committee member, "We cannot single out for special attention the unique needs of the American-fathered child and ignore that large number of other children who have a right to our concern and assistance."[15] Instead, the experts wanted Congress and the president to act on behalf of all children victimized by the war. USAID and the State Department agreed with Cherney's assessment that South Vietnam's long-term health relied on a robust child welfare system that prioritized in-country solutions over transnational adoption.[16] The alliance between USAID and child welfare experts blended, and consequently blurred, the paradigms of development and child welfare in the 1960s and 1970s.

Although the study mission hesitated to support a large-scale adoption program, they did consider black-Vietnamese orphans a special case that required a separate institutional strategy. Two members from the 1967 subcommittee mission to Vietnam—Dr. James Dumpson, dean of Fordham University's School of Social Service, and Wells Klein, executive director for the American Council for Nationalities Service and former head of ISS-American branch (known in the 1970s as TAISSA)—became key advisors to USAID and the Senate on this issue. Led by Dumpson and Klein, the study mission and subcommittee agreed that they needed a "concerted effort," not a "divided" one, to meet the needs of black GI children. Thus, Dumpson suggested that a temporary "consortium of agencies" would be the best approach and would interfere the least with those mainly private organizations already working in South Vietnam. USAID officials, leaning heavily on the study mission's recommendations, responded by hosting a conference on Vietnamese orphans. Representatives from USAID, study mission members, and voluntary agency personnel who met in July 1973 proposed that a steering committee reconvene in New York in September to work out the details.

Through the committee's recommendation and USAID's blessing, the Interagency Vietnam Adoption Committee (IVAC) was formed on October 3, 1973, with Dumpson as its consultant. A consortium of sixteen voluntary agencies, the committee had two governing mandates: one, to protect the interests of children fathered by black Americans in Vietnam, and two, to place those black-Vietnamese orphans released for adoption with black U.S.

families.[17] IVAC was unique because it brought together the key players in black and white child welfare efforts, a veritable Who's Who of the adoption world. Afro-American Family Services, Black Child Development, Inc., Harlem-Dowling Children's Service, Homes for Black Children, and the NAACP Adoptive Parents Recruitment and Education Project all represented programs devoted to placing only black children. One spot went to Spence-Chapin, a New York-based adoption agency that had been successful at recruiting black adoptive families, and another slot went to NABSW. The mainstream or "white" agency representation came from the primary national regulatory body for state departments of public welfare, the Child Welfare League of America, religiously affiliated charitable organizations including Church World Service, U.S. Catholic Conference, Lutheran Council, National Conference of Catholic Charities, and World Vision, and the international adoption agencies working in South Vietnam—Holt Adoption Program, Friends of Children of Vietnam, and TAISSA/ISS.[18]

When the study of Vietnamese children began in the mid-1960s, modernization theory was at the apex of its influence. But by the end of the decade, the escalating conflict in Vietnam had tarnished its academic sheen and it was increasingly critiqued as, at best, ethnocentric and, at worst, imperialist. By the time IVAC convened its first meeting in 1973, Nixon and Kissinger had rejected the ephemeral hope of making Southeast Asia modern, swapping it instead for the flesh and blood pragmatism of "realpolitik." But the ideology of modernization lingered. In David Ekbladh's insightful words, "it is hard to provide a tidy conclusion for a set of ideas that had such powerful sway on international affairs." Nowhere was this more evident than in USAID efforts to handle the orphan "problem" in the early 1970s, where it infused the culture of relief long after its height. Kissinger might have been espousing realism, but the development models for child welfare still reflected modernization's influence.[19]

The Domestic Roots of the Interagency Vietnam Adoption Committee

At a time when black agencies felt antagonized and disappointed by the efforts of both mainstream agencies and the U.S. government to reform the child welfare system, IVAC's composition seemed an ostensible ray of interracial hope for intercountry and domestic adoption policy. As co-chair

Alfred Herbert of the Black Child Development Institute remarked to the black press, "For the first time agencies with roots in the black community and international social welfare agencies have joined together in a cooperative effort to meet the needs of black children"—an effort that would have seemed unimaginable even several years earlier.[20] Before the late 1960s, transracial adoptions of black children were virtually nonexistent. As nonrelative adoption continued to grow in popularity and prominence in the post-World War II era, children with special needs, including children from minority backgrounds, remained "unadoptable." While social workers struggled to find acceptable homes for all special needs children, those with visible black ancestry were often the hardest to place. Racial matching standards and cultural taboos against interracial relationships meant that agencies needed to find willing black couples who also fulfilled rigorous public and private agency requirements. Despite publicity campaigns in newspapers and magazines throughout the 1950s and 1960s, most agencies failed to complete more than a handful of adoptions for black children annually.[21]

Early attempts by the African American community to recruit black adoptive parents and reform the child welfare system were only marginally more successful. The National Urban League's pioneering Foster Care and Adoptions Project worked in the mid-fifties to link local agencies and social workers nationally. Barred from relaxing standards for black applicants and unable to use black professionals in some cities because of Jim Crow laws, the program made little progress. The Urban League's second attempt, Adopt-A-Child, placed almost 1,000 black and Puerto Rican children with families over its five-year tenure.[22] Seeking structural changes as well, recommendations to Adopt-A-Child member agencies included eliminating minimum income and age requirements, permitting mothers to work outside the home, holding interviews on weekends and evenings, and approving homes even in "congested" areas. Unfortunately, while some agencies instituted a selection of these recommendations, no agency ever implemented all of them, leading the black community to blame the structural injustices built into the social welfare system. An NABSW president would later reflect: "for all these years, white agencies have not really been trying to find black families for black children."[23]

Thus, by the mid-1960s, as civil rights reforms loosened the legal and cultural ties of segregation, most mainstream social welfare agencies gave up trying to place black children with only black families. Still, there were exceptions. The Los Angeles County Department of Adoptions, Division of Adoptions of the New York City Department of Public Social Services, Children's Division of the Cook County Department of Public Aid, Louise Wise Services, New York Foundling Hospital, Spence-Chapin Adoption Service, and Chicago Child Care Society all tried to avoid transracial placements. But even these agencies would perform transracial placements as a last resort.[24] Both single mother and transracial adoptions came in response to the perceived dearth of eligible black families and the sudden eagerness of white families to adopt black or part-black children. Single mother adoptions actually opened the door to a few black women as adoptive mothers, a placement strategy black social workers supported. Given, however, that most adoption agencies preferred placing children with two parents, transracial placements were far more popular than single-mother adoptions.[25] Even though the number of white families adopting black children was never large—at their 1971 peak they only totaled 2,600 placements—these adoptions had a significant cultural influence because of the parents' elite status: 98 percent were married, most were under age forty and attended church regularly, 66 percent earned at least $10,000 annually, and more than half were college educated.[26]

As early as 1969, African American professionals worried about the implications of such adoptions, but these fears came to a crescendo as transracial adoptions rose.[27] In 1971, Alvin Poussaint, a black psychiatrist, expressed his unease that white liberals "might keep telling the child that color doesn't matter."[28] In a study foreshadowing NABSW's position, researchers suggested that if transracial adoptions increased, they would conveniently "solve" the oversupply of black children without forcing the white child welfare system to confront its endemic racism.[29] The president of the Philadelphia chapter of the Alliance of Black Social Workers, Audrey Russell, explained how racial identity was being remapped through the process: "By immutable law, a drop of black blood has made one black for generations, and now to satisfy the whims of arrogant white America, they have suddenly become different and they are adopting the whiteness in them."[30] The NABSW statement elaborated on how this social shift affected hybrid children. "Those born of black-white alliances are no longer black as decreed . . . for centuries." Instead, "they are now black-white, interracial, bi-racial," stressing "whiteness as the adoptable quality; a further subtle, but vicious design to further diminish black and accentuate white."[31]

Certainly not all black child welfare professionals responded similarly to transracial adoption's threat to the black community. Cornell psychologist James L. Curtis repudiated the stance that foster care or an institution would be better than a white home, calling it "the most destructive position that could be taken," because of the shared belief "that a child has a right to grow up in an adoptive home." A black social worker adopting a more moderate position agreed that NABSW's recruitment strategies for black families and singles seemed promising. She cautioned, however, that these strategies shouldn't be "alternatives to transracial placement, but as additional methods of placing children in homes." Yet, as another black social worker unequivocally contended, "The implication that whites can—whether they have goodwill, good intentions or not—produce viable solutions for black problems is a notion that no longer has credibility—if it ever really did have any."[32] The latter viewpoint received the most media coverage, provoked white adoptive families, and caused a significant—albeit temporary—downturn in transracial placements.

Black social workers believed that adoption should be a last resort in child welfare solutions for a host of reasons. Formal adoption was permanent and decreased chances for family reunification—a fact especially harmful for poor, minority families with fewer resources. Through the creation of NABSW, black professionals articulated that for hundreds of years, whether through slavery, coerced labor, foster care, or transracial adoption by white families, black families were denied the ability to parent their children. As Laura Briggs argues, "single black mothers lost their children as part of the fight over civil rights, an event made more likely by the long history of slavery that normalized taking black mothers' children."[33] Even though organizations like the Children's Bureau and Child Welfare League emphasized family preservation in theory, black scholars found that practice deviated from this standard. For instance, in families receiving benefits from Aid for Families with Dependent Children (AFDC), social workers removed an average of 66 percent of children from their parents.[34] Black social workers knew that economic vulnerability often led to familial vulnerability in African American communities.

For IVAC's black social workers, this context was inseparable from the conversations over part-black children in Vietnam. As a former colonial state, South Vietnam in the late 1960s had become a symbol of U.S. neocolonialism for black nationalists. Black Panther leader Huey Newton observed, "We see very little difference in what happens to a community in

North America and what happens to a community in Vietnam."[35] Drawing on the language of worldwide decolonization struggles, NABSW, at its 1969 conference, advocated for "complete self-determination" in its advocacy work for black families. Black social workers further contended in the 1972 statement that only self-determination would protect the black family from cultural "genocide." This rhetorical gesture evoked the Black Power movement's 1967 indictment of the Johnson administration's birth control funding for poor blacks as "comparable to speaking in favor of genocide." Just as advocates like the Panthers, NAACP, and Fannie Lou Hamer agreed that blacks needed to protect the ability to procreate on their own terms, NABSW insisted that black families needed similar autonomy from state control.[36] The identification with self-rule, and resistance to government oppression, linked African Americans to decolonizing nations around the globe, including South Vietnam.[37] It was within this framework that IVAC's black representatives strove to protect Vietnamese family structure and authority—a point of view that would set them apart in the debate over discrimination.

Debating Discrimination

IVAC's existence rested on one pivotal assumption: that black children would be ostracized and discriminated against in Vietnam, as they had been historically in the United States. But this was a deeply contested assumption. Initially, the State Department and USAID dismissed media accounts that American-fathered children would face discrimination. According to USAID reports, Vietnam, unlike Japan and Korea, countries that had previously grappled with large populations of GI children, did not have a history of discrimination based on racial purity.[38] As Edward Ruoff, a USAID official serving in South Vietnam, acknowledged, "a welcome climate for the acceptance of racial difference in Vietnam" made it better than Korea—a country that he described as a "state of rampant racism."[39] A 1971 USAID study found that "contrary to statements contained in these [media] reports, discrimination against racially mixed children is generally unknown in Vietnam. The great majority of children of American fathers born to Vietnamese women are accepted by the families of their mothers in the same way as any other children."[40] The State Department further refuted reports that the Vietnamese were abandoning large numbers of the estimated 25,000 American-fathered youth. Instead, officials argued that the mothers' families took the children in, evidenced by the fewer than 5 percent abandoned in orphanages.[41]

At first, the official wishes and responses of the South Vietnamese government about American-fathered orphans influenced the State Department and USAID's views. State Department officials reported that "the Government of Vietnam has shown great concern for these children, and this concern makes no distinction between children of fully Vietnamese parentage and children of mixed parentage."[42] South Vietnamese officials publicly affirmed their desire to care for American-fathered children. In a letter to Wells Klein, Minister of Social Welfare Dr. Tran Nguon Phieu acknowledged that adoptions could be considered if no other options existed. But overall, he unequivocally stated, "my Ministry does not agree to mass adoptions under which a large number of orphans, whether racially mixed or not, are to be taken overseas in order to become adopted children."[43] Even as adoption became an increasingly popular solution in the United States, South Vietnamese officials continued to assert their ability to care for American-fathered children. Responding to concerns that children would be rejected when older, the Assistant Minister of Social Welfare in South Vietnam, Dr. Vu Ngoc Oanh, pointed to the "integration of 400 older children fathered by French African soldiers and Vietnamese women" as evidence that black children would be fine. Dr. Tran elaborated: "Having suffered through 100 years of colonialization, we are tolerant of other races. Racial mixing makes for a more vigorous nation." Although admitting that both black and white part-Vietnamese children "may suffer a little now," he predicted, "in two generations, all will be the same."[44] As late as 1974, Vietnamese social workers stressed that "racially-mixed children" were their responsibility, regardless of color.[45]

Social welfare experts, however, were more skeptical of South Vietnamese acceptance of part-black children from the start. In 1965 during the first Vietnam subcommittee study mission, Paul Cherney, head of both ISS and the study mission, argued that American-fathered children would face discrimination. Basing his findings on the U.S. history in South Korea, Cherney compared "the current situation in Viet Nam . . . to conditions in Korea" without ever explaining the details of this connection.[46] South Korea was a sending nation for GI children because of its tradition of racial purity and eager government leaders who advocated for large-scale international adoption as a solution to their social welfare crisis. Since Vietnam had neither of these conditions, Korea hardly seemed like a transferable case study.[47] The ISS 1971 conference on the Special Needs of Vietnamese Children built on Cherney's conclusions. Conference participants agreed with USAID findings that Vietnam did not have a tradition of racial purity because of its colonial history. While some attendees speculated that the Vietnamese favored whiter skin, Klein clarified that "much of this is conjecture and many Vietnamese are unclear as to the future status of the Caucasian-Vietnamese children." Overwhelmingly, however, participants expressed concerns about the acceptance of part-black children. Drawing on the experiences of French-Senegalese troops, the report bleakly stated that the "Negro-Vietnamese child . . . faced dim prospects," a prediction that Klein claimed the Vietnamese unanimously upheld.[48] The conference came to no conclusion about how best to address the discrimination that part-black children would encounter. Since the South Vietnamese government had severely curtailed adoptions in 1969, and U.S. legislative attempts to counteract this had failed, the only solution that could be pursued was increased U.S. government aid to the orphanages to improve living conditions.

These preliminary reports influenced the 1973 study mission's ideas about part-black children. The study mission too expressed skepticism about the successful, long-term integration of part-black children into Vietnamese society, based on three factors: the struggles of Senegalese French-Vietnamese orphans who "live[d] in relative social isolation" during the 1950s, the lack of an extant black community in Vietnam, and the previous discrimination against black GI children in Korea. Dumpson and Klein predicted that the black child "will face serious problems of social rejection" if left in South Vietnam. Though Dumpson qualified that both black and white children could face discrimination "because their mothers, 'did business with the Americans,' as was expressed by one child's grandmother," he argued that a black child would face hardship "simply . . . because he is black." Yet, Dumpson contradicted himself shortly after his first statement. When one mother of two GI children—one part-black, one part-white—was asked what she planned to do with her children, she responded, "Take care of them as long as we can. These are our children."[49]

Would black-Vietnamese children have endured discrimination if left in Vietnam? Of the estimated twenty-five thousand American-fathered children, all but a thousand of them lived with their families. And of the one thousand American-fathered children in orphanages, only one-quarter were part black, pointing to the fact that either there were not many black-Vietnamese children or that most of them remained with their families.[50] The study mission admitted this, noting that "the great majority of the American-fathered children have not been abandoned by their mothers—and we saw much love and warmth for many of these children."[51] Another USAID report, written by John Thomas, director general for the Intergovernmental Committee for European Migration, and his wife Jean, a Washington, D.C., public school administrator, further argued that the problem of discrimination against black-fathered orphans "was grossly exaggerated."[52] Although some officials insisted that the Vietnamese themselves had "preference for light skin coloring," there was little evidence besides media reports to support this assertion, which often contained conflicting or untrue information.[53] For instance, an *Ebony* article reported that when in the sun women wore long pants and carried parasols because of a "secret color preference." Yet in the same piece the author also found that the Vietnamese considered white-mixed children "beautiful" and black-mixed children "cute."[54]

The few concerns expressed by Vietnamese families about potential racial discrimination were more likely cultivated in the racially divisive U.S. military base context and not in Vietnamese culture at all. Tensions between white and black soldiers intensified over the 1960s, leading to segregated brothels. Some white soldiers "thought it humorous to tell the Saigon bargirls that blacks were 'animals' and 'had tails.'" Even worse, if white GIs discovered that a Vietnamese prostitute also serviced black men, they would most likely kill her. Since U.S. forms of racism had seemingly been "imported" to South Vietnam—so much so that the military established race relations councils starting in 1969—it was likely that the study mission was unable to separate U.S. practice from Vietnamese anxieties.[55]

Moreover, experts' insistence that black-Vietnamese children needed immediate adoption by U.S. families seemed confusing in light of stateside discrimination. In the early 1970s, blacks in the United States faced rejection and isolation in housing, jobs, and facilities—certainly no better than the conditions of the part-Senegalese who still lived in Vietnam. When considering the discrimination that blacks faced domestically, the study mission's insistence that black-Vietnamese children should be evacuated from South Vietnam for racial protection seemed naïve. Following Dumpson's subcommittee statement, Senator Philip Hart, a Michigan Democrat with a liberal track record, acknowledged this naïveté, incredulously remarking, "I hope I am dead wrong, but we don't do very well by mixed children in America."[56] The Thomas 1973 study also found that black-fathered children faced a "stateside problem," far exceeding potential discrimination in South Vietnam.[57] In 1970, a three-judge federal court ruling in a transracial adoption case admitted that because of "the realities of American society . . . an interracial home in Louisiana presents difficulties for a child, including the possible refusal by a community to accept the child"—almost identical language to that used in a policy report to explain why part-black children could not safely remain in South Vietnam.[58] Even the Vietnamese expressed concern about the fate of part-black children in the United States. One newspaper article reported that a South Vietnamese official lamented the evacuation of Vietnamese orphans because the United States was such a racist country.[59]

Maybe the most telling response was that of the black agencies that visited South Vietnam as part of the IVAC delegation in early 1974. When in South Vietnam, officials from NABSW, Black Child Development, Inc., and Afro-American Family and Community Services witnessed firsthand how "mothers were making concerted efforts to keep their Black children," making them reluctant to promote adoption for race-based reasons. They speculated that "there may be problems in the future" with black-Vietnamese children integrating; however, overall, the delegates "did not sense an attitude of rampant racism in Vietnam." The delegation left South Vietnam feeling reassured that black-Vietnamese children should be recognized first and foremost as South Vietnamese citizens, even though IVAC's co-chair, Alfred Herbert, thought that this would make the American public uncomfortable.[60] Because they understood the endemic nature of U.S. racism, and their advocacy focused on preserving biological families, IVAC's black representatives were also less inclined to hurry part-black children out of South Vietnam and officially recommended that they should remain in Vietnam if at all possible.

Although USAID had initially agreed with black social workers that black-Vietnamese children were better off remaining in South Vietnam, in 1973 the agency reversed its stance. In testimony before the 1973 subcommittee hearing and a subsequent memo, high-level USAID officials agreed with nearly all the study mission's recommendations, including the proposal that international adoption efforts focus on part-black children because they were more likely to experience targeted discrimination. Why did USAID change its position? What convinced child welfare experts and foreign policymakers to promote adoption based on the *possibility* of discrimination? Especially when, in so doing, they downplayed Vietnamese efforts to care for part-black children as their own, ignored the racism these children would face in the United States, and contradicted their own stance that adoption should be a last resort?

Making sense of this shift requires a racial lens. For both the development and the humanitarian paradigms, assimilability into whiteness was the standard by which multiracial children were measured. This manifested itself in a complicated and contradictory racial taxonomy of black-Vietnamese children—one in which USAID and child welfare experts identified black-fathered children as black, or inherently inassimilable, and international adoption agencies and humanitarian volunteers considered the same children through the lens of colorblindness, or capable of being whitened. In either case, it obscured children's Vietnamese and multiracial identities while simultaneously designating Vietnamese society as racist. When viewed through the lens of race, a different narrative of IVAC's founding and short life emerges and reveals how competing paradigms led to new kinds of racemaking—a process that was complex, ambiguous, and contested.[61]

Racemaking: USAID and Social Welfare Experts

As debates over discrimination demonstrated, USAID and social welfare experts maintained a white-black color line among American-fathered orphans. Despite the GVN's insistence that the South Vietnamese would care for all racially mixed children and not discriminate against them, USAID Administrator Daniel Parker determined that black children created "special problems" that demanded a separate strategy. Officials feared that a child's black heritage could create new racial categories in Vietnam that would threaten the country's fragile social structure. As in much of U.S. adoption history, the policy to place only black-fathered children reinforced that, once again, black orphans were the "problem." To justify an exception to their anti-adoption position, USAID labeled black children as "hard to place." While this euphemism accurately described an earlier era of domestic adoption, it was a misnomer for Vietnam since international adoption agencies had no problem finding families for black-Vietnamese children.[62] Still, moving part-black children out of South Vietnam, ostensibly for their own protection, would convince the Senate subcommittee that the Nixon administration, through USAID, was "doing enough" for American-fathered children.

But there were other reasons to focus on black-Vietnamese children instead of American-fathered children in general. Superficially, it made racism a Vietnamese problem and one that no longer plagued the United States. Exporting part-black children out of Southeast Asia to the West offered evidence that America was now a haven for diversity. But, at its core, this venture projected a distinctly American black/white racial binary on Vietnamese soil that signified blackness was a threat to nation building. Such thinking revealed how "out of control" postwar liberals felt amid persistent racial crises and urban poverty: reminders of where development had failed. Showing their hand, USAID officials explicitly peppered their prose with racialized discussions of the "culture of poverty," welfare, and prostitution, making it difficult to ascertain where the discussions of Vietnam ended and the United States began. Through the language of race, officials and experts at times conflated the "backwardness" of the Vietnamese with the moral depravity of African American families, revealing how Third World development campaigns ultimately reflected frustration with the lack of domestic modernization.[63]

Because South Vietnam represented the ideal model of how U.S. social welfare institutions could be exported to a decolonizing nation, it was particularly important that USAID eliminate any potential racial tension. Officials described how South Vietnam had a strong network of orphanages, school-based programs, and professional social workers. Building on existing institutions gave the United States an opportunity to see programs multiply quickly and validate American relief efforts.[64] USAID and congressional Democrats also believed these strong social safety nets reinforced democratic government and hedged against demands for communist intervention.[65] As one USAID memo explained, "disadvantaged children in Vietnam—more than any other single group—provide a highly visible index of both social problems and measures taken by the respective governments to demonstrate their humanitarian concern." When articulating their philosophy of development, USAID administrators drew heavily from a 1970 United Nations paper titled "Social Welfare Planning in the Context of National Development Plans," which argued that social welfare was instrumental in helping countries "deal successfully with the social requirements of change."[66]

On the surface, IVAC also expressed the intention to include the South Vietnamese in the "policymaking" for orphaned children, representing the philosophy of USAID and the study mission as well as the State Department's goal of indigenous leadership in Southeast Asia. USAID Assistant Administrator Robert Nooter emphasized, "these [child welfare programs] have to be Vietnamese programs if they are to be successful."[67] When the IVAC delegation visited South Vietnam in early 1974, representatives met with an array of Vietnamese social workers, Ministry of Social Welfare officials, and Vietnamese consultants to USAID. In each of these meetings, the Vietnamese impressed upon the delegates how they wanted to be given full authority over the relief funds, allocating them as they saw fit.[68] Crucial to USAID's work in South Vietnam was a slate of programs designed to train Vietnamese social workers, develop and fund South Vietnamese voluntary agencies, and plan for future child welfare needs. As one report claimed, "the importance of community self-help activities designed to engage the citizens in participating in their own future, has been given substantial attention in Vietnam."[69]

The State Department's approach "both invited and delimited" the GVN's political agency in nation building.[70] In theory, USAID wanted the South Vietnamese to manage relief funds and develop programs that would outlast the U.S. occupation, and thus tried to protect South Vietnam's Ministry of Social Welfare from too much U.S. direction. Officials reminded in-country agents that "the U.S. Mission must not undermine the [ministry's] confidence and integrity . . . at this critical juncture where [it] is beginning to exercise leadership." USAID's pattern of relief distribution, however, suggested that officials were skeptical about the ability of Vietnamese agencies to handle the money properly. While some foreign aid went directly to the ministry, other funding was routed to private voluntary agencies, many of which operated without Vietnamese representation.[71] In fact, after years of congressional relief monies that were supposed to be directed to Vietnamese agencies, the Senate Subcommittee on Refugees found that only a quarter of promised aid had been dispersed.[72]

When aid did go directly to the Ministry of Social Welfare, it still came back to foreign NGOs. Of the twenty voluntary agencies working under the ministry and approved for relief funds in 1973, eight, or almost half, were U.S.-based. USAID defended its reliance on voluntary agencies by explaining that South Vietnam lacked a cadre of professional social welfare leaders. Yet, USAID and voluntary agencies lagged behind in offering necessary training programs so that, as some IVAC officials observed, Vietnamese social workers "could assume responsibility for administering their own voluntary agency welfare programs."[73] Social welfare officials also made it seem unlikely that the GVN could capably handle the orphan crisis. As Dumpson asked in a 1972 committee statement, "Who better than we Americans know the crippling effects in the development of children of the stigma of difference based on color and mixed ethnic parentage? Who better than we should provide the choice for children to escape that stigma and its damaging effects on the individual and the society of which he is a member?"[74] In his 1973 testimony before the subcommittee, Dumpson's position was more ambivalent. While he stressed that the GVN must have primary control over social welfare decisions, he also cautioned that "serious questions must be raised concerning the capability of the Government of Vietnam, at this time, to meet the special needs of these children."[75]

Amid this ambivalence, U.S. social welfare officials and policymakers refused to admit that helping needy foreign children had political cachet. Dumpson argued that children "do not have political leverage" and the nation had a collective responsibility to help them. The study mission also depicted children as "above politics."[76] In this rendering, child welfare became a safe space where politicians could look past partisan disagreements by funding humanitarian efforts directed at children. UNICEF's growing influence in the 1970s illustrates how nations "came together" when efforts centered on global child protection. For the study mission, making children apolitical, a safe target for publicly acceptable U.S. intervention, meant that they could appeal to "both sides" to help further their child welfare agenda in South Vietnam. The assertion that children were "above politics" belied the reality that child welfare policy carried significant political weight. Senator Edward Kennedy and Senate Democrats saw the administration's lack of support for child welfare as part of its hawkish foreign policy agenda. NABSW's moratorium on transracial adoption came from black social workers' desire to influence the domestic politics of child placement. As the 1975 study mission report on South Vietnam concluded unequivocally, "Economic assistance obviously has political implications," even in the name of humanitarianism.[77]

Nowhere was this association clearer than in the demarcation of racial difference. Influenced by the specter of modernization theory, USAID embraced the Western, and largely white, model as the standard for how institutions should be governed and how authority should be appropriated.

Western institutions were modern, democratic, capitalist, professional, complex, and independent, while non-Western institutions were backward, totalitarian, socialist, disorganized, simple, and dependent. USAID's goal for social welfare and training programs would create South Vietnam's welfare state in the American image: "the success of the [social worker training] program would be measured by the growth of financially secure Vietnamese agencies with salaried staff, the sophistication of their agency operations, and the increased role of the private Vietnamese welfare sector in national and community planning."[78] Even in the 1970s, officials acknowledged that South Vietnam still had a long way to travel from "traditional" to "modern." The vice consul at the U.S. Embassy in Vietnam, Lauralee Peters, blatantly voiced this paternalism. In a 1974 letter, she wrote, "Viet Nam will, I'm afraid, always be a difficult place to work in the manner we would all like to work. Any country where every child is known by at least four names and where modern 'Western-style' hospitals refuse to admit children under their correct names lest 'evil spirits seek them out' is not likely to produce an easy working situation for anyone."[79]

Making South Vietnamese systems modern and "white" required large amounts of aid, placing USAID in a relief conundrum. Officials did not want South Vietnam to become dependent on U.S. aid by establishing systems "too expensive" to maintain. In the plans for Vietnamese training programs, USAID specified that the design should enable "each agency program or project [to] stand alone on its own merits," requiring no "outside technical assistance that is not already available in Vietnam." To ensure that the South Vietnamese system would not rely on public funds, officials assembled a network of private U.S. voluntary agencies that administered the funds. As USAID administrator Robert Nooter explained, "Social programs of this kind require complex and time-consuming procedures and controls if they are to be administered properly, as we have learned in our own U.S. welfare programs. The Vietnamese . . . cannot take on responsibilities which exceed their ability to administer." Officials further worried that South Vietnam's systemic reliance on U.S. relief would make South Vietnamese citizens entitled and overly dependent on government aid. Nooter expressed his apprehension that, in establishing a social safety net in South Vietnam, "welfare recipients do not receive benefits in excess of the regular members of society, which would lead to a massive influx of those on public welfare rolls."[80] The language here underscored how the racially tinted language of welfare "dependency" had seeped into USAID policymaking in

South Vietnam. Here, as in the United States, those receiving welfare payments were not "regular members of society" and were seen as morally unfit because they relied on government support. One *Newsweek* article included in the Senate subcommittee report reinforced that "the ideal rescuers, the Vietnamese, do not seem up to the task—in part because of their own poverty, in part because of their demoralized state of mind." Citing a child psychologist, the article stressed that "negative values" like corruption, greed, and self-interest demonstrated that "morality has simply disappeared in much of society." Striking an ominous concluding note, the reporter darkly warned: "If . . . help does not come from the United States, it may not come at all."[81]

Indeed, the media's language describing the Vietnamese as "demoralized," and thus immoral, was strikingly similar to the rhetoric directed at African Americans from policymakers. The "culture of poverty" thesis, crafted by anthropologist Oscar Lewis to explain Puerto Rican and Mexican communities and applied to the U.S. context by Michael Harrington, asserted that economic marginalization had left indelible social and moral marks on the poor. In this algorithm, poverty, immorality, and passivity were intrinsically related and cyclical, becoming embedded in poor communities. Liberal intellectuals used the culture of poverty thesis to "explain" why African Americans remained in ghettos and required external intervention. It was in this context that Daniel Patrick Moynihan drafted his infamous 1965 report for President Johnson, "The Negro Family: The Case for National Action." Moynihan, the assistant secretary of labor, argued that "pathological" black families were responsible for the deficiencies and poverty of the black community. "At the heart of the deterioration of the fabric of the Negro society is the deterioration of the Negro family," Moynihan contended, calling it "the fundamental source of the weakness of the Negro community" and one that would be handed down to future generations if intervention did not occur.[82] Although Moynihan blamed these conditions partly on male unemployment, the media instead emphasized "cultural explanations of poverty . . . that assumed passivity and disorganization among the poor" as seen in female-headed families, delinquency, crime, low test scores, and race-based segregation. This shrouded the realities of black men's unemployability under cultural deficiencies. By the late 1960s, these ideas were stripped of their economic causes and appropriated by conservatives to justify why the African American poor were "undeserving" of government support.[83]

To be sure, it might have been impossible to discuss welfare programs in 1970s America without implicitly or explicitly talking about race. As welfare costs increased dramatically, AFDC (formally ADC) came under public scrutiny in the 1960s. Over the course of the decade, participation climbed from 3.5 to 11 million women and children. Even though the majority of AFDC recipients were actually white mothers, and the increases were due to program publicity, the general perception was that aid went predominantly to African American women and children. Politicians convinced the public, according to Rickie Solinger, that "the money to pay for the consequences of [black women's] sexual behavior came out of the white families' wallet." Despite the fact that AFDC's paltry payouts only supplemented wages or offered temporary support between jobs, debates over welfare reform had influenced USAID's perceptions of black families as nonviable homes for adoptive children.[84] When IVAC delegates met with Edward Ruoff, these racialized constructions of dependency came to the surface. The USAID administrator asked whether IVAC represented the views of the entire black community or just those of agencies serving "welfare families." This question revealed how the administrator perceived welfare families as predominantly African American.[85] USAID worked hard to ensure that their policies and programs would not promote "welfare families" in South Vietnam.

In the case of Vietnamese families, social welfare officials at first praised the resilience of the extended family structure. Although the war had upset Vietnamese village life—turning a primarily rural society into an urban one in less than two decades—its extended family structure remained fairly intact. One official reported to the Brookings Institution in 1971, "Despite more than 25 years of war, the extended family is still a strong institution."[86] While some social workers continued to see the extended family structure as resilient in 1973 and 1974, most thought the war had left the South Vietnamese family at least temporarily crippled, if not completely beyond repair. In his testimony concerning the state of South Vietnam, study mission member Dr. John Levinson explained, "because of the American servicemen often being involved with the women of the country . . . families were destroyed" and the "moral fiber" was lost.[87] One 1971 NBC news broadcast report highlighted the instability of the new urban extended family structure in Vietnam and galvanized Congress to resend the study mission in 1973. The reporter chronicled the rough lot of American-Vietnamese children. To illustrate the bereft lives of these "orphans," he visited the home of Nguyen Van Cuong, the son of a military police officer who had already returned to the States. The reporter described the family's house as a "lean-to over a sidewalk," suggesting ramshackle and temporary housing. The boy lived with his mother, grandmother, grandfather, and stepfather—an extended family arrangement common in Vietnam but when mentioned directly after the small quarters, emphasized the family's poverty and inadequate living conditions. To further express the bleakness of this future, the reporter described Cuong's mother as a criminal drug addict who had recently been incarcerated for shooting up on the street. In the reporter's words, "the whole family is addicted to drugs," including the grandfather, who "could not be roused from his opium induced sleep." Since the grandfather worked as a beggar most days, the newscaster observed that he used the American Vietnamese boy "to heighten the pathos of his appeal" to GIs.[88]

As this press coverage suggested, it was hard to uphold the Vietnamese extended family structure as whole and healthy when officials were simultaneously criticizing the same types of families in the United States. As Moynihan stressed in a 1972 article, "Poverty is now inextricably associated with family structure," arguing that poverty had forced black families away from a two-parent model.[89] Black families were depicted as unstable because they often lacked "traditional" married parents. Instead, the African American community, especially in the urban Northeast, relied on extended kinship networks to raise children and provide a social and economic safety net. NABSW recognized this and proposed that "exploration for resources within a child's biological family can reveal possibilities for permanent planning. The extended family of grandparents, aunts, cousins, etc. may well be viable resources if agencies will legitimize them."[90] But just as welfare policymakers could not envision a successful family apart from two parents, neither would agencies legitimize extended families by placing children there.

Debates over welfare reform also revealed how gendered notions of breadwinning contributed to perceptions of welfare dependence. In 1970, President Nixon proposed reforms to AFDC, called the Family Assistance Plan (FAP), which would provide families with a small guaranteed income. Since payments would go to families instead of women, FAP intended to promote male breadwinning and give black women a reason to marry. As Marisa Chappell has argued, FAP failed to generate enough support from either conservatives or liberals to pass, but it brought debates over welfare to the fore and highlighted the centrality of a male-breadwinner model to welfare policymakers.[91] While conservative lawmakers depicted AFDC mothers as oversexed, immoral, and lazy, liberals found fault with the deserting men and wanted policies that reunited families rather than punishing single mothers.[92]

In a similar vein, a 1971 *New York Times Magazine* article proclaimed: "Wanted: A Dr. Spock for Black Mothers." The author stressed that while black mothers had "tremendous strength and resilience," they had less support than white mothers and needed extra resources because they parented alone. This article, like a 1968 *Times* article, uniformly categorized black fathers as "deserters."[93] Even the majority of social scientists ostensibly working to help the poor portrayed the black family as fatherless. In her influential 1970s study, anthropologist Carol Stack noted the prevalent view among academics that all black families were matriarchal and most accepted "uncritically that poor black families are fatherless families," based on the father's residence apart from his biological kin. In her survey of AFDC, however, Stack found that "fathers openly recognized 484 (69 percent) of 700 children," drawing children into their extended kinship networks for financial and emotional support.[94]

Similar emphasis on the deserted mother also emerged when considering how to handle the orphan crisis in South Vietnam. Senator Kennedy asked study mission member Wells Klein to address the media rumors that Vietnamese mothers were both selling and abandoning their American-fathered children. Klein confirmed the rumors but cautioned the subcommittee not to blame the abandoning mother, because she had few options. He insisted that mothers were the victims: "The mothers are in dire circumstances. They have been deserted by their husbands or the various men they have been living with, and they have children that they need to care for, that they are responsible for, but they don't have money and they don't have resources."[95] For the study mission representatives, as in the FAP debate, the true villains were the absent fathers and, even more systemically, the lack of two-parent families.

Policymakers hardly left women "off the hook," however, especially because in their view the link between American-fathered children and prostitution sullied women's moral authority as mothers. Just as conservatives during the FAP debate depicted black mothers as loose and immoral, Vietnamese women's occupation of prostitution—sometimes the only work available for uneducated and unskilled women—marked them as deviant. While one *Newsweek* reporter insisted that "GIs are often good with their mixed-blood children," the Vietnamese mothers were dismissed as bar girls and prostitutes.[96] Some officials reasoned that American-fathered children would face discrimination for perceptions about their mothers' work. "There is some indication," Wells Klein speculated, "that [the American-fathered child] may have problems relating to his peers," possibly "from the implication that the child is illegitimate or that his mother was a prostitute."[97] The Asian woman as prostitute was a stereotype employed throughout nineteenth- and twentieth-century U.S. culture. Popularized by policies like the 1875 Page Act, which restricted immigration of Chinese women "imported for the purposes of prostitution," these laws unfairly made all Chinese women seem suspect and hampered family reunification.[98] Characterizations of Asian women as prostitutes continued to have a cultural hold in the second half of the twentieth century. The U.S. military presence in Japan, South Korea, and South Vietnam during the post-World War II era led to a prostitution industry particularly tied to bases.[99] Many U.S. bases officially welcomed Vietnamese prostitutes, as the military command left prostitution regulation up to field commanders. Most often prostitutes worked as base service personnel and sometimes as personal maids to individual soldiers. As scholar Cynthia Enloe has argued, "Prostitution was not simply a matter of personal choices or private sexual decisions. There were institutional decisions, there were elaborate calculations, there were organizational strategies, there were profits."[100] Thus, even though the U.S. military perpetuated the existence of GI children, the women bore the responsibility as immoral sex workers.

Part of popular Vietnam War mythology about prostitutes also reflected conceptions of Vietnamese ethnic inferiority. Official U.S. Army training cautioned soldiers about "gook whores and Vietnamese women in general." One especially gruesome legend recounted how Viet Cong prostitutes would prey on innocent GIs by lining their vaginas with razor blades and then engaging GIs in intercourse as an act of resistance. Through the image of clandestine castration, this myth depicted North Vietnamese women as a scheming communist collective, ready to take advantage of GIs by injuring them both morally and physically. Historian Susan Zeiger attributes this to Orientalist ideas depicting Asian women as "sexually dangerous . . . dragon ladies." Echoing Zeiger's analysis, another scholar reflects that "the majority group symbolizes the anxieties about minority groups by seeing them as sexual threats to our innocent males . . . the virtue is on our side, the aggression on theirs."[101]

As the interweaving of racialized notions of dependency, welfare, and prostitution illustrated, South Vietnamese child welfare policies reflected black/white racial tensions. Despite racially charged images of Vietnamese prostitutes, children's Asian identity barely registered in the debates over the adoption of American-fathered children. When referring to the children available for adoption, study mission chair James Dumpson observed, "I think we are so accustomed in our country to say white and black, that we forget that we have other ethnic groups, too. I am sure some of those [part-black] children were fathered by Puerto Ricans and Asian Americans. When we say black, we tend to mean nonwhite."[102] This surprisingly imprecise assumption of whiteness illustrated how the racial categories of black and white hid other racial and ethnic identities when it came to children. At the USAID conference several months later, Dumpson again referred to American-fathered black and Puerto Rican children as nonwhite, but this time he grouped Asian children with part-white American-fathered orphans in the "white" category.[103]

Dumpson's elision reflected Asians' liminal place in U.S. society during the Cold War. As historian Charlotte Brooks has argued, while the Chinese were regarded as "alien neighbors" in the 1930s, by the 1950s they became "foreign friends" because of their alliance during World War II and the Cold War. For Asian Americans, in Brooks's words, "American foreign policy was the most effective domestic civil rights program of all." Although Asian Americans continued to experience challenges to their "Americanness" throughout the 1950s and 1960s, including entry into certain neighborhoods, African Americans bore the brunt of the housing color line. In 1960, Asian Americans could increasingly purchase homes in suburban developments still off-limits to blacks.[104] When the Hart-Celler Act ended the national origins quota system in 1965, instituting a new hierarchy based on family reunification and occupation in its place, it gestured to such "abstract notions of formal equality" by increasing the opportunities for Asians to migrate to the United States (even as it correspondingly curtailed migration from Latin America).[105] Still, even as most officials deemphasized adopted children's Asian identity, this didn't mean that tensions, or stereotypes, disappeared. One family, who adopted their Vietnamese daughter in 1967, experienced resistance from their friends. A close friend cautioned: "I'm not sure it's such a hell of a good idea to bring a Gook into a WASP environment"—an unsurprising statement given that U.S. military officials and government workers frequently called the Vietnamese "primitive, lazy, and effeminate."[106]

An influential leader in the world of social welfare policymaking, Dumpson himself was African American. He had held many prestigious positions and was the first social worker appointed New York City Commissioner of Welfare. As part of the liberal mainstream, he was a favorite of President Johnson, Governor Nelson Rockefeller, and New York City mayor Robert Wagner, serving frequently as an international expert for the United Nations, the U.S. Senate, and the White House. When some black social workers walked out of the 1968 National Conference of Social Work (NCSW) and started their own organization, which would later become NASBW, he remained.[107] Even though in 1970 the NCSW featured sessions and focus groups aimed at black and Latino participants, Dumpson's remarks revealed that they had limited influence on liberals' thinking about race in an international context. Dumpson spoke the language of the liberal center by identifying race in terms of white and black. Although some scholars have depicted liberals as embracing "rights consciousness," Marisa Chappell argues that liberals tried to appeal to the mainstream as much as possible, working for a broad consensus or "new majority" in American politics, not one fractured by niche "identity politics."[108] This applied to U.S. humanitarian relief efforts in South Vietnam, where part-Vietnamese meant white when it came to children.

In sum, USAID's position on finding U.S. homes for part-black children implied that while the South Vietnamese child welfare system could handle children who looked Asian or white, only sophisticated U.S. institutions could manage the social and structural challenges of being black. Such thinking deflected attention from the failures of liberalism to provide economic opportunity to the poor at home. USAID did not set out to promote the adoption of black American-fathered children. Officials compromised to meet Congress and the study mission halfway, most likely as a result of an intensifying media blitz about the "abandoned" children of the Vietnam War. Yet they were able to compromise because the study mission conveniently fitted into familiar racial categories and existing ideas of how foreign aid worked. Regardless whether the study mission and USAID efforts to remove black children from South Vietnam were inherently or intentionally racist, the policy marked part-black orphans as different from part-white orphans.

Racemaking: Humanitarians and Adoptive Parents

While IVAC's international adoption agency members often agreed in principle that foreign adoption should be a last resort, they rarely upheld this
in practice. Few in-country resources, coupled with pressure from politicians and prospective adoptive parents, made international adoption a convenient, efficient, and humanitarian solution. Since international adoption
agencies served a largely white clientele, they could place children much
faster and more efficiently in the white community, leading agencies to
espouse a race-blind philosophy that protected their interests in arranging
adoptions. Yet, agencies also held deep-seated biases against the black community. By stressing colorblindness and giving only half-hearted support to
IVAC, these agencies worked to maintain their historic control over international adoption mechanisms and outcomes.

From the start, volunteer humanitarians were hesitant to support
IVAC's formation and mission. Six months before IVAC's founding, Holt
Adoption Program voiced its concern that "the mixed-race child, particularly the black child, does need adoption as the best solution to meet his
needs," directly contradicting the study mission's findings. Rather than
soliciting members for relief funds or sending supplies overseas, the
Lutheran Council in the United States had instead recruited homes for
one thousand Vietnamese orphans by early 1973.[109] The most active international adoption agency, Friends of Children of Vietnam (FCVN), was
also the most reluctant to accede to the study mission and USAID's philosophy of deemphasizing adoption and focusing solely on placement of
part-black children.[110] FFAC's services "concentrated primarily on rescuing the 'dying infant' who might be racially-mixed but in most cases is an
ethnic Vietnamese, abandoned child." At the time of IVAC's founding,
only FFAC and Holt conducted adoptions in South Vietnam, yet both
resisted the consortium's approach on several counts.[111] In an interesting
reversal of the mission's argument, both agencies contended that focusing
on only part-black children would direct too many resources to a small
group rather than addressing the needs of all Vietnamese orphans. Furthermore, agency representatives hesitated to establish another organization that could undermine the existing system, which had faithfully
supported the efforts of volunteer humanitarians for two decades. After
voicing their objections, they were the only member agencies to vote
against IVAC's formation.[112]

Unlike the proponents of the development paradigm, international adoption agencies had no patience for South Vietnamese self-rule, since they viewed it as inefficient. Friends of Children of Vietnam worried that South Vietnamese officials would only interfere, making their work harder. Holt Adoption Program expressed frustration with the Ministry of Social Welfare's policy toward orphanage directors. Since the GVN paid orphanage directors based on how many children they took in, Holt had difficulty locating orphanages willing to release children for adoption and wanted this system reformed.[113] When the ministry refused to grant Welcome House authority to conduct adoptions in South Vietnam (it only had approval for humanitarian assistance), Pearl Buck's agency lobbied representative Benjamin Gilman (R-N.Y.) to try and circumvent South Vietnamese policies. Without hearing the South Vietnamese perspective, legislators took the U.S. agencies' side, assuming that Welcome House had been wrongly treated.[114] International adoption agencies perceived the South Vietnamese government as an inconvenience to their objectives and relied on U.S. legislators and government agencies to help them avoid foreign child welfare regulations.

Further complicating the identity of black-Vietnamese children, international adoption agencies used a different racial taxonomy from USAID's, drawn on the humanitarian paradigm. Since they viewed international adoption as the best form of relief, private agencies wanted to expedite adoptions for as many children as possible. To achieve this goal, international adoption agencies downplayed black-Vietnamese children's race, arguing that an orphan's need for a family trumped any concerns over racial difference. Volunteers would have agreed with Pearl Buck's subcommittee testimony: "I can offer only one part of one solution which is ageless, tried and true. Love and a family given to a lonely, homeless child will save that child."[115] Indeed, adoption agencies emphasized that their primary mission was necessary to save lives. Quoting a World Vision relief worker, one *Newsweek* article stated, "The question is not whether a child will be better off being raised in his own culture. The choice is not there. I see so many babies in orphanages who are simply going to die unless somebody rescues them."[116] Another agency representative explained, "The name of the game in Vietnam is to keep kids alive. . . . Color is a stateside problem."[117] The notion that color was a "stateside problem" failed to stop social workers from placing part-black children with white families. Instead, adoption workers minimized racial difference in placing adoptive children, justifying their approach by insisting "they were color-blind in their services" and sometimes not even bothering to collect racial data on prospective adoptive parents. In 1974, black agencies determined that "virtually all of the Black children on their caseloads were being placed with White families in Europe, the United States, and Canada."[118]

International adoption was popularly depicted as a time-sensitive rescue mission, justifying the speedy removal of children into adoptive families. At Halfway House, a World Vision center for sick children, the superintendent had placed six children for adoption overseas who had never been relinquished by their parents. After "causing an uproar" with the GVN, the World Vision official refused to accept any children without the proper orphanage or parental relinquishment papers. As ISS Hong Kong representative Patricia Nye noted, "the superintendent has a reluctance to return children after they are well to their parents or the orphanage," because they would only become sick again. While Nye conceded that this was happening, she confessed being "uncomfortable" about the "dilemma" parents faced, "either releasing the child or let[ting] it die from lack of treatment and care."[119] Many relief workers contended that unless children were transported out of South Vietnam immediately, they would become casualties of war. By setting the terms of the debate as life or death, aid workers stressed that Vietnamese families were unable to protect their kin. A similar kind of urgency had also framed the conversation over domestic adoption. To justify transracial adoptions, international social workers and agencies argued that if the children were not adopted quickly, they would lose their chances to be permanently placed and would remain in institutions indefinitely.

Promoting adoptions for the sake of expediency often undermined families without as many resources and gave those already in power the upper hand. In one Vietnam adoption case file, the background story, recounted from the perspective of a Catholic nun, explained that one man surrendered his grandson Hai because his daughter was unmarried. According to Sister Germaine, "the family is ashamed and decided to give the little boy to the orphanage without the mother's knowledge. She thought that he died at the hospital."[120] In this case, the mother's will was deemphasized ostensibly for cultural reasons, although it was unusual in South Vietnam for children to be relinquished out of shame. More realistically, the child's family was encouraged by the nuns to place Hai in the orphanage because they were unable to support him financially. In domestic placements, similar logic justified the need for transracial adoptions. Social workers argued that since no black families were willing to adopt black children, someone had to act. In the name of urgency, the humanitarian volunteers minimized family preservation and child welfare "best practices."

The rhetoric of urgency also deemphasized the need for systemic or political change. Some humanitarians insisted that children were people, not projects, and their lives would be wasted if aid workers waited around for slow structural changes to take effect. As advocates contended, "These children can't wait for social programs to eliminate poverty and racism. We must act now to move them from their destructive families and neighborhoods into stable homes."[121] Those focused on changing international structures or, like USAID, interested in promoting South Vietnamese development also faced criticism. As one *New York Times* article reported, "many amateurs say that the professionals are too wrapped up with policy and not sufficiently concerned about the welfare of the children." An adoptive mother of twins expressed her frustration with U.S. agencies: "The most discouraging thing was the attitude of American social service agencies who could only ask whether the children would be better off in the United States . . . at least in this country there is no war and plenty of food."[122]

One of the reasons that white social workers and adoption agencies could increasingly minimize color differences in U.S. adoptions was because the "language of color blindness . . . resonated nationwide."[123] No longer limited to intellectual elites and political liberals, groups like Nixon's "silent majority," made up of the middle-class center, also incorporated colorblind rhetoric to assert meritocratic access to education, work, and resources.[124] Nowhere was this clearer than in the adoption of black children by white families. As National Urban League executive director Whitney M. Young, Jr., entreated in 1965, "We need a major effort to break the color line in child adoptions, such as we have achieved in employment."[125] Liberal white families took up this mantle, and the public and press celebrated their transracial adoptions as "courageous," "brave," and "humane." Families embraced transracial adoption for a range of reasons: some believed in the "one-world concept," some wanted to help the "neediest" children, and others didn't want to contribute to the already overcrowded globe. For one father, interracial adoption was "the only way to understand the race problem in our country."[126]

But most adoptive parents embraced the rhetoric of colorblindness by deemphasizing racial difference. Barbara Dolliver's 1968 article in *Good*

Housekeeping in 1968 detailed the reasons she chose to adopt a black child. Two-year-old Jennifer, with her "deep amber face and dark brown legs," became the fifth and only adoptive child of the Dollivers. The Seattle family considered adopting a "part-Oriental" child but settled on "part-Negro because they're the hardest to place." Expecting her neighbors and community to resist her family's newest member, Dolliver was pleasantly surprised. Although she did get some "looks" from strangers, she found that most people were extremely kind and open to reeducation about racial difference. When her friends were unable to find baby arrival cards with a nonwhite child on them, they became examples of this reeducation. Dolliver worried that Jennifer could face discrimination as she grew, especially when she reached "dating age," but this, and the implications of miscegenation remaining taboo even among transracial adopters, was brushed aside as something to think about later. Reflecting on how the adoption had most affected the family, Dolliver concluded, "Jennifer has enlarged our family in another, special way. Before she came to us I used to categorize people as 'we' and 'they.' 'They' were strangers, member of other races than my own. But once I had taken Jennifer into my arms and felt her tiny dark arms curl trustingly around my neck, 'they' became part of the 'we.' Jennifer has made the term 'the human family' a reality."[127] In this depiction, racial difference was only "skin deep" and color lines could be swept away through the work of willing families and welcoming communities.

Stories like the Dollivers' made racial barriers seem like problems of an earlier, less tolerant era. While vestiges of this racist past still remained—such as looks from strangers or the inability to purchase a card featuring a nonwhite baby—these also seemed on the verge of extinction as more middle-class families enlightened their friends and communities through transracial adoptions.[128] When asked why they adopted a black boy, a New York City couple answered, "Why not? Love is love, and a child is a child no matter what his color." Another mother explained, "Our children are not manifestations of our rationalism or ideas about racial relations. . . . These are children I love." Like the Dollivers, most adoptive parents downplayed their children's racial differences, insisting, in the words of one journalist, "we must stop separating people—in our minds as well as in fact—if we are ever to achieve peace and unity."[129] A 1973 study by Thomas Nutt and John Snyder affirmed these sentiments, observing that transracially adoptive parents saw "the world as a place to be made humane. They have grown up in a world [of] power and control, and found lacking their application through the conventional institutions of society. [They] are refocusing on the family as the locus for creating a new definition of the world."[130] As one scholar noted about the Nutt and Snyder study, however, "it is considerably easier to reject power and control if one has been exposed to these factors or has been socialized in a culture where one had access to these. It is vastly different, however, if this access has been denied."[131] To some, only those families with racial and economic privilege could make the color line disappear.

As interracial families grew in number and visibility, they formed groups that offered empathetic and like-minded communities. By the early 1970s, over fifty interracial adoptive parents' groups had emerged across the nation, concentrated on both coasts. Some evolved from mainstream adoptive parent groups started in the 1950s and simply reflected the changes in adoption resulting from fewer available white infants. Others were started especially to meet the special needs of transracial families. Despite the fact that the transracial adoptions of black children garnered more attention, in these affinity associations the term "transracial adoption" was not limited to white adopters of black children but also applied to Japanese, Korean, Vietnamese, and Puerto Rican youth—most adopted internationally. The Seattle Interracial Family Association, for instance, had two founding families: one had adopted their part black children domestically and the other had adopted their Korean and Taiwanese children internationally.[132] Just months after NABSW issued its statement, the *New York Times* featured an adoptive parent group in Westchester County, New York, that boasted all types of interracial adoptive families. When pressed about the recent concerns raised by black social workers, one of the fathers admitted, "We were aware of all the problems" in adopting transracially, "but our assumption was that these were children not being adopted."[133] In response to the charge that whites simply couldn't raise black children in a racist world, the group planned to offer a panel discussion to discuss the issues around developing their children's racial identity. These groups, and transracial adoptions themselves, offered white Americans a chance to have, in the words of historian Karen Dubinsky, "extended conversation[s] about the social meaning of race . . . a group not accustomed to such exchanges."[134]

What made this conversation so palatable for white adoptive parents was that it took place in the key political and social unit for middle-class white Americans—the nuclear family. Amid a rights revolution where women, homosexuals, and ethnic minorities destabilized all kinds of "traditional" hierarchies and relationships, the nuclear family became a rallying cry for the right and a middle ground for the mainstream left. Joyce Ladner, a social welfare scholar in the 1970s, authored an important sociological work on transracial families that situated the NABSW debate in terms of a racial divide over the idea of family. "Whereas black social workers emphasize group solidarity, political control, and a developing social consciousness among blacks as black people," Ladner contended, "the white parents emphasize the value of the nuclear family unit and the necessity for it to be allowed to develop and function to its fullest capacity in the manner in which the parents decide."[135] According to Ladner, the interests and collective identity of the black community trumped individual family autonomy. Formal adoption through social welfare channels reinforced the nuclear family as the crucial unit of identity and the parents as the ultimate arbiters of authority. As black social workers well understood, there was little room in this model for a collective identity based on group consciousness and solidarity. Since social workers and policymakers crafted adoption to meet the needs of their clients (almost all middle-class, white couples) it championed and protected a very particular idea of family—one that made less sense in nonwhite or poorer communities that relied on extended family networks for survival.

Because of white parents' willingness to adopt across the color line, IVAC's black social workers struggled to convince NGOs in South Vietnam that black children belonged in black families. Similar to most domestic adoption agencies, international agency representatives expressed deep skepticism that black families wanted to adopt at all, a doubt that permeated their meetings with IVAC. Some representatives expressed reservations that looking for black homes would take too long. In the meantime reception centers would become bogged down and unable to admit critically ill children. To justify their placement of part black children with white parents, humanitarians ignored "in-between" racial categories while reifying black and white as the only meaningful differences. In an especially revealing moment, one Saigon worker questioned how they were supposed to distinguish between "dark-skinned" groups like Cambodians and Filipinos versus American blacks or know "how Black is Black?"[136] Questions like these revealed how constructing racial difference was a complex social and institutional process, one that required calculated, and patently absurd, definitions. Since part-black children were still subject to inferior status under the U.S. "one-drop rule," black social workers considered other racial heritage as immaterial. Yet, in an international context, blackness was less monolithic and mixed-race identities had different meanings, which U.S. racial patterns ignored.[137] These muddied racial waters also reinforced the limits of colorblindness. International adoption agency staff believed that placing nonwhite children in white families diminished the importance of a child's Cambodian or Filipino heritage, when it in fact upheld whiteness as the ideal racial norm. The question—"how Black is Black?"—suggested that while international adoption agencies would allow IVAC to redirect "truly black" children to the black community, the remaining nonwhite orphans "belonged" to any white family willing to adopt them.

Styling black-Vietnamese children's race as unimportant also helped mainly white international adoption workers to mitigate their anxieties about the black community. These fears and misconceptions arose in IVAC meetings with adoption agency representatives from FFAC, Holt, Catholic Relief Services, and World Vision. One "fear" was that "IVAC planned to select welfare families as prospective adoptive parents resulting in the need for heavy subsidies." Black agencies responded defensively, insisting that children wouldn't be placed with "welfare cases"—an understandable response given the incendiary political climate toward AFDC.[138] Black social workers also justified the legality and mainstream acceptability of adoption subsidies that covered the fees for poorer families, which certain representatives understood as just more "welfare." As the IVAC report concluded, "Foreign workers in Vietnam stressed the abundance of superior 'white' adoptive homes [and] indicated their fear that 'Black' was synonymous with 'Welfare.'"[139]

Another fear was the intrusion of black militants into international adoption policymaking. As race riots swept throughout U.S. cities in the late 1960s and early 1970s, media reports and government officials pointed to Black Power and other separatist movements as destroying the civil rights consensus. Along with most of middle America, the white international adoption community held a suspicious view of blacks as dysfunctional, ungrateful, and dependent.[140] IVAC delegates had to reassure adoption agency representatives that they were not "Black militants intent on making trouble for all concerned," nor were they "collecting Black children from orphanages or elsewhere for adoption in the United States."[141] By placing part-black children with white families, and diminishing their blackness, international adoption agencies circumvented the black community and mitigated white fears about black militancy and welfare dependence.

The whitening of black-Vietnamese children's' racial identity underscored precisely what drove NABSW's 1972 statement—the unwillingness of white agencies to reconsider child welfare procedures and structures to prioritize the maintenance of black families. Of the two adoption agencies licensed in South Vietnam in 1973, both Holt and FFAC admitted that they had no ties with agencies in the black community. This was apparent in international placements. In fall 1972, TAISSA/ISS had nine black-Vietnamese children they were working to place in U.S. homes. While they found two black families who agreed to take two of the children, the remaining seven children were placed in white families who had previously adopted black children.[142] The IVAC delegates also discovered that as of July 1973, "no systematic procedures had yet been established to place children in the Black Community in the United States." Because of this, the committee concluded, "Black children continue to be placed primarily in White homes."[143] Despite IVAC's efforts, international adoption remained the unequivocal domain of white parents.

Conclusion

In 1973, one couple wrote an anonymous article in the theologically liberal *Christian Century* explaining how challenging transracial adoption had become. Although they wanted to adopt their foster child, a black social worker had removed the child from their home, explaining that the little boy would be better off in a black family where he would be raised to appreciate his racial identity. Hurt and confused, the couple questioned the larger implications of this policy in a global context: "Is the principle involved in the rejection of black-white adoption to be applied to all other transracial and transcultural adoptions? Are we prepared to affirm this rigid principle in a world that suffers from the lack of international or transracial contacts that might demonstrate a new humanity?"[144] In one rhetorical leap, this query put international and domestic adoptions in the same conversation, questioning whether Americans were willing to consider adoptions of foreign Asians in the same light.

Earlier contests between the child welfare paradigm and the humanitarian paradigm centered on voluntarism's authority to shape adoption policy.

In the 1960s and early 1970s, the terms of the debate shifted to reveal national insecurities about race. The introduction of the development paradigm of child placement showed how racial rhetoric played a key role in revealing the divergent interests of USAID, volunteer agencies, and the fragile interracial composition of IVAC. Transracial adoptions also shed light on how Americans' perceptions of racial tensions at home influenced modernization efforts abroad. No group was able to picture a South Vietnamese future without referencing its own racial moorings. This mooring divided white and black multiracial children into strict categories while minimizing children's Asianness. USAID officials imagined a black American-fathered child as a hindrance to successful nation building in South Vietnam while simultaneously an affirmation of American exceptionalism in civil rights. International adoption agencies minimized race when it came to adoptive placements. In their humanitarian paradigm formulation, black-Vietnamese children just needed loving families—color didn't matter. This belief, that the United States had moved beyond its racist past and could now set an example for other nations, demonstrated how pervasive the colorblind myth had become by the early 1970s.

And yet, as NABSW's statement portended, race absolutely mattered. Black social workers and activists contended that the system itself was unable to handle the placement of black children because it was steeped in racism, a claim that persists today. IVAC's fragility highlighted the tenuous cross-racial alliances of the seventies, the skepticism in black child welfare agencies toward white structures, and the uncertainty of a U.S. future in South Vietnam. Superficially, IVAC appeared to meet the needs of the black community by giving black agencies a voice in international child welfare policy. Yet, as IVAC's internal challenges and short life reveal, it was never designed to change the system that black social workers decried for punishing the poor black community. White agencies simply would not allow black agencies a significant foothold in the international placement process.

While the power of volunteers in international adoption ebbed somewhat in the late 1960s and early 1970s, circumscribed by the South Vietnamese government, public outcry against the war in Vietnam, and USAID's fiduciary control, their influence was merely dormant and would reemerge as joint private-public efforts evacuated thousands of South Vietnamese children to the United States. To an American public weary of an unpopular war, disenchanted with Watergate-era abuses of power, and sensitive to civil rights concerns, Operation Babylift epitomized the problems with the

Vietnam War. The next chapter will examine how Babylift's reliance on the actions of private agencies, coupled with the lack of clearly marked regulatory boundaries, compromised the rights of Vietnamese children and their extended families. This action, for the first time, sparked a national debate over the ethics of intercountry adoption.

CHAPTER 6

"Children of Controversy"

Operation Babylift and
the Crisis of Humanitarianism

FILM DIRECTORS COULD NOT have invented the drama that unfolded the night of April 2, 1975, and continued to escalate over the next three weeks. As the North Vietnamese Army (NVA) inched steadily toward the south, U.S. military officials and policymakers debated whether to evacuate children from American-sponsored orphanages. Before officials chose their course of action, and with reports that NVA soldiers would soon capture Da Nang, Ed Daly, president of World Airways, an airline working as a contractor during the war, commanded his pilot to take off with 55 orphans on board. The flight landed in Oakland, California, with press swarming the plane, some balanced on ladders to capture the best shot. The next day, President Gerald Ford officially sanctioned Operation Babylift, authorizing the action that would bring 2,000 orphans to the United States by the end of April, using $2 million in government aid.[1]

Even with official support and generous funding, Operation Babylift faced numerous setbacks. On April 5, the first military aircraft used to transport orphans—packed full with 230 children—crashed in a Vietnamese rice field, killing 138 orphans and volunteers.[2] During the first week, a bevy of commercial and military planes shuttled hundreds of children at a time to homes and bases in the United States, Canada, and Australia. These flights became increasingly erratic in the following weeks as the government of South Vietnam (GVN) stopped and started evacuations three times, waffling because of domestic and international pressures. At least nine children died en route and planeloads of sick children needed to be quarantined on bases in Japan and the Philippines. When the Babylift ended on April 26, it had weathered operational tragedies, confusion, and panic while transporting more than 2,200 children to the United States.

The U.S. government's decision to authorize a mass evacuation, after World Airways had already done so, sheds light on the public-private partnerships that had become fundamental to the structure of international adoption. While to most observers Babylift seemed like a reflexive, last-minute action, it was in fact the result of established policy choices and the decades-old paradigm of humanitarianism. Reminiscent of the authority of voluntarism in 1950s Korean adoptions, the leeway afforded volunteers fostered an environment conducive to "can-do" policymaking. Exemplified by urgency, improvisation, and decentralization, this kind of policymaking maintained that private agencies created and implemented humanitarian procedures better than governments did in the mid-1970s.[3] A rift between Congress and the State Department, and a growing public distrust of government in the 1970s, provided an opportunity for private interests to conduct on-the-ground policymaking in South Vietnam with less regulatory oversight than they might otherwise have had. The détente between the development and the humanitarian paradigms that governed Vietnamese adoptions in the 1960s and the first half of the 1970s imploded under Babylift's logistical and political weight. Contrary to media reports, the U.S. government was not the singular force behind the orphan evacuations; Operation Babylift would not have happened without the aid of volunteer organizations.

Significantly, Babylift also emphasized anxieties over Vietnamese children's citizenship and the ethics of international adoption. The U.S. media and public questioned where Babylift children belonged. Was it with their biological families in Vietnam or their adoptive families in the United States? Were children's human rights violated when officials removed them from their homeland? Was U.S. intervention in the name of universal democracy an insincere front for a further extension of Cold War power or a legitimate effort to take care of the less fortunate? The lawsuit that followed Babylift attempted to answer these questions. Even as parties divided over whether children's individual rights trumped an orphan's right to protection from harm, these debates demonstrated a growing concern for international children's rights, especially for children caught in between countries and governments. Despite attempts in the mid-1970s to cast children as global citizens, Babylift demonstrated how national objectives ultimately overcame universalist rhetoric. Indeed, in contrast to the labored naturalization process for "average" South Vietnamese refugees in the 1970s, Babylift children's expedited immigration path revealed their privileged place as U.S. citizens.

It was, and is, tempting to paint Operation Babylift as either a mass kidnapping or a mass rescue. Press reports gave in to this temptation, going back and forth depending on the sentiment of the day. Headlines such as "From Forced Urbanization to Mass Baby-Snatching," "Orphans as Propaganda," and "The Orphans: Saved or Lost?" illustrated the media's tendency to paint the action in black and white.[4] Even in contemporary adoption scholarship, these categories persist.[5] Yet, overgeneralizations establish historical straw men—manufacturing categories and motivations that never existed while glossing over the sticky realities of systems that maintained child welfare inequities. What can look like kidnapping or rescue from afar changes when situated within the social policy context of the mid-1970s. By depicting legislators, humanitarians, mavericks, social workers, and adoptive parents as nuanced historical actors, the story of Operation Babylift becomes less about kidnappers and rescuers, and more about the legacy of voluntarism in international adoption and U.S. foreign policy objectives.

Behind Babylift

The mass importation of children was not an unprecedented event in postwar America. As Chapter 3 illustrated, the Holts made national headlines in the 1950s when they airlifted hundreds of South Korean orphans at a time to U.S. adoptive homes. Children displaced during the Hungarian Civil War and Cuban Revolution also spurred international aid efforts to give thousands of children temporary homes in the United States.[6] Although official and unofficial government policy sanctioned these efforts, civilian humanitarian aid organizations or individuals initiated and orchestrated the evacuations of Korean, Hungarian, and Cuban children. While the mass evacuation of children during wartime was hardly unprecedented, Operation Babylift differed from previous evacuations because the U.S. government through military action *appeared* to the American people to have the chief administrative responsibility—a particularly unfortunate association given the unpopularity of the Vietnam War. Yet in the weeks that followed, trying to ascertain which agency or individual issued the orders proved tricky since so many conflicting narratives emerged. Tracking who initiated the action sheds light on international adoption's spotty regulatory framework, jurisdictional complexities, and public-private structure.

On April 4, President Ford officially launched Operation Babylift, ordering government agencies "to cut red tape and other bureaucratic obstacles preventing these children from coming to the United States."[7] Various groups claimed responsibility for prodding Ford to issue the order. According to communication and hearing testimony, the Agency for International Development (USAID) administrator Daniel Parker took responsibility for initiating the airlift. The media reported that it was a joint effort between the administration and GVN officials. Adoption workers from Friends for All Children (FFAC) credited their organization for bringing it to the attention of government officials. Scholars have also framed Operation Babylift as a push from voluntary agencies.[8]

In fact, the instigation for a mass evacuation appeared to come from the U.S. Embassy. On Friday, March 28, Lauralee Peters, a Foreign Service officer for the U.S. Embassy in Vietnam, sent a memo to the Bureau of Security and Consular Affairs (SCA). Peters, an adoptive mother of a Vietnamese girl herself, had spent two years working with USAID, voluntary agencies, and the GVN Ministry of Social Welfare to establish a coordinated childcare effort. In the memo, Peters reported that public pressure had mounted to remove the orphans and that the workload for orphan processing could become overwhelming. She argued that expediting paperwork for those children already in the "adoption pipeline" would free staff to concentrate on emergency cases that would undoubtedly arise in the following weeks. The following Tuesday, Peters met with SCA and visa office officials, who decided to refer the matter to INS and the Attorney General's office. While still deliberating how to approach the evacuation, officials learned of Daly's flight. After receiving direction from the SCA, early Wednesday morning Peters consulted with USAID to organize transportation. According to her chronology, this was the first time USAID had been consulted. Although Leonard Walentynowicz, administrator of the SCA, formally credited Peters with initiation of the action, the timeline and Peters's testimony indicated that the SCA, under direction of the State Department, were the ultimate decision makers.[9]

Yet in congressional testimony, Administrator Parker took credit for initiating the airlift after consulting with voluntary agencies in South

Vietnam. The memo Parker sent to White House staff identified USAID as the initiator of the action and central organizer of evacuation transport. USAID officials reported to the State Department with only limited accountability to Congress for funding. When pressed by Subcommittee chairman Joshua Eilberg (D-Pa.) to name other government agencies that he consulted with, Parker was initially unable to name even one other agency. Only after intense questioning did Parker point to the April 2 meeting as the point that USAID gained approval from others in the executive branch.[10] While this differed from Peters's account, other sources show that a USAID representative was at that meeting.[11] This discrepancy is worth noting because it illustrates the confusion surrounding the action—so much so that by April 7 officials had yet to align their stories.

Voluntary agencies' accounts, however, disputed the testimony from USAID and the Embassy. According to Rosemary Taylor, director of FFAC, "the idea of the evacuation . . . certainly did not originate with the U.S. government." While she admitted that her agency did "use our contact with USAID to assist in obtaining the authorization," Taylor argued that, along with a representative from Holt Adoption Program, she had requested a laissez-passer (block of exit visas) directly from Dr. Phan Quang Dan, South Vietnam's Deputy Minister of Social Welfare, as soon as they heard of troop movement. When Dan denied the visas because the order could create panic in Saigon, FFAC's stateside director Wende Grant threatened Dan that she would fly to San Francisco to give a press conference notifying adoptive parents that the GVN would not release their children.[12] On the evening of March 31, Ambassador Martin met with both Dr. Dan and the GVN president. In Taylor's account, it was at this point that Dan changed his mind and issued the laissez-passer. Once given the green light from the GVN, Taylor and Grant worked to book a private charter through Ed Daly on March 30, days before USAID started offering government transport. Indeed, it was the letter from Dr. Dan that gave permission from the GVN for Daly's flight on April 2.[13] As this timeline illustrates, pressure from voluntary agencies, the Ministry of Social Welfare's issuing of emergency exit visas from South Vietnam, and urgent actions such as Daly's worked together to mobilize government resources at the time that State Department agencies were still deciding what course of action to take.

The media, however, focused only on the meeting between Ambassador Martin and GVN officials as the driving force behind Babylift. In a letter

Figure 6. President Ford carries a Vietnamese baby from "Clipper 1742," April 5, 1975.
Courtesy Gerald R. Ford Library.

from Graham Martin to Dr. Dan, Martin depicted the Babylift as a way to "reverse the current of American public opinion to the advantage of the Republic of Vietnam."[14] USAID vehemently denied Babylift's political association, however. When asked by representative Elizabeth Holtzman (D-N.Y.) if the sudden evacuation had anything to do with the political considerations detailed in Dr. Dan's letter, Parker retorted, "Absolutely not. It was the overcrowding of the orphanages, the fact that the Government had indeed accelerated its processing and the agencies were confronted with a logistical problem on how to move those that had been cleared."[15] Like other skeptics, Holtzman was undoubtedly influenced by reports of the administration's keen interest in these orphans. For instance, when 319 children arrived in San Francisco, President Ford made a special late-night flight from his vacation home in Palm Springs to greet the flight, "dramatizing the nation's growing concern for the orphans," in the words of one reporter. Visits like Ford's kept the cameras focused on public officials and brought allegations of political pandering to the fore.[16]

The military's role in the evacuation further complicated Babylift's origin narrative. Throughout its tenure in South Vietnam, the U.S. military had performed humanitarian work, often collaborating with civilian aid organizations. Established in February 1962, military divisions such as MAC-V (Military Assistance Command-Vietnam) and CORDS (Civil Operations and Revolutionary Development Support) assisted foreign and Vietnamese humanitarian efforts, including orphanage care and in-country adoption.[17] Initially, military officials resisted policymakers' efforts to give them responsibility for the airlifts, insisting that agencies like USAID were better equipped to head the relocation. Once Daly's flight was in the air on April 2, military commanders received an "unorthodox request" from Alexander Schnee, the assistant to Kempton Jenkins, acting assistant secretary of state for congressional relations. In the name of the "national interest," Schnee pleaded with Colonel Robertson to "support the program" by taking the children into the San Francisco Presidio, urging him to "please do it" because of congressional backing. According to House and Senate subcommittee records, however, Congress only learned of Babylift's launch through media reports, which made Schnee's plea seem disingenuously political.[18] In responding to Schnee, Lieutenant Colonel Oneto and Major Cutler both agreed that the orphan evacuation and reception should be conducted by USAID. Colonel Robertson hoped to "avoid any action that could be construed as acceptance by the army of a commitment to accept the orphans."

Although army officers kept expecting USAID to assume responsibility, without the appropriate visas (which INS had yet to grant) USAID was unwilling to accept liability for the Babylift. Only because of continued insistence from the State Department and executive branch were the officers, in effect, ordered to take the orphans and command the operation.[19] In an internal memo on April 4, army vice chief of staff General Walter T. Kerwin acknowledged that the action had been "poorly and improperly handled" since it violated established procedures to separate military leadership from mass humanitarian action.[20]

Over the course of the evacuations, the military review of Operation Babylift highlighted how the involvement of so many government agencies made a clear chain of command under one operating authority impossible. According to military hierarchy charts, tasks were so minutely divided that no one agency could be held accountable for the actions. The State Department provided funds and designated drop-offs, USAID approved eligible orphans, the Chief Military Command authorized planes, MAC-V assumed operational control of aircraft, the secretary of defense offered procedural guidance, and the U.S. Embassy in Saigon verified all alien personnel. When the Embassy tried to get the ceiling lifted on the 2,000 orphans, the State Department waffled on the decision. On April 26, department officials confirmed that the attorney general had approved an increase of the ceiling to 2,279 so that two planes of waiting children would be able to take off. But when the joint chiefs of staff tried to get further clarification on how the ceiling would affect future flights, "neither the Embassy in Saigon nor any other available documented source made further reference to the existing Babylift ceilings." Since most estimates placed Babylift evacuations around 2,900, this number significantly exceeded the original ceiling and the April 26 extension.[21]

Military officials also bemoaned the complications of relying on private airlines. The Pacific Command captain reflected, "Although the military C-141 evacuation flights from Saigon were under strict military control, no such control could be enforced over the commercial carriers." For example, on April 21 a World Airways flight delivered 271 orphans to Oakland, California—an unapproved government destination. Private flights also required military resources for which officers were often unprepared. When several planes lay over in Guam or Japan, military staff treated children on board needing emergency medical attention. More important, since many of these flights did not inform the military command of their authorization or course, officials frequently had to request emergency diplomatic allowances, especially in Japan. Military command in Japan "noted that the ad hoc approach for handling these flights to date had been cumbersome and disruptive to all echelons." As early as April 14, MAC-V recommended that a "single coordination point" at a high level of authority was necessary to choreograph the joint military and civilian effort, noting that "this would eliminate duplication of effort and poor utilization of valuable aircraft, manpower, and materiel resources."[22] Communication was particularly inefficient because no one understood who was in charge of what aspect of the process, leading to multiple requests for the same piece of information.

No one person, organization, agency, or government could definitively claim responsibility for launching or coordinating Babylift. Many agencies and organizations, both public and private, took some role in the process, whether or not officially acknowledged. The only body not consulted was Congress—a point that reinforced to legislators the inappropriate extension of executive power. The long-time practice of "informal consultation" between the State Department and both congressional judiciary committees before recommending parole visas to the Justice Department was overlooked in the launch of Babylift.[23] Even if Congress had no formal role in initiating Babylift, less than a month before, Rep. Paul Tsongas (D-Mass.) had introduced legislation to remove orphans—evidence that some legislators wanted to be a step ahead of the administration. In his address before the House, Tsongas insisted that of the many "tragedies of war" the Vietnamese had faced, this was "one of the few which we [the U.S. government] might erase," highlighting that some legislators thought something had to be done.[24]

A Government Divided

Public and congressional suspicion of presidential power and a breakdown of the early Cold War foreign policy "consensus" profoundly shaped the debate over child welfare policy. The funding for orphans and promotion of international adoption in South Vietnam occurred as Congress was trying to wrest power away from the administration. When President Lyndon Johnson deployed U.S. troops to South Vietnam without a joint legislative-executive action in 1965, it signaled to legislators that Johnson's exercise of presidential power was becoming inappropriate and excessive—a sentiment that gained traction in the late 1960s. Senate hearings on President Nixon's secret bombings of Cambodia and the Watergate exposé culminated in Congress passing the War Powers Act in 1973, after overriding Nixon's veto. The act stipulated that the president consult and report to Congress before authorizing military action, and gave legislators increased oversight of executive branch agencies and departments.[25] At the same time, Congress also passed the Foreign Assistance Act of 1973, reflecting the new internationalist bent in Congress that called for a demilitarized foreign policy upholding human rights. By mandating that aid to Indochina go to war victims and refugees, Congress sent a clear signal that humanitarian aid would have priority.[26]

Indeed, the 1973 Foreign Assistance Act authorized $10 million in aid to South Vietnam's children, even though USAID had only requested $8 million, gesturing to a pattern of increased congressional humanitarian spending. Just as Congress granted USAID more money than it requested for aid to children, it simultaneously approved much less military funding than the administration asked for. In Senator Harrison Williams's (D-N.J.) words, "I think Congress must redirect our emphasis in Vietnam away from military actions and toward alleviating the social problems there."[27] Yet, as Congress appropriated increasing funds throughout the 1970s for children, legislators discovered that only a fraction of this money actually reached orphanages and daycare centers. Of the $10 million designated for 1974–1975, a mere $3.9 million had been disbursed during the fiscal window.

These funding decisions seemed to come from the top. After congressional and public pressure put Vietnamese orphans in the spotlight, the State Department scrambled to do something to regain political credibility. In a memo to the National Security Council Ad Hoc Group on Viet Nam, Secretary of State Henry Kissinger asked the officials to come up with a strategy. Three weeks later, USAID approved a grant of $100,000 to ISS to expand their adoption referral services and staffing—a paltry amount in the world of foreign relief but one that USAID pointed to repeatedly as evidence that it was responding to Congress.[28] The administration's reluctance to prioritize humanitarian interests over military expenses and economic development drew the ire of Senator Edward Kennedy (D-Mass.). In a heated 1973 statement to President Nixon in the *Congressional Record*, Kennedy urged USAID to stop holding conferences and study missions and instead make funding available to voluntary organizations.[29]

Brewing beneath the surface of these tensions there were also power struggles within the State Department over adoption jurisdiction. While USAID supervised volunteer agencies that operated orphanages in South Vietnam, the Embassy staff processed the paperwork in conjunction with INS so that visas could be issued to children GVN authorities approved for adoption. In early March 1973, a string of memos exposing an inter-agency fissure circulated between Deputy Ambassador Charles Whitehouse and USAID officials. Despite objections from USAID, Embassy officials reacted to "public and Congressional pressures" by circumventing the Ministry of Social Welfare to expedite adoption cases when a number of the children had not been in fact released for adoption. The Embassy also released a statement that blamed "bureaucratic ineptitude and sluggishness" for adoption delays, a not-so-subtle dig at USAID field officers. In a scathing retort, USAID officials argued that the blatant promotion of intercountry adoption was "completely unacceptable," foremost because it "undermine[d] the confidence and integrity of the Ministry of Social Welfare at this critical juncture where the Ministry is beginning to exercise leadership."[30] James Dumpson, Vietnam task force consultant, interpreted the conflict between USAID and the Embassy as an indication that the U.S. government lacked "a clear-cut policy [and] commitment on the part of the American Government and its people for doing what must be done in terms of the welfare of the children in Vietnam."[31] As Dumpson suggested, even though the Embassy and USAID both fell under the State Department's jurisdiction, this conflict revealed the lack of a cohesive philosophy and policy approach to orphan care within the executive branch itself. It also reflected the often confusing and decentralized social welfare hierarchy that characterized Vietnamese adoption.

Some legislators, coming from the humanitarian position that had worked in South Korea, tried to address what they saw as USAID's "ineptitude" in South Vietnamese child welfare. Starting in 1971, the House Republican Research Committee identified the abysmal lack of executive branch interest in the plight of American-fathered orphans. In their words, "The Pentagon has rather unofficially declared that 'as far as we are concerned, they (half-American, half-Vietnamese children) don't exist.' It appears that the Government considers this problem out of its realm."[32] Earlier that year, Senators Harrison Williams (D-NJ), Mark Hatfield (R-OR), and Harold Hughes (D-Iowa) had introduced a bill (S. 2497) in response to the NBC News broadcast "Sins of the Fathers," a sensationalist account exposing alleged discrimination against GI-fathered children.[33] Their bill, representing the bipartisan interest in orphan legislation, proposed the creation of a temporary childcare agency that would provide in-country services for South Vietnam's children and facilitate adoptions to the United States. This agency, under executive branch oversight with Senate approval, would offer increased funds to orphanages for feeding, clothing, and facilities while also training more social welfare workers. In many ways, the bill specified exactly what USAID and professional agencies wanted—money directed toward the children who would remain in South Vietnam and training Vietnamese staff. Only 10 percent of the aid allocation under S. 2497 could be spent toward facilitating adoptions. In addition, it met the crucial need for volunteer agency support by authorizing one centralized adoption authority to give "direct assistance to public or private nonprofit organizations."[34]

The hearing over S. 2497 accentuated the divisions between Congress and the Nixon Administration. For members of the Senate Committee on

Foreign Relations, this bill both proposed a needed fix to an urgent humanitarian problem and satisfied constituent pressure to "do something" about
the suffering of South Vietnamese children. While USAID claimed to support the provisions of the bill, Deputy Administrator Robert Nooter
objected to the creation of a new agency because it duplicated efforts that
his organization was already implementing. When senators pushed him to
justify USAID's current program, however, Nooter reluctantly admitted
that his agency's program was not, in fact, fully "adequate." Nooter's
admission verified what the authors of the bill already knew: that USAID
only pursued child welfare goals as an afterthought. Long-time task force
consultant James Dumpson agreed with legislators' assessment, pointing to
the 1967 recommendations to strengthen child welfare programs USAID
had ignored. In a perceptive summary that foreshadowed Babylift, Dumpson argued that the administration fostered "a crisis-oriented approach to
human problems in South Vietnam, a narrow perception of human need,
and a short-range, inadequate allocation of funds that fail to reflect any
intent on the part of our government to share with the Vietnamese our
technical and financial capability for the pursuit of social as well as economic development."[35]

Despite USAID's resistance, S. 2497 drew support from nearly all of the
social welfare agencies operating in South Vietnam. Winburn Thomas of
the National Council of Churches noted that the bill was "the most satisfactory to volunteer agencies." As a show of their support, ISS staff even
coached the bill's authors by helping them to refine phrasing and make it
compatible with the current Immigration and Nationality Act.[36] Relief
workers agreed that the U.S. government needed to protect the interests of
all Vietnamese orphans, not just those available for adoption. They also
wanted a more consistent and supportive child welfare authority. In the
words of ISS Director Wells Klein, "I and my colleagues feel that it would
be more effective and [guarantee greater continuity] if a special agency was
established for this purpose."[37] Representatives from Friends for All Children and Friends of Children of Vietnam echoed this sentiment. While
USAID protested that the bill duplicated the work Congress had already
funded for the next fiscal year, volunteer agencies argued that USAID support was insufficient because the requirement to renew funding annually
made long-range planning impossible.

In the end, Congressmen expressed concern that creating a new agency
would contribute to an already "cumbersome bureaucracy," ignoring social

workers' insistence that better administration would solve long-term child welfare concerns. In a desperate attempt to still get his legislation through, Senator Williams added an amendment to the Foreign Assistance Act of 1972, requesting $5 million of aid to South Vietnam's orphans. While primarily intended to fund development assistance programs, the act also included what the Nixon Administration referred to as "security expenses" that would finance military arms and personnel.[38] Unlike the earlier bill, the new proposal would route relief through USAID, a significant shift for Williams, who two months before had critiqued the agency's ability to ensure that appropriated funds actually reached those in need of assistance. Even though some initial holdouts considered the amendment a "balanced, moderate response," this bill too failed in a 42–48 vote. Even the "pure humanitarianism" of assisting needy children could not save a bill with excessive military spending from a Congress less inclined than ever to support the administration's war.[39]

Legislators also produced bills that reflected a more opportunist approach. For example, the Griffin Bill, proposed in the Senate in 1972 by Senator Robert Griffin (R-Mich.), came shortly after the failure of S. 2497. Unlike S. 2497, Griffin's legislation focused only on meeting the needs of American-fathered children through international adoption, and social workers criticized its limited scope and simplistic rendering of orphans as all adoptable. One provision of the bill was prescient, however. Section Six specified that adopted children be transported via military aircraft on an emergency "space-available" basis. Although dismissed by social welfare officials and others as inappropriate, given the long time period necessary for professional adoptions, this became the arrangement during Operation Babylift.[40] Government disunity over humanitarian priorities continued to escalate throughout 1973 and 1974, reaching a climax with the execution of Operation Babylift. As chair of the Subcommittee on Immigration, Citizenship, and International Law, Representative Joshua Eilberg confronted Administrator Parker on USAID's failure to consult with or even notify Congress of the action. When Parker apologized for not consulting the House committee, Eilberg quickly pointed out that the administrator also neglected to communicate with the Senate subcommittee, leaving both legislative houses without input or oversight.[41]

In addition to the lack of notification, a particular sticking point for some legislators was the use of the attorney general's parole power to admit the orphans. Introduced under the Eisenhower administration to admit individual political refugees on a moment's notice, it was most often used for airlifting large numbers of migrants. The most notable parole actions were for refugees seeking immediate political asylum—including those displaced by the Hungarian Civil War in 1956 and the Cuban Revolution in 1959. Yet legislators expressed unease with this application of parole. In the 1965 Hart-Celler Act hearings, legislators made clear that the congressional intent behind the parole power was to admit individuals and not large groups.[42] Since the parole power did not require oversight from Congress, it seemed just another blatant misuse of executive authority to circumvent the legislative branch. When used in Babylift, it reinforced to legislators that the administration in general, and the secretary of state in particular, had no respect for congressional oversight, a point emphasized by Senator Kennedy. Not until the Refugee Act of 1980 did Congress explicitly limit the attorney general's parole power, a move certainly influenced by the parole of over 130,000 Vietnamese refugees as part of Operation New Life.[43]

It is possible that if S. 2497 had passed, Operation Babylift would have been substantially more organized. One central authority would have offered volunteer agencies, government officials, and military officers a clear chain of command during Babylift's urgent hours, instead of what Representative Eilberg characterized as "a total lack of direction, leadership, and coordination."[44] It also might have allayed some tension between Congress and the executive branch as a tangible symbol of the move away from militarism and toward relief-based humanitarianism. But the bill would have only solved the administrative issues and had little effect on the more foundational policy procedures that gave volunteer agencies generous authority on the ground, a move resoundingly supported in Congress. This "can-do" policymaking complicated an already unstable process and perpetuated a culture of mavericks, with significant implications for the progression of Babylift.

"Can-Do" Policymaking

The story of informal policymaking in adoption certainly did not begin in South Vietnam. As Chapters 2 and 3 showed, philanthropic and for-profit adoption agencies used the proxy process and individual bills to complete adoptions from Greece and South Korea. With the outlawing of proxy adoptions in 1961 immigration law, professional social welfare agencies and government regulators thought they had "solved the problem" of volunteer agencies asserting too much influence over adoption policymaking. Yet, rather than Korea serving as a "lesson learned" about volunteer power, the divisions in government opened up an opportunity for private interests to conduct on-the-ground policymaking in the Vietnam War era. This, coupled with the growing public distrust of government in the 1970s, gave voluntary agencies with humanitarian sensibilities less oversight than they would have had under the development and child welfare paradigms. "Can-do" policymaking, characterized by urgency, decentralization, and improvisation, rested on the assumption that private agencies created and implemented humanitarian policies better than governments did.

Starting in the late 1960s, a bipartisan effort endorsed volunteer agencies as the solution to foreign humanitarian crises. Legislators argued that by privatizing relief, it would become less politically motivated. As Senator Kennedy put it, "there has been clear congressional intent for a considerable period of time about the desirability of providing humanitarian aid through the specialized U.N. and voluntary agencies, and to take it out of the area of the political arm of the government, which is the AID program"—ironic given that the original intent in creating USAID was to depoliticize humanitarian relief. Legislators further justified the extension of more authority to private groups because "the American people want[ed] aid to be conducted through voluntary/church agencies." Senator Kennedy summarized, "[Voluntary agencies] have really led the way in providing relief assistance wherever people need it . . . they've been ahead of our Government by their moral leadership and example, and have contributed greatly to America's claim to humanitarianism." Not limited to humanitarian efforts, USAID also backed the work of private agencies in international development. Administrator Parker and Deputy Administrator Robert Nooter frequently testified to their reliance on voluntary organizations. In a statement to the Senate Judiciary Committee, Administrator Parker "paid tribute" to the private sector in South Vietnam, characterizing their work as "critical."[45] By relying on voluntary agencies, USAID could serve in a supervisory role that would minimize the agency's costs and responsibilities. But some key private players doubted that the private sector had the financial resources to fully replace state action. In a 1971 letter to National Security Council staff assistant John Negroponte, ISS director Wells Klein expressed his concern that USAID was exclusively "looking to the voluntary agencies for the maintenance of present programs and the development of new child welfare services." Klein asserted that "the voluntary agencies are not in a position to assume additional responsibilities," and recommended "that the American Government assume a greater degree of responsibility for child welfare services in [South] Vietnam."[46]

Because of the "critical" role that voluntary agencies played in the field, Congress and USAID allowed them to set standards and procedures that government players were unequipped to manage. As ISS was the only international organization arranging adoptions from South Vietnam to the United States in 1971, it attempted to fashion a policy that stressed in-country services but still arranged adoptions. In Wells Klein's words, "We have de-emphasized inter-country adoption but have quite clearly said that intercountry adoption is an alternative for some children on a case by case basis," even though adoption "must be handled by professionally competent persons . . . in order to protect the child and the adopting parents."[47] While Klein legitimized this case-by-case standard by couching it in professionalism, his disclaimer did little to ensure that other agencies would follow ISS's lead and left too much authority and discretion in the hands of individual agencies.

While Congress appeared set on the "moral leadership" and impartiality of private agencies, this belied voluntary agencies' own interests and motivations. When the GVN licensed Holt and FFAC in 1973, these organizations quickly surpassed ISS as the dominant adoption agencies in South Vietnam. ISS board members then used these more prolific programs as their benchmark for success. In documenting the inefficiency of its staffing, ISS compared its staff ratio of one caseworker to two children to Holt's, noting that the other agency had a much more sustainable ratio of one caseworker to twenty-five children. Even though ISS had a reputation as a leader in intercountry adoption, executives admitted that "in reality we have produced minimal results in our total adoption program in respect to the amount of money received for adoption work, and in relation to the amount of work we have completed on the regular ISS program."[48] In this case, ISS determined success by placement rates instead of by how rigorously staff scrutinized such placements. Allowing private agencies the largest role in "legislating" international adoption made child welfare policies less subject to standardized regulations.

Furthermore, since many relief agencies—particularly ISS, Holt, World Vision, and Welcome House—also conducted international adoptions, this blurred an already muddy line between adoption and humanitarianism.

Wells Klein admitted this problematic connection in a 1971 letter to the ISS bureau chief in Hong Kong. At first, Klein described ISS's success in getting Congress to recognize the need to expand child welfare support to all South Vietnamese orphans and not just those with American fathers. Then, he expressed the quandary of continuing to conduct intercountry adoptions, even on a small scale. International ISS headquarters, for instance, strongly cautioned the American Branch about promoting intercountry adoption to appease U.S. families when they should be focused on in-country aid.[49] Yet without a "rounded program which includes intercountry adoption services," Klein expressed concern that ISS would be unable to maintain its costly presence in South Vietnam.[50] The media reinforced this link between adoption and humanitarianism. A 1973 *Newsweek* article focused on sick children in Vietnam; yet at least one-third of the article highlighted adoption complications and bemoaned the clichéd "red tape." Even at the subcommittee hearing where the study mission urged Congress to deemphasize adoption, the hearing's published report summarized the media coverage on Vietnamese children by including six news articles. Four of the six, or two-thirds, focused predominantly on adoption—a reflection of what most media outlets considered newsworthy when covering war orphans.[51]

Because the U.S. and South Vietnamese governments relied heavily on private agencies to administer Vietnamese child welfare programs, they fostered a social welfare culture that supported maverick humanitarians like Rosemary Taylor and Wende Grant of Friends for All Children. Taylor had worked independently in South Vietnam since the 1960s. An Australian initially supported by a Catholic diocese in Australia, Taylor began working in 1968 as the in-country representative for the Denver agency Friends of Children of Vietnam (FCVN). When FCVN split into two agencies in 1973, Taylor went with Grant to the new organization, FFAC. Even before the Ministry of Social Welfare formally licensed FFAC in 1973, Taylor was the primary adoption practitioner in South Vietnam. From 1968 to 1972 her orphanage placed 1,132 orphans, mostly in Europe and Australia. In comparison, ISS only arranged twenty-six adoptions over the same period. Policymakers recognized Taylor's informal authority in South Vietnamese adoption and frequently sought her opinion. In August 1971, the Senate Committee on Labor and Public Welfare asked for her advice on proposed intercountry adoption legislation. In a telegram from Ambassador Bunker to Secretary of State Kissinger on October 31, 1972, Bunker recommended that Congress speak with Taylor about the process for locating adoptable children in South Vietnam since she was the "outstanding authority on Vietnamese adoptions." When Taylor completed her first two adoptions to the United States on November 25, 1968, the U.S. consul personally escorted the children to their adoptive parents as a personal favor to the Australian powerhouse.[52]

Despite having no official role, Taylor's influence illustrated the possibility for improvisational policymaking in South Vietnam. In a submission from Holt Adoption Program in support of S. 2497, Director Jack Adams noted Taylor's effectiveness. "The parallels between her spirit and methods and those of Harry Holt are striking," Adams reflected. "She is not recognized by the Vietnamese government [GVN] and in official disclosures she does not exist, yet she receives substantial support from Vietnamese and foreigners alike, including a number who are highly placed."[53] Taylor used her relationships to expedite cases, move children out of South Vietnamese orphanages and into her Western one, and make sick children "adoption ready." In her memoir, she remembered that, in the beginning, "these adoptions were a tremendous amount of work, as I had to discover the procedure step by step."[54] If Taylor could get GVN and U.S. authorities to "sign off" on an adoption, she considered it a success—even if the "system" forbade it.

While she worked easily with U.S. Embassy and GVN officials and was well known to legislators, she had a less positive relationship with USAID. Taylor explicitly distrusted USAID's investment in South Vietnam because, in her view, they failed to understand the context. For instance, when Daniel Parker tried to assure lawmakers that USAID had accurate statistics because of new surveys, Taylor argued that he still underestimated the true numbers. She "knew how certain orphanages resented the interference and arranged their own statistics." During a meeting with USAID staff in 1973, Taylor confessed to Grant that she reduced the chairman to "table-thumping madness" because she disagreed with how little money USAID was allocating to orphan care. Perhaps because of interactions like these, when Taylor's entrance visa to South Vietnam was denied in January 1973, she blamed USAID officials for the subterfuge.[55]

Taylor's colleague Wende Grant shared this disregard for "traditional" adoption authorities, which she conflated with a bureaucratic social welfare citadel. In a 1966 letter, Grant, who had bypassed social agencies to adopt her Vietnamese child through an attorney, contended, "when Americans are so willing to take a chance of killing hundreds of 'suspected' Communists by dropping napalm on villages, why not be just as reckless in taking a chance on saving the lives of a few of the babies there[?]"[56] This logic used the government's dubious actions as justification for social workers to bend the rules in getting children to the United States faster and cheaper. It also suggested that bending those rules to save babies could offer penance for the U.S. government's arbitrary killing of Vietnamese civilians.

USAID's strained relationship with certain volunteers became a serious problem during Babylift. When Taylor and Grant refused to put FFAC children on Daly's April 2 flight because of safety concerns, Cherie Clark, director of Friends of Children of Vietnam, saw an opportunity to get dozens of her children evacuated. In Clark's rendition, even though she received approval from USAID to use Daly's flight, the next morning USAID assistant director Edward Ruoff called an impromptu meeting where he castigated Clark in front of agency representatives. To Clark, this miscommunication underscored the lack of central authority in decision-making. Her reactions confirmed both the gulf between USAID and certain volunteer agencies and the conflict between the development paradigm and the humanitarian paradigm. In Clark's words, "We were worlds apart. I lived down at street level while he prowled around neat, air-conditioned offices, cushioned from the reality we lived in. We had never seen eye-to-eye; we each saw the problems in Saigon from opposite viewpoints."[57] Taylor had also recognized the gulf between USAID officials and South Vietnam's needy. When invited to a send-off for a U.S. delegation visit at an elegant Saigon club, Taylor demurred, quipping snidely that she "thought to save a little of the tax-payers' money."[58]

Orphans' Airlift, a Presidio-based group led by Dr. Alex Stalcup and comprised of physicians, Red Cross volunteers, and media interests, also complained about USAID's support. In spite of his organization's assistance in processing, feeding, and caring for the orphans flown to San Francisco, a USAID official called the group a "bootleg operation," which he felt "no obligation to cooperate with." Stalcup pointed out a stark inconsistency here: while USAID didn't want to cooperate with them, it also didn't want legal custody of the children—a role that Orphans' Airlift temporarily fulfilled until the children could be released to their adoptive parents. Just as in South Vietnam, USAID wanted to maintain control of the children without any legal ties, necessitating their reliance on private groups.[59] For those in the trenches, like Stalcup and Taylor, USAID's critique of the volunteer effort seemed misdirected and out of touch with the life-and-death decisions that were an integral part of their daily experiences.

Established agencies, such as ISS and Holt, acted more cautiously to follow procedures amid the rushed evacuations. Holt's director, Jack Adams, reflected that his agency "carefully avoided the hasty intake of children in the emotional atmosphere of those April days at some risk of being considered unhumanitarian."[60] After only ten days of the Babylift, Patricia Nye of ISS's Vietnam office determined that she would not participate in more airlifts, despite frantic calls from desperate prospective parents. Nye reasoned that it lacked professionalism to play on the panic of birth parents, prospective adoptive parents, and orphanages when ISS would be unable to perform proper relinquishment counseling.[61] Regardless of its stated position, however, no agency was above reproach. Agencies largely insisted that the Babylift was only a large-scale finalizing of already processed placements. Yet, an Army report issued in late April determined that many children remained in the Presidio without anywhere to go.[62] ISS's Patricia Nye admitted, "although [Operation Babylift] was originally aimed at taking out matched children, many unmatched and uncleared children were taken out, some without government permission."[63] While Holt maintained that they only admitted children who had previously been placed with adoptive families, in May they still had thirty-four children without permanent placements.[64]

More startling was the carelessness that both FFAC and FCVN staff exhibited when maintaining children's records. When children were hurried on to flights, and separated from the staff who had cared for them in the nursery, volunteers were left responsible for ensuring accurate identification. FCVN marked nursery boxes with infants' names, but during the long flights chaperones often put children back in the wrong boxes. The practice of using "nursery names" only magnified the confusion. When customs officials used formal names for visa paperwork, staff who only knew children by their nursery names had a much harder time locating mis-assigned paperwork.[65] But even agencies keeping careful records made mistakes. Of the ninety-six children ISS evacuated, INS officials determined that sixty-nine had proper documentation and twenty-seven lacked sufficient relinquishment papers.[66]

USAID wanted an unattainable arrangement—to have the dispersed responsibility and resources that came from using private agencies while maintaining complete control over the process. This loose public-private coalition backfired during Babylift because the confusing collaboration between government divisions, the military, and volunteer agencies gave individual interests too much authority. In an April 16 point paper to the White House, Air Force Gen. M. F. Casey cited this as Babylift's main problem. "Despite the official State/AID/DOD system, certain individuals have operated as free agents making arrangements for contract flights and direct liaison with orphanages," which he argued, "caused considerable confusion and resulted in less than desirable service for the orphans."[67] Even when private adoption agencies chartered flights, the State Department stepped in to sponsor and give "official" approval.[68] Casey's identification of volunteers as mere "free agents," working outside a clearly defined system, missed the mark since such private-public cooperation was a hallmark of "the system."

Cultivating policies that encouraged private agencies to have autonomy made policing those who transgressed unmarked boundaries tricky. World Airways President Ed Daly was the most visible example of a private interest gone awry. The airline had a long-time contract with the U.S. government to airlift rice and other provisions to South Vietnam and Cambodia. When Daly began shuttling refugees from Da Nang to Saigon, he notified the State Department and the president that he had moved nearly 2,000 refugees. While it was not clear if he began the refugee transport on a government order or his own initiative, by the end of March Daly's theatrical tactics (taking off with people hanging on to wheel wells and such) had made him notorious to executive branch staff.[69] At the end of March, the military command in Vietnam notified Daly that World Airways' contract had been terminated, ostensibly because of the dangerous conditions. With classic Daly showmanship, on April 14 he sent an outraged telegram to the president, cabinet members, Congress, state governors, and the press. Because Daly still had $22 million of flight equipment in Saigon without the compensation to get it back to the states, he was more than a little miffed. Feeling betrayed, Daly tried to put the weight of global geopolitics into his jeremiad: "There is no wonder that the peoples of the world have lost their confidence in the U.S. government and its people . . . I strongly urge that you get the incompetents out of here immediately and appoint someone with the intelligence, competency and the guts necessary to get the job done. You don't have days or weeks—you only have minutes."[70]

While Daly attracted criticism for his recklessness, he also became something of a hero—a can-do, if brazen, contrast to the ineffectiveness of government. When Betty Ford claimed that she would "like to adopt all" of the Vietnamese orphans, Daly responded with his standard candor, quipping, "I'm sending her a cable right now telling her if she'll have her husband get the ambassador and Weyand [general of U.S. Military Airlift Command] out of the way I'll return to Saigon with my own aircraft and at my own expense I'll bring her out 1,500 of them."[71] After Daly's initial evacuation, letters to the president called for the pilot to win the Distinguished Service Medal and the President's Citizen Medal for his decisiveness and courage. A Beverly Hills dentist described Daly as a hero. "Under great duress," he wrote, Daly "obviated traditional behavior, slashed through what would have been tragic red tape, and flew those Vietnamese youngsters to the safety and sanctity of the United States." A writer from Detroit rued, "Too bad there aren't more men of his kind in this world." White House aides scrambled to balance this tricky political situation. Since Daly's flight was unauthorized, and had outraged USAID staff, it rigged a potential landmine for the president. White House adviser Jack Marsh told his staff to not "encourage Daly" and to "disengage" from attempts to appear that they were promoting Daly's course of action. By late May, the White House had determined that singling Daly out for this award when he was not officially sanctioned to airlift orphans would send the wrong message, even though they agreed that he had displayed "initiative and compassion."[72]

Perhaps the most unsettling example of the U.S. government's reliance on private interests came during the crash of a C-5A Galaxy, the first authorized flight of Babylift. Loaded with approximately 300 children and adult chaperones, all associated with Taylor's organization, the huge military aircraft turned back to Tan Son Nhut Airport when two cargo doors blew off. Before it could land, the plane crashed in a rice paddy, killing 138 adults and children.[73] The continual shifting of blame on the C-5A incident highlighted the precarious balance between public and private interests in Babylift's execution and administration. After the crash, White House chief of staff Richard Cheney scrambled to figure out why a C-5A plane was issued. Administrator Parker explained in an April 3 letter that they were "lining up one or two C-5A planes and equipping them to ensure safe transportation and care en route." According to Theodore Marrs, special assistant to the president for human resources, a joint State Department and Defense Department coordination group issued the directive.[74] Both Lockheed and the U.S. attorney general faced a barrage of criticism from the press, adoptive families, and adoption agencies for their handling of the incident.[75]

The lawsuit over the C-5A Galaxy crash, which lasted until the mid-1980s, accentuated the competing private interests at stake. FFAC accused both Lockheed and the U.S. government of bowing to corporate and political interests, trumping the need for a safe and reliable Air Force medivac plane as originally promised. According to FFAC accounts and court records, both Lockheed and government officials knew that the C-5A had defects and had spent several years debating who should cover the expense of a redesign. Expert witnesses testified that Lockheed wanted the C-5A to be used for the orphan evacuation, instead of the readily available medivac planes, hoping that positive publicity would push Congress to finance the repairs. For child welfare workers, who lost several committed staff and seventy-eight children, the official response represented the worst kind of pandering to corporate interests. After several earlier juries awarded plaintiffs as much as $1 million in damages, the federal government finally negotiated a settlement for the remaining cases. The government assumed 65 percent of the liability, while Lockheed made up the remaining 35 percent. In the end, the court ordered that a total of $8.775 million be paid, which came to $300,000 per infant or adult who died. Even though the amount was agreed to in 1976, the government and Lockheed did not pay out until the mid-1980s.[76] Agencies had hoped that the foundation they had established for Southeast Asian refugees would receive the compensation funds. The courts instead ruled that the settlement would go to adoptive parents. Since some had been matched with their intended child only a few days before, it revealed the cultural and legal power adoption held by the 1980s.[77]

As the initiation and execution of Babylift revealed, the years of decentralized leadership and improvisational policies in Vietnam adoptions exacted a steep toll. The action's mismanagement stemmed from a divided government, an uneven reliance on private agencies to make and enforce policies, and the lack of a central agency to manage child welfare. Without stronger regulatory boundaries, mavericks could and did enforce their own visions of child protection, which often prioritized humanitarian rescue over conscientious procedures. The end of Babylift, along with the final evacuation of U.S. troops from South Vietnam, should have been the denouement to a drawn-out story. But instead of resolution, the evacuations produced a series of questions and lawsuits that persisted well into the 1980s, contributing to a discourse on international adoption's ethics that resonated long after April 1975.

"Children of Controversy"

Not until Operation Babylift did the inherent complications of international adoption receive attention outside professional and government circles. In Babylift's wake, media outlets and activists started questioning the ethics of removing children from their native countries, provoking debates over citizenship, custody, and human rights. These themes all surfaced in an especially charged California court case, *Nguyen Da Yen v. Kissinger* (1975). One volunteer, Muoi McConnell, was assisting evacuees at the Presidio's transition facility when she discovered that some of the children did not consider themselves orphans. Shocked that any child had been improperly removed from South Vietnam, McConnell approached San Francisco attorney Tom Miller and his wife Tran Thong Nhu, head of International Children's Fund, for advice. After a failed effort to confront the agencies and government directly, Tran and Miller contacted the Center for Constitutional Rights (CCR) to file a suit against the federal government and participating adoption agencies.[78]

Arguing for the plaintiffs, Morton Cohen, a San Francisco-based attorney, and Nancy Stearns, from the CCR, contended that holding unorphaned Babylift children violated their Fifth Amendment rights to due process and liberty. Entering on parole visas instead of the standard I-600 visas gave the children "undetermined immigrant status." Moreover, they argued that the children were being held in the United States "against their will and the will of their parents or legal guardian."[79] The defendant's attorneys countered, however, that the attorney general's discretionary power of parole was unquestionable when the reasons were "strictly in the public interest." They further asserted that the attorney general did not abuse his discretion because children were inherently moldable, based on the impermanence of their memories and language abilities. Finally, the attorneys explained that "the power to provide the necessary information [adoption records] is with the adoption agencies" and relieved the government of its responsibility, further illustrating how the diffused authority made no one ultimately responsible.[80] In a November 1975 opinion, the three-judge District Court ordered an INS review of adoptive children's records over several months and set in motion plans for repatriation. Both sides appealed, the plaintiffs because the timing was too slow and the defendants because the attorney general's "discretionary exercise of the parole power was not subject to judicial review."[81]

The initial appeal favored the plaintiffs, expediting the timetable and requiring all Babylift children to be investigated by INS, but especially those with insufficient documentation, whom the judge referred to as "Children of Controversy."[82] The justices rejected the defense's call for the protection of the attorney general's discretionary power by ruling that discretion can never violate constitutional rights. Still, in February 1976, the Ninth Circuit Court of Appeals came down on the government's side, determining that *Nguyen* could no longer be considered a class action suit, and that it was only viewed as a class action suit in the 1975 opinion for discovery purposes. The justices stressed how each orphan came from a different orphanage with discrete procedures and relationships with foreign agencies, underscoring that there was no "typical" class of Babylift orphan. Even the plaintiff's counsel Nancy Stearns acknowledged this when she asked for a release of individual files during oral argument. In her words, "I think when you see the files you will understand that you can't just make the generalizations. Because there are very very great differences in the problems in the different files."[83] Also, the judges ordered the adoption records sealed, which made returning children to their parents cumbersome and unlikely. From this point on, only when Vietnamese families located their children through their own efforts could they file a lawsuit. Ultimately, the process reunited only twelve children with their Vietnamese parents and never did locate the families of the three children named in the lawsuit.[84]

As the lawsuit revealed, those involved in Operation Babylift fundamentally disagreed about the children's best interests. One side cast Babylift as a "kidnapping mission" to serve as the final act of U.S. imperialism in South Vietnam, while the other believed the airlift "rescued" children who would not survive, either physically or emotionally, if left in the now communist-controlled Vietnam. By arguing for children's fundamental human rights and their Fifth Amendment rights to due process and liberty, the plaintiffs prioritized children's individual rights and identities as the most important factors. In this view, Vietnamese orphans were primarily South Vietnamese citizens with self-articulated needs and rights, not just dependents "in the position of being governed."[85] The other side, represented by volunteer agencies and the defense, argued that the protection from harm superseded all other rights. By transporting them out of Vietnam, they not only saved the orphans' lives but also offered them "forever families." Groups like FFAC contended that *Nguyen* limited the agencies from "defend[ing] the position of the children," whose best interest was the permanence of adoptive placements. As FFAC's Rosemary Taylor averred, "Life itself must take precedence over questions of colour, culture, legal documentation, national image, or possible adolescent confusion."[86] In other words, protection from harm trumped identity, citizenship, and social rights.

As the *Nguyen* plaintiffs underscored, one of the key problems with the discourse around Babylift and the subsequent litigation was how legislators, volunteer workers, and media presented Vietnamese children as mere pawns of adult will. In one scholar's assessment, "because of adult practice 'the child' appears for public consumption only as victim and a source of trouble."[87] Edward Zigler, a self-stated "long-time advocate for children," renowned Yale psychologist, and future head of the Children's Bureau, presented his response paper to Babylift during the congressional hearings in April of 1975. Even Zigler never once used evidence from children or a Vietnamese orphan's perspective during his lengthy presentation, minimizing the evacuees' agency.[88] Characterizing Vietnamese children as helpless was striking given that the children's responses, as depicted both by the plaintiffs and in the media, undoubtedly galvanized the lawsuit. The CCR considered Babylift children's testimony crucial and requested that INS officials conduct systematic interviews. Media stories abounded about children who told aid workers or volunteers that they were not orphans.[89] Children also resisted their adoptive placements. In one story released in several news accounts, an eight-year-old boy was beside himself when delivered to his foster mother. Even though the boy walked on crutches with heavy braces on both feet, he refused to go with his new mother. One reporter observed that "both the Vietnamese woman who had accompanied the boy and the foster mother broke into sobs while an airport employee picked up the crying child and carried him to an exit."[90] Stories like these highlighted children's efforts to advocate for themselves in the best way they knew how: by expressing raw emotions that transcended all barriers of language and culture.

The argument for protection was a publicly compelling one because it drew on a larger, centuries old cultural debate over childhood itself. In Vietnam, as in other countries with long-term instability, the boundaries of adulthood were constantly in flux as mandatory education laws became unenforceable and children needed to work to support their families.[91] Since boys could be conscripted into the army at age fourteen and children as young as ten earned money by running shoe shining businesses, children had a great deal more autonomy in Vietnam than in the United States.

Legislators, journalists, and aid workers all lamented this "loss" of childhood since part of the way they understood protecting children was keeping them separate from adult responsibilities. One columnist wrote, "Some of the attention, as every experienced observer knows, is spurious. Hypocritical. Based on a guilt complex. But much is real. Full of genuine concern for kids who've never had a chance to have a childhood."[92]

After conducting a fifteen-year war that killed tens of thousands of civilian women and children, the North Vietnamese could not fathom that Operation Babylift was simply a way to protect childhood. When the Viet Cong captured Saigon in late April 1975, it established a provisional government in the South that North Vietnam dissolved in 1976 so that the country could be reunified under northern control. Upset that the United States questioned the North's ability to care for South Vietnamese children, Viet Cong Foreign Minister Nguyen Thi Binh called Babylift "an effort by the United States to indoctrinate children who will later be used to try to subvert the revolutionary government. No one will believe the United States wants to help the Vietnamese people after slaughtering millions of them."[93] Americans also voiced these concerns. One soldier on a humanitarian mission in South Vietnam asked, "Now is it better for a child here to die or be maimed for life or to risk his being screwed up by well-intentioned people back home?"[94]

One of the most common critiques that volunteer agencies faced from the media, liberal legislators, and *Nguyen* plaintiffs was that they were placing children who were not true orphans. These accusations had merit. In countless anecdotes, some Babylift children had mothers who had been forced to give up their children or had only placed them temporarily in institutional care. In Babylift's immediate aftermath, ISS received an inquiry from a father about the location of his child.[95] Decades later, writer Dana Sachs discovered letters posted online by birth parents still searching for "lost" children. The story of two Danang birth mothers sheds light on how unorphaned children arrived in the United States as part of Babylift. Both women's husbands abandoned them in the early days of the war. To make ends meet, they worked on U.S. military bases and relied on extra support from American soldiers, trading sex for financial and social stability. As the northern army encroached, their neighborhood gossip network reported that American-fathered children would be tortured and killed. These mothers, like many others, surrendered American-fathered children for overseas adoption because they thought they had no other choice for their children's survival. In the panic of the coming invasion, families hastily abandoned children, sometimes throwing them over orphanage walls, with the hope of being reunited later.[96]

It was not the journey to the United States of which families were unaware, but the permanence of that arrangement. Representative Elizabeth Holtzman's claim that children were sent to the United States without a family's knowledge was unsubstantiated. In her testimony before the House subcommittee, Embassy official Lauralee Peters confirmed that most Vietnamese-run orphanages did house children whose parents placed them there as a temporary measure, but these children were designated "unavailable" for adoption. Peters also clarified that Western agencies rarely took permanently relinquished children. Only ISS and Holt had the trained staff to work with birth mothers and accept relinquishments. The other five agencies, including FFAC, only accepted children who had already been abandoned or relinquished to a Vietnamese-run orphanage. According to Peters, it was the responsibility of South Vietnamese orphanages and the GVN Ministry of Social Welfare to give proper relinquishment counseling. In fact, only one-quarter to one-third of Vietnamese orphanages would even allow children to transfer to facilities that conducted international adoptions. So when journalist Judith Coburn argued that "American adoption agencies have never taken into account the fact that many of the children in South Vietnamese orphanages are not orphans," she was making a broad statement that did not apply to the bulk of American-run orphanages or orphans transported to the United States.[97]

Arguments like these were still powerful, however, because they reinforced South Vietnamese orphans' dependence and vulnerability. Without the mantle of social, political, and civil citizenship, children relied on adult advocates to represent "their best interests," making it easy to focus on the protection of children above any other considerations.[98] Highlighting children's rights exposed how traditional definitions of citizenship that focused on individuality, obscured the interdependence that underlies social citizenship and marginalized children's social and economic contributions.[99] In the case of Babylift, and international adoption in general, immigration law made foreign children legal citizens through their incorporation into U.S. families. The governing immigration statute, the Hart-Celler Act, stipulated that "no natural parent or prior adoptive parent of any such child shall thereafter, by virtue of such parentage, be accorded any right, privilege, or status under this Act," solidifying adoptive parents' permanent legal and cultural right to their adopted children.[100] This was supported by decades of social welfare research, which demonstrated that orphans' outcomes improved significantly if they were raised in families. By the 1960s, foster care had replaced institutions as the primary care unit for orphaned Americans, and most Americans agreed that growing up in a family was preferred, if not an inalienable right of childhood.[101]

Part of the *Nguyen* defense strategy was to emphasize this "right" to a family. One notable witness for the defense was Joseph Goldstein, a Yale professor and psychoanalyst who collaborated with Anna Freud and Alfred Solnit on the landmark 1973 book, *Beyond the Best Interests of the Child*. Their book argued that a child's primary relational tie, what they called a "psychological parent," was paramount in producing secure and healthy development. This parent could be "biological, adoptive, foster, or common-law," as long as the relationship was stable and consistent.[102] In his testimony, Goldstein contended that Babylift children born between October 1973 and April 1975 could suffer dramatically if forced to return to what he termed their "absent parents." Since the "psychological parent" for these younger children was the prospective adoptive parent, Goldstein testified that every effort should be made to preserve this relationship. He even suggested that "reparation be made to the natural parent in the form of cash, for property is a moveable object . . . children are not," implying that Vietnamese families could be consoled for the right price.[103] By calling on Goldstein as a witness for the defense, lawyers pointed to loving and nurturing adoptive parents as one legitimizing factor in Vietnamese children's U.S. citizenship, one that surpassed cultural or national origins. Of course this testimony deemphasized the possibility that some children also had loving and nurturing biological families.

While few disagreed that children would be better off in families, advocates parted ways over what kind of family was best. For Vietnamese expats, liberal doves, and some social workers, the best place for Vietnamese orphans was to remain in Vietnam until their birth or extended families could care for them. As Martin Teitel, director of the American Friends Service Committee Asian program, remarked, "It is insulting to the Vietnamese to suggest that they are unable to care for their own children."[104] One Vietnam resident further highlighted the importance of national and cultural ties: "Many people cannot help sighing as to whether or not in [the] future these Vietnamese orphans will still remember that they are Vietnamese and that their fatherland is Viet Nam, the land where they were born."[105] For aid workers, certain policymakers, and adoptive parents, U.S. families provided the most opportunities and the greatest stability for children raised in a war-torn country where the extended family system had "broken down."[106] Perhaps Rosemary Taylor best captured this perspective in her memoir:

> No one is suggesting that a Western family has any child-raising talent superior to that of an Asian family, nor that it is better to grow up in the West than in the Far East. Surely, let a child grow up with biological parents in his own country, if the option exists. But for abandoned children, such an option does not exist. To continue confronting a real and immediate problem with an ideal and hypothetical solution is unintelligent. . . . It is so much more convenient for the conscience to believe that the child should stay in his country of birth. It absolves everyone from the guilt of personal involvement.[107]

Babylift's dramatic and contentious implementation compelled Americans to consider the larger implications of children's rights, international adoption in general, and citizenship.

As these debates suggest, children held a privileged position in U.S. discourses of citizenship because of their legal bonds to U.S. families, young age, and assimilability. This becomes even more striking when Babylift is situated within Operation New Life, the refugee evacuation that relocated 130,000 Vietnamese refugees to the United States in 1975. The media and intellectuals generally perceived Operation New Life, like Babylift, as a way to assuage guilt. As MIT Professor and former modernization theorist Lucian Pye explained, "we are trying to prove that we are not really abandoning these people. The guilt feeling is very deep cutting across hawk and dove alike. We want to know we are still good, still decent." Yet, in spite of this "guilt feeling," a Gallup Poll found that 54 percent of Americans thought the refugees should be resettled outside the United States.[108]

The resettlement authority's placement strategy revealed the massive social and cultural undertaking of relocating a large group of racially different refugees. The agency dispersed migrants throughout the country and assigned them a "sponsoring family" that would serve as a cultural bridge, providing help with job hunting, grocery shopping, and neighborhood transition. This strategy emphasized individuality over social connections to other Vietnamese, an ideology that suggested these refugees lacked the ability to become autonomous and responsible U.S. citizens as residents of ethnic enclaves.[109] Since the resettlement agency had to combat media stories that reported refugees "going on welfare shortly after arriving in a community," it foregrounded autonomy and self-reliance as the keys to citizenship. Resettlement officials argued that when recent refugees relied on American-resident relatives instead of a sponsoring family or volunteer agency, they were more likely to seek state assistance. A strong connection with a sponsoring family, officials believed, would help the newcomers navigate the cultural road to self-sufficiency while avoiding the stigma of welfare.[110] Although there were no explicit references to racial or ethnic difference in the resettlement report, the resettlement plan clearly stated that race-based communities worked against forming assimilated and independent citizens.[111]

The perception of Vietnamese refugees as dependent was reinforced by their immigration status. Initially admitted to the United States under the same parole provision as the Babylift children, adult refugees had parole visas, which granted them entrance but not residency. Highlighting the parole statute's "dichotomy between physical presence and legal status," these visas offered "a false kind of freedom" because they relied on the attorney general's discretion—meaning that the refugees had no constitutional rights, since Attorney General Edward Levi could revoke parole without a hearing or explanation. Furthermore, as one scholar argued, "since the decision to grant an adjustment is wholly discretionary, a parolee has no guidelines to follow in attempting to argue the merits of an application."[112] Without resident status, refugees had little chance of finding steady work or pursuing more education, significantly derailing their road to "self-sufficiency." President Jimmy Carter emphasized this in a 1977 letter to Congress in which he blamed the parolee status for refugees' need to supplement their jobs with federal assistance programs. Not until October 1977, in an amendment to the Indochina Migration and Refugee Assistance Act of 1975, did Vietnamese refugees have the opportunity to become permanent residents with a clear route to citizenship.[113] Even then, Congress approved increased spending for refugee support programs until 1981 or until economic realities changed, signaling that "dependence" on social programs had less to do with refugees' questionable mores and more to do with a lack of living-wage jobs.[114] This was ironic, considering that the mission's name—Operation New Life—signified that coming to the United States was akin to being reborn in a much better place.

Unlike the fluctuating status of most Vietnamese refugees, Babylift children's status did not remain in flux or require an act of Congress; adoptive parents needed only to process readoption paperwork for orphans to become citizens. The easiest route to naturalized citizenship in the United States was, in fact, through adoptive parents, sending a message that family marked the model path to U.S. citizenship. From the late 1960s, the Nixon administration made it clear that there was no other path to citizenship open to American-fathered Vietnamese children, despite French precedent. In colonial Vietnam, the child of a French father and Vietnamese mother was considered *enfant reconnu* or an "acknowledged child." Although not technically "legitimate," they received French citizenship, education, and social support.[115] When pressed by legislators, the State Department rejected this precedent, arguing that "American citizenship laws are fundamentally different from those of France, and under existing American laws the U.S. government cannot adopt a policy similar to that of France." Furthermore, administration officials insisted that Vietnamese laws offered all children born in Vietnam to Vietnamese mothers the same citizenship protections, so there was no need for the United States to intervene. Congress tried to pass orphan legislation because of this history, but the bill never gained widespread support. In the words of one Vietnamese bargirl, "The Americans take five minutes of fun and forget about the consequences. The French were better. When they had a child, they paid for his education. Why don't you Americans do the same thing?"[116]

For U.S. officials, it had less to do with an inability to take responsibility than with the implications of such responsibility. If the United States conferred citizenship privileges on American-fathered Vietnamese children, this would not only set a precedent for future military occupations, but would officially color the nation as an empire like France, a connotation that would be damaging to raising multilateral Cold War support for U.S. democratic missions.[117] Over the course of the war, it served U.S. interests better to shepherd South Vietnam as a tactical ally and have the Vietnamese and American voluntary agencies care for children in Vietnam. In cases where children could not thrive in South Vietnam, they could be made citizens through U.S. adoptive parents, showing solidarity with the Third World.

"Citizens of the World"?

As the "children of controversy" debates affirmed, many still viewed international adoptees as the "best possible immigrants"—those most assimilable into the American way of life. But the assumption that all children were better off as Americans was challenged in the 1970s. The widespread distrust of government power, both at home and abroad, made the public leery of associating international adoption with Cold War military campaigns. Amid the critiques, a new image of international adoptees emerged. As relief efforts became increasingly international and nongovernmental, so did the children they came to serve. Characterizing children as global rather than national subjects, humanitarian agencies claimed that needy youth belonged to the international community first and foremost, just as relief agencies insisted that they served universal interests over national ones. Tired of wrestling with individual government restrictions and regulations, FFAC staff member Margaret Moses argued that nationalism and bureaucracy limited the ability to help children in need. Moses envisioned a sympathetic brotherhood of volunteers free from hierarchy where "children would be *citizens of the world*," without national affinity.[118] The image of children as "citizens of the world" served by a nonpartisan and international relief community depoliticized transnational adoption, ensuring its ability to weather whatever storms would come.

Much changed from the early days of anticommunist propaganda, this ideology deemphasized nationalism, and even modernization, while still upholding Western values of democracy, free enterprise, and equality. When reflecting in 1976 on the fallout after Babylift, Holt director Jack Adams contended, "For over 19 years, the Holt Adoption Program has attempted to provide the best service possible for children without regard to race, nationality or region. . . . We deeply regret any events which seem to tie together American military assistance and the serving of these children [and] cannot accept . . . that communists do not love children and will not accept them."[119] A significant shift from founder Harry Holt's open patriotism and anti-communism, Adams's remarks illustrated how much had changed in the relief community by the mid-1970s. Even more striking was child protection advocates' emphasis on global cooperation. Reflecting on the increasing expectation of international cooperation, one prospective adoptive parent wrote to his senator, "It seems to me that regardless of the ideological differences between nations, we could still help rear these children who have no one or nothing else [because] our children are the best hope for a peaceful world in the future."[120]

One *Newsweek* journalist's journey to adopt a Vietnamese child in 1973, featured in a Senate report, serves as a fitting allegory for how international adoption transcended nation and relied on global connectivity. When Paul and his wife Kathleen decided to adopt, they visited an orphanage in Saigon. Immediately mobbed by dozens of desperate waifs, the couple was overwhelmed by the children's deprivation. They finally picked an eleven-month-old girl, Duong Muoi, covered with bedsores and rat bites, incapable of even sitting up. After being abandoned by her mother who had twelve other children to care for, the infant spent months in hospitals where she was "half forgotten." Once Paul and Kathleen brought Duong Muoi home to their apartment in Japan, they worked tirelessly to make her well again. The parents recalled, "We put a pink ribbon in her hair, dressed her in a smock and tried to sit her up on the couch. She fell over. But with Kathleen filling Duong Muoi with U.S. baby formula supplied by an American doctor, and our Chinese maid and Vietnamese cook filling the baby with protein-rich fish sauce, Duong Muoi was sitting up in a few weeks. Soon, she was smiling too." Without a doubt, the Brinkley-Rogers knew they had saved this little girl.[121]

This story demonstrated the global collaboration that international adoptions made possible. The Brinkley-Rogers family lived at a cosmopolitan intersection between Japanese, Chinese, Vietnamese, and American cultures. Connected through a child's universality, they could combine U.S. formula with a Vietnamese "protein-rich fish sauce" to produce the ideal potion to make Duong Muoi well. The piece, titled the "Americanization of Duong Muoi," also told a story of American superiority, however. As the couple's orphanage visit recounts, all Vietnamese children longed for an American to rescue them from their poverty, disease, and hopelessness. Only the most needy, determined by her inability to even sit up unassisted, was lucky enough to be adopted—the chosen beneficiary of U.S. largesse. In this account, China and Vietnam acted as selfless and faithful servants of U.S. interests and supported the rescued waif without pause or question. Yet the couple trusted only an American doctor to provide the proper medical advice, even in a technologically advanced country like Japan. This narrative affirmed American superiority as benign and paternal while simultaneously celebrating multilateral, multiethnic help under white leadership.

Regardless of the cultural power inherent in describing needy children as "citizens of the world," Operation Babylift demonstrated how national objectives ultimately overcame universalist rhetoric. Under USAID's development program, the administration wanted to prove that South Vietnam could address its own child welfare needs through modernization. But when the North Vietnamese takeover became imminent, suddenly taking national ownership of the same children that the State Department had insisted since the mid-1960s were South Vietnam's responsibility became of paramount importance. For all the talk of cooperation with the South Vietnamese and multilateral action, in the last minutes of the war, the remaining American Embassy staff, civilian personnel, and military trainers flew to safety while the South Vietnamese military remained to deal with the fallout. Perhaps this transferable population of adoptable children ameliorated the failure of nation building. Officials could hope that Babylift children, housed and fed through U.S. dollars, would serve as global ambassadors, ultimately justifying the Vietnam War. Even naming the mission "Operation Babylift" implied that the United States was intoxicated by its unique ability to rescue the needy. As one columnist contended, this was the worst kind of nationalism since it came under the auspice of global interest: "We . . . will never wave a white flag. Instead we fill the skies with innocents, tiny human peace symbols borne aloft in the same planes that flew the bombs that made them orphans in the first place."[122]

No one captured the tensions between U.S. nation building and the expansionist global vision better than Garry Trudeau in *Doonesbury*, a nationally syndicated comic strip that won the Pulitzer Prize in 1975 for its editorial cartoons. Over the course of a dozen strips, Trudeau featured a Babylift orphan named Kim adopted by a Santa Monica, California, couple. Trudeau exposed Operation Babylift as a government effort to justify the loss of South Vietnam to the North Vietnamese. But by chronicling Kim's average American family, the cartoonist also stressed the normality of international adoption. Trudeau first depicts Kim on her airlift evacuation, looking out a window over the United States. The nurse accompanying her, a representation of a U.S. "savior," chirps: "You're a very lucky young lady . . . an important symbol of hope for the free world!" This positions Kim as the benefactor of U.S. policies in Vietnam since her evacuation offered freedoms and privileges only available in a democracy. While Vietnam itself was lost as "an important symbol" of freedom, Babylift protected the most vulnerable from communist control while reaffirming American humanitarianism.

When Kim arrived at the airport, she was brought to the immigration health inspector. As the pediatrician examined her, Kim identified herself not through her Vietnamese identity but through her value in the eyes of the U.S. government, exclaiming to the physician in a thought bubble, "You better not hurt me—I'm a symbol you know!" Kim might have been a symbol; however, what is notable about this cartoon is the normality of the encounter. Her routine, twenty-minute physical, administered by a "regular" pediatrician in his office as he might for any other young patient, stood in contrast to the global drama that brought her there. While earlier Asian immigrants would have faced restrictive immigration policies and invasive procedures, Trudeau instead illustrated how a colorblind nation welcomed Vietnamese adoptees with open arms.[123]

Trudeau also uses adoptive parents as caricatures of U.S. government interests. In the press conference strip, almost certainly a parody of White House press conferences about Babylift, Kim's adoptive parents are overwhelmed with happiness. For childless couples, many of whom had waited years to adopt, the orphan evacuations signaled the beginning of their families. Calling Babylift "heroic," "courageous," and an "extraordinary gesture," their personal stake in the process understandably influenced their interpretation of the action.[124] In Trudeau's parody of the process, they served as veritable "Babylift Boosters" in the press, glorifying the government's decisive action. Even though for most Americans the orphan evacuations appeared inseparable from politics, as demonstrated by the reporters' question about "aton[ing] for our collective national guilt through individual action," adoptive families refused to see Babylift as another act of U.S. "aggression." Lana Noone, a prominent advocate and adoptive mother of two Babylift children, contended, "I consider Babylift to be the uniting thread of the Vietnam era. No matter what your politics on the Vietnam War, the best thing to do was to evacuate the children."[125] By downplaying the clear political motivations, adoptive parents could reimagine the Babylift as the U.S. government looking out for their interests as childless couples. Yet, Trudeau's interpretation suggests that the government abused this trust, using adoptive parents' vulnerability to serve U.S. objectives.

Conclusion

It is hard to read the story of Operation Babylift without seeing it as an allegory for the Vietnam War as a whole. With power struggles between the executive branch and Congress, a State Department committed to military spending over humanitarian aid, rampant administrative secrecy, and knee-jerk reactions to public pressure, the connections abound. During Babylift, Congress was the last to know about Ford administration decisions, the State Department failed to streamline the humanitarian chain of command because of its focus on militarism, and all sides prioritized reactive decisions over conscientious procedures. Babylift epitomized failed Cold War policies in South Vietnam that had terrorized the Southeast Asian nation for nearly two decades. Ironically, the Babylift became exactly what President Kennedy had hoped to avoid when he commissioned USAID in 1961—humanitarianism inseparable from military and political power.

Operation Babylift perhaps offered the most dramatic example of how the international adoption process dispersed authority through a complicated network of public and private interests. Built on established policy choices and the humanitarianism paradigm, the evacuation mobilized a range of players, including government agencies, congressional committees, volunteer agencies, and foreign governments. Although the media presented Babylift as primarily a government action, in fact it only had a veneer of officialdom, instead relying heavily on the actions and decisions of private agencies. Without clearly marked regulatory boundaries, can-do policymakers operated without a sufficient central authority, and administration officials evaded their responsibility to protect the rights of South Vietnam's children.

Still looking to win the "hearts and minds" of the Third World, the United States used the mass evacuation of Vietnamese children to bolster its waning national image. Even though the State Department and USAID did not initially plan to act on child protection, both organizations used Babylift as a convenient public relations campaign to cloak militarism in humanitarianism and offer a distraction from the failed nation-building project in South Vietnam. Amid calls for children to become "citizens of the world," lawsuits like *Nguyen* undermined the argument that these orphans belonged to no one and challenged the United States' image as a benevolent rescuer. Babylift litigation further exposed the internal contradictions inherent in simultaneously protecting children while obscuring their national identities. As one Vietnamese social worker concluded, "We felt the children have been used by almost all governments involved as a political ploy . . . that everyone was using the children to wave their flag."[126]

The Legacy of Voluntarism

International Adoption
in the Twenty-First Century

I N THE WAKE OF OPERATION BABYLIFT, it seemed that international adoption had finally reached its denouement. Babylift's intense media attention, coupled with the 1976 *Nguyen Da Yen* lawsuit, produced the first widespread public backlash against the adoption of foreign children. Such critiques echoed rising fears of American decline that circulated throughout the 1970s amid a string of economic and political crises, from stagflation to the Watergate scandal. Furthermore, with the United States no longer engaged in an on-the-ground war, there were no ready replacements for Vietnamese adoptees. In fact, after 1976, the number of international adoptions gradually fell. Was it possible that this thirty-year tenure was merely a deviation and the institution would simply fade away? But international adoption did not go away. After a multiyear dip, the adoption of foreign children reached a historic high by 1983. Although countries like Greece and Vietnam no longer sent children to the United States, Korean adoptions grew throughout the 1980s, driven by government pressures on single mothers to relinquish their children for overseas adoption in response to rapid urbanization and industrialization. Over the next twenty-five years, annual totals grew significantly and only dipped below the 1983 number twice. And as in the past, large-scale geopolitical changes meant new sending countries for foreign children. When the Cold War ended, for instance, there was a large uptick in children adopted from the orphanages of Romania, Ukraine, and Russia.[1]

If the critiques of transnational adoption did not lead to its end, then the spotlight on the rights of children and birth families during the Babylift era gradually influenced efforts to establish international laws governing adoptions. U.S. child welfare professionals considered a cross-border adoption statute beginning in the 1940s, but lacked both a central international body capable of enacting and enforcing laws and the necessary public support.[2] As part of its larger human rights campaign, the United Nations adopted the first Declaration of the Rights of the Child in 1959. Although the principles stated that young children should only be separated from their mothers in "exceptional circumstances" and should never "be the subject of traffic, in any form," these were broad guidelines without any methods for implementation.[3] But as the international community grew increasingly wary of U.S. global authority over the course of the Vietnam War, the UN General Assembly passed a resolution in December 1972, proposing a conference on international adoption law.[4] This resolution, and the subsequent conferences, eventually culminated in the 1989 Convention on the Rights of the Child, which was the first international statute to mention adoption explicitly. In Article 21, the document specified that international adoption should only be considered a solution if all of the options in the child's home country had been exhausted.[5] Unlike previous resolutions, the 1989 UN resolution became internationally enforceable in 1993, through the Hague Convention on Protection of Children and Cooperation in Respect of Intercountry Adoption. These reforms acknowledged the power differentials in intercountry adoption and sought to protect the rights of poor children and families.

Despite these reforms, the U.S. government lagged behind other countries in compliance. Although the United States signed the 1989 Convention, it remains the only country besides Somalia that has yet to ratify it.[6] Additionally, even though U.S. officials signed the Hague Convention in 1994, it took fourteen years to go into effect, during which time international adoptions to the United States soared to their highest levels. Nevertheless, these international laws have started to close some of the regulatory gaps that propelled post-World War II-era adoptions. Because of the Hague Convention, the U.S. government has now designated the State Department as the central authority responsible for enforcing adoption regulations nationwide—a reform that ISS's Susan Pettiss had longed to see in the 1961 immigration law that made intercountry adoption a permanent U.S. institution. The State Department also ensures that only agencies accredited by child welfare authorities can conduct permanent child placements, another landmark change to international adoption regulations.[7]

Yet, even with a more comprehensive network of international law and increased regulations governing private agencies, international adoption's historic emphasis on voluntarism remains. Following the massive earthquake in Haiti on January 12, 2010, American families rushed to local adoption agencies, hoping to adopt a child orphaned by the disaster.[8] Although Haitian officials, in partnership with UNICEF, put an almost immediate moratorium on new adoptions, U.S. representatives hurried to expedite the adoptions already in process. On January 19, secretary of the Department of Homeland Security Janet Napolitano approved humanitarian parole visas for children already matched with U.S. families—the same legislative mechanism used in Operation Babylift. The next day, secretary of state Hillary Clinton organized a joint task force, comprised of the State Department, Department of Homeland Security, and Department of Health and Human Services, to further oversee that these 150 adoptions would be legal and ethical.[9] U.S. officials decried hasty adoptions that could be mistaken for child trafficking. Nevertheless, the Obama administration's emergency actions opened the legislative door for adoption of 1,150 Haitian children; 1,000 more children than originally planned.[10]

As the official actions suggested, although non-state actors and adoptive parents operated within tighter strictures, they still commanded significant institutional clout. One week after the earthquake, Pennsylvania governor Ed Rendell chartered a private airplane to bring fifty-four children from the flattened Brebis de Saint Michel de l'Attalaye (BRESMA) orphanage to Pittsburgh, Pennsylvania, where they would meet their adoptive families. In a scene reminiscent of Operation Babylift, Haitian government workers stopped the plane on the runway, insisting that seven of the children did not have the appropriate paperwork to leave. After hours of diplomatic negotiations with the White House, Rendell's flight was allowed to take off, evacuating the children from the ruins below. Even with stricter international regulations, Rendell was never officially censured for his rescue mission.[11] The Haitian case shows that the U.S. international adoption system continues to extend authority to those operating under the umbrella of humanitarianism, especially during "emergencies."

The conflation of adoption and humanitarianism works because, in the twenty-first century, children remain the most worthy subjects of foreign relief. From 1945 to 1976, legislators, the media, and the U.S. public deemed the children rescued from Cold War hotspots the "best possible immigrants." By naming international adoptees the "best possible immigrants," it embedded into both law and culture the practice of bringing foreign children into U.S. families. Indeed, this designation persists, as seen in adopted children's privileged immigration status and the ongoing use of parole visas to bypass naturalization queues. But, with the turn toward internationalizing aid and the increasing prominence of transracial families, another term became even more resonant in the post-Vietnam War era— "citizens of the world." A more expansive expression that applied to all children regardless of nation, race, or creed, "citizens of the world" was first used by Friends of Children of Vietnam Director Wende Grant in the mid-1970s. As international citizens, orphans were no longer national subjects, but global subjects: belonging simultaneously to no one and to everyone.

The image of borderlessness complements the contemporary message of adoptive parents, humanitarians, and lawmakers that children's universal need is for a family to love and nurture them, regardless of where that family is located. In a *Huffington Post* article, one adoptive father affirmed this, contending, "I simply don't believe in borders when it comes to children needing families."[12] Although most adoptive parent and orphan advocacy groups concur with The Hague's recommendation that children should be raised in their home countries if at all possible, recent efforts have focused on expediting the placement of foreign children into U.S. families. An entrepreneur and adoptive father of three Haitian children, Craig Juntunen, launched a nonprofit in 2012, for instance, with the mission to "revitalize international adoption" in the United States through policy and publicity. Calling current mechanisms to screen adoptive families "inefficient," Juntunen aims to increase international adoptions to five times their 2011 levels by "informing and educating" foreign officials and "standardizing" the process among sending nations.[13]

To serve this mission, Juntunen's organization, Burning Both Ends, produced a documentary on the hazards of Hague regulations for those trying to adopt internationally. Titled *Stuck*, the film depicted the harrowing experiences of several adoptive families as they navigated the hostility of foreign governments, excessive paperwork, and unhelpful U.S. bureaucrats to be united with their adoptive children. Told almost exclusively from the perspective of adoptive parents, the film juxtaposed impoverished scenes of foreign orphanages with tree-lined suburban streets dotted with two-story brick colonials. Without taking time to differentiate between places, the filmmaker transitioned quickly from Ethiopia and Vietnam to Romania and Cambodia, blurring the differences between origin countries as if they were irrelevant to the end goal—simplifying international adoption for children "stuck" in the system. Such a cursory survey implied that all of these countries were poor and corrupt, institutionalizing children because they devalued their lives; in contrast to U.S. adoptive parents whom the film shows waiting with beautifully decorated bedrooms and expansive homes. Perhaps these dueling images—depicting developing countries as interchangeable and constructing childhood as borderless and universal—are fitting in a world increasingly governed by the norms of globalization where national boundaries can seem to have less meaning.[14] But they also reveal the importance of perspective. For governments, maintaining sovereignty over one's citizens demonstrates the freedom to govern. For U.S. adoptive parents, national sovereignty matters less than the universality of all children.

Given the coverage after the Haitian earthquake, it appears that the media still consider these "citizens of the world" as "the best possible immigrants," for their presumed adaptability and link to largely white, middle-class families. Two Haitian children on Rendell's flight went to a Nebraska family of four. The Heatons, who had been waiting for adoption approval for nearly three years, initially chose Haiti because of its extreme poverty. The couple was stricken by the number of children who starved to death under age four.[15] When Bettania and Dieunette finally arrived at their new six-bedroom home situated on five acres in the rural Midwest, the girls' reversal of fortune was not lost on one *New York Times* reporter, who stressed their new world of material comfort. While "Dieunette arrived caked in dried diarrhea [and] Bettania's clothing had to be burned," the writer gushed how they now "spent the weekend . . . cuddling on a plush sofa, feet warmed by a fire, outfitted like princesses, being hugged and kissed as they ate and drank, laughed and played with a toy poodle." Comforted by a mother who could afford to stay home with them, Bettania and Dieunette "looked thoroughly contented," in the reporter's words, "perhaps for the first time in their short lives."[16] As the *Times* reporter summarized, "Now Bettania and Dieunette have, among so many other things, a new last name—if not quite by law yet, the Heatons say, then by the often stronger rules of love and attachment."[17] Along with the *Times*, *Essence* and *Huffington Post* also featured the family's adoptive success as a "magnificent story," all echoing that the girls had easily adjusted to life as middle-class Americans.[18] As these vignettes illustrated, they had been transplanted across national borders with great success by those in a position to help.

But are transplanted children ever fully moldable or "free" of their national affiliations. Only two months after the piece on the Heatons, the *New York Times* ran quite a different story. On April 7, 2010, the mother of a seven-year-old adopted boy "returned" the youth to Moscow. Torry Ann Hansen had adopted Artyom Savelyev in 2009 from Russia, renamed him Justin, and finalized his citizenship. But when she was unable to cope with what she deemed "psychopathic issues," she delivered him to the Russian Education and Science Ministry via a hired courier. Appropriately, the media and the social welfare community rebuked Hansen for child abandonment. Yet, absent from the coverage was the question of belonging.[19] Why did Hansen put a U.S. citizen on a plane for Russia, rather than seeking her agency's help to place Justin with another family in the United States? In Hansen's mind, Artyom, or "Justin," belonged to Russia, not the United States. The Hansen story illustrates that the national identity of foreign children lingers. And sometimes adoptees choose that identity themselves. A 2015 *New York Times Magazine* article explored "why a generation of adoptees is returning to South Korea" and forming a robust ex-pat community. One of the article's highlights was a series of photographs that featured adoptees living in Seoul and the surrounding countryside. Titled "Homing Signals," the montage gestured to the inherent embeddedness of nation and people.[20]

Even beneath the ostensibly triumphal assimilation of the Haitian adoptees was also a story of a homeland in crisis, magnified by the very borders that international adoption sought to minimize. One of the adopted girls, Dieunette, was born with a rare condition that left her brain partly exposed. Through the advocacy of BRESMA, the orphanage featured in Governor Rendell's airlift, an international aid group flew Dieunette to an Omaha hospital for corrective surgery, and the Heatons fostered the infant during her recovery. According to the *New York Times* reporter, even though the family was "already attached" to the fragile child, the Heatons sent Dieunette back to her birth mother, who planned to care for the now one-year-old.[21] Yet, only a week after they returned to Haiti, Hurricane Gustav devastated and then flooded Dieunette's home town.

In a painfully familiar story, Dieunette's mother called the BRESMA orphanage, stranded and panicking as dead bodies floated past her, unable to locate food or clean water. It took twenty-four hours for BRESMA staff to reach the child, whom they found alone with only a bottle of "dirty water." The staff took this suddenly "adoptable" child—"orphaned" by the combined blows of poverty and a natural disaster—back to the Port-au-Prince orphanage and began adoption paperwork for the Heatons immediately. Although the conditions in Haiti seemed exceptional, such relinquishments are not uncommon. In *Stuck*, the filmmaker interviews an Ethiopian birth mother after she relinquished her child to the local orphanage. When asked why she chose to give up her daughter, the woman remarked simply that she was unable to feed her.[22] In both of these cases, it is clear that the children are worth saving, and the mothers are not. As these examples show, designating children as orphans remains culturally loaded and reveals the trickiness of disentangling the rights of adoptive parents from the rights of a child. Calls to further restrict immigration continue to ring in the background of the appeals to make international adoption laws more generous. Without any sense of irony, when speaking to a local reporter about the remaining children in Haiti who still needed homes, Kristin Heaton concluded, "I guess my plea is just a cry for the orphans."[23]

In an opinion piece on Haitian adoption, law professor David Smolin contended that actions like the Haitian airlift demonstrate how the system itself remains flawed: "Since you can't fix what you will not admit is broken, there is a perverse tendency to repeat, over and over again, the same mistakes in intercountry adoption."[24] This book has challenged the notion that incidents like the Haitian airlifts are mistakes. It has, instead, argued that what seem like mistakes are instead intentional "patterns" in the U.S. social welfare state.[25] The reliance of U.S. child welfare and international relief programs on non-state actors fostered an environment where NGOs and volunteers catered to the interests of individual players, minimized bureaucracy, and avoided regulations. Indeed, volunteers and humanitarians responded nimbly to crises, developing informal and improvisational policies to provide immediate child welfare solutions. Since voluntary leadership was extremely popular with prospective adoptive parents, legislators enacted few policies that limited either the power or the on-the-ground policymaking of volunteers. By offering legitimacy and funding to an array of private interests, all with competing visions of child saving, the state unwittingly perpetuated a series of conflicts among these private interests: those who viewed international adoption as under the jurisdiction of professional social work; those who viewed international adoption as an act of humanitarianism, religious faith, and/or relief; and those who viewed international adoption as a solution to the domestic demand for "adoptable" babies. While the world of international adoption has certainly changed since the 1970s, the current system bears the whispers and imprints of these long-established adoption paradigms and the influence of volunteers.

In the early 1950s, one report captured the essence of international adoption's legacy on American policy and culture. The U.S. Committee for the Care of European Children attributed the agency's success in relocating the displaced children of World War II to the "flexibility of a democracy in which it is possible for national and local, sectarian and nonsectarian, governmental and voluntary efforts to be pooled together for one common goal—the happiness of the individual child."[26] In the twenty-first-century United States, international adoptees continue to play integral roles in the construction of American families, friendships, and communities. Their presence remains because international adoption—as a system and a story—is still in the interest of many.

Selected Immigration Legislation and Refugee Action Chronology, 1945–1976

1945	**War Brides or GI Brides Act** Permitted U.S. military to bring children fathered overseas with foreign women. Excluded Asian women as "racially non-admissible aliens."
December 1945	**Special Directive** President Truman issues a special directive giving displaced orphans "preferential treatment" in visa distribution. USCOM brought 1,387 orphans to the United States in 1946–48 for primarily relative adoption.
1948	**Displaced Persons Act** Provided 3,000 non-quota visas to orphaned European children. Redefined the term "orphan" in international law to include children with two surviving parents.
1950	**Alien Brides Act, Public Law 717** Extended a citizenship waiver to the foreign wives and children of U.S. military forces, regardless of race.
1952	**McCarran-Walter Act** Removed ban on immigration from Asia, but upheld national quota rules. Ended exclusion on Asian migration and citizenship but maintained small quotas for these nations.
July 1953	**House Joint Resolution for Military Families** Permitted admission of 500 orphans adopted by military families abroad.

August 1953   **Refugee Relief Act**
                 Provided 4,000 non-quota visas to orphaned children in
                 Europe, Asia, and Palestine.
1956   **Refugee Relief Act, Revised**
                 Extended the RRA for one more year and increased non-
                 quota visas to 9,000 total.
1957   **Refugee-Escapee Act**
                 Placed RRA under the Immigration and Nationality Act.
                 Extended the RRA two more years and offered unlimited
                 visas to foreign orphans adopted into U.S. families.
Dec 1960–1962   **Operation Pedro Pan**
                 Parole evacuation of over 14,000 Cuban youth that lasted
                 two years in the wake of the Cuban Revolution.
                 Placements were largely temporary.
1961   **Immigration and Nationality Act, Revised**
                 Made international adoption a formal part of
                 immigration law and ended adoptions by proxy.
1965   **Hart-Celler Act**
                 Ended national origins quota system. Prioritized family
                 reunification and occupation in admission of new
                 migrants. Added overall numerical limits and established
                 quotas in Western Hemisphere.
1975   **Operation New Life**
                 Parole action by attorney general to admit over 130,000
                 Southeast Asian refugees, predominantly from Vietnam
                 and Cambodia.

NOTES

Introduction. The Interest of Many:
The Foundations of International Adoption

1. Statistics, Bureau of Consular Affairs, U.S. Department of State webpage, http://travel.state
.gov/content/adoptionsabroad/en/about-us/statistics.html (accessed January 13, 2015); Adam
Pertman, *Adoption Nation: How the Adoption Revolution Is Changing America* (New York: Basic,
2001).

2. David Crary, "Why Are Foreign Adoptions in the U.S. on the Decline?" *Christian Science
Monitor*, March 21, 2014; John M. Simmons, "Why the Decline in International Adoptions?,"
Huffington Post, April 8, 2014; Rachel L. Swarns, "U.S. Adoptions from Abroad Decline Sharply,"
New York Times, January 24, 2013, sec. World; Landrieu Introduces CHIFF Legislation, September
19, 2013, http://childreninfamiliesfirst.org/landrieu-introduces-chiff-legislation/. For analysis on
CHIFF, see Nila Bala, "The Children in Families First Act: Overlooking International Law and
the Best Interests of the Child," *Stanford Law Review Online* 66 (April 18, 2014): 135–42.

3. Domestic and transracial adoption statistics are uneven and spotty from 1945 to 1955,
since they relied on states to report data and social welfare experts did not have reliable sources
to track the number of independent adoptions conducted. These figures are estimates based on
the following sources: Penelope L. Maza, "Adoption Trends: 1944–1975," Child Welfare Research
Notes #9 (U.S. Children's Bureau, August 1984), 1–4, Box 65, Folder: Adoption-Research-
Reprints of Articles, CWLA papers; Lena Heyman to Alan Olschwang, June 14, 1965, Box 1033,
Folder: Non-resident Problems (includes Juvenile Immigration, Transient Boys), June 1965, 1963–
68, USCB papers; Barbara Melosh, *Strangers and Kin: The American Way of Adoption* (Cambridge,
Mass.: Harvard University Press, 2002), 160.

4. Christina Klein, *Cold War Orientalism: Asia in the Middlebrow Imagination, 1945–1961*
(Berkeley: University of California Press, 2003), 188; Christian G. Appy, ed., *Culture Politics and
the Cold War* (Amherst: University of Massachusetts Press, 2000).

5. Senate Committee on the Judiciary, *Authorizing Additional Visas for Orphans*, 84th Cong.,
2nd sess., 1956, S. Rpt. 2684, 3; Betsy Carrington, Vice Chairperson of the ISS Intercountry Adoption Committee, to Charles Akre, Chairperson, July 31, 1963, Box 3, Folder: Administration:
Comm Intercountry Adoption Correspondence, 1963–1966, ISS papers. In this case, orphans were
envisioned as "modular" entities, capable of "merg[ing]" with a particular political and cultural
landscape. This is a more literal rendering of Benedict Anderson's argument about nationalisms.
See Anderson, *Imagined Communities*, rev. ed. (London: Verso, 2006), 4.

6. Andrew J. F. Morris, *The Limits of Voluntarism: Charity and Welfare from the New Deal
Through the Great Society* (New York: Cambridge University Press, 2009). For private organizations' influence on foreign policy, see Sara Fieldston, *Raising the World: Child Welfare in the*

American Century (Cambridge, Mass.: Harvard University Press, 2015); and David Ekbladh, *The Great American Mission: Modernization and the Construction of an American World Order* (Princeton, N.J.: Princeton University Press, 2010), 6.

7. The literature on the welfare state and public-private collaboration is vast. The following is a small sample: Jennifer Klein, *For All These Rights: Business, Labor, and the Shaping of America's Public-Private Welfare State* (Princeton, N.J.: Princeton University Press, 2006); Michael Katz, *In the Shadow of the Poorhouse: A Social History of Welfare in America* (New York: Basic, 1996); Susan J. Pearson, *The Rights of the Defenseless: Protecting Animals and Children in Gilded Age America* (Chicago: University of Chicago Press, 2011); Meg Jacobs, *Pocketbook Politics: Economic Citizenship in Twentieth-Century America* (Princeton, N.J.: Princeton University Press, 2007); Alan Brinkley, *The End of Reform: New Deal Liberalism in Recession and War* (New York: Knopf, 1995); Jacob Hacker, *The Divided Welfare State: The Battle over Public and Private Social Benefits in the United States* (Cambridge: Cambridge University Press, 2002); and Walter W. Powell and Elisabeth S. Clemens, eds., *Private Action and the Public Good* (New Haven, Conn.: Yale University Press, 1998).

8. Lizabeth Cohen, *A Consumers' Republic: The Politics of Mass Consumption in Postwar America* (New York: Vintage, 2003).

9. As Regina Kunzel aptly argues, professionalization was an uneven process with expansions and contractions. Kunzel, *Fallen Women, Problem Girls: Unmarried Mothers and the Professionalization of Social Work, 1890–1945* (New Haven, Conn.: Yale University Press, 1993), 163. Rickie Solinger also argues this but in the post–World War II era. See Solinger, *Wake Up Little Susie: Single Pregnancy and Race Before Roe v. Wade* (New York: Routledge, 1992), 15–16. In her book that examines commercial and independent adoptions across the U.S.-Canadian border, Karen Balcom highlights the uneven role of the welfare community in shaping and implementing adoption policies, but does not stress the pivotal role of independent actors in policymaking. See Balcom, *The Traffic in Babies: Cross-Border Adoption and Baby-Selling Between the United States and Canada, 1930–1972* (Toronto: University of Toronto Press, 2011). For the argument that social workers solidified their professional authority from the Progressive Era throughout the Cold War, see Melosh, *Strangers and Kin*; Ellen Herman, "The Paradoxical Rationalization of Modern Adoption," *Journal of Social History* 36, no. 2 (Winter 2002): 350–55; and Julie Berebitsky, *Like Our Very Own: Adoption and the Changing Culture of Motherhood* (Lawrence: University of Kansas Press, 2001).

10. Michael Mann, "The Autonomous Power of the State: Its Origins, Mechanisms, and Results," in *States in History*, ed. John A. Hall (Oxford: Oxford University Press, 1986), 109–36, as cited in William Novak, "The Myth of the 'Weak' American State," *American Historical Review* 113, no. 3 (June 2008): 763, 770. Also see Gary Gerstle, "A State Both Strong and Weak," *American Historical Review* 115, no. 3 (June 2010): 779–85.

11. For more on this intersection, see James T. Campbell, Matthew Pratt Guterl, and Robert G. Lee, eds., *Race, Nation, and Empire in American History* (Chapel Hill: University of North Carolina Press, 2007). While Western European countries and Australia did conduct some foreign adoptions from Korea and Vietnam, the numbers were small compared to the U.S. program.

12. Carl Bon Tempo, *Americans at the Gate: The United States and Refugees During the Cold War* (Princeton, N.J.: Princeton University Press, 2008).

13. Until the Refugee Act of 1980, lawmakers included refugee provisions under general immigration law. Bon Tempo; Mae M. Ngai, *Impossible Subjects: Illegal Aliens and the Making of*

Modern America (Princeton, N.J.: Princeton University Press, 2004); Gary Gerstle, *American Crucible: Race and Nation in the Twentieth Century* (Princeton, N.J.: Princeton University Press, 2002); and Roger Daniels, *Guarding the Golden Door: Immigration Policy and Immigrants Since 1882* (New York: Macmillan, 2005).

14. Arissa Oh has argued that even though international adoptions did not begin in South Korea, it was this Asian nation that most influentially shaped international adoption's "culturally powerful practice." See *To Save the Children of Korea: The Cold War Origins of International Adoption* (Stanford, Calif.: Stanford University Press, 2015), 2.

15. There is a growing literature that tackles the history of international adoption. Arissa Oh's 2015 book, *To Save the Children of Korea*, notably explores both the push factors from Korea and the pull factors to the United States, offering a true transnational history. Catherine Ceniza Choy's 2013 book attempts to survey international adoption in Asia, but only considers the International Social Service-American Branch papers and neglects to examine Vietnam, anchoring her conception of policy formation to child welfare professionals. See Choy, *Global Families: A History of Asian International Adoption in America* (New York: New York University Press, 2013). Laura Briggs effectively situates the domestic transracial adoptions of African American and American Indian children alongside adoptions and rescue campaigns in Asia and Guatemala. See Briggs, *Somebody's Children: The Politics of Transracial and Transnational Adoption* (Durham, N.C.: Duke University Press, 2012). For other works that consider international adoption in the past and present, see Karen Dubinsky, *Babies Without Borders: Adoption and Migration Across the Americas* (New York: New York University Press, 2010); Balcom, *The Traffic in Babies*; Sara K. Dorow, *Transnational Adoption: A Cultural Economy of Race, Gender, and Kinship* (New York: New York University Press, 2006); and Klein, *Cold War Orientalism*. Works on the history of adoption in America typically include a chapter on international adoption. See Ellen Herman, *Kinship by Design* (Chicago: University of Chicago Press, 2008); Melosh; *Strangers and Kin*; E. Wayne Carp, ed., *Adoption in America: Historical Perspectives* (Ann Arbor: University of Michigan Press, 2004).

16. Ngai, *Impossible Subjects*, 9.

17. Peggy Pascoe attributes the conservative adoption of colorblindness to the decision in the *Loving v. Virginia* (1967) case. Matthew Lassiter points to its grassroots suburban origins in the North Carolina debates over busing in the early 1970s. See Pascoe, *What Comes Naturally: Miscegenation Law and the Making of Race in America* (Cambridge: Oxford University Press, 2008); Lassiter, "The Suburban Origins of 'Color-Blind' Conservatism: Middle-Class Consciousness in the Charlotte Busing Crisis," *Journal of Urban History* 30, no. 4 (May 2004): 549–82; and Jacquelyn Dowd Hall, "The Long Civil Rights Movement and the Political Uses of the Past," *Journal of American History* 91, no. 4 (March 2005): 1237–38.

18. Charlotte Brooks, *Alien Neighbors, Foreign Friends: Asian Americans, Housing, and the Transformation of Urban California* (Chicago: University of Chicago Press, 2009), 227–29, 238–39. Also see Klein, *Cold War Orientalism*; Henry Yu, *Thinking Orientals: Migration, Contact, and Exoticism in Modern America* (Oxford: Oxford University Press, 2001); and Chiou-Ling Yeh, *Making an American Festival: Chinese New Year in San Francisco's Chinatown* (Berkeley: University of California Press, 2008).

19. Michael Omi and Howard Winant, *Racial Formation in the United States: From the 1960s to the 1990s*, 2nd ed. (New York: Routledge, 1994).

20. Ruth Frankenberg, *White Women, Race Matters: The Social Construction of Whiteness* (Minneapolis: University of Minnesota Press, 1993), 17; Pamela Anne Quiroz, *Adoption in a Color-Blind Society* (New York: Rowman & Littlefield, 2007); Michael K. Brown et al., *Whitewashing*

Race: The Myth of a Color-Blind Society (Berkeley: University of California Press, 2003); Neil Gotanda, "A Critique of "Our Constitution Is Colorblind," *Stanford Law Review* 44, no. 1 (November 1991): 18; and Dubinsky, *Babies Without Borders*, 68.

21. Gina Miranda Samuels, "Beyond the Rainbow: Multiraciality in the 21st Century," in *Our Diverse Society: Race and Ethnicity Implications for 21st Century American Society*, ed. David Engstrom (Washington, D.C.: National Association of Social Workers Press, 2006), 52.

22. For the nineteenth- and twentieth-century interpretations and usages of humanitarianism in the West in general and the United States in particular, see Michael Barnett, *Empire of Humanity: A History of Humanitarianism* (Ithaca, N.Y.: Cornell University Press, 2011).

23. Chief Julia Lathrop to Dr. H. H. Hart, August 14, 1918; Lulie Jones to Julia Lathrop, November 20, 1918; Julia Lathrop to Lulie Jones, November 21, 1918; Immigration Commissioner to Anthony Caminetti, March 25, 1916, all in Box 67, Folder: War in Relation to Dependency, USCB papers.

24. Melosh, *Strangers and Kin*, 158; E. Wayne Carp, *Family Matters: Secrecy and Disclosure in the History of Adoption* (Cambridge, Mass.: Harvard University Press, 1998), 34; and Klein, *Cold War Orientalism*.

25. Laura Briggs, "Mother, Child, Race, Nation: The Visual Iconography of Rescue and the Politics of Transracial and Transnational Adoption," *Gender & History* 15 (2003): 179–200; and Arissa Oh, "A New Kind of Missionary Work: Christians, Christian Americanists, and the Adoption of Korean GI Babies, 1955–1961," *Women's Studies Quarterly* 33 (Fall/Winter 2005): 161–88.

26. Penny Von Eschen, *Satchmo Blows Up the World: Jazz Ambassadors Play the Cold War* (Cambridge, Mass.: Harvard University Press, 2004); Mary L. Dudziak, *Cold War Civil Rights: Race and the Image of American Democracy* (Princeton, N.J.: Princeton University Press, 2000); and Dudziak, "Josephine Baker, Racial Protest, and the Cold War," *Journal of American History* 81, no. 2 (September 1994): 543–70.

27. See Yara-Colette Lemke Muniz de Faria, "Germany's 'Brown Babies' Must Be Helped! Will You? U.S. Adoption Plans for Afro-German Children," *Callaloo* 26, no. 2 (2003): 342–62.

28. As works by Melani McAlister and Amy Kaplan have shown, intersecting these ostensibly disparate ideological spaces sheds light on state power not as a "one-way imposition" but a multi-lane migration of people, ideas, and policies. See Kaplan, *The Anarchy of Empire in the Making of U.S. Culture* (Cambridge, Mass.: Harvard University Press, 2005); and McAlister, *Epic Encounters: Culture, Media, and U.S. Interests in the Middle East Since 1945* (Berkeley: University of California Press, 2005).

29. James Scott, *Domination and the Arts of Resistance: Hidden Transcripts* (New Haven, Conn.: Yale University Press, 1992).

30. For example, see Jane Jeong Trenka, Julia Chinyere Oparah, and Sun Yung Shin, eds., *Outsiders Within: Writing on Transracial Adoption* (Cambridge, Mass.: South End Press, 2006); Tobias Hubinette, *Comforting an Orphaned Nation: Representations of International Adoption and Adopted Koreans in Korean Popular Culture* (Seoul: Jimoondang, 2006); Kim Jackson, Heewon Lee, Jae Ran Kim, Kim Park Nelson, and Wing Young Huie, *Here: A Visual History of Adopted Koreans in Minnesota* (St. Paul, Minn.: Yeong & Yeong, 2010).

31. Senate Committee on the Judiciary, *Authorizing Additional Visas for Orphans*, 84th Cong., 2nd sess., 1956, S. Rpt. 2684, 3. Also see Dubinsky, *Babies Without Borders*, esp. chap. 2.

32. For more on this construction of orphans in the late nineteenth and early twentieth centuries, see Linda Gordon, *The Great Arizona Orphan Abduction* (Cambridge, Mass.: Harvard

University Press, 1999). For an argument on how the legal definitions of orphans often depended on social and cultural conceptions of worthy parents, see Rickie Solinger, *Beggars and Choosers: How the Politics of Choice Shapes Adoption, Abortion, and Welfare in the United States* (New York: Hill and Wang, 2001), 22, 32.

Chapter 1. "Babyselling Rings," "Adoption Mills," and "Baby Rackets": Formalizing Policies and Manufacturing Markets

1. Eleanor Roosevelt, "The Cradle Society Improves Scientific Child Care Methods," *Washington Daily News*, February 4, 1944, Box 169, Folder: Adoption, 1941–1944, USCB papers.

2. Maurine Thompson, Secretary to Mrs. Roosevelt, to Martha Eliot, February 19, 1944; Katharine Lenroot to Eleanor Roosevelt, March 4, 1944, both in Box 169, Folder: Adoption, 1941–1944, USCB papers; and Ellen Herman, *Kinship by Design: A History of Adoption in the Modern United States* (Chicago: University of Chicago Press, 2008), 43–45.

3. An Act to Provide for the Adoption of Children, General Court of Massachusetts, Sect. 5, May 24, 1851, in *Families by Law: An Adoption Reader*, ed. Naomi R. Cahn and Joan Heifetz Hollinger (New York: New York University Press, 2004), 9–10.

4. Naomi Cahn, "Perfect Substitutes or the Real Thing?" in *Families by Law*, ed. Cahn and Hollinger, 22–23.

5. Herman, *Kinship by Design*, 21.

6. Kriste Lindenmeyer, *"A Right to Childhood": The U.S. Children's Bureau and Child Welfare, 1912–46* (Urbana: University of Illinois Press, 1997).

7. Herman, *Kinship by Design*, 57.

8. Ibid., 58–60; and Robyn Muncy, *Creating a Female Dominion in American Reform, 1890–1935* (New York: Oxford University Press, 1991).

9. Herman, *Kinship by Design*, 61.

10. Bertha Holt, *Bring My Sons from Afar* (Eugene, Ore.: Holt International Children's Services, 1986), 131–32.

11. Some professionals, like Arnold Gesell, went against this grain, arguing instead that a "good" home was better than a "bad" home. See Herman, *Kinship by Design*, 164–76.

12. See Molly Ladd-Taylor, *Mother-Work: Women, Child Welfare, and the State, 1890–1930* (Urbana: University of Illinois Press, 1994); and Theda Skocpol, *Protecting Soldiers and Mothers: The Political Origins of Social Policy in the United States* (Cambridge, Mass.: Harvard University Press, 1992).

13. Regina Kunzel, *Fallen Women, Problem Girls: Unmarried Mothers and the Professionalization of Social Work, 1890–1945* (New Haven, Conn.: Yale University Press, 1993), 128–10, 169; and Rickie Solinger, *Wake Up Little Susie: Single Pregnancy and Race Before* Roe v. Wade (New York: Routledge, 1992).

14. Ellen Herman, "The Paradoxical Rationalization for Modern Adoption," *Journal of Social History* 36, no. 2 (Winter 2002): 350–55.

15. Barbara Melosh, *Strangers and Kin: The American Way of Adoption* (Cambridge, Mass.: Harvard University Press, 2002), 15; Julie Berebitsky, *Like Our Very Own: Adoption and the Changing Culture of Motherhood, 1851–1950* (Lawrence: University of Kansas Press, 2000), chap. 2; and Brian Paul Gill, "Adoption Agencies and the Search for the Ideal Family, 1918–1965" in *Adoption*

in America: Historical Perspectives, ed. E. Wayne Carp (Ann Arbor: University of Michigan Press, 2002), 160.

16. Herman, *Kinship by Design*, 134–35.

17. Ibid., 143.

18. Henrietta L. Gordon, *Adoption Practices, Procedures, and Problems: Report of Workshop Material and Proceedings of the Adoption Conference, Held May 19–21, 1948 in New York City* (New York: Child Welfare League of America, 1949), 25–26.

19. Mary Ryan, *Cradle of the Middle Class* (Cambridge: Cambridge University Press, 1981), ch. 4; and Gary Cross, *The Cute and the Cool: Wondrous Innocence and Modern American Children's Culture* (New York: Oxford University Press, 2004), 27–29.

20. Marilyn Irvin Holt, *The Orphan Trains: Placing Out in America* (Lincoln: University of Nebraska Press, 1992); Stephen O'Connor, *Orphan Trains: The Story of Charles Loring Brace and the Children He Saved and Failed* (Boston: Houghton Mifflin, 2001); and Herman, *Kinship by Design*, 24–25.

21. Viviana A. Zelizer, *Pricing the Priceless Child* (New York: Basic, 1985), 72; and Michael B. Katz, *In the Shadow of the Poorhouse: A Social History of Welfare in America* (New York: Basic, 1986). This protection of innocence did not extend to black children until the mid-twentieth century. See Robin Bernstein, *Racial Innocence: Performing American Childhood from Slavery to Civil Rights* (New York: New York University Press, 2011).

22. Zelizer, *Pricing the Priceless Child*, 173–77; Herman, *Kinship by Design*, 31–36; and Sherri Broder, *Tramps, Unfit Mothers, and Neglected Children: Negotiating the Family in Nineteenth-Century Philadelphia* (Philadelphia: University of Pennsylvania Press, 2002). See also Viviana Zelizer, *The Social Meaning of Money* (New York: Basic, 1994), chaps. 4–5.

23. Zelizer, *Pricing the Priceless Child*, 171, 193; and Berebitsky, *Like Our Very Own*, 11.

24. Catherine Ross, "Society's Children: The Care of Indigent Youngsters in New York City, 1875–1903," in *Families by Law*, ed. Cahn and Hollinger, 15.

25. Herman, *Kinship by Design*, 36–39; and Zelizer, *Pricing the Priceless Child*, 192.

26. Herman, *Kinship by Design*, 40–43; and Zelizer, *Pricing the Priceless Child*, 190–92.

27. Program Research Branch, Social Statistics Section, Children's Bureau, April 3, 1951, Box 449, Folder: Adoptions, 1949–52, USCB papers. Also see Evelyn Smith to Hazel Ferguson, November 24, 1952, Box 445, Folder: Traffic in Children, Baby Farms, 1949–52; and Martha Eliot to Warren Olney III (DOJ), December 13, 1954, Box 674, Folder: Traffic in Children, Baby Farms, 1953–56, both in USCB papers.

28. See Herman, *Kinship by Design*; and Balcom, *The Traffic in Babies*.

29. Zelizer, *Pricing the Priceless Child*, 11.

30. Berebitsky, *Like Our Very Own*, 60; and Zelizer, *Pricing the Priceless Child*, 196–97.

31. Mona Gardner, "Traffic in Babies," *Collier's*, September 16, 1939, 14; and Zelizer, *Pricing the Priceless Child*, 199.

32. Virginia Reid, "Black Market Babies," *Woman's Home Companion*, December 1944, 30–31. See also Herman, *Kinship by Design*, 139–42.

33. Balcom, *The Traffic in Babies*, 60–62.

34. The sale of children is still a "purchase of intimacy" that most economists reject. See Viviana A. Zelizer, *The Purchase of Intimacy* (Princeton, N.J.: Princeton University Press, 2005), 80–88.

35. Balcom, *The Traffic in Babies*, 62; " 'Phony Mothers' and Border-Crossing Adoptions: The Montreal-to-New York Black Market in Babies in the 1950s," *Journal of Women's History* 19, no. 1 (2007): 107–16; and Zelizer, *Pricing the Priceless Child*, 202.

36. Balcom, *The Traffic in Babies*, 62.

37. Zelizer, *Pricing the Priceless Child*, 203–5; and Balcom, *The Traffic in Babies*, 63.

38. Herman, *Kinship by Design*, 107, 136.

39. Maud Morlock, "Babies on the Market," reprint from USCB Survey Midmonthly, March 1945, Box 159, Folder: Adoption, January 1945–June 1945, USCB papers.

40. Ralph N. Kallock, "So You're Buying a New Automobile," *University of Pittsburgh Law Review* 10 (1948–1949): 42; and Scott D. Gilbert, Eugene A. Ludwig, and Carol A. Fortine, "Federal Trademark Law and the Gray Market: The Need for a Cohesive Policy," *Law and Policy in International Business* 18, no. 1 (1986): 103–43.

41. Edith M. Stern, "Gray-Market Babies," *Woman's Home Companion*, June 1949, 32–33. Other early examples are Coleman to Moss, August 31, 1949, Box 449, Folder: Adoptions, 1949–52, USCB papers; Ellis Michael, "The Shame of Illegitimacy," *Coronet*, September 1949, 27; and Albert Maisel, "Why You Can't Adopt a Baby," *Woman's Home Companion*, March 1950. Even the *Yale Law Journal* article "Moppets on the Market," which the USCB considered the best expert perspective on independent adoptions, included the term in a footnote. See "Moppets on the Market: The Problem of Unregulated Adoption," *Yale Law Journal* 59, no. 4 (March 1950): 715–36; and Dorthea Andrews to Raymond Schuessler, January 29, 1952, Box 445, Folder: Traffic in Children, Baby Farms, 1949–52, USCB papers.

42. A. Katsenelinboigen, "Coloured Markets in the Soviet Union," *Soviet Studies* 29, no. 1 (January 1977): 62–85; Herman, *Kinship by Design*, 36–40; "Babies on the Market," clipping from *Survey Midmonthly*, March 1945, Box 159, Folder: Adoption, January 1945–June 1945, USCB papers; Dorthea Andrews to Daniel Button, October 25, 1951, Box 445, Folder: Traffic in Children, Baby Farms, 1949–52, USCB papers; and Zelizer, *Pricing the Priceless Child*, 203.

43. Balcom, *Traffic in Babies*, 62; and Herman, *Kinship by Design*, 138–39.

44. Zelizer, *Pricing the Priceless Child*, 11.

45. Meg Jacobs, *Pocketbook Politics: Economic Citizenship in Twentieth-Century America* (Princeton, N.J.: Princeton University Press, 2005), 202, 204, 220; Jacobs, "'How About Some Meat?': The Office of Price Administration, Consumption Politics, and State Building from the Bottom Up, 1941–1946," *Journal of American History* 84, no. 3 (December 1997): 917; and Emily Bentley, *Eating for Victory: Food Rationing and the Politics of Domesticity* (Urbana: University of Illinois Press, 1998), 36–37.

46. Herman, *Kinship by Design*, 154.

47. Memo to State Welfare Directors, "'Black Market' in Babies," October 11, 1951, Box 445, Folder: Traffic in Children, Baby Farms, 1949–52, USCB papers.

48. Zelizer, *Pricing the Priceless Child*, 189–95.

49. Memo: Orville Crays to Louise Noble, November 2, 1951, Box 445, Folder: Traffic in Children, Baby Farms, 1949–52, USCB papers; Robert Mills, "Lawyer on Trial in Unwed Mom Adoption Mill," *New York Post*, June 17, 1952; Natalie Tiranno and Harry Cohen, "Baby Mother Gave Away Sold to Grocer at $1,300," *New York Daily Mirror*, June 19, 1952; "Baby Black Market Case Begun by State," *New York Herald Tribune*, June 19, 1952; and "Suing Siegal in Baby Racket, Judge Is Sorry," clipping in Box 445, Folder: Traffic in Children, Baby Farms, 1949–52, USCB papers. See also Jess Stearn, "There Are 10 Takers for Every Child," *Sunday News* (New York), April 17, 1949, 6–7.

50. Henry F. Pringle and Katharine Pringle, "Babies for Sale," *Saturday Evening Post*, December 22, 1951, 11–13.

51. Press Form Letter, October 11, 1951, Box 445, Folder: Traffic in Children, Baby Farms, 1949–52; and Morlock, "Babies on the Market."

52. Division of Social Services, "Summary of Discussion on 'Black Market' in Babies," February 12, 1954, Box 674, Folder: Traffic in Children, Baby Farms, 1953–56, USCB papers.

53. "Progress Report, Project on Prevention of Black Market in Babies and Other Unprotected Adoptive Placements," April 5, 1955, 3, Box 674, Folder: Traffic in Children, Baby Farms, 1953–56, USCB papers.

54. Herman, *Kinship by Design*, 45.

55. Balcom, *The Traffic in Babies*, 4.

56. Minutes, "Salt Lake Conference on Interstate and International Placements," June 4–5, 1951, 1, Box 445, Folder: Interstate Transportation of Dependents, 1949–52, USCB papers.

57. Herman, *Kinship by Design*, 43; "Dead Director Blamed in Black Baby Market," *Chicago Daily News*, September 16, 1950, 8; " 'Baby Market' Charged: Memphis Foundling 'Sales' Estimated at $1,000,000," *New York Times*, September 13, 1950, 23; Linda Austin, *Babies for Sale: The Tennessee Children's Home Adoption Scandal* (Westport, Conn.: Praeger, 1993); and Barbara Raymond, *The Baby Thief: The Untold Story of Georgia Tann, the Babyseller Who Corrupted Adoption* (New York: Carroll & Graf, 2007).

58. Ellis Michael, "The Shame of Illegitimacy," *Coronet*, September 1949, 27.

59. Report of Current Adoption Agency Practices in Connecticut-Independent and Agency Placement, May 1948, Box 449, Folder: Adoptions, 1949–52, USCB papers.

60. Program Research Branch, Social Statistics Section, Children's Bureau, April 3, 1951, Box 449, Folder: Adoptions, 1949–52, USCB papers. Also see Smith to Ferguson, November 24; and Eliot to Olney (DOJ), December 13, 1954, Box 674; E. Wayne Carp, *Family Matters: Secrecy and Disclosure in the History of Adoption* (Cambridge, Mass.: Harvard University Press, 1998), 26; and Melosh, *Strangers and Kin*, 108.

61. Children's Bureau Press Release, November 4, 1951, Box 445, Folder: Traffic in Children, Baby Farms, 1949–52, USCB papers.

62. "Conference with Mr. Reid and Mr. Schapiro of the Child Welfare League, and Miss Arnold," October 29, 1954, Box 674, Folder: Traffic in Children, Baby Farms, 1953–56, USCB papers.

63. Alfred Melucci to Margaret Thornhill, March 15, 1955, Box 674, Folder: Traffic in Children, Baby Farms, 1953–56, USCB papers.

64. Maxine Harrigan to Dr. Eliot, October 14, 1954, Box 685, Folder: Adoptions, September 1954, 1954–1956, USCB papers.

65. Pearl S. Buck, "The Children Waiting," *Woman's Home Companion*, September 1955, 131.

66. Draft letter, Elizabeth Ross to Charles Schottland, August 25, 1955, Box 684, Folder: Adoptions, May 1956, 1953–1957, USCB papers; Joseph Reid to Mr. Paul C. Smith, Editor-in-Chief of *Woman's Home Companion*, September 15, 1955, Box 23, Folder: Welcome House, ISS papers; and Buck, "The Children Waiting," 32–33.

67. J. G. Riddle to Frank DeBlois, January 16, 1948, Box 158, Folder: Adoptions, January 1948, USCB papers.

68. See Linda Gordon, *Pitied But Not Entitled: Single Mothers and the Origins of Welfare* (Cambridge, Mass.: Harvard University Press, 1995).

69. Only fifteen states had laws against so-called "baby-selling": Alabama, Arizona, Colorado, Delaware, Florida, Georgia, Kentucky, Maryland, Massachusetts, Michigan, Minnesota,

New Jersey, New York, Utah, and Washington. J. G. Riddle to Frank De Blois, January 16, 1948; De Blois to Riddle, January 6, 1948, both in Box 158, Folder: Adoptions, January 1948, USCB papers; and "Progress Report, Project on Prevention of Black Market in Babies and Other Unprotected Adoptive Placements," April 5, 1955, 8–9, Box 674, Folder: Traffic in Children, Baby Farms, 1953–56, USCB papers. Also see "States Tighten Adoption Laws," *Parade*, May 1947, 183; and Marybeth Weinstein, "The Markets—Black and Gray—in Babies," *New York Times*, November 27, 1955, 248.

70. "Progress Report, Project on Prevention of Black Market in Babies and Other Unprotected Adoptive Placements," April 5, 1955, 6, Box 674, Folder: Traffic in Children, Baby Farms, 1953–56, USCB papers.

71. Helen Witmer to Margaret Thornhill, November 4, 1954, Box 674, Folder: Traffic in Children, Baby Farms, 1953–56, USCB papers.

72. "Conference with Mr. Reid and Mr. Schapiro of the Child Welfare League, and Miss Arnold," October 29, 1954, Box 674, Folder: Traffic in Children, Baby Farms, 1953–56, USCB papers.

73. Weinstein, "The Markets—Black and Gray—in Babies," 248; and Balcom, *The Traffic in Babies*, 64, 157, 171, 177–78.

74. Herman, *Kinship by Design*, 229–38.

75. Smith to Johnson, June 15, 1951; Johnson to Smith, May 25, 1951; Report of Current Adoption Agency Practices in Connecticut—Independent and Agency Placement, May 1948; all in Box 449, Folder: Adoptions, 1949–52; and Taylor to Shulsky, November 10, 1950, Box 450, Folder: Adoptions, 1949–52, USCB papers. Also see Herman, *Kinship by Design*, 143–44.

76. Miss Shepperson to Martha Eliot, February 24, 1944, Box 169, Folder: Adoption, 1941–1944, USCB papers.

Chapter 2. "An International Baby Hunt": The "Gray Market" in Greece

1. Ernest Mitler, "Report on Inter-Country Adoptions," December 28, 1959, 19, Box 17, Folder 1, Child Welfare League of America papers, Social Welfare History Archives, University of Minnesota (hereafter CWLA papers). Mitler also examined independent adoptions from Italy.

2. The larceny and bootlegging both happened in the 1920s during Prohibition and were related to liquor purchases and trafficking. He served a total of nine months at a work farm and county jail. Mitler, "Survey of Greek-U.S. Proxy Adoptions," 4, Box 11, Folder: Adoption Manual and Other Printed Material, ISS papers.

3. Mitler, "Report on Inter-Country Adoptions," 2, 7–8, 18–19.

4. "AHEPA Order Elects Officers," *New York Times*, August 21, 1950, 17; and George J. Leber, *The History of the Order of AHEPA* (Washington, D.C.: Order of AHEPA, 1972), 393, 408–9, 494, 506.

5. For more on the links between consumerism and foreign and domestic policies, especially during the Cold War, see Lizabeth Cohen, *A Consumers' Republic: The Politics of Mass Consumption in Postwar America* (New York: Knopf, 2003); Reinhold Wagnleitner, *Coca-Colonization and the Cold War: The Cultural Mission of the United States in Austria After the Second World War* (Chapel Hill: University of North Carolina Press, 1994); Victoria De Grazia, *Irresistible Empire: America's Advance Through Twentieth-Century Europe* (Cambridge, Mass.: Belknap Press of Harvard University Press, 2005); and Laura A. Belmonte, *Selling the American Way: U.S. Propaganda*

and the Cold War (Philadelphia: University of Pennsylvania Press, 2008). This chapter also hopes to help historicize the current literature on adoption markets. For instance, see Michele Bratcher Goodwin, ed., *Baby Markets: Money and the New Politics of Creating Families* (Cambridge: Cambridge University Press, 2010); and Kim Park Nelson, "Shopping for Children in the International Marketplace," in *Outsiders Within: Writing on Transracial Adoption*, ed. Jane Jeong Trenka, Julia Chinyere Oparah, and Sun Yung Shin (Cambridge, Mass.: South End Press, 2006), 89–104.

6. Christina Klein, *Cold War Orientalism: Asia in the Middlebrow Imagination, 1945–1961* (Berkeley: University of California Press, 2003), 22, 36. Scholars typically use the Cold War to explain why Americans suddenly started being open to adopting across racial and national boundaries, but have not explored how the Cold War also affected social policy structures.

7. The *New York Times* reported that petitions to adopt increased 30 percent from 1944 to 1953. "New Laws Sought by Adoption Units," *New York Times*, June 25, 1956, 24. Also see Elaine Tyler May, *Barren in the Promised Land: Childless Americans and the Pursuit of Happiness* (Cambridge, Mass.: Harvard University Press, 1997), ch. 4.

8. Victoria De Grazia's work, on what she calls the Market Empire, informs my understanding of international adoption as another aspect of the United States asserting its global leadership. See De Grazia, *Irresistible Empire*, 6–7.

9. Mrs. Kanes to Miss Lenroot, June 5, 1945, Box 161, Folder: Appeals from People Wishing Children for Adoption, May–June 1945; Emery to London, December 16, 1947, Box 160, Folder: Appeals from People Wishing Children for Adoption, July–December 1947; and Ford to Lenroot, July 22, 1947, Box 160, Folder: Appeals from People Wishing Children for Adoption, July–December 1947, USCB papers.

10. Hall to the U.S. Committee for the Case of European Children (forwarded to USCB), December 27, 1949, Box 445, Folder: Interstate Transportation of Dependents, 1949–52, USCB papers.

11. Bolton to Lenroot, February 24, 1950, Box 445, Folder: Interstate Transportation of Dependents, 1949–52, USCB papers.

12. For example, see Campbell to USCB, February 20, 1950, Box 452. Boxes 451 and 452 are filled with these types of requests and staff replies that emphasize how adoptive parents significantly outnumber available children. Also see Mildred Arnold to Staff, Division of Social Services, March 27, 1950, Box 449, Folder: Adoptions, 1949–52, USCB papers; and Viviana Zelizer, *Pricing the Priceless Child: The Changing Social Value of Children* (New York: Basic, 1985), 200.

13. Harry S. Truman, "Statement and Directive by the President on Immigration to the United States of Certain Displaced Persons and Refugees in Europe," December 22, 1945, *The American Presidency Project*, http://www.presidency.ucsb.edu/ws/?pid=12253 (accessed March 29, 2012); and Memorandum Concerning Official Basis of the Program of the United States Committee for the Care of European Children, Inc., 1953, 2–8, Box 23, Folder: U.S. Committee for the Care of European Children, ISS papers.

14. House Subcommittee on Immigration and Naturalization, Hearings: Regulating Powers of Attorney General to Suspend Deportation of Aliens, 80th Cong., 1st sess., April 21, 1947, 59.

15. "Problems in the International Placement of Children," July–August 1948, 4–7.

16. Truman, "Statement and Directive by the President on Immigration."

17. Senate Judiciary Committee, *Hearing on S. 830*, July 18, 1947, 80th Cong., 1st sess., 4–5.

18. Henry La Cossitt, "We Adopted a War Orphan," *Saturday Evening Post*, December 15, 1951, 26.

19. Clipping, "Why Does Christina's Mother Cry?" n.d., Box 133, Folder: Publicity, Displaced Person Commission Records.

20. Klein, *Cold War Orientalism*, 152–59; and Laura Briggs, "Mother, Child, Race, Nation: The Visual Iconography of Rescue and the Politics of Transnational and Transracial Adoption," *Gender & History* 15, no. 2 (August 2003): 179–200.

21. Alice B. Hiteman to Katherine Welch, USCB, November 6, 1950, Box 451, Folder: Adoptions, 1949–52, USCB papers.

22. "Orphans Clothed," *Life*, November 17, 1947, 57–60.

23. "Bread and Meat Amaze 67 DP Orphans in by Air," *New York World-Telegram*, March 17, 1949; "War Orphans Happy Learning United States Ways-102 Here from DP Camps-Waiting at Center for Foster Homes," *New York Sun*, March 17, 1949; "DP Children Here, Dazzled but Happy-Little Balts Are Bewildered by Pot Roast, Oranges, and Things in General," *New York Times*, March 17, 1949; "Ringlings to Play Santa Claus as Two DP Kids See First Circus," *Washington Times-Herald*, April 1, 1949. Additional articles include Melita Spraggs, "Jam on Their Bread: Help for 500 War Orphaned Allied Children," *Christian Science Monitor Magazine*, April 29, 1944, 5; and Gertrude Samuels, "Children Who Have Known No Childhood: Orphans of the Nazi Ghettos and Slave Labor Camps," *New York Times Magazine*, March 9, 1947, 12.

24. Julie Berebitsky, *Like Our Very Own* (Lawrence: University of Kansas Press, 2000), ch. 2; and Zelizer, *Pricing the Priceless Child*, 193.

25. Walter Davenport, "Uncle! Uncle! Hearts of America's Soldiers Go Out to Britain's War Orphans," March 27, 1943, *Colliers*, 54, 80.

26. *Hollywood Reporter*, February 10 and February 25, 1942, Folder: Woman of the Year-publicity, #3198, Box 272, George Stevens Papers, Margaret Herrick Film Library.

27. Herbert L. Larson, "Woman of Year Career Drama," February 13, 1942, *Portland Oregonian*, Folder: Woman of the Year-reviews, #3200, Box 272, George Stevens Papers, Margaret Herrick Film Library. Also see *Woman of the Year*, Lists-Subject Files, 1940–44, Margaret Herrick Film Library.

28. *Woman of the Year*, dir. George Stevens (1942; Culver City, Calif.: Metro-Goldwyn-Mayer Studios).

29. Bosley Crowther, "Movie Review: Woman of the Year (1942)," *New York Times*, February 6, 1942.

30. On the psychological stability of fathers, see Robert Griswold, *Fatherhood in America: A History* (New York: Basic, 1993).

31. Script, 130, Folder: Woman of the Year-script, #3186, Box 272, George Stevens Papers, Margaret Herrick Film Library.

32. Crowther, "Movie Review: Woman of the Year (1942)."

33. *The Return of Rusty*, dir. William Castle (1946; Los Angeles: Columbia Pictures); *The Vicious Years*, dir. Robert Florey (1950; USA: Emerald Productions); *Great Expectations*, dir. David Lean (1946; USA: Cineguild); *Oliver Twist*, dir. David Lean (1948; USA: Cineguild); *The Secret Garden*, dir. Fred M. Wilcox (1949; Culver City, Calif.: Metro-Goldwyn-Mayer Studios); and *Les Misérables*, dir. Lewis Milestone (1952; USA: Twentieth Century Fox).

34. Mildred Arnold to Administrators of State Public Welfare Agencies and Directors of Child Welfare, "Problems in the International Placement of Children," July–August 1948, 3–4, Box 154, Folder: Interstate Transportation of Dependents, April 1948, USCB papers.

35. *West's Encyclopedia of American Law*, 2nd ed. (New York: Thomson Gale, 2008); and "Memo on Consultations with United States Committee on the Care for European Children

looking toward their liquidation," March 20, 1953, Box 23, Folder: U.S. Committee for the Care of European Children, ISS papers.

36. I. Evelyn Smith, USCB, to Visa Division, State Dept., September 2, 1947; and H. J. L'Heureux, Visa Division Chief, October 3, 1947, both in Box 158, Folder: Adoptions, September 1947–October 1947, USCB papers. Also see Margaret Emery to Viola Frister, December 17, 1947, Box 158, Folder: Adoptions, November 1947–December 1947, USCB papers.

37. James McTigue, General Counsel, to Robert Corkery, European Coordinator, August 3, 1951, Box 65, Folder: Orphans, Displaced Persons Commission records.

38. Senate Committee of the Judiciary, *To Permit Certain Displaced Persons Under 14 Years of Age Orphaned as a Result of World War II to Enter the United Sates as Non-Quota Immigrants: Hearings on S. 830*, July 18, 1947, 28–30, 51; and Biographical Directory of the United States Congress, http://bioguide.congress.gov/scripts/biodisplay.pl?index = I000050 (accessed February 12, 2008).

39. Senate Committee of the Judiciary, *Certain Displaced Persons*, 5, 47.

40. Displaced Persons Act, Section 2(e) and 3(b).

41. Senate Committee of the Judiciary, *Certain Displaced Persons*, 17.

42. "Orphans of the European Storm: The DP Children," *Congressional Record*, House, April 5, 1949, A2130–31.

43. See Carl Bon Tempo, *Americans at the Gate: The United States and Refugees During the Cold War* (Princeton, N.J.: Princeton University Press, 2008). The next chapter explores more extensively the use of orphans as refugees in immigration law.

44. Displaced Persons Act of 1948, as amended June 1950, Public Law 555; and Minutes, "Salt Lake Conference on Interstate and International Placements," June 4–5, 1951, 5, Box 445, Folder: Interstate Transportation of Dependents, 1949–52, USCB papers.

45. Displaced Persons Act of 1948, Public Law 774, *U.S. Statutes at Large* 1009 (June 25, 1948); and Displaced Persons Act of 1948, as amended June 1950, Public Law 555, Sections 2(e) and 2(f).

46. McTigue to Corkery, August 3, 1951, 3, 5.

47. Memorandum Concerning Official Basis of the Program of the United States Committee for the Care of European Children, Inc., 1953, 2–8, Box 23, Folder: U.S. Committee for the Care of European Children, ISS papers.

48. List of Inquiries Received from Displaced Persons Commission, January 31, 1949, Box 30, Folder: Orphans List to USCEC, Displaced Persons Commission records; Kanes to Lenroot, June 5, 1945; and Alice Nutt to Kanes, June 23, 1945, both in Box 161, Folder: Appeals from People Wishing Children for Adoption, May–June 1945; Margaret Emery to Ada London, December 16, 1947, Box 160, Folder: Appeals from People Wishing Children for Adoption, July–December 1947; K. L. Osmun to Children's Bureau, November 27, 1948; and I. Evelyn Smith to Osmun, December 3, 1948, both in Box 154, Folder: Interstate Transportation of Dependents, April 1948, all in USCB papers. For more inquiries about war orphans, see Boxes 451–52, USCB papers.

49. Emery to Viola Frister, December 17, 1947, Box 158, Folder: Adoptions, November–December 1947, USCB papers.

50. Arnold to Administrators of State Public Welfare Agencies and Directors of Child Welfare, "Problems in the International Placement of Children," July–August 1948, 6–7, Box 154, Folder: Interstate Transportation of Dependents, April 1948, USCB papers.

51. Arnold to A. S. Waiss, October 4, 1949, Box 445, Folder: Interstate Transportation of Dependents, 1949–52, USCB papers; "Smith to Pepper," March 4, 1948, Box 164, Folder: Non-Resident Unwed Mothers (Interstate Problems), November 1947; and Arnold to Administrators of State Public Welfare Agencies "Problems in the International Placement of Children," 5.

52. Rauch to O'Connor, August 16, 1951, Box 58, Folder: Orphans-Public Law 555, Displaced Persons Commission records.

53. Martha Gellhorn, "Little Boy Found," *Saturday Evening Post*, April 15, 1950, 168.

54. "Adopted Greek Baby Meets U.S. Mother," January 14, 1955, *New York Herald Tribune* clipping; Maurice Johnson, IMP Photo, January 13, 1955, both in Box 13, Folder: Orphans, Refugee Relief Program Files; and "Greek Orphan Coming to New Home," January 3, 1955, *New York Times*, clipping in Box 31, Folder: ISS-Greek Branch, Adoptions File 1955–58, ISS papers.

55. Gellhorn, "Little Boy Found," 29.

56. Mark Mazower, "Introduction," in *After the War Was Over: Reconstructing the Family, Nation, and State in Greece, 1943–1960*, ed. Mazower (Princeton, N.J.: Princeton University Press, 2000), 6–7.

57. Robert M. Mages, "Without the Need of a Single American Rifleman: James Van Fleet and His Lessons Learned as Commander of the Joint United States Military Advisory and Planning Group During the Greek Civil War, 1948–1949," in *The U.S. Army and Irregular Warfare, 1775–2007*, ed. Richard G. Davis (Washington, D.C.: Center of Military History, 2007), 195–212.

58. Mazower, "Introduction," 7.

59. Mando Dalianis and Mark Mazower, "Children in Turmoil During the Civil War: Today's Adults," in *After the War Was Over*, ed. Mazower, 91–104; Loukianos Hassiotis, "Relocating Children During the Greek Civil War," in *The Disentanglement of Populations: Migration, Expulsion and Displacement in Post-War Europe, 1944–9*, ed. Jessica Reinisch and Elizabeth White (New York: Palgrave Macmillan, 2011), 271–88; Minutes, "Salt Lake Conference on Interstate and International Placements," June 4–5, 1951, 5, Box 445, Folder: Interstate Transportation of Dependents, 1949–52, USCB papers; and Note from the Greek Foreign Ministry, June 9, 1950, Box 133, Folder: Position of European Governments re Release of Children, Displaced Persons Commission records.

60. Lena Cochran and Helen McKay to Corkery, May 21, 1951, Box 132, Folder: Greece, Displaced Persons Commission records.

61. Hassiotis, "Relocating Children During the Greek Civil War," 275.

62. Eftihia Voutira and Aigli Brouskou, " 'Borrowed Children' in the Greek Civil War," in *Abandoned Children*, ed. Catherine Panter-Brick and Malcolm T. Smith (Cambridge: Cambridge University Press, 2000), 108.

63. Note from the Greek Foreign Ministry, June 9, 1950, Box 133, Folder: Position of European Governments re Release of Children; Robert Brown, U.S. Embassy to Department of State, September 6, 1950, Box 133, Folder: Position of European Governments re Release of Children; Child Welfare Officer to Robert Corkery, Monthly Report, March 10, 1952, Box 133, Folder: Monthly Field Reports (Greece), all in Displaced Persons Commission records; and Leber, *The History of the Order of AHEPA*, 378.

64. Cochran and McKay to Corkery, August 24, 1951, 3; and Rausch to Elliott Shirk, Bi-Annual Report from June 30, 1950 to February 1, 1951, May 8, 1951, Box 58, Folder: Orphan Program Monthly Report, both in Displaced Persons Commission records.

65. UN General Assembly, "Repatriation of Greek Children," October 16, 1951, Box 9, Folder: Displaced Persons Committee (Orphans Program) Order of AHEPA-Correspondence, U.S. Foreign Assistance Agency records.

66. "Orphan Greece," *Senior Scholastic*, March 1947, 5–6.

67. Ibid., 5; for more on efforts to engage the U.S. public with Greece's reconstruction, see De Grazia, *Irresistible Empire*, 347–49.

68. Senate Subcommittee, Hearing on Displaced Persons, 235.

69. Cohen, *A Consumer's Republic*, 126; and Diane Kunz, *Butter and Guns: American's Cold War Economic Diplomacy* (New York: Free Press, 1997).

70. McTigue to Corkery, August 3, 1951, 5.

71. For more on the Cold War propaganda wars, see Walter L. Hixson, *Parting the Curtain: Propaganda, Culture, and the Cold War* (New York: Palgrave Macmillan, 1997); and Stephen J. Whitfield, *The Culture of the Cold War* (Baltimore: Johns Hopkins University Press, 1996).

72. Matthew Frye Jacobson, *Whiteness of a Different Color: European Immigrants and the Alchemy of Race* (Cambridge, Mass.: Harvard University Press, 1998), 90–94.

73. Charles C. Moskos, *Greek Americans, Struggle and Success* (Piscataway, N.J.: Transaction, 1989), 40, 42. Also see Anna Karpathakis and Dan Georgakas, "Demythologizing Greek American Families," *Journal of the Hellenic Diaspora* 36, no. 1, 2 (2010): 45–61.

74. Editorial, *Observer (Fayetteville, N.C.),* n.d., as quoted in Leber, *The History of the Order of AHEPA*, 374–75. (Contextual evidence suggests that this ran sometime between 1954 and 1957.)

75. Mrs. Robert Todd to Children's Bureau, August 27, 1949, Box 452, Folder: Appeals for People Wishing Children for Adoption, 1949–52, RG 102, Archives II.

76. Mae Ngai, "'A Nation of Immigrants': The Cold War and Civil Rights Origins of Illegal Immigration," Paper 38 (Princeton, N.J.: Institute for Advanced Study, School of Social Science, April 2010), 5.

77. Senate Subcommittee, *Hearings on Displaced Persons*, 223.

78. Ibid.

79. Robert O. Self, *American Babylon: Race and the Struggle for Postwar Oakland* (Princeton, N.J.: Princeton University Press, 2003); Thomas Sugrue, *The Origins of the Urban Crisis: Race and Inequality in Postwar Detroit* (Princeton, N.J.: Princeton University Press, 1998); and Arnold R. Hirsch, *Making the Second Ghetto: Race and Housing in Chicago, 1940–1960* (Chicago: University of Chicago Press, 1998).

80. House Subcommittee, *Hearings: Regulating Powers of Attorney General*, 58–60, 62; Senate Subcommittee, *Hearings on Displaced Persons*, 233.

81. "Orphan Support Project of the Greek War Relief Association, Inc., USA," March 28, 1947, Box 154, Folder: Foreign Work and Organizations for Delinquent Children, Jan. 1945, USCB papers.

82. AHEPA collaborated with the Greek War Relief Association in raising $750,000 for a hospital in Greece. Arthur H. Lalos to Advisory Committee on Voluntary Foreign Aid, July 18, 1950, Box 9, Folder: Displaced Persons Committee (Orphans Program) Order of AHEPA, A and B, RG 469: Records of the U.S. Foreign Assistance Agencies, 1948–1961, Archives II.

83. Leber, *The History of the Order of AHEPA*, 361.

84. Senate Subcommittee, *Hearings on Displaced Persons*, 227, 229.

85. Leber, *The History of the Order of AHEPA*, 364, 366, 368, 374, 377, 381.

86. In theory, AHEPA membership was open to all ethnicities, but in practice most members were Greek. Moskos, *Greek Americans*, 40.

87. Harold H. Martin, "Greeks Know How to Die," *Saturday Evening Post*, July 7, 1951, 26; and Leber, *The History of the Order of AHEPA*, 385.

88. Leber, *The History of the Order of AHEPA*, 377, 385, 435–39.

89. House Committee, *Hearings on Admission of 300,000 Refugees*, 205.

90. For more on how the myth of U.S. expansiveness toward immigrant "super-citizens" reinforces U.S. democratic and liberal exceptionalism; see Ali Behdad, *A Forgetful Nation: On*

Immigration and Cultural Identity in the United States (Durham, N.C.: Duke University Press, 2005), 13.

91. Smith to M. Ingeborg Olsen, July 20, 1950, Box 450, Folder: Adoptions, 1949–52, USCB papers.

92. Senate Subcommittee on Amendments to Displaced Persons Act, *Hearing Displaced Persons*, 81st Cong., 1st sess., 1949, 221–24; and Leber, *The History of the Order of AHEPA*, 370, 372.

93. AHEPA prospective adoptive parent form letter, May 29, 1951, Box 9, Folder: Displaced Persons Committee (Orphans Program) Order of AHEPA-Correspondence, Foreign Service records; and House Committee on the Judiciary, Hearings on Admission of 300,000 Immigrants, 82nd Cong., 2nd sess., 1952, 205.

94. Memo on Consultations with United States Committee on the Care of European Children . . . , March 20, 1953; and M. Ingeborg Olsen to Ruth Larned, April 2, 1953, both in Box 23, Folder: U.S. Committee for the Care of European Children, ISS papers.

95. George Polos to Arthur C. Ringland, February 20, 1951, Box 58, Folder: Orphans-Public Law 555, Displaced Persons Commission records.

96. Rausch to Shirk, May 8, 1951.

97. Cochran and McKay to Corkery, August 24, 1951, 3, Box 58, Folder: Orphans-Public Law 555, Displaced Persons Commission records.

98. Joan Kain to Ben Dixon, October 23, 1951, Box 9, Folder: Displaced Persons Committee (Orphans Program) Order of AHEPA-Correspondence, U.S. Foreign Assistance Agency records.

99. "Meeting with Miss Olsen re U.S. Committee for Care of European Children and AHEPA DP Committee," Department of State Memorandum of Conversation, October 4, 1951, Box 9, Folder: Displaced Persons Committee (Orphans Program) Order of AHEPA-Correspondence, U.S. Foreign Assistance Agency records.

100. Kain to Dixon, October 23, 1951.

101. Mildred Arnold to Dept. of Social Services Staff, November 19, 1951, Box 131, Folder: AHEPA, Displaced Persons Commission records.

102. Barbara Penney to Elliott Shirk, November 16, 1951, Box 131, Folder: AHEPA, Displaced Persons Commission records.

103. Senate Subcommittee to Investigate Juvenile Delinquency in the U.S., *Hearings on Juvenile Delinquency (Pittsburgh)*, December 7, 1955, 84th Cong., 1st sess., 12–14.

104. Senate Special Subcommittee to Investigate Problems Connected with Emigration of Refugees or Escapees from Western European Nations, *Hearings on Amendments to Refugee Relief Act of 1953*, 84th Cong., 1st sess., 1955, 146–47.

105. Senate Special Subcommittee, *Hearings on Amendments to Refugee Relief Act of 1953*, 37.

106. Olsen to Larned, April 2, 1953.

107. Elliott Shirk to Gibson, O'Connor, Rosenfield, February 4, 1952, Box 58, Folder: Orphans-Public Law 555, Displaced Persons Commission records; and Child Welfare Officer to Robert Corkery, March 10, 1952, 5.

108. Child Welfare Officer to Robert Corkery, March 10, 1952; and Child Welfare Officer to Robert Corkery, Monthly Report, July 5, 1952, Box 133, Folder: Monthly Field Reports (Greece), Displaced Persons Commission records.

109. "Memo on Consultations with United States Committee on the Care for European Children looking toward their liquidation," March 20, 1953.

110. Senate Special Subcommittee, *Hearings on Amendments to Refugee Relief Act of 1953*, 140.

111. Antonio Micocci to John Rieger, November 5, 1954, Box 2, Folder: RRP-Orphan Cases, State Department records.

112. "Possibilities for Inter-Country Adoption in Greece," October 29, 1954, 3, Box 31, Folder: ISS-Greek Branch, Adoptions File 1955–58; and Ernest Mitler, "Survey of Greek-U.S. Proxy Adoptions," n.d., 3, Box 11, Folder: Adoption Manual and Other Printed Material, both in ISS papers.

113. Pettiss to Elliott, July 18, 1956, Box 674, Folder: Interstate Placement, Non-Resident Problems, Juvenile Immigration, 1953–57, USCB papers.

114. Refugee Relief Act, Public Law 203, *U.S. Statutes at Large* 400 (August 7, 1953), Sec. 5(a).

115. Cochran to Rausch, March 7, 1952; Cochran to Rausch, March 19, 1952, 2, both in Box 132, Folder: Greece, Displaced Persons Commission records; and Koutsoumaris to Kirk, Case #1, June 13, 1958, Box 10, Folder: Proxy Adoptions, 1954–56, ISS papers.

116. Koutsoumaris to Kirk, Case #3, June 13, 1958, Box 10, Folder: Proxy Adoptions, 1954–56, ISS papers. U.S. parents still occasionally "return" their adoptive children to foreign countries, even when they have been readopted in the United States and are U.S. citizens. See Damien Cave, "In Tenn., Reminders of a Boy Returned to Russia," *New York Times*, April 10, 2010, A16.

117. Antonio Micocci to John Rieger, November 5, 1954; and Robert Alexander to Scott McLeod, March 1, 1954, both in Box 2, Folder: RRP-Orphan Cases, State Department records.

118. Pettiss to Kefauver, May 15, 1956, 1, Box 227, Folder: Press Releases-Witness List, Senate Subcommittee records.

119. Memo from Staff of the Senate Juvenile Delinquency Subcommittee, July 2, 1957, Box 229, Folder: S. 588 Adoption Bill, 1957, Senate Subcommittee records; and Senate Committee on the Judiciary, *Making Unlawful Certain Practices in Connection with the Placing of Minor Children for Permanent Free Care or for Adoption*, July 25, 1956, 84th Cong., 2nd sess., S. 3021, 3.

120. Kefauver reintroduced the bill throughout the 1960s and it still failed. Memorandum Concerning Official Basis of the Program of the United States Committee for the Care of European Children, Inc., 1953, Box 23, Folder: U.S. Committee for the Care of European Children, ISS papers. Also see U.S. Senate Committee on the Judiciary, "Investigation of Juvenile Delinquency in the United States," S. Res. 62, July 15–16, 1955, 84th Cong., 1st sess.; and U.S. Senate Committee on the Judiciary, "Investigation of Juvenile Delinquency in the United States," S. Res. 62, November 15–16, 1955.

121. Senate Special Subcommittee, *Hearings on Amendments to Refugee Relief Act of 1953: Hearings*, 43.

122. "12 Greek Orphans Fly in to Begin Life as Americans in 9 States," *New York Times*, July 13, 1956; and "AHEPA Greek Orphans Start Migrating," Press Release, July 1956, Box 13, Folder: Orphans, State Department records.

123. Senate Special Subcommittee, *Amendments to Refugee Relief Act of 1953: Hearings*, 37–39.

124. Memo from Lamberson to State Department Representative, July 1956, Box 13, Folder: Orphans, State Department records. Mitler argues that all AHEPA's placements were shady and that they were never truly authorized. He dates the "diversion of the AHEPA program into commercial channels" to this 1956 airlift. Mitler, "Survey of U.S.-Greek Proxy Adoptions," 6.

125. Pettiss to Winford Oliphant, June 17, 1958, Box 10, Folder: Independent Adoptions Schemes, AHEPA, 1954–59, ISS papers. Also see Leber, *The History of the Order of AHEPA*.

126. Katherine Kuplan to Susan Pettiss, May 8, 1958, Box 10, Folder: Independent Adoptions Schemes, AHEPA, 1954–59, ISS papers.

127. Theodore Waxter to A. W. Pilavashi, February 10, 1960, Box 883, Folder: Non-Resident Problems (Include Juvenile Immigrant, Transient Boys), June 1962, 1958–1962, USCB papers.

128. Mitler claims that in 1955–56 Lamberson charged a moderate fee of $643. See Mitler, "Survey of U.S.-Greek Proxy Adoptions," 5, 7.

129. Mark Mazower, *Inside Hitler's Greece: The Experience of Occupation, 1941–44* (New Haven, Conn.: Yale University Press, 2001), ch. 19.

130. By 1955, authorities reported that there was one available child for every twenty-five prospective Jewish parents. See Ellen Herman, "The Difference Difference Makes: Justine Wise Polier and Religious Matching in Twentieth-Century Child Adoption," *Religion and American Culture* 10, no. 1 (Winter 2000): 69; Maud Morlock, "Babies on the Market," reprint from USCB Survey Midmonthly, March 1945, Box 159, Folder: Adoption, January 1945–June 1945; and "Progress Report, Project on Prevention of Black Market in Babies and Other Unprotected Adoptive Placements," April 5, 1955, 4, 7–10, Box 674, Folder: Traffic in Children, Baby Farms, 1953–56, both in USCB papers.

131. Mitler, "What's Wrong with Adoption Agencies in the Eyes of the Lay Public," n.d., Box 227, Folder: Mitler: Speech, adoption, Senate Subcommittee files.

132. "Progress Report, Project on Prevention of Black Market in Babies and Other Unprotected Adoptive Placements," April 5, 1955, 3, Box 674, Folder: Traffic in Children, Baby Farms, 1953–56, USCB papers; Arnold to Emery, May 19, 1959, Box 884, Folder: Non-Resident Problems (Include Juvenile Immigrant, Transient Boys), June 1960, 1958–1962, USCB papers. See also *Congressional Record*, May 15, 1959, 7398; and Mitler, "Report on Inter-Country Adoptions," 7–8.

133. While authorized social welfare agencies resisted charging fees in the first half of the twentieth century, by 1950 almost all agencies assessed fees, Ellen Herman, *Kinship by Design: A History of Adoption in the Modern United States* (Chicago: University of Chicago Press, 2008), 45, 224–25; and Zelizer, *Pricing the Priceless Child*, 204.

134. Susan Pettiss to Bolton Smith, July 5, 1957, Box 10, Folder: Proxy Adoptions, 1954–56; Rollin Zane to Edwin May, March 25, 1957, Box 10, Folder: Adoption: Individual Schemes, American Mission to Greeks, 1957–60; and "Report: Arrival in U.S. of 33 Greek Orphans," January 15, 1957, Box 31, Folder: ISS-Greek Branch, Adoptions File 1955–58, all in ISS papers.

135. Mitler, "Survey of U.S.-Greek Proxy Adoptions," 6.

136. Interstate Adoption Practices, Interim Report of the Subcommittee to Investigate Juvenile Delinquency to the Committee on the Judiciary U.S. Senate, 1956, Box 227, Folder: GPO Copy for Interim Report-Interstate Adoption, Senate Subcommittee files.

137. Cohen, *A Consumer's Republic*, 108, 331.

138. "Possibilities for Inter-Country Adoption in Greece," October 29, 1954, 1, Box 31, Folder: ISS-Greek Branch, Adoptions File 1955–58, ISS papers; and Barbara Melosh, *Strangers and Kin: The American Way of Adoption* (Cambridge, Mass.: Harvard University Press, 2002), 55–69.

139. Cochran to Rausch, March 7, 1952, 2, and Cochran to Rausch, March 19, 1952, 2, both in Box 132, Folder: Greece, Displaced Persons Commission records.

140. ISS-Greek Branch to ISS-American Branch, May 14, 1957, Box 31, Folder: ISS-Greek Branch, Adoptions File 1955–58, ISS papers.

141. John Tompert to Estes Kefauver, December 4, 1955, Box 226, Folder: Adoption Correspondence-1955, Subcommittee to Investigate Juvenile Delinquency files.

142. "Greek Branch Report," April 11, 1955, 9, Box 3, Folder: Inter-Country Adoptions Committee-ISS Reports, ISS papers.

143. Greek adoptive parents had to be childless and over fifty years old. "Greek Branch Report," April 11, 1955, 11, Box 3, Folder: Inter-Country Adoptions Committee-ISS Reports; "Possibilities for Inter-Country Adoption in Greece," October 29, 1954, 3–4, Box 31, Folder: ISS-Greek Branch, Adoptions File 1955–58; and Eleanor Linse, "Report on Visit to Greek Branch of

International Social Services, Inc.," July 17, 1956–August 4, 1956, 2, Box 31, Folder: Greece 1952–59, Vol. I, all in ISS papers.

144. Law Decree No. 4532 entitled "A Decree for the Adoption of Minors up to the age of 18," August 1966, Article 14, Box 31, Folder: ISS-Greek Branch, Adoptions File 1955–58, ISS papers; Albert Clattenburg, Jr., to Clare Golden, October 12, 1959, Box 883, Folder: Non-Resident Problems (Include Juvenile Immigrant, Transient Boys), June 1962, 1958–1962, USCB papers; and "Greece Is Revising Her Adoption Laws," *New York Times*, July 12, 1959, 6.

145. Mitler, "Report on Inter-Country Adoptions," 11–12.

146. Ibid., 17.

147. Marguerite Windhauser to Dwight H. Ferguson, June 1, 1955, Box 675, Folder: Interstate Placement, Non-Resident Problems, Juvenile Immigration, June 1955, 1953–1957, USCB papers.

148. Donna Gabaccia, *Immigration and American Diversity: A Social and Cultural History* (Malden, Mass.: Blackwell, 2002), 139; Linda Reeder, "Conflict Across the Atlantic: Women, Family, and Mass Male Migration in Sicily, 1880–1920," *International Review of Social History* 46, no. 3 (December 2001): 371–91; and Arodys Robels and Susan Cotts Watkins, "Immigration and Family Separation in the U.S. at the Turn of the Twentieth Century," *Journal of Family History* 18, no. 3 (July 1993): 191–211.

149. Alexopoulos to Saunders, February 22, 1954, Box 31, Folder: Greece 1952–59, vol. I, ISS papers.

150. Mitler, "Report on Inter-Country Adoptions," 17; Cochran to Rausch, March 7, 1952, 1; and Cochran to Rausch, March 19, 1952, both in Box 132, Folder: Greece, Displaced Persons Commission records.

151. Letter excerpt from Greek Branch ISS, April 17, 1956, Box 230, Folder: International Adoption, Subcommittee to Investigate Juvenile Delinquency files, NARA.

152. Zane to May, March 25, 1957, Box 10, Folder: Proxy Adoptions, 1957–66, ISS papers.

153. Mitler, "Report on Inter-Country Adoptions," 18.

154. Karen Balcom, *The Traffic in Babies: Cross-Border Adoption and Baby-Selling Between the United States and Canada, 1930–1972* (Toronto: University of Toronto Press, 2011) 192–94; Ernest Mitler to Mrs. Richard H. (Phoebe) Davis, April 23, 1957, Box 226, Folder: Adoption Correspondence-1955, Subcommittee to Investigate Juvenile Delinquency files; and Zelizer, *Pricing the Priceless Child*, 202.

Chapter 3. "The Great Heart of America": Volunteer Humanitarians and Korean Adoptions

1. Bertha Holt, *Bring My Sons from Afar* (Eugene, Ore.: Holt International Children's Services, 1986), 61–64; Thayer Waldo, "Smiles, Tears Hail Korean Orphans," *Oakland Tribune*, February 1, 1958, 4; Gene Kramer, "'Pied Piper' Corrals 12 Korean Babies, Flies Them to America for Adoption," *Washington Post*, October 14, 1955, 71; AP, "Tubercular Waifs Can't Get State Treatment," *Register-Guard* (Eugene, Ore.) January 1, 1958.

2. "Oregon Farmer Brings 12 More Orphans from Korea for New Homes in America," *Oregonian*, April 8, 1956, 18.

3. Ellen D. Wu, *The Color of Success: Asian Americans and the Origins of the Model Minority* (Princeton, N.J.: Princeton University Press, 2014); Arissa Oh, *To Save the Children of Korea: The Cold War Origins of International Adoption* (Stanford, Calif.: Stanford University Press, 2015);

Christina Klein, *Cold War Orientalism: Asia in the Middlebrow Imagination, 1945–1961* (Berkeley: University of California Press, 2003); Chiou-Ling Yeh, "'A Saga of Democracy': Toy Len Goon, American Mother of the Year, and the Cultural Cold War," *Pacific Historical Review* 81, no. 3 (Fall 2012): 432–61; Henry Yu, *Thinking Orientals: Migration, Contact, and Exoticism in Modern America* (Oxford: Oxford University Press, 2002).

4. Karen Balcom, *The Traffic in Babies: Cross Border Adoption and Baby-Selling Between the United States and Canada, 1930–1972* (Toronto: University of Toronto Press, 2011); Michael Barnett, *Empire of Humanity: A History of Humanitarianism* (Ithaca, N.Y.: Cornell University Press, 2011), 107. Credit goes to Alice O'Connor for suggesting the terminology "policy vacuum."

5. Most scholars have framed independent or proxy adoptions as loopholes as well. See Jae Ran Kim, "Scattered Seeds: The Christian Influence on Korean Adoption," in *Outsiders Within: Writing on Transracial Adoption*, ed. Jane Jeong Trenka, Julia Chinyere Oparah, and Sun Yung Shin (Cambridge, Mass.: South End Press, 2006), 151–62; Catherine Ceniza Choy, *Global Families: A History of Asian International Adoption in America* (New York: New York University Press, 2013).

6. Klein, *Cold War Orientalism*, 225.

7. Senate Committee on the Judiciary, *Final Report of the Administrator of the Refugee Relief Act of 1953, As Amended*, 85th Cong., 1st sess., November 15, 1957, 1, 15; Barnett, *Empire of Humanity*, 124.

8. Carl Bon Tempo, *Americans at the Gate: The United States and Refugees During the Cold War* (Princeton, N.J.: Princeton University Press, 2008); Michael Gill Davis, "The Cold War, Refugees, and U.S. Immigration Policy, 1952–1965" (Ph.D. dissertation, Vanderbilt University, 1996), 99–100; J. Bruce Nichols, *The Uneasy Alliance: Religion, Refugee Work, and U.S. Foreign Policy* (Oxford: Oxford University Press, 1988), 84–85, 99.

9. Robert H. Weil, "International Adoptions: The Quiet Migration," *International Migration Review* 18, no. 2 (Summer 1984): 280–81.

10. Act of August 19, 1950, Public Law 717, *U.S. Statutes at Large* 464 (1950).

11. Immigration and Nationality Act, Public Law 414, *U.S. Statutes at Large* 163 (June 27, 1952), sec. 323.

12. To Permit the Entry of Certain Eligible Orphans, HJ Res 228, 83rd Cong., 1st sess., *Congressional Record* 607, no. 605 (July 21, 1953).

13. Ibid., 2–3.

14. Refugee Relief Act, Public Law 203, *U.S. Statutes at Large* 400 (August 7, 1953), Sec. 5(a).

15. *Final Report of the Administrator of the Refugee Relief Act of 1953*, 57. For a complete list of the voluntary agencies, see 134.

16. The *New York Times* reported that petitions to adopt increased 30 percent from 1944 to 1953. "New Laws Sought by Adoption Units," *New York Times*, June 25, 1956, 24.

17. Because the desire for children was so acute, differences in race and religion became less important than in the past, as noted in the *Final Report of the Administrator of the Refugee Relief Act of 1953*, 57. See Elaine Tyler May, *Barren in the Promised Land: Childless Americans and the Pursuit of Happiness* (Cambridge, Mass.: Harvard University Press, 1995), ch. 4; Barbara Melosh, *Strangers and Kin: The American Way of Adoption* (Cambridge, Mass.: Harvard University Press, 2002), 160; Carp, *Family Matters: Secrecy and Disclosure in the History of Adoption* (Cambridge: Harvard University Press, 2000), 34.

18. Beverly Moeller, "Column: Over the Hill: In Simi Valley," *Van Nuys News* (Van Nuys, Calif.), February 23, 1961, 13.

19. Lou Jorst, "Yoo and Kim Get 200 Mothers, Dads," *Independent*, November 24, 1958.

20. Letter from Scott McLeod to Rep. Adam Clayton Powell, March 29, 1955, Box 2, Folder: RRP-Orphan Cases, Bureau of Security and Consular Affairs, Decimal Subject Files, 1953–56, Department of State papers.

21. Senate Committee on the Judiciary, *Authorizing Additional Visas for Orphans*, 84th Cong., 2nd sess., 1956, S. Rpt. 2684, 3; and Intercountry Adoption Program Under the Refugee Relief Act, January 1, 1954-July 1, 1957, Box 674, Folder: Interstate Placement, Non-Resident Problems, Juvenile Immigration, 1953–57, USCB papers.

22. "Unwanted Find a Home," *Look*, October 30, 1956, 106.

23. H. P. Sconce, "Lenten Guideposts," *Vidette-Messenger*, April 19, 1957, 7.

24. "From Korea to America—Three Children Now Citizens," *Lincoln Star* (Lincoln, Neb.), April 23, 1963, 6.

25. James Bulse, "Sparks Family Provides Home for Four Korean Girls," *Nevada State Journal*, July 31, 1960, 32. Also see Al Carr, "Korean Tots Find Love with County Families," *Los Angeles Times*, April 21, 1963.

26. *Final Report of the Administrator of the Refugee Relief Act of 1953*, 57; Authorizing Additional Visas for Orphans, 3.

27. *Final Report of the Administrator of the Refugee Relief Act of 1953*, 65.

28. Ibid., 62.

29. Senate Committee on the Judiciary, *World Refugee Problems: Hearings before the subcommittee to investigate problems connected with refugees and escapees*, 87th Cong., 1st sess., 1961, 6.

30. *Authorizing Additional Visas for Orphans*, 3. See Christina Klein, "Family Ties and Political Obligation: The Discourse of Adoption and the Cold War Commitment to Asia," in *Cold War Constructions: The Political Culture of United States Imperialism, 1945–1966*, ed. Christian G. Appy (Amherst: University of Massachusetts Press, 2000), 35–66.

31. For more on this, see Karen Dubinsky, *Babies Without Borders: Adoption and Migration Across the Americas* (New York: New York University Press, 2010), esp. chap. 2.

32. Flyer, "Newspapers in which Dondi appears regularly," Oversized Box 2, Folder: Dondi (film); Film promo, Oversized Box 2, Folder: Dondi (film); and The Trib, *Chicago Tribune Magazine*, May 1962, 7, Box 1, Folder: Clippings, National Cartoonists Society, all in Gus Edson papers. Oral Interview of Gus Edson and Irwin Hasen by Vern Green (The Cartoonist's Art series), National Cartoonists Society Interviews, 1959–62, Belfer Audio Archive.

33. Award certificates, Oversize Box 4, Folder: Awards; Background on Edson, Oversize Box 3; Clipping, 8 November 1949, "Cartoonists Are First-Rate Husbands, Say Their Wives," Box 1, Folder: Newspaper Clippings; National Cartoonists Society Newsletter, January 1966, Box 1, Folder: Clippings, National Cartoonists Society; *The Stars and Stripes: European Edition*, December 24, 1952, 6–7; *National Cartoonists Society Newsletter*, Spring 1953, both in Box 1, Folder: Clippings, National Cartoonists Society, all in Edson papers; and Oral Interview of Gus Edson and Irwin Hasen by Vern Green, Belfer Archive.

34. *Dondi* strip, March 18, 1956, Irwin Hasen Cartoons.

35. Oversized box 2, Bound book, Cover; Shooting Script, 117, both in Edson papers.

36. *Dondi*, March 18, 1956, Hasen Cartoons. See Elaine Tyler May, *Homeward Bound: American Families in the Cold War Era* (New York: Basic Books, 1988).

37. *Dondi*, November 6, 1955, Hasen Cartoons; Shooting Script, 104, Edson papers. In the film, Whitey McGowan was renamed Dealey and Monique was called Liz. For clarity's sake, I have used McGowan and Monique throughout to express the same character type.

38. Shooting Script, 118, Edson papers.

39. Shooting Script, 132–33.

40. Mae M. Ngai, *Impossible Subjects: Illegal Aliens and the Making of Modern America* (Princeton, N.J.: Princeton University Press, 2004).

41. Shooting Script, 71A, Edson papers.

42. Oral Interview of Gus Edson and Irwin Hasen by Vern Green, Belfer Audio Archive.

43. Oral Interview.

44. Photo of Colonel Dean Hess handing card to Korean officials, n.d., Box 1, Folder: Photographs, 1949, undated, Edson papers; and *Battle Hymn*, dir. Douglas Sirk (1957; Los Angeles: Universal International Pictures); Hye Seung Chung, "Hollywood Goes to Korea: Biopic Politics and Douglas Sirk's *Battle Hymn* (1957)," *Historical Journal of Film, Radio and Television* 25, no. 1 (March 2005): 51–80.

45. Memorandum received from American Council of Voluntary Agencies for Foreign Service, Inc., January 1955, 1, Box 10, Folder 29, ISS papers; "Holt 'Babylift' Slows Only for Diaper Shift," *The Oregonian*, April 7, 1956. Amendment of Refugee Relief Act of 1953," 84th Cong., 2nd sess., *Congressional Record*, vol. 102, part 6 (April 30, 1956): 7247–49, as cited in Oh, "A New Kind of Missionary Work: Christians, Christian Americanists, and the Adoption of Korean GI Babies, 1955–1961," *Women's Studies Quarterly* 33 (Fall/Winter 2005): 161–88; Susan Pettiss, Report of Meeting with Dr. Pierce of World Vision, March 13, 1956, Box 10, Folder 29, ISS papers.

46. Report of Meeting with Dr. Pierce of World Vision, March 13, 1956; Bertha Holt and David Wisner, *The Seed from the East* (Los Angeles: Oxford Press, 1956), 25, 27; Holt, *Bring My Sons from Afar*, 8.

47. H. P. Sconce, "Lenten Guideposts," *Vidette-Messenger* (Valparaiso, Ind.), April 19, 1957.

48. Holt and Wisner, *The Seed from the East*, 54.

49. Richard Neuberger, "What Has Happened to American Spirit?" *Washington Calling* IV, January 1958, as cited in Holt, *Bring My Sons from Afar*, 61.

50. Certain Korean War Orphans Act, 84th Cong., 1st sess. (July 28, 1955).

51. Holt and Wisner, *The Seed from the East*, 124–26; Michael Barone, Grant Ujifusa, and Douglas Matthews, *The Almanac of American Politics* (Chicago: Gambit, 1972), 675.

52. Holt and Wisner, *The Seed from the East*, 114.

53. Holt, *Bring My Sons from Afar*, 9, 17.

54. Arissa Oh has completed the most thorough research on the Holts' religious motivation and how it gained support amid a surge of what she calls Christian Americanism—a mainstream, tolerant form of Protestantism focused on the national good. See Oh, *To Save the Children of Korea*.

55. Holt, *Bring My Sons from Afar*, 156.

56. Andrew Preston, *Sword of the Spirit, Shield of Faith: Religion in American War and Diplomacy* (New York: Knopf, 2012), 481; Nathan O. Hatch, "Evangelicalism as a Democratic Movement," in *Evangelicalism in Modern America*, ed. George Marsden (Grand Rapids, Mich.: Eerdmans, 1984), 78; and William R. Hutchison, *Errand to the World: American Protestant Thought and Foreign Missions* (Chicago: University of Chicago Press, 1987), 192–93. There is a large body of literature on the Western missionary tradition's work to rescue women and children, especially in Asia, in the eighteenth and nineteenth centuries. For example, see Maina Chawla Singh, *Gender, Religion, and "Heathen Lands": American Missionary Women in South Asia, 1860s–1940* (New York: Garland, 2000); Eliza F. Kent, *Converting Women: Gender and Protestant Christianity in Colonial South India* (Oxford: Oxford University Press, 2004); Patricia Ruth Hill,

The World Their Household: The American Women's Foreign Mission Movement and Cultural Transformation, 1870–1920 (Ann Arbor: University of Michigan Press, 1985); Ann Laura Stoler, *Carnal Knowledge and Imperial Power: Race and the Intimate in Colonial Rule* (Berkeley: University of California Press, 2002).

57. Joel A. Carpenter, "From Fundamentalism to the New Evangelical Coalition," in *Evangelicalism and Modern America*, ed. Marsden, 3–16; Barnett, 120–22.

58. Holt and Wisner, *The Seed from the East*, 201.

59. Ibid., 156.

60. Ibid., 221. Also see Ellen Herman, "The Paradoxical Rationalization of Modern Adoption," *Journal of Social History* 36, no. 2 (2002): 339–85.

61. Holt and Wisner, *The Seed from the East*, 161; Henry Chang, "From Korea to Creswell: Waifs, 'Aboji,' Eye Departure," *Register-Guard*, October 5, 1955.

62. Richard Eves, "'Black and White, a Significant Contrast': Race, Humanism, and Missionary Photography in the Pacific," *Ethnic and Racial Studies* 29, no. 4 (2006): 739.

63. Holt, *Bring My Sons from Afar*, 21.

64. Holt and Wisner, *The Seed from the East*, 240.

65. Susan Pettiss, Memo to Files regarding ISS trip to visit County Department of Public Welfare, World Vision, and Holt family, Box 10, Folder 29, ISS papers.

66. Holt, *Bring My Sons from Afar*, 9. Throughout her book, Bertha refers to ISS as the American Social Agency and Susan Pettiss as Miss Perry.

67. Letter from Holts to supporters, February/March 1956, 2, Box 10, Folder: Independent Adoption Schemes, 1955–57, vol. 1, Harry Holt, ISS papers. See "Adopted Korean Kids Cleared for U.S. Entry," *Register-Guard*, September 25, 1955. See also Holt, *Bring My Sons from Afar*, 12; "89 Korean Orphans Here for New Homes," *San Mateo Times* (Calif.), December 17, 1956.

68. Letter from Holts to supporters, February/March 1956, 2, Box 10, Folder: Independent Adoption Schemes, 1955–57, vol. 1, Harry Holt, ISS papers.

69. Holt, *Bring My Sons from Afar*, 10, 12, 18.

70. Senate Judiciary Committee, *Hearing on S. 830*, July 18, 1947, 80th Cong., 1st sess., 42.

71. Displaced Persons Act, June 25, 1948, Public Law 774, S. 2242, 80th Cong., 2nd sess., 1009.

72. "89 Korean Orphans Here for New Homes," *San Mateo Times*, December 17, 1956.

73. "Adopted Korean Kids Cleared for U.S. Entry," *Register-Guard*, September 25, 1955. Also see Holt, *Bring My Sons from Afar*, 12.

74. Christ is the Answer Foundation and Everett Swanson Evangelistic Association are two other groups studied by Catherine Ceniza Choy, "Institutionalizing International Adoption: The Historical Origins of Korean Adoption in the United States," in *International Korean Adoption: A Fifty-Year History of Policy and Practice*, ed. Kathleen Ja Sook Berquist, M. Elizabeth Vouk, Dong Soo Kim, and Marvin D. Feit (Binghamton, N.Y: Haworth, 2007), 25–42.

75. Senate Committee on the Judiciary, *Final Report of the Administrator of the Refugee Relief Act of 1953, As Amended*, 85th Cong., 1st sess., November 15, 1957, 135. "Holt Annual Report," 1965, Box 10, Folder: Independent Adoption Schemes, 1955–57, vol. 3, Harry Holt, ISS papers.

76. *Congressional Record*, July 30, 1955, vol. 101, no. 130, 10706 in Box 10, Folder: Independent Adoption Schemes, 1955–57, vol. 1, Harry Holt, ISS papers.

77. Holt, *Bring My Sons from Afar*, 8; "Holt Plane Arrives at Portland Airport," *Register-Guard*, October 14, 1955, 1.

78. "Mr. Holt 'Moves the World'," *Oregonian*, April 9, 1956; Ron Moxness, "Good Samaritan of Korea," *American Mercury*, October 1956, 86.

79. Moxness, 86.

80. ISS-American Branch website, http://www.iss-use.org/site/subsection.asp?IdSection = 1& IdSub = 19 (accessed January 19, 2008); "Expediting Adoption of Korean Orphans," *Christian Century*, July 11, 1962, 857.

81. Helen L. Witmer, Elizabeth Herzog, Eugene A. Weinstein, and Mary E. Sullivan, *Independent Adoptions: A Follow-Up Study* (New York: Child Welfare League of America, 1963), 43. See also *Child Welfare League of America Standards for Adoption Service* (New York: Child Welfare League of America, 1958), 4; Michael Schapiro, *A Study of Adoption Practice: Adoption Agencies and the Children They Serve* (New York: Child Welfare League of America, 1956).

82. ISS website, http://www.iss-use.org/site/subsection.asp?IdSection = 1&IdSub = 19 (accessed January 19, 2008).

83. AP, "Differences in Religion Held No Bar to Adoption," *New York Times*, January 25, 1957, 45.

84. UP, "Baltimore Couple Lose Plea for Boy," *New York Times*, November 26, 1957, 35.

85. For more on the legal implications of adoptive family construction, see Naomi Cahn and Joan Heifetz Hollinger, eds., *Families by Law: An Adoption Reader* (New York: New York University Press, 2004).

86. Child Welfare League of America, *Standard for Adoption Service*, 1959 ed., 24.

87. Memo, December 3, 1963, attached to the front of *Standard for Adoption Service*, 1959.

88. *Standards for Adoption Service*, 1959, 68.

89. Letter from William Kirk to Eugene Carson Black, June 17, 1958, Box 10, Folder: Independent Adoption Schemes, Harry Holt, vol. 2, ISS papers.

90. Holt, *Bring My Sons from Afar*, 11.

91. Holt Newsletter, n.d., Box 10, Folder: Independent Adoption Schemes, 1955–57, vol. 1, Harry Holt, ISS papers.

92. Pettiss, Itinerary of Trip and More Notes, March 13, 1956, Box 10, Folder 29, ISS papers.

93. Pettiss, Memo to Files, Box 10, Folder 29, ISS papers.

94. Ibid.

95. Helen Fradkin, *The Adoption Home Study* (Trenton: State of New Jersey, Department of Institutions and Agencies, Division of Public Welfare, and Bureau of Children's Services, August 15, 1963), 65.

96. Laurin and Virginia P. Hyde, "A Study of Proxy Adoptions," 1958, Box 17, Folder 1, CWLA papers. This language was also picked up in the press; see UP, "Agencies Urge Bill to Prohibit Proxy Adoptions," *Albuquerque Journal*, August 1, 1958, 45.

97. Pettiss to Elliott, July 18, 1956, Box 674, Folder: Interstate Placement, Non-Resident Problems, Juvenile Immigration, 1953–57, USCB papers.

98. Senate Committee on the Judiciary, *To Amend the Refugee Relief Act of 1953*, 83rd Cong., 2nd sess., H.R. 3005 (April 7, 1954). A White House official also expressed disbelief over the idea of a "loophole"; see Katherine Oettinger to W. L. Mitchell, Telephone Conversation with Mr. Brad Patterson, White House, April 23, 1959, Box 883, Folder: Non-Resident Problems (Include Juvenile Immigrant, Transient Boys), June 1962, 1958–1962, USCB papers.

99. Credit to Karen Balcom for this insight.

100. *Final Report of the Administrator of the Refugee Relief Act of 1953*, 65.

101. Mildred Arnold to Miss Emery, May 15, 1959, Box 884, Folder: Non-Resident Problems (Include Juvenile Immigrant, Transient Boys), June 1960, 1958–1962, USCB papers.

102. List of Prospective Adoptive Parents, April 4, 1956; Mrs. Henry Luehr to William Langer, April 1, 1956; William Langer to Mrs. Henry Luehr, April 9, 1956, all in Box 4-Subcommittee on Immigration, 1955–59, NARA.

103. Letter from William Langer to Jocelyn Ames, Adoptive Parents Committee, July 6, 1959; Letter from Langer to Richard Neuberger, May 18, 1959, re: Mr. & Mrs. P. N. Haakenson; Lawrence Newhouse to Langer, July 30, 1957; Newhouse to Eleanor Guthridge, December 23, 1958, all in Box 4-Subcommittee on Immigration, 1955–59. On adoptive parents, see Mrs. Kenneth L. Lucas to Katherine Oettinger, April 21, 1959; Ruby Pletsch to Katherine Oettinger, April 1959; Edward A. Ruestow to Rep, Steven B. Derounian, April 14, 1959, all in Box 884, Folder: Non-Resident Problems (Include Juvenile Immigrant, Transient Boys), June 1959, 1958–1962, USCB papers.

104. Letter from George Wooley to William Langer, May 12, 1959, Box 4-Subcommittee on Immigration, 1955–59.

105. Holt to Arnold, May 8, 1959, Box 884, Folder: Non-Resident Problems (Include Juvenile Immigrant, Transient Boys), June 1960, 1958–1962, USCB papers.

106. Letter from Susan Pettiss to ISS Headquarters and Branches, July 28, 1958, Box 10, Folder: Children—Intercountry Adoption Seminar (1960), ISS papers; Holt and Wisner, *The Seed from the East*, 169.

107. Senate Committee on the Judiciary, *Authorizing Additional Visas for Orphans*, 84th Cong., 2nd sess., 1956, S. Rpt. 2684, 2–3; and Holt, *Bring My Sons from Afar*, 17.

108. Senate Committee on the Judiciary, *A Bill for the Relief of Judy-Ellen Kay (Choi Myosoon)*, 85th Cong., 1st sess., S. Rpt. 914 (August 14, 1957), 1–3.

109. Refugee-Escapee Act, Public Law 85–316, *U.S. Statutes at Large* 639 (September 11, 1957), sec. 101(e).

110. Memo from Susan Pettiss to ISS HQ and Branches, July 28, 1958, Box 10, Folder: Children-Intercountry Adoption Seminar (1960), ISS papers.

111. ISS News Release, n.d., Box 11, Folder: Adoption Manual and Other Printed Material, ISS papers.

112. Letter from Lawrence E. Laybourne to Miss Virginia Smucker, January 14, 1958, Box 10, Folder: Independent Adoption Schemes, vol. 2, Harry Holt, ISS papers; Memo from Susan Pettiss to ISS HQ and Branches, July 28, 1958, Box 10, Folder: Children-Intercountry Adoption Seminar (1960), ISS papers. For more on their lobbying efforts, see ISS Newsletters, Summer and October 1959, Box 16, Folder 21: ISS/American Branch Publications, ISS papers.

113. Draft letter from William T. Kirk to Erabelle Thompson, managing editor for *Ebony* magazine, June 11, 1958, Box 23, Folder: Welcome House, ISS papers; Pearl S. Buck, "Should White Parents Adopt Brown Babies?," *Ebony*, June 1958, 26–31.

114. President Eisenhower, *Message to Congress Recommending Certain Changes in the Refugee Relief Act of 1953*, on May 27, 1955, 84th Cong., 1st sess., 3.

115. "Lane County Tuberculosis Assn. Hears Mrs. Holt, Salem Doctor," *Register-Guard*, April 25, 1958.

116. Refugee-Escapee Act of 1957, Public Law 85–316, *U.S. Statutes at Large* 639 (September 11, 1957), sec. 6. When Oregon refused to admit the GI children into its state tuberculosis facilities, sectarian organizations like Denver's Jewish hospital and a handful of Catholic hospitals in California took the children instead.

117. Letter from William Kirk to Eugene Carson Blake, ISS Board Member, June 17, 1958, Box 10, Folder: Independent Adoption Schemes, vol. 3, Harry Holt, ISS papers.

118. Letter from Susan Pettiss to Lorena Scherer, January 8, 1957, Box 10, Folder 29, ISS papers.

119. Letter to Harry Holt from Wilmer Tolle, March 20, 1958, Box 10, Folder: Independent Adoption Schemes, vol. 2, Harry Holt, ISS papers. Also see Pettiss to George A. Richardson, April 15, 1960; Clare Golden to Susan Pettiss, February 17, 1960, both in Box 883, Folder: Non-Resident Problems (Include Juvenile Immigrant, Transient Boys), June 1962, 1958–1962, USCB papers.

120. Laurin and Hyde, "A Study of Proxy Adoptions."

121. Letter from William Kirk and Joseph Reid to Member Agencies, July 28, 1958, Box 17, Folder 1, CWLA papers; Mildred Arnold to Miss Emery, Mrs. Eveland's Report, May 5, 1959, Box 883, Folder: Non-Resident Problems (Include Juvenile Immigrant, Transient Boys), June 1959, 1958–1962, USCB papers.

122. Letter from Joseph Reid to Harry Holt, July 15,1959, Box 10, Folder: Independent Adoption Schemes, vol. 2, Harry Holt, ISS papers; Elsie Carper, "Hearing to Air Refugee Needs," *Washington Post*, June 22, 1959, A9; Susan Pettiss to Clare Golden, May 13, 1959, Box 883, Folder: Non-Resident Problems (Include Juvenile Immigrant, Transient Boys), June 1962, 1958–1962, USCB papers.

123. Senate Subcommittee on Immigration, *Hearings on S. 1468, S. 1532, S. 1610, S. 2004*, 86th Cong., 1st sess., June 23, 1959, 56.

124. Ibid., 41–43; Floor Speeches Introducing S. 1468, March 19, 1959, Box 884, Folder: Non-Resident Problems (Include Juvenile Immigrant, Transient Boys), Sept 1958, 1958–1962, USCB papers.

125. Mary Dudziak, *Cold War Civil Rights: Race and the Image of American Democracy* (Princeton: Princeton University Press, 2001).

126. Mildred Arnold to Margaret Emery, June 8, 1959, Box 884, Folder: USCB papers; Associated Press, "North Korea Attacks U.S. on Orphans," *Washington Post*, June 8, 1959, A6.

127. Amendment to Refugee-Escapee Act of 1957, Public Law 86–253, *U.S. Statutes at Large* 490 (1959); Internal memo, September 16, 1959, box 10, folder: Independent Adoption Schemes, vol. 2, Harry Holt, ISS papers; Holt, *Bring My Sons from Afar*, 102. This legislation extended Section 4 of PL 85–316 until June 30, 1960. Holt, *Bring My Sons from Afar*, 98. The Holts failed to specify whom INS designated to perform these home studies.

128. Amendment to Refugee-Escapee Act of 1957, Public Law 86–648, *U.S. Statutes at Large* 504 (1960); Jacob K. Javits, News Release, May 20, 1959, Box 4, Folder: Sen. 86A-F12, "H" Adoptions-Orphans, Subcommittee on Immigration of Refugees and Escapees, Senate Judiciary Committee papers, NARA; HAP Annual Report, 1965, Box 10, Folder: Independent Adoption Schemes, 1955–57, vol. 1, Harry Holt, ISS papers.

129. All but four states allowed readoption. The four states that did not—California, Minnesota, Ohio, and Michigan—required that families travel to the country to adopt their child. See Holt, *Bring My Sons from Afar*, 157.

130. Ibid.

131. Ibid., 171.

132. Act of September 26, 1961, Public Law 87–301, *U.S. Statutes at Large* 650 (1961), sec. 25(b); House of Representatives, *Amending the Immigration and Nationality Act and for Other Purposes*, 87th Cong., 1st sess., September 12, 1961, H. Rpt. 1172; and Holt, *Bring My Sons from Afar*, 144.

133. President Dwight Eisenhower, *Special Message to the Congress on Immigration Matters*, January 31, 1957; and Department of Health, Education, and Welfare Summary of Specifications,

January 30, 1959, Box 883, Folder: Non-Resident Problems (Include Juvenile Immigrant, Transient Boys), June 1962, 1958–1962, USCB papers.

134. Susan *Pettiss* to State Public Welfare Departments, September 18, 1961, Box 883, Folder: Non-Resident Problems (Include Juvenile Immigrant, Transient Boys), June 1962, 1958–1962, USCB papers; Arissa Oh, "From War Waif to Ideal Immigrant: The Cold War Transformation of the Korean Orphan," *Journal of American Ethnic History* 31, no. 4 (June 2012): 41.

135. Evan B. Donaldson Adoption Institute, http://www.adoptioninstitute.org/FactOver view/international.html#22 (accessed March 3, 2008). For statistics on domestic adoptions, see Penelope L. Maza, "Adoption Trends: 1944–1975," Child Welfare Research Notes #9 (USCB, August 1984), 1–4, Box 65, Folder: "Adoption-Research-Reprints of Articles," CWLA Papers.

136. Susan Pettiss to State Public Welfare Departments, September 18, 1961; Pettiss to Margaret Emery, September 13, 1961; Emery to Pettiss, September 20, 1961; Martin Gula to Mildred Arnold, August 23, 1961, all in Box 883, Folder: Non-Resident Problems (Include Juvenile Immigrant, Transient Boys), June 1962, 1958–1962, USCB papers.

Chapter 4. Coming Out of the Shadows:
Adoptive Parents as Public Figures, 1945–1965

1. Madalon Neuvirth to Katherine Lenroot, January 5, 1948, Box 158, Folder: Adoptions, January 1948, USCB papers.

2. Julie Berebitsky makes the argument that single mothers also helped to push this boundary. Berebitsky, "Family Ideals and the Social Construction of Modern Adoption," in *Adoptive Families in a Diverse Society*, ed. Katarina Wegar (New Brunswick, N.J.: Rutgers University Press, 2006), 30.

3. Some scholars have argued that adoptive parents were powerless outsiders. See, for instance, Elaine Tyler May, *Barren in the Promised Land: Childless Americans and the Pursuit of Happiness* (Cambridge, Mass.: Harvard University Press, 1995); and Betsy Smith, Janet L. Surrey, and Mary Watkins, " 'Real' Mothers: Adoptive Mothers Resisting Marginalization and Recreating Motherhood," in *Adoptive Families in a Diverse Society*, ed. Wegar, 146–61.

4. E. Wayne Carp, *Family Matters: Secrecy and Disclosure* (Cambridge, Mass.: Harvard University, 1998), ch. 4; and Keith Monroe, "A Better Way to Adopt a Baby," *Harper's Magazine*, January 1957, 54–58. See also Julie Berebitsky, *Like Our Very Own* (Lawrence: University of Kansas Press, 2000), chs. 3–11 and epilogue; and Ellen Herman, "The Paradoxical Rationalization for Modern Adoption," *Journal of Social History* 36, 2 (2002): 339–85.

5. Thomas P. Hughes, *American Genesis: A Century of Invention and Technological Enthusiasm, 1870–1970* (Chicago: University of Chicago Press, 2004); and Adam Rome, *Bulldozer in the Countryside: Suburban Sprawl and the Rise of American Environmentalism* (Cambridge: Cambridge University Press, 2001).

6. Rima Apple, *Perfect Motherhood: Science and Childrearing in America* (New Brunswick, N.J.: Rutgers University Press, 2006), 107–10. Also see Margaret Lock and Judith Farquhar, "Introduction" in *Beyond the Body Proper: Reading the Anthropology of Material Life*, ed. Lock and Farquhar (Durham, N.C: Duke University Press, 2007), 2; and Jacqueline Low and Claudia Malacrida, eds., *The Sociology of the Body: A Reader* (Don Mills, Ontario: Oxford University Press, 2008).

7. Barbara Melosh, *Strangers and Kin: The American Way of Adoption* (Cambridge, Mass.: Harvard University Press, 2002), 110–11; Rickie Solinger, *Wake Up Little Susie: Single Pregnancy and Race Before* Roe v. Wade (New York: Routledge, 1992); Wendy Kline, *Building a Better Race: Gender, Sexuality, and Eugenics from the Turn of the Century to the Baby Boom* (Berkeley: University of California Press, 2001); and Betty Jean Lifton, "Bad/Good, Good/Bad: Birth Mothers and Adoptive Mothers," in *"Bad" Mothers: The Politics of Blame in Twentieth-Century America*, ed. Molly Ladd-Taylor and Lauri Umansky (New York: New York University Press, 1998), 191–97.

8. Mary L. Dudziak, *Cold War Civil Rights: Race and the Image of American Democracy* (Princeton, N.J.: Princeton University Press, 2000); Penny Von Eschen, *Race Against Empire: Black Americans and Anticolonialism, 1937–1957* (Ithaca, NY: Cornell University Press, 1997); and Thomas Borstelmann, *The Cold War and the Color Line: American Race Relations in the Global Arena* (Cambridge, Mass: Harvard University Press, 2001).

9. Although the terms "childless" and "childlessness" are concise, they are problematic. When possible, I describe prospective adoptive parents as without children to detach the existence of children from their core identity.

10. "Faith and a Child," *Newsweek*, July 18, 1955, 20–21.

11. C. C. Cawley, "The Outlaws," *Christian Century*, April 3, 1957, 420. See also Massachusetts Statute 1950, c. 737, §3. Now G.L. (Ter. Ed.) c. 210, §5B.

12. "A Girl Got Affection," *Newsweek*, June 3, 1957, 29–30; and "Hildy," *Time*, July 22, 1957, 65.

13. "Hildy," 65; and "Mother to Appeal Hildy McCoy Ruling," *New York Times*, July 12, 1957, 10. See also "Adoption Backed by Florida Judge," *New York Times*, July 11, 1957, 52; "Hildy Is an Ellis Now Court Rules," *Chicago Defender*, July 11, 1957, 4; and "Ellises Are Held Fit to Rear Child," *New York Times*, July 9, 1957, 33.

14. "Fight for Hildy," *Time*, July 18, 1955, 38.

15. Doris Patterson to Mamie Eisenhower, April 7, 1957, Box 682, Folder: Adoptions, April 1957, 1953–1957, USCB papers; and "Book on Adoption Tells Procedure," *New York Times*, July 16, 1957, 40.

16. Samuel C. Heilman, *Portrait of American Jews: The Last Half of the 20th Century* (Seattle: University of Washington Press, 1995), 17, 45; Arthur Hertzberg, *The Jews in America* (New York: Columbia University Press, 1997), 298–99, 309–11, 322; and Hasia R. Diner, *A New Promised Land: A History of Jews in America* (New York: Oxford University Press, 2000), 93–95.

17. "Faith and a Child," *Newsweek*, July 18, 1955, 20–21; and "Fight for Hildy," July 18, 1955.

18. Cawley, "The Outlaws," 420–22.

19. "Ellises Are Held Fit to Raise Child," *New York Times*, July 9, 1957, 33.

20. "Fight for Hildy," *Time*, July 18, 1955, 38.

21. Florida Lets Jewish Couple Keep Catholic Child There," *New York Times*, May 24, 1957, 1.

22. "Fight for Hildy."

23. May, *Barren in the Promised Land*, 153.

24. See Linda Gordon, *The Great Arizona Orphan Abduction* (Cambridge, Mass.: Harvard University Press, 1999).

25. "Press and TV Chided on Hildy Coverage," *New York Times*, June 1, 1957, 8.

26. Francis J. Lally, "Reflections on 'Hildy' McCoy," *America*, June 8, 1957, 303–4.

27. "Fight for Hildy," 38.

28. "Reporter and Babies," *Newsweek*, November 28, 1955, 96; and "A Girl Got Affection," *Newsweek*, June 3, 1957. Also, Carp, *Family Matters*; and Melosh, *Strangers and Kin*.

29. "Florida Lets Jewish Couple Keep Catholic Child There," *New York Times*, May 24, 1957, 1.

30. "A Girl Got Affection," 29–30. Also see photo in "Florida Lets Jewish Couple Keep Catholic Child There," *New York Times*, May 24, 1957, 1.

31. "Florida Lets Jewish Couple Keep Catholic Child There," 1; and Editorial, "Home for Hildy," *New York Times*, May 26, 1957, E2.

32. James Gilbert, *A Cycle of Outrage: America's Reaction to the Juvenile Delinquent in the 1950s* (New York: Oxford University Press, 1986), 7–9, ch. 8; and Jason Barnosky, "The Violent Years: Responses to Juvenile Crime in the 1950s," *Polity* 38, no. 3 (July 2006): 314–44, esp. 318, 323, 326–27.

33. Hyde, "A Study of Proxy Adoptions"; and Balcom, "'Phony Mothers' and Border-Crossing Adoptions," *Journal of Women's History* 19, no. 1 (Spring 2007): 107–16.

34. "City's Gang Wars Ascribed to Girls," *New York Times*, March 10, 1961, 29.

35. U.S. Senate Committee on the Judiciary, *Investigation of Juvenile Delinquency in the United States*, S. Res. 62, 84th Cong., 1st sess., July 15–16, 1955, 3, 36.

36. U.S. Senate Committee on the Judiciary, *Investigation of Juvenile Delinquency in the United States*, S. Res. 728, 894, 1088, 1832, 84th Cong., 1st sess., July 6 & 8, 1955, 42, 50.

37. Frances Palmer, *And Four to Grow On* (New York: Holt, Rinehart, 1959), 221.

38. Mary Louise Mitchell to Estes Kefauver, July 19, 1955; Kefauver to Mitchell, July 26, 1955; and "The Roots of Delinquency," brochure, n.d., all in Box 226, Folder: Adoption Correspondence-1955, Senate Subcommittee on Juvenile Delinquency; and U.S. Senate Committee on the Judiciary, July, 6 & 8, 1955, 121. Also see Ira Henry Freeman, "50% of the Juvenile Delinquents in City Said to Be Rehabilitated," *New York Times*, July 2, 1956, 1.

39. Lisa Jacobson, *Raising Consumers: Children and the American Mass Market in the Early Twentieth Century* (New York: Columbia University Press, 2004), 173–75.

40. Marilyn Irvin Holt, *The Orphan Trains: Placing Out in America* (Lincoln: University of Nebraska Press, 1992); and Stephen O'Connor, *Orphan Trains: The Story of Charles Loring Brace and the Children He Saved and Failed* (Boston: Houghton Mifflin, 2001).

41. Regina Kunzel, *Fallen Women, Problem Girls: Unmarried Mothers and the Professionalization of Social Work, 1890–1945* (New Haven, Conn.: Yale University Press, 1993), 128–30; and Ellen Herman, "The Difference Difference Makes: Justine Wise Polier and Religious Matching in 20th Century Adoption," *Religion and American Culture* 10 (Winter 2000): 57–98.

42. Solinger, *Wake Up Little Susie*, 86–87.

43. Dorothy Barclay, "'Chosen Children': A Fresh Look," *New York Times Magazine*, November 9, 1958, 60; Melosh, *Strangers and Kin*; E. Wayne Carp, ed., *Adoption in America: Historical Perspectives* (Ann Arbor: University of Michigan Press, 2002); and Solinger, *Wake Up Little Susie*, 15–16.

44. "New Laws Sought by Adoption Units," *New York Times*, June 25, 1956; and Herman, "The Difference Difference Makes," 69.

45. Maud Morlock, "Babies on the Market," reprint from USCB Survey Midmonthly, March 1945, Box 159, Folder: Adoption, Jan. 1945–June 1945; and "Progress Report, Project on Prevention of Black Market in Babies and Other Unprotected Adoptive Placements," April 5, 1955, 4, 7–10, Box 674, Folder: Traffic in Children, Baby Farms, 1953–56, USCB papers.

46. U.S. Senate Committee on the Judiciary, July 15–16, 1955, 75.

47. Elaine Tyler May, *Homeward Bound: American Families in the Cold War*, 120.

48. John E. Twomey, "The Citizens' Committee and Comic Book Control: A Study of Extra-governmental Restraint," *Law and Contemporary Problems* 20, no. 4 (Autumn 1955): 621–29; William Cuyler Sullivan, *Nuclear Democracy: A History of the Greater St. Louis Citizen's Committee for Nuclear Information, 1957–1957* (St. Louis: Washington University, 1982); and Citizens Committee to Save Elysian Park records, Environmental History Archival Collections, USC Libraries Special Collections.

49. Wesley La Fever to Board of Directors, Rosenberg Foundation, February 1, 1952, Box 167, Folder 3: CCAC, 1950–1952, CA Public Welfare Law records. Even though the composition list reported only one adoptive parent, this did not match other documents' reports. For instance, in Los Angeles County Mary Stanton reported that her committee had a group of adoptive parents. I interpret this statistic to mean a person who *only* identified him/herself as an adoptive parent as opposed to an adoptive parent who put her first association down as a "PTA" member, "lay woman," or "nurse." See Mary Stanton, "Highlights from Eleven Months with the Citizen's Adoption Committee of Los Angeles," June 1951, 2–5, Box 167, Folder 3: CCAC, 1950–1952.

50. California Planning Conference on Adoption and Child Care, Bellevue Hotel, San Francisco, September 26–27, 1949; and Irene Liggett to Katherine Lenroot, February 7, 1950, both in Box 449, Folder: Adoptions, 1949–52, USCB papers; and Constitution and Code of By-Laws of CCAC, Art. II, Sec. 1, Box 167, Folder 4: CCAC, 1952–1954.

51. The state committee established local subcommittees in Alameda, Contra Costa, Fresno, Kern, Los Angeles, San Bernardino, San Diego, San Francisco, San Mateo, Santa Barbara, and Santa Clara.

52. Draft of Minutes of Meeting of CCAC Held in Los Angeles, August 1, 1950, Box 167, Folder 3: CCAC, 1950–1952; Mildred Arnold to Administrators of State Public Welfare Agencies and Directors of Child Welfare, March 1, 1952, Box 450, Folder: Adoptions, 1949–52, USCB papers; and CCAC, "A Report of the Project Planning Committee with Recommendations for a Research and Study Program," May 15, 1963, 21, Box 23, Folder 41: CCAC, Wycoff papers.

53. Robert E. G. Harris, "What's Wrong with the Adoption System?" *Los Angeles Times*, May 26, 1950.

54. "Request to Rosenberg and Columbia Foundations for Grant to Underwrite Adoption Project Recommended by Planning Conference on Adoption and Child Care," September 26–27, 1949, 1, Box 449, Folder: Adoptions, 1949–52, USCB papers.

55. Mary Stanton, "Highlights from Eleven Months with the Citizens' Adoption Committee of Los Angeles," June 1951, 2–5, Box 167, Folder 3: CCAC, 1950–1952.

56. Draft of Minutes of Meeting of CCAC Held in Los Angeles, August 1, 1950, 5; and (Draft) Interim Report of the Citizens Committee on Adoption of Children in California, January 1, 1951, 5, Box 167, Folder 3: CCAC, 1950–1952.

57. List of Adoption Questions, n.d., 1, Box 167, Folder 3: CCAC, 1950–1952.

58. Carp, *Family Matters*, ch. 4.

59. "A Case Study in Human Tragedy!" leaflet reprinted by CCAC, n.d., Box 167, Folder: CCAC, 1950–1952.

60. Bess Wilson, "Aid to Unwed Mothers Given Approval of Adoption Group," *Los Angeles Times*, February 4, 1951, article reprinted by CCAC with accompanying text; Charles Schottland, "A Report on Services for Unmarried Mothers in California," November 14, 1952, both in Box 167, Folder: CCAC, 1950–1952.

61. Mary Stanton to Kathryn Niehouse and meeting proceedings, October 18, 1950, Box 167, Folder: CCAC, 1950–1952.

62. Donald Tollefson, Chairman, Committee on Services to the Unmarried Mother, "Suggested Plan for Services to the Unmarried Mother," n.d.; John F. Hall, "An Experimental Program for Unmarried Mothers," *Child Welfare* 15, no. 5 (May 1951), reprinted by CCAC, Box 167, Folder: CCAC, 1950–1952.

63. Citizens Committee, "Unwed Motherhood—A Community Problem and Challenge," n.d., Box 167, Folder 4: CCAC, 1952–1954; and Rickie Solinger, *Beggars and Choosers: How the Politics of Choice Shapes Adoption, Abortion and Welfare in the United States* (New York: Hill and Wang, 2001).

64. Draft of Minutes of Meeting of CCAC Held in San Francisco, June 1, 1951, 3, Box 167, Folder 3: CCAC, 1950–1952.

65. CCAC Membership List, Report to Rosenberg Foundation, January 1, 1964, Box 23, Folder 42: CCAC, Wycoff papers; "Trends in Agency Services Compared to Independent Adoption Petitions," in Report to Rosenberg Foundation, January 1, 1964, Box 23, Folder 42: CCAC, Wycoff papers; and Letter Sent to Adoption Agencies, October 18, 1963, Box 23, Folder 42: CCAC, Wycoff papers.

66. CCAC "Initial report to Project Planning Committee," March 8, 1963, 1–2, 14, Box 23, Folder 38: CCAC, Wycoff papers.

67. H. David Kirk, *Shared Fate: A Theory and Method of Adoptive Relationships*, rev. ed. (1964; Port Angeles, Wash.: Ben-Simon, 1984), 107–9, 113.

68. Kirk dates the earliest adoptive parent association as The Adopted Children's Association of Los Angeles in 1948. He also argues that all adoptive parent societies were named as "adoptive child" groups rather than "adoptive parent" groups, until New York's Adoptive Parents' Committee formed in 1958. Archival records show that Ohio's Chosen Parent League predated this by over a decade. See Madalon Neuvirth to Katherine Lenroot; and Kirk, *Shared Fate*, 64.

69. *National Adoptalk*, October 1964, 2, Box 22, Folder: National Council of Adoptive Parents, ISS papers. Also see Bertha Holt, *Bring My Sons from Afar*, (Eugene, Ore.: Holt International Children's Services, 1986), 117.

70. Neuvirth to Lenroot, January 5, 1948.

71. As of 1966, NCAPO's member organizations included Adopted Children's Association of Los Angeles, Inc., Adoptive Parents' Committee of N.J., Inc., Adopted Children's Association of Whittier, Inc., Adoptive Parents' Committee of N.Y., Inc., Adoptive Parents' League of New Jersey, Colorado Adoptive Parents Association, Holtap of New Jersey, Little Church of Abandoned Children (Wisconsin), Mid-Continent Parents Organization, Nebraska Orphan Aid and Hope, Open Door Society of Canada, Inc., Parents for Overseas Adoption (of New York), and Society of Arkansas Parents. See *National Adoptalk*, February 1965 issue, 3, Box 22, Folder: National Council of Adoptive Parents, ISS papers.

72. Ellen Herman, *Kinship by Design: A History of Adoption in the Modern United States* (Chicago: University of Chicago Press, 2008), 246–48; and *National Adoptalk*, February 1966, 3, Box 22, Folder: National Council of Adoptive Parents, ISS papers.

73. "Question: Where Vanished the Tragic Piper," *Slattery's People*, first broadcast November 2, 1964 by CBS, directed by Lamont Johnson and written by Anthony Lawrence; "C.B.S. and Mr. Holt," *National Adoptalk*, November–December 1964, 1, Box 22, Folder: National Council of Adoptive Parents, ISS papers.

74. "Youngsters Lobby to Extend Orphan Bill," *Los Angeles Times*, July 23, 1961, OC13.

75. Daryl Lembke, "State Accused in Row over Korean Adoptions," *Los Angeles Times*, April 30, 1963, 2; and "State Senate Passes Bill to Ease Adoptions," *Los Angeles Times*, May 11, 1963, B11.

76. Mary Sarah King, "Battle for Adopted Child Won by Woman Crusader," *Boston Globe*, November 19, 1967, A10; Carol Liston, "One Woman's Battle Wins Equality for Adopted Children," *Boston Globe*, April 11, 1965, 34; and Mr. and Mrs. William L. Schultz, Jr., "Letter to the Editor: Adoption Law Hearings," *Boston Globe*, February 11, 1967, 4.

77. Jane Pierce, "When Adoption Is a Crusade," *Boston Globe*, March 16, 1969, A1.

78. "New York Bills Pass," *National Adoptalk*, May–June 1965, 1, Box 22, Folder: National Council of Adoptive Parents, ISS papers. Even though federal law still required special legislation for permission to adopt a third, this allowed New York state residents to take advantage of the federal exception.

79. Jean Dietz, "Adoption Inheritance Rights Urged," *Boston Globe*, March 1, 1967, 8; and "Editorial: Help for Adopted Children," *Boston Globe*, March 20, 1967, 10.

80. "Thumbs Down!" *National Adoptalk*, October 1964, 1–3, Box 22, Folder: National Council of Adoptive Parents, ISS papers.

81. "Moppets on the Market: The Problem of Unregulated Adoption," *Yale Law Journal* 59, no. 4 (March 1950): 715–36.

82. From major presses: Ernest Cady, *We Adopted Three* (New York: William Sloane, 1952), reprinted three times; Helen Doss, *The Family Nobody Wanted* (Chicago: Peoples Book Club, 1954, rep. Little, Brown, 1955, 1960, 1966); Harry Bell, *We Adopted a Daughter* (Boston: Houghton Mifflin, 1954); Marjorie Winter, *For Love of Martha* (New York: Julian Messner, 1956); Frances Palmer, *And Four to Grow On* (New York: Holt, Rinehart, 1959), went through four editions; and Robert Hyde, *Six More at Sixty* (Garden City, N.Y.: Doubleday, 1960). In his memoir, Hyde cites the influence of adoptive couples such as the Holts and Dosses on his own experience. From religious or vanity presses: Bertha Holt and David Wisner, *The Seed from the East* (Los Angeles: Oxford Press, 1956); E. Jane Mall, *P.S. I Love You* (St. Louis: Concordia, 1961); Edna Violet Stride, *Led By His Hand* (Upland, Calif.: Amko News, 1963), 10, 35, 40; Grace Connor, *Don't Disturb Daddy!* (Boston: Branden, 1965); Helen Louise West, *Adopted Four and Had One More* (St. Louis: Bethany Press), 1968; Maia Pederson, *At Sixes and Sevens* (New York: World, 1969); and Frank W. Chinnock, *Kim: A Gift from Vietnam* (New York: World, 1969).

83. Margaret A. Blanchard, *History of the Mass Media in the United States* (Chicago: Fitzroy Dearborn, 1998), 341; and Paul Lazarsfeld and Robert Merton, "Mass Communication, Popular Taste, and Organized Social Action," in *The Communication of Ideas*, ed. Eric Lenneberg (Cambridge, Mass.: MIT Press, 1948), 23–63, esp. 101.

84. May, *Barren in the Promised Land*, 147; and Margaret Marsh and Wanda Ronner, *The Empty Cradle: Infertility in America from Colonial Times to the Present* (Baltimore: Johns Hopkins Press, 1996), 209.

85. Rima Apple, *Mothers and Medicine: A Social History of Infant Feeding, 1890–1950* (Madison: University of Wisconsin Press, 1987), 3, 128, 131, 165–66; Linda M. Blum, *At the Breast: Ideologies of Breastfeeding and Motherhood in the Contemporary United States* (Boston: Beacon, 2000), 28–32; and Gwendolyn Mink, *The Wages of Motherhood: Inequality in the Welfare State* (Ithaca, N.Y.: Cornell University Press, 1995).

86. Benjamin Spock, *Baby and Child Care* (New York: Cardinal, 1957), 67–68. This recommendation was removed in later editions.

87. Apple, *Mothers and Medicine*, 3, 131; Blum, *At the Breast*, 31.

88. May, *Homeward Bound*, 121, 125; and Kirk, *Shared Fate*, 113.

89. Doss, *The Family Nobody Wanted*, 3; Winter, *For Love of Martha*, 34; and Mall, *P.S. I Love You.*

90. Doss, *The Family Nobody Wanted*, 232.

91. Winter, *For Love of Martha*, 144; Bell, *We Adopted a Daughter*, 2–3; and Jane Cobb, "A Delight Ever Since," *New York Times*, May 9, 1954, Book Reviews, 23.

92. Cady, *We Adopted Three*, 26; Elinor Haynes, "He Rescued 3,000 Orphans," *Oakland Tribune*, 30 April 1964, 2; and Ben, "A World Inside One Household: Review," *New York Times*, November 21, 1954, sec. BR. For more on the rescue of childless couples during the early twentieth century, see Berebitsky, *Like Our Very Own.*

93. Bell, *We Adopted a Daughter*, 74; Mall, *P.S. I Love You*, 118.

94. Winter, *For Love of Martha*, 40, 74.

95. Bell, *We Adopted a Daughter*, 80. See also Cobb, "A Delight Ever Since," 23.

96. Winter, *For Love of Martha*, 19; and "Advertisement *For Love of Martha*," *New York Times*, March 3, 1957.

97. Palmer, *And Four to Grow On*, 70; Jane Cobb, "Their Need Was Love," Book Review; and "Advertisement," *Chicago Daily Tribune*, May 24, 1959.

98. Hyde, *Six More at Sixty*, 157, 164–65.

99. Bradford, "A World Inside One Household: Review," 34; "Unwanted Find a Home," *Look*, October 30, 1956, 106–8, "'The Lord Is Their Sponsor': Korean Octet Gets a U.S. Home," *Life*, December 26, 1955, 58; Pearl S. Buck, "Should White Parents Adopt Brown Babies?" *Ebony*, June 1958, 26–31; and May, *Homeward Bound*, 132.

100. Joanne Meyerowitz, "Beyond the Feminine Mystique: A Reassessment of Postwar Mass Culture, 1946–1958," in *Not June Cleaver: Women and Gender in Postwar America, 1945–1960*, ed. Meyerowitz (Philadelphia: Temple University Press, 1994), 234; "'Babylift' Bribe Charges Rejected by Mrs. Holt," *Register-Guard*, June 26, 1959; "Mrs. Harry Holt Pleased with TV Presentation," *Register-Guard*, February 2, 1959; and "Lane County Tuberculosis Assn. Hears Mrs. Holt, Salem Doctor," *Register-Guard*, April 25, 1958.

101. May, *Homeward Bound*, 16; and Hyde, *Six More at Sixty.*

102. Lillian D. Poling, *Mothers of Men: A Twenty-Five-Year History of the American Mothers of the Year, 1935–1959* (Bridgeport, Conn.: Kurt H. Volk, 1959), 56–57; and American Mothers Committee, *34th Anniversary Yearbook, 1935–1969* (acquired by author through American Mothers, Inc. staff).

103. "Bertha Holt" in *All Believers Are Brothers*, ed. Roland Gammon (Garden City, N.Y.: Doubleday, 1969), 108–9.

104. Poling, *Mothers of Men*, 11; and Chiou-Ling Yeh, "'A Saga of Democracy': Toy Len Goon, American Mother of the Year, and the Cultural Cold War," *Pacific Historical Review* 81, no. 3 (Fall 2012): 432–61.

105. Ralph La Rossa, "The Culture of Fatherhood in the Fifties: A Closer Look," *Journal of Family History* 29, no. 1 (January 2004): 47–70. Also M. J. E. Senn, "What Only a Father Can Give," *Woman's Home Companion*, November 1956, 11; Robert L. Griswold, *Fatherhood in America: A History* (New York: Basic Books, 1993).

106. "Adopter of 8 Koreans off to Get 200 More," *New York Times*, March 26, 1956; Elinor Haynes, "He Rescued 3,000 Orphans," *Oakland Tribune*, April 30, 1964, 2; "New Faces," *Time*, December 23, 1957.

107. Ron Moxness, "Good Samaritan of Korea," *American Mercury*, October 1956, 86; "An Airlift for 89 Orphans Flies Korean Children 'Home' to U.S.," *New York Times*, December 18, 1956, 33; "Pair Mortgage Home to Adopt Baby Girl," *Los Angeles Times*, January 18, 1962; and "Orange Couple Adopt Second Korean Waif," *Los Angeles Times*, August 2, 1962.

108. May, *Homeward Bound*, 130–31; and "Father's Place in the Home," *Ladies Home Journal*

109. Cady, *We Adopted Three*, 103–4.

110. "In a Nutshell," *Washington Post*, July 20, 1952; Joseph Henry Jackson, "Bookman's Notebook: They Adopted Three," *Los Angeles Times*, May 27, 1952; Frances Dunlap Heron, "For Doubters of Adoption Practicality," *Chicago Daily Tribune*, July 13, 1952, sec. Part 4; and Dorothy Barclay, "A Playmate for Jeff," *New York Times*, October 5, 1952, sec. Book Review.

111. May, *Homeward Bound*, 21; William H. Chafe, *The Unfinished Journey: America Since World War II*, 5th ed. (New York: Oxford University Press, 2003), 115–16; and "Religious Faiths List Large Gains," *New York Times*, September 3, 1957, 52. Also see John Butler, *Awash in a Sea of Faith: Christianizing the American People* (Cambridge, Mass.: Harvard University Press, 1992); and Arissa Oh, "Into the Arms of America: The Korean Roots of International Adoption" (Ph.D. dissertation, University of Chicago, 2008), chap. 3.

112. See Mall, Stride, Holt, Doss, Palmer, and West. Carl Doss and Jane Mall's husband were also ministers.

113. Stride, *Led by His Hand*, 25, 41, 42. Also see Holt and Wisner, *Seed from the East*; and Holt, *Bring Your Sons from Afar*.

114. "'The Lord Is Their Sponsor': Korean Octet Gets a U.S. Home," *Life*, December 26, 1955, 58; Elinor Haynes, "He Rescued 3,000 Orphans," *Oakland Tribune*, April 30, 1964, 2; H. P. Sconce, "Lenten Guideposts," *Vidette-Messenger*, April 19, 1957, 7; and Dan Sellard, "Work Abroad Scatters Harry Holt Clan," *Register-Guard*, December 5, 1960.

115. Lou Jorst, "Yoo and Kim Get 200 Mothers, Dads," *Independent*, November 24, 1958, 1.

116. Bell, *We Adopted a Daughter*, 17, 26, 122, 114.

117. "Family's Reward: The Multi-Racial Dosses Hit a $10,000 Jackpot," *Life*, January 14, 1952, 41–44.

118. See Jacobson, *Raising Consumers*; Gary Cross, *Kids' Stuff: Toys and the Changing World of American Childhood* (Cambridge, Mass.: Harvard University Press, 1997); and William Leach, "Child-World in the Promised Land," in *The Mythmaking Frame of Mind: Social Imagination and American Culture*, ed. James Gilbert et al. (Belmont, Calif.: Wadsworth, 1993).

119. May, *Homeward Bound*, 11, 146.

120. George Putnam, newscast in documentary film by The Archives Project, *The Atomic Café*, 1982, Thorn Emi Video, as cited in May, *Homeward Bound*, 150. See also Lizabeth Cohen, *A Consumer's Republic: The Politics of Mass Consumption in Postwar America* (New York: Vintage, 2003), ch. 6.

121. "A Famous Orphan Finds a Happy Home," *Life*, May 14, 1956, 129–30.

122. "New American Comes Home," *Life*, November 30, 1953, 25–29. See J. Hoberman, *An Army of Phantoms: American Movies and the Making of the Cold War* (New York: New Press, 2011); and Matthew J. Costello, "Rewriting High Noon: Transformations in American Popular Political Culture During the Cold War, 1952–1968," in *Hollywood's West: the American Frontier in Film, Television, and History*, ed. Peter C. Rollins and John E. O'Connor (Lexington: University Press of Kentucky, 2005).

123. Bradford, "A World Inside One Household: Review," 43; and Doss, *The Family Nobody Wanted*, 32.

124. Stride, *Led by His Hand*, 10, 35, 40.

125. Mall, *P.S. I Love You*, 107, 143.

126. "Life Visits a One-Family U.N.," *Life*, November 12, 1951, 157–60; and "Family's Reward: The Multi-Racial Dosses Hit a $10,000 Jackpot," 41–44.

127. Dan Fowler, "A Rare Lesson About Love," *Look*, April 30, 1957, 42–46.

128. May, *Homeward Bound*, xix; and Stephanie Coontz, *The Way We Never Were* (New York: Basic, 1993), 30–31.

129. "Farmer Who Adopted 3,000 Orphans Dies," *Los Angeles Times*, April 29, 1964.

130. "Benefactor Visits 30 Korean Orphans Here," *Los Angeles Times*, February 13, 1959.

131. James Bulse, "Sparks Family Provides Home for Four Korean Girls," *Nevada State Journal*, July 31, 1960, 32.

132. Al Carr, "Korean Tots Find Love with County Families," *Los Angeles Times*, April 21, 1963.

133. Moxness, "Good Samaritan of Korea," 86; and Sol Padlibsky, "Weekly Column: Of All Things," *Charleston Daily Mail*, September 24, 1956, 5.

134. Doss, *The Family Nobody Wanted*, ch. 13.

135. Coontz, *The Way We Never Were*, 31.

136. Christina Klein, "Family Ties and Political Obligation: The Discourse of Adoption and the Cold War Commitment to Asia," in *Cold War Constructions: The Political Culture of United States Imperialism, 1945–1966*, ed. Christian G. Appy (Amherst: University of Massachusetts Press, 2000), 38.

137. Doss, *The Family Nobody Wanted*, 193.

138. West, *Adopted Four and Had One More*, 94.

139. Cady, *We Adopted Three*, 9.

140. Ibid., 14.

141. "New Laws Sought by Adoption Units," *New York Times*, June 25, 1956. Also see Cady, *We Adopted Three*.

142. West, *Adopted Four and Had One More*, 54.

143. Doss, *The Family Nobody Wanted*, 4.

144. Cady, *We Adopted Three*, 43.

145. "Our Adopted Children," Report of Workshop for Adoptive Parents, March 24, 1956, Box 684, Folder: Adoptions, March 1956, 1953–1957, USCB papers.

146. Carl Doss and Helen Doss, *If You Adopt a Child* (New York: Holt, 1957); Ernest Cady and Frances Cady, *How to Adopt a Child* (New York: Whiteside and Morow, 1956); and Carp, *Family Matters*, 124.

147. Mall, *P.S. I Love You*, 11.

148. Doss, *The Family Nobody Wanted*, 27.

149. Winter, *For Love of Martha*, 114.

150. West, *Adopted Four and Had One More*, 62.

151. Palmer, 57–59, 94.

152. Winter, *For Love of Martha*, 19, 112.

153. Solinger, *Beggars and Choosers*, 28–35.

154. Holt, *Bring My Sons from Afar*, 12. More recent Korean birth mothers' own stories indicate that they had myriad reasons for relinquishing their children. See Sara Dorow, *I Wish for You a Beautiful Life: Letters from the Korean Birth Mothers of Ae Ran Won to Their Children* (St. Paul, Minn.: Yeong & Yeong, 1999).

155. Holt, *Bring My Sons from Afar*, 13 (emphasis mine).

156. Eleana Kim, *Adopted Territory: Transnational Korean Adoptees and the Politics of Belonging* (Durham, N.C.: Duke University Press, 2010). See also Oh, *To Save the Children of Korea: The Cold War Origins of International Adoption.*

157. Solinger, *Beggars and Choosers*, 25, 28, 31; and Ann Laura Stoler, *Carnal Knowledge and Imperial Power: Race and the Intimate in Colonial Rule* (Berkeley: University of California Press, 2002).

158. Holt, *Bring My Sons from Afar*, 16.

159. "Unwanted Find a Home," *Look*, October 30, 1956, 106; and Oh, *To Save the Children of Korea.*

160. In other correspondence, Paek is spelled "Paik." See Munro to Cherney, November 23, 1962, Box 34, Folder: Korea-Adoptions to '62, ISS papers.

161. Memo from ELH to Adoption Staff, August 14, 1967, Box 10, Folder: Adoption Correspondence, ISS papers.

162. Etienne Balibar and Immanuel Wallerstein, *Race, Nation, Class: Ambiguous Identities* (London: Verso, 1991), 96.

Chapter 5. A New Kind of Racial Alchemy: International Development, Transracial Adoption, and the Vietnam War, 1965–1974

1. "Orphans of the Storm," June 25, 1973, *Chicago Defender (Daily Edition)*, 13; and Andrew Billingsley and Jeanne Giovannoni, *Children of the Storm* (New York: Harcourt Brace, 1972).

2. Ursula M. Gallagher, "Adoption in a Changing Society," *Children Today*, September–October 1972, 2, clipping in RG 46: Senate Judiciary Committee, Box 16, Folder: Subcommittee on Children, 1972–1976, Archives I; "Black Social Workers Oppose Placement of Black Children in White Homes, 1972," in *Children and Youth in America: A Documentary History*, vol. 3, *1933–1973*, ed. Robert H. Bremner (Cambridge, Mass.: Harvard University Press, 1974), 777–80; and Judy Klemesrud, "Furor over Whites Adopting Blacks," *New York Times*, 12 April 1972, 38, reprint *New Pittsburgh Courier*, April 22, 1972, 36.

3. Nils Gilman, *Mandarins of the Future: Modernization Theory in Cold War America* (Baltimore: Johns Hopkins University Press, 2003), 71.

4. Gilman, *Mandarins of the Future*, 12; Michael Omi and Howard Winant, *Racial Formation in the United States: From the 1960s to the 1990s*, 2nd ed. (New York: Routledge, 1994), 55; and Matthew Frye Jacobson, *Whiteness of a Different Color: European Immigrants and the Alchemy of Race* (Cambridge, Mass.: Harvard University Press, 1999).

5. Andrew J. Rotter, "The Causes of the Vietnam War," in *The Oxford Companion to American Military History*, ed. John Whiteclay Chambers II (New York: Oxford University Press, 1999); Allison Stanger, *One Nation Under Contract: The Outsourcing of American Power and the Future of Foreign Policy* (New Haven, Conn.: Yale University Press, 2011), 110–12; and Michael Latham, *Modernization as Ideology: American Social Science and "Nation Building" in the Kennedy Era* (Chapel Hill: University of North Carolina Press, 2000), 57, 83.

6. Hearing Before the Subcommittee to Investigate Problems Connected with Refugees and Escapees, Senate Committee on the Judiciary, 94th Cong., 1st sess., 8 April 1975, 7.

7. Latham, *Modernization as Ideology*, 2–5, 151, 213; Michael Katz, *The Undeserving Poor: From the War on Poverty to the War on Welfare* (New York: Pantheon, 1989), 23; and Gilman,

Mandarins of the Future, 3–4. Also see Michael E. Latham, *The Right Kind of Revolution: Modernization, Development, and U.S. Foreign Policy from the Cold War to the Present* (Ithaca, N.Y.: Cornell University Press, 2011).

8. Depp to Wells Klein, June 7, 1971; Klein to Edward Zigler, June 24, 1971; and Klein, "The Special Needs of Vietnamese Children—A Critique," September 1971, all in Box 38, Folder: Vietnam—Conference on the Special Needs of Children in Vietnam—July 19, 1971, ISS papers.

9. Senate Subcommittee to Investigate Problems Connected with Refugees and Escapees, *Hearing: Relief and Rehabilitation of War Victims in Indochina, Part II: Orphans and Child Welfare*, 93rd Cong., 1st sess., May 11, 1973.

10. Paul R. Cherney, General Director, ISS, Statement to Subcommittee on Refugees and Escapees, U.S. Senate Committee on the Judiciary, RE: Vietnam, August 4–5, 1965, Box 38, Folder: ISS International, Vietnam Administrative Files, January 1965–December 1965, ISS papers.

11. Klein to Zigler, June 24, 1971; Klein, "The Special Needs of Vietnamese Childreners.

12. Mrs. Marcia Burke to Sen. Walter F. Mondale, n.d.; Mondale to Ellen Winston, June 29, 1965; and Winston to Mondale, July 12, 1965, Box 1033, USCB papers.

13. Internal Memo, Dept. of State: Agency for International Development, 5/71, Box 38, Folder: Vietnam—Conference on the Special Needs of Children in Vietnam—July 19, 1971, ISS papers.

14. Agency for International Development, "Operation Babylift Report (Emergency Movement of Vietnamese and Cambodian Orphans for International Adoption)," Washington, D.C., April–June 1975, 2, Box 56, Folder: Adoption-Intercountry, Vietnam Babylift, Media, CWLA papers.

15. Senate Subcommittee, *Relief and Rehabilitation of War Victims in Indochina*, May 11, 1973, 7.

16. Robert Lewis to Paul Cherney, December 15, 1965, Box 38, Folder: ISS International, Vietnam Administrative Files, January 1965–December 1965, ISS papers.

17. Study Mission Report, Subcommittee to Investigate Problems Connected with Refugees and Escapees, Committee on the Judiciary, U.S. Senate, *Relief and Rehabilitation of War Victims in Indochina: One Year After the Ceasefire*, 93rd Cong., 2nd sess., January 27, 1974, 157, 168.

18. Alfred B. Herbert, Jr., to IVAC Committee Members, Re: Updating of IVAC Activities, May 9, 1974, Box 39, Folder: IVAC, Interagency Vietnam Adoption Committee, ISS papers; and "Atlanta NAACP Adoption Agency Voices Concern for Viet Orphans," *Atlanta Daily World*, November 27, 1973, 5.

19. Latham, *Modernization as Ideology*, 207; Natasha Zaretsky, *No Direction Home: The American Family and the Fear of National Decline, 1968–1980* (Chapel Hill: University of North Carolina Press, 2007), 74; David Ekbladh, *The Great American Mission: Modernization and the Construction of an American World Order* (Princeton, N.J.: Princeton University Press, 2010), 10; and Christopher T. Fisher, "Nation Building and the Vietnam War: A Historiography," *Pacific Historical Review* 74, no. 3 (August 2005): 441–56.

20. "Place Viet Kids Here," *Chicago Defender (Daily Edition)*, October 30, 1973, 4.

21. Ellen Herman, *Kinship by Design: A History of Adoption in the Modern United States* (Chicago: University of Chicago Press, 2008), ch. 7.

22. Herman, *Kinship by Design*, 238.

23. Billingsley and Giovannoni, *Children of the Storm*, 164–65; and Steven Morris, "Fight for Black Babies," *Ebony*, September 1973, 32–42.

24. See Billingsley and Giovannoni, *Children of the Storm*, ch. 7.

25. Billingsley and Giovannoni, *Children of the Storm*, 197–98. For the history of single-mother adoption, see Herman, *Kinship by Design*, 203–4. For contemporary concerns regarding single-parent adoption, see Christine Ward Gailey, "'Whatever They Think of Us, We're a Family': Single Mother Adopters," in *Adoptive Families in a Diverse Society*, ed. Katarina Wegar (New Brunswick, N.J.: Rutgers University Press, 2006), 162–74. There are a few cases of single-father adoption, but these were rare. See Charles and Bonnie Remsberg, "Baby Everyone Wanted," *Redbook*, January 1973, 73, 125–27; and Peter Bailey, "Malcolm Bailey Finds a Father," *Ebony*, August 1974.

26. Randall Kennedy, *Interracial Intimacies: Sex, Marriage, Identity, and Adoption* (New York: Pantheon, 2003), 452; and "White Parents, Black Children," *Time*, August 16, 1971, 42–45.

27. For a critical stance on interracial adoption in the black press, see Helen H. King, "It's Easier to Adopt Today," *Ebony*, December 1970, 120–28. For a more supportive perspective, see "Beau Bridges Starts a New Family," *Ebony*, October 1970, 96–104; Barbara Cowan, National Urban League, to Margaret Penn, Catholic Family Services to Black Families, October 18, 1972, Box III, Folder 84: Adoption 1972–77, National Urban League papers; and Pamphlet, "The A-B-C's of Adoption," 1968, Box VI F130, Folder: NAACP Adoptive Parent Recruitment and Education Project, NAACP papers.

28. Joseph Morgenstern, "New Face of Adoption," *Newsweek*, September 13, 1971, 67.

29. Billingsley and Giovannoni, *Children of the Storm*, 17. Laura Briggs has challenged traditional interpretations that argue NABSW was aimed only at adoption and white families. Instead, she argues convincingly that the statement was a plea to stop the white social welfare system's removal of black children from their families and into foster care. See Briggs, *Somebody's Children: The Politics of Transracial and Transnational Adoption* (Durham, N.C.: Duke University Press, 2012), 421–54.

30. "Black Orphans in White Homes," *Sun Reporter*, June 24, 1972.

31. "Black Social Workers Oppose Placement of Black Children in White Homes, 1972," 779.

32. Frontiers in Adoption newsletter, July 1972, Box 19, Folder: Adoptive Parent Groups, ISS papers; and Judy Klemesrud, "Furor over Whites Adopting Blacks," *New York Times*, April 12, 1972, 38.

33. Briggs, *Somebody's Children*, 46–48, 58.

34. Billingsley and Giovannoni, *Children of the Storm*, 68–69.

35. David Hilliard and Lewis Cole, *This Side of Glory: The Autobiography of David Hilliard and the Story of the Black Panther Party* (New York: Lawrence Hill, 1993), 320.

36. Simone M. Caron, "Birth Control and the Black Community in the 1960s: Genocide or Power Politics," *Journal of Social History* 31, no. 3 (Spring 1998): 545–69; and Dorothy Roberts, *Killing the Black Body: Race, Reproduction, and the Meaning of Liberty* (New York: Pantheon, 1997), 99, 102.

37. "Black Renaissance," *Chicago Defender (Daily Edition)*, March 5, 1969, 15; Thomas F. Jackson, *From Civil Rights to Human Rights: Martin Luther King, Jr., and the Struggle for Economic Justice* (Philadelphia: University of Pennsylvania Press, 2009). Also see Penny M. Von Eschen, *Race Against Empire: Black Americans and Anticolonialism, 1937–1957* (Ithaca, N.Y.: Cornell University Press, 1997); and Kevin K. Gaines, *African Americans in Ghana: Black Expatriates and the Civil Rights Era* (Chapel Hill: University of North Carolina Press, 2008).

38. Ebony Mail Response, clipping, and Heller to Prospective Adoptive Parents, September 1967, Box 10, Folder: Adoption Correspondence, ISS papers; and Department of State: Agency for International Development, "Children in Vietnam of Mixed American-Vietnamese Parentage."

39. "Report of IVAC Delegation Visit to South Vietnam, January 10–20, 1974," vi, Folder: IVAC, Interagency Vietnam Adoption Committee, Box 39, Folder: IVAC, Interagency Vietnam Adoption Committee, ISS papers.

40. Department of State: Agency for International Development, "Children in Vietnam of Mixed American-Vietnamese Parentage."

41. Internal Memo, Department of State: Agency for International Development, May 1971, Box 38, Folder: Vietnam—Conference on the Special Needs of Children in Vietnam.

42. Department of State: Agency for International Development, "Children in Vietnam of Mixed American-Vietnamese Parentage.

43. Minister of Social Welfare to Klein, July 9, 1971, Box 38, Folder: Vietnam—Conference on the Special Needs of Children in Vietnam.

44. Era Bell Thompson, "Plight of Black Babies in South Vietnam," *Ebony*, December 1972, 104–16.

45. "Report of IVAC Delegation Visit to South Vietnam."

46. Paul R. Cherney, Statement to Subcommittee on Refugees and Escapees, Committee on Judiciary, U.S. Senate, Re: Viet Nam, August 4–5, 1965, Box 38, Folder: ISS International, Vietnam Administrative Files, January 1965–December 1965, ISS papers.

47. See Arissa Oh, "Into the Arms of America: The Korean Roots of International Adoption," (Ph.D. dissertation, University of Chicago, 2008).

48. Depp to Klein, June 7, 1971; Klein to Zigler, June 24, 1971; and Klein, "The Special Needs of Vietnamese Children—A Critique," September 1971, all in Box 38, Folder: Vietnam—Conference on the Special Needs of Children in Vietnam.

49. Senate Subcommittee, *Relief and Rehabilitation of War Victims in Indochina*, May 11, 1973, 6, 12, 22.

50. Senate Subcommittee, *Relief and Rehabilitation of War Victims in Indochina*, May 11, 1973, 6; and *Relief and Rehabilitation of War Victims in Indochina: One Year After the Ceasefire*, January 27, 1974, 31.

51. Senate Subcommittee, *Relief and Rehabilitation of War Victims in Indochina*, May 11, 1973, 6.

52. House Subcommittee on Immigration, Citizenship, and International Law, "A Second Visit to Vietnam—A Report on Child Care Activities," in *Refugees from Indochina Hearings*, April 9, 1975, 97th Cong., 1st sess., 115.

53. Senate Subcommittee, *Relief and Rehabilitation of War Victims in Indochina*, May 11, 1973, 159.

54. Thompson, "Plight of Black Babies in South Vietnam."

55. Cynthia Enloe, *Maneuvers: The International Politics of Militarizing Women's Lives* (Berkeley: University of California Press, 2000), 67; and James Westheider, *Fighting on Two Fronts: African Americans and the Vietnam War* (New York: New York University Press, 1997), 46, 133.

56. Senate Subcommittee, *Relief and Rehabilitation of War Victims in Indochina*, May 11, 1973, 22.

57. "A Second Visit to Vietnam—A Report on Child Care Activities," 115, 119.

58. *Compos v. McKeithen*, 341 F. Supp. 266 (1970) as cited in Kennedy, *Interracial Intimacies*, 389; and "Children in Vietnam of Mixed American-Vietnamese Parentage," May 1971, ISS papers.

59. Military Press Summaries, April 8, 1975, Box 4, Folder: Press Releases, April 7–23, 1975, Records of the Army Staff, Archives II.

60. "Report of IVAC Delegation Visit to South Vietnam, January 10–20, 1974," Appendix B, p. v, 8, ISS papers.

61. Robert Vitalis, "The Graceful and Generous Liberal Gesture: Making Racism Invisible in American International Relations," *Millennium—Journal of International Studies* 29, no. 2 (2000): 341.

62. Senate Subcommittee, *Relief and Rehabilitation of War Victims in Indochina: One Year After the Ceasefire*, January 27, 1974, 171; and Ann Laura Stoler, "Carnal Knowledge and Imperial Power: Gender and Morality in the Making of Race," in *Women in Asia*, vol. 4: *Constructions of the Feminine*, ed. Louise Edwards and Mina Roces (London: Routledge, 2009), 3.

63. Gilman, *Mandarins of the Future*, 20.

64. Senate Subcommittee, *Relief and Rehabilitation of War Victims in Indochina*, May 11, 1973, 34–35.

65. Robert David Johnson, *Congress and the Cold War* (Cambridge: Cambridge University Press, 2006), 126–28.

66. "Background Memoranda on the Development of a Child Welfare Program in South Vietnam: Officials USAID Memoranda for the Record" as recorded in Senate Subcommittee, *Relief and Rehabilitation of War Victims in Indochina*, May 11, 1973, 75, 82.

67. Senate Subcommittee, *Relief and Rehabilitation of War Victims in Indochina*, May 11, 1973, 32.

68. "Report of IVAC Delegation Visit to South Vietnam," 4.

69. "Background Memoranda on the Development of a Child Welfare Program in South Vietnam: Officials USAID Memoranda for the Record," 83.

70. Paul A. Kramer, *The Blood of Government: Race, Empire, the United States, and the Philippines* (Chapel Hill: University of North Carolina Press, 2006), 5.

71. "Report of IVAC Delegation Visit to South Vietnam," 4.

72. Senate Subcommittee, *Relief and Rehabilitation of War Victims in Indochina: One Year After the Ceasefire*, January 27, 1974, 154–57.

73. "Report of IVAC Delegation Visit to South Vietnam," 4.

74. Senate Committee on Foreign Relations, *Hearing on S. 2497*, April 5, 1972, 92nd Cong., 2nd sess., 126.

75. Senate Subcommittee, *Relief and Rehabilitation of War Victims in Indochina*, May 11, 1973, 6.

76. Ibid., 4–5, 7.

77. Senate Subcommittee to Investigate Problems Connected with Refugees and Escapees, Study Mission Report, *Humanitarian Problems in South Vietnam and Cambodia: Two Years After the Ceasefire*, 94th Cong., 1st sess., January 27, 1975, 37.

78. "Background Memoranda on the Development of a Child Welfare Program in South Vietnam: Officials USAID Memoranda for the Record," 80.

79. Lauralee M. Peters to William M. Taylor, May 29, 1974, Box 39, Folder: Vietnam, ISS papers.

80. Senate Subcommittee, *Relief and Rehabilitation of War Victims in Indochina*, May 11, 1973, 32, 35, 80.

81. Loren Jenkins, "Vietnam's War-Torn Children," *Newsweek*, May 28, 1973. Also cited in *Relief and Rehabilitation of War Victims in Indochina*, 1973, 97.

82. Daniel Patrick Moynihan, "The Negro Family: The Case for National Action," March 1965, Office of Policy Planning and Research, U.S. Department of Labor, quote from Chapter II: The Negro American Family; and Katz, *The Undeserving Poor*, 20, 23–25.

83. Rickie Solinger, *Wake Up Little Susie: Single Pregnancy and Race Before* Roe v. Wade (New York: Routledge, 1992), 43, 79; Katz, 28–29; and Ortiz and Briggs, "The Culture of Poverty, Crack Babies, and Welfare Cheats: The Making of the 'Healthy White Baby Crisis,'" *Social Text* 76 (2003): 39–58.

84. Zaretsky, *No Direction Home*, 13–14; Solinger, *Wake Up Little Susie*, 42; and Marisa Chappell, *The War on Welfare: Family, Poverty, and Politics in Modern America* (Philadelphia: University of Pennsylvania Press, 2010), 11, 50, 143.

85. "Report of IVAC Delegation Visit to South Vietnam," vi.

86. "A Summary of Discussion on Special Needs of Vietnamese Children," July 19, 1971; and Nazli Kibria, *Family Tightrope: The Changing Lives of Vietnamese Americans* (Princeton, N.J.: Princeton University Press, 1993), 51.

87. Senate Subcommittee, *Relief and Rehabilitation of War Victims in Indochina*, May 11, 1973, 22.

88. "Text of April 25th NBC Broadcast Re Racially Mixed Children in Vietnam," April 25, 1971, Box 38, Folder: Vietnam—Conference on the Special Needs of Children in Vietnam—July 19, 1971, ISS papers.

89. As quoted in James Patterson, *Freedom Is Not Enough: The Moynihan Report and America's Struggle over Black Family Life—From LBJ to Obama* (New York: Basic, 2010), 97, 129.

90. "Black Social Workers Oppose Placement of Black Children in White Homes, 1972," 779.

91. Chappell, *The War on Welfare*, 103.

92. Ibid., 53. Also see Patricia Hill Collins, "Producing the Mothers of the Nation: Race, Class and Contemporary US Population Policies," in *Women, Citizenship and Difference*, ed. Nira Yuval-Davis and Pnina Werbner (London: Zed, 1999), 124–26.

93. Joanne Dann, "Wanted: A Doctor Spock for Black Mothers," *New York Times Magazine*, April 18, 1971, 88; and Chappell, *The War on Welfare*, 48, 56.

94. Carol B. Stack, *All Our Kin: Strategies for Survival in a Black Community* (New York: Harper & Row, 1974), 24, 51.

95. Senate Subcommittee, *Relief and Rehabilitation of War Victims in Indochina*, May 11, 1973, 18.

96. Ibid.

97. App IV, Wells Klein report on Special Needs of Korea in Senate Subcommittee Hearing, May 11, 1973, 86.

98. Page Act of 1875, 43rd Cong., 2nd sess., 1875, Chap. 141, Sec. 5; and Ronald Takaki, *Strangers from a Different Shore: A History of Asian Americans* (New York: Penguin, 1989), 126.

99. Yuki Fujime, "Japanese Feminism and Commercialized Sex: The Union of Militarism and Prohibitionism," *Social Science Japan Journal* 9 (2006): 33–50; Mire Koikari, "Rethinking Gender and Power in the U.S. Occupation of Japan, 1945–1952," *Gender & History* 11, no. 2 (July 1999): 313. See also Jin-Kyung Lee, *Service Economies: Militarism, Sex Work, and Migrant Labor in South Korea* (Minneapolis: University of Minnesota Press, 2010).

100. Enloe, *Maneuvers*, 66–67.

101. Susan Zeiger, *Entangling Alliances: Foreign War Brides and American Soldiers in the Twentieth Century* (New York: New York University Press, 2010), 215–16; and John Baky, "White Cong and Black Clap: The Ambient Truth of Vietnam War Legendry," *Vietnam Generation* 5 (1994): 166–68.

102. Senate Subcommittee, *Relief and Rehabilitation of War Victims in Indochina,* May 11, 1973, 19.

103. Senate Subcommittee, *Relief and Rehabilitation of War Victims in Indochina,* January 27, 1974, 163.

104. Charlotte Brooks, *Alien Neighbors, Foreign Friends: Asian Americans, Housing, and the Transformation of Urban California* (Chicago: University of Chicago Press, 2009), 227–29, 238–39.

105. Mae M. Ngai, *Impossible Subjects: Illegal Aliens and the Making of Modern America* (Princeton, N.J.: Princeton University Press, 2004); 258–63.

106. Andrew J. Rotter, "Culture, the Cold War, and the Third World," in *The Cold War in the Third World,* ed. Robert J. McMahon (New York: Oxford University Press, 2013), 159; and Frank W. Chinnock, *Kim: A Gift from Vietnam* (New York: World, 1969), 11, 197.

107. Chappell, *The War on Welfare,* 114–15; and Dr. James Dumpson, Career Highlights, accessed July 25, 2011, http://www.fordham.edu/academics/colleges__graduate_s/graduate__ profession/social_service/centers__institutes/the_james_r_dumpson_/dr_james_r_dumpson_697 49.asp.

108. Chappell, *The War on Welfare,* 108.

109. *Relief and Rehabilitation of War Victims in Indochina,* May 11, 1973, 59, 68.

110. Friends of Children of Vietnam became Friends for All Children in late 1973. The acronym FFAC reflects this shift. Friends of Children of Vietnam continued to operate as a separate group, an institutional change that Chapter Six examines more extensively.

111. While TAISSA had conducted adoptions previously in Vietnam, its program ended in late 1960s when GVN halted adoptions. Before restarting its program in 1973, it worked on migration and family reunification.

112. Senate Subcommittee, *Relief and Rehabilitation of War Victims in Indochina,* 1974, 159–60.

113. Senate Subcommittee, *Relief and Rehabilitation of War Victims in Indochina,* 1973, 60.

114. Senate Committee on International Relations, *The Vietnam-Cambodia Emergency, 1975, Part I: Vietnam Evacuation and Humanitarian Assistance,* 94th Cong., 1st sess., April/May 1975, 32.

115. Senate Subcommittee, *Relief and Rehabilitation of War Victims in Indochina,* 1973, 72.

116. Jenkins, "Vietnam's War-Torn Children."

117. "Report of IVAC Delegation Visit to South Vietnam," ix.

118. "Proposal from the Interagency Vietnam Adoption Committee (IVAC) to the Department of Health, Education, and Welfare (HEW)," March 1974, 5, Box 39, Folder: IVAC, Interagency Vietnam Adoption Committee, ISS papers.

119. Memo: ISS Hong Kong to ISS American Branch, August 6, 1971, Box 39, Folder: Vietnam ISS, 1971, ISS papers.

120. "Social History of Little Nguyen Van Hai," February 1973, Box 39, Folder: Vietnam, ISS papers.

121. As quoted in Dorothy Roberts, *Shattered Bonds: The Color of Child Welfare* (New York: Basic, 2002), ix.

122. Winthrop A. Rockwell, "Efforts Grow to Bring Here Babies That G.I.'s Left in Vietnam," *New York Times,* January 8, 1972.

123. Jacquelyn Dowd Hall, "The Long Civil Rights Movement and the Political Uses of the Past," *Journal of American History* 91, no. 4 (March 2005): 1255.

124. Matthew Lassiter, "The Suburban Origins of 'Color-Blind' Conservatism: Middle-Class Consciousness in the Charlotte Busing Crisis," *Journal of Urban History* 30, no. 4 (May 2004): 557, 558; and Omi and Winant, *Racial Formation*, 90.

125. "Urban Group Plan Bared," *Baltimore Sun*, August 2, 1965, 4.

126. Phyllis Feinstein, "Report on Interracial Adoption," *Parents*, December 1968, 48, 82–84; Ivan Doig, "Interracial Adoptions: How Are They Working?" *Parents*, Feb. 1971, 63–65; and "Beau Bridges Starts a New Family," *Ebony*, October 1970, 96–104.

127. Barbara Dolliver, "We're the Lucky Ones!" *Good Housekeeping*, December 1969, 90–91, 148–53.

128. Joyce Ladner, *Mixed Families: Adopting Across Racial Boundaries* (Garden City, N.Y.: Anchor/Doubleday, 1977), 93.

129. Feinstein, "Report on Interracial Adoption"; Doig, "Interracial Adoptions: How Are They Working?"; John Devaney, "Children No One Wanted," *Redbook*, December 1971, 68–70, 201–4; Regina Carlson, "Why Nursing a Baby Means Love to Me," *Redbook*, December 1973, 59–62; Gary Brooten, "Multiracial Family," *New York Times Magazine*, September 26, 1971, 78–80; and Charles Mangel, "Nine 'Unadoptable' Children Joined by Love," *Look*, October 19, 1965, 55–58.

130. Thomas E. Nutt and John A. Snyder, *Transracial Adoption* (Cambridge, Mass.: MIT, 1973), 36.

131. Ladner, *Mixed Families*, 94.

132. Phyllis LaFrage, "When the Adopted Child Comes Home: Adoptive Parent Societies," *McCall's*, October 1972, 66; Mrs. Frank Tschabold to Wells Klein, January 5, 1972, Box 19, Folder: Adoptive Parent Groups, ISS papers; and Doig, "Interracial Adoptions," 63.

133. Linda Greenhouse, "After Adoption, Their Families Are Interracial," *New York Times*, August 15, 1972, 26.

134. Karen Dubinsky, *Babies Without Borders: Adoption and Migration Across the Americas* (New York: New York University Press, 2010), 63.

135. Ladner, *Mixed Families*, 93.

136. "Report of IVAC Delegation Visit to South Vietnam," ix.

137. The one-drop rule is what anthropologists term a "hypodescent rule" because of its implications for a mixed person's status. See F. James Davis, "Defining Race: Comparative Perspectives," in *Mixed Messages: Multi-Racial Identities in the "Color-Blind" Era*, ed. David L. Brunsma (Boulder, Colo.: Lynne Rienner, 2006), 17. Also see David Parker and Miri Song, eds., *Rethinking "Mixed-Race"* (London: Pluto, 2001).

138. "Report of IVAC Delegation Visit to South Vietnam," 6.

139. "Proposal from the Interagency Vietnam Adoption Committee (IVAC) to the Department of Health, Education, and Welfare (HEW)," March 1974, 6.

140. Robert O. Self, *American Babylon: Race and the Struggle for Postwar Oakland* (Princeton, N.J.: Princeton University Press, 2005).

141. "Report of IVAC Delegation Visit to South Vietnam," 5.

142. Wells Klein to Onesta Carpene, September 19, 1972, Box 39, Folder: Vietnam ISS, 1972, ISS papers.

143. "Report of IVAC Delegation Visit to South Vietnam," 6.

144. "White Family, Black Child," *Christian Century*, May 9, 1973, 527.

Chapter 6. "Children of Controversy": Operation Babylift and the Crisis
of Humanitarianism, 1974–1976

1. Gerald R. Ford, "The President's News Conference," April 3, 1975, online by Gerhard Peters and John T. Woolley, *The American Presidency Project*; Military Press Summaries, April 3, 4, 1975, Box 2, Folder: Press Releases, April 2–7, 1975, Records Relating to Operations New Life and New Arrivals, 1975–1976, Records of the Army Staff.

2. Military Press Summaries, April 4, 5, 1975.

3. I borrow the term "can-do" policymaking from Penny Von Eschen in her masterful work of cultural diplomacy and policymaking, *Satchmo Blew Up the World: Jazz Ambassadors Play the Cold War* (Cambridge Mass.: Harvard University Press, 2004), 5. She uses the term to describe the foreign policy culture that gave U.S. legislators "extraordinary confidence" in using American institutions to shape world systems.

4. "From Forced Urbanization to Mass Baby-Snatching," *Viet Nam Courier*, May 1975, Douglas Pike Collection; Martin Woollacott, "Orphans as Propaganda," April 12, 1975, Douglas Pike Collection; and "Indo-China: The Orphans: Saved or Lost?" *Time*, April 21, 1975.

5. This is best exemplified by the perspectives of Elizabeth Bartholet and Rickie Solinger. Bartholet, a Harvard Law professor and adoptive mother of two Peruvian children, has become a champion for international and domestic adoption as the best solution for needy children. Solinger has countered that foreign adoption is a "consumer-related entitlement," akin to international kidnapping. In an assessment of Bartholet's book *Family Bonds*, Solinger posits, "a critic of ICA might identify Bartholet's acquisition of 'Peruvian treasures'—the boys she adopted—with the depredations of European invaders." See Rickie Solinger, *Beggars and Choosers: How the Politics of Choice Shapes Adoption, Abortion, and Welfare in the United States* (New York: Hill and Wang, 2001), 31–32; and Elizabeth Bartholet, *Family Bonds: Adoption and the Politics of Parenting* (New York: Houghton Mifflin, 1993).

6. Maria de los Angeles Torres, *The Lost Apple: Operation Pedro Pan, Cuban Children in the U.S., and the Promise of a Better Future* (Boston: Beacon, 2003); and Karen Dubinsky, *Babies Without Borders: Adoption and Migration Across the Americas* (New York: New York University Press, 2010).

7. Ford, "The President's News Conference," April 3, 1975.

8. Kathleen Ja Sook Berquist, "Operation Babylift or Babyabduction?: Implications of the Hague Convention on the Humanitarian Evacuation and Rescue of Children," *International Social Work* 52 (2009): 622.

9. House Subcommittee on Immigration, Citizenship, and International Law, *Hearing on Refugees from Indochina*, 94th Cong., 1st sess., April 8, 1975, 41, 43.

10. House Subcommittee, *Hearing on Refugees from Indochina*, April 8, 1975, 23

11. Daniel Parker to Theodore C. Marrs, April 3, 1975, Box 10, Folder: Indochina Refugees—Orphan Airlift, Theodore C. Marrs files.

12. Rosemary Taylor, *Orphans of War: Work with the Abandoned Children of Vietnam* (London: Collins, 1988), 154. Although Taylor published her book thirteen years after Babylift's end, she relied on journals, letters, and other documents from the period rather than her memory. Based on this, and my cross-checking with other sources, I find her account a reliable one.

13. At the last minute, Taylor and Grant backed out of Daly's flight, uncomfortable with his sensationalist bent. Cherie Clark's organization, Friends of Children in Vietnam, sent fifty

children instead. See Taylor, *Orphans of War*, 154; and Cherie Clark, *After Sorrow Comes Joy: One Woman's Struggle to Bring Hope to Thousands of Children in Vietnam and India* (Westminster, Colo.: Lawrence & Thomas, 2000), 136–38.

14. Letter reprinted in Dana Sachs, *The Life We Were Given: International Adoption, Operation Babylift, and the Children of War in Vietnam* (Boston: Beacon, 2010), 43–44. Bernardine Dohrn, Editorial, *New York Times*, April 18, 1975, clipping in Douglas Pike Collection, Vietnam Archive.

15. House Subcommittee, *Hearing on Refugees from Indochina*, April 8, 1975, 21.

16. UPI, Carl Ingram, Military Press Summaries, April 6, 1975, Box 4, Folder: Press Releases, April 2–7, 1975, Records of the Army Staff.

17. For example, the U.S. Air Force launched a mission in 1962 called Operation Lifeline that provided support to six orphanages. See Captain Rex Sullivan to Susan Pettiss, January 8, 1963, Box 38, Folder: ISS International, Vietnam Administrative Files, 1960–1964, ISS papers.

18. House Subcommittee, *Hearing on Refugees from Indochina*, April 8, 1975, 12–13.

19. Chronology of Actions, "1000 Vietnamese Orphans Action," April 3, 1975, Box 1, Folder: Army Staff Situation Reports, 1975. April 2–May 3, Records of the Army Staff.

20. General Walter Kerwin to DAS, April 3, 1975, Box 1, Folder: Army Staff Situation Reports, 1975. April 2–May 3, Records of the Army Staff.

21. Capt. H. M. Smith, Commander in Chief Pacific Command History, 1975, Appendix III, Babylift, 2–3, Douglas Pike Collection, Vietnam Archive.

22. Smith, Appendix III, Babylift, 2–5, 20, 29.

23. House Subcommittee, *Hearing on Refugees from Indochina*, April 8, 1975, 36. This "regular" or "informal consultation" dates from the Gulf of Tonkin resolution. See William C. Gibbons, "Vietnam and the Breakdown of Consensus," in *Foreign Policy and Domestic Consensus: The Credibility of Institutions, Policies and Leadership*, ed. Richard A. Malanson and Kenneth W. Thompson, vol. 11 (Lanham, Md.: University Press of America, 1985), 115.

24. *Congressional Record*-House, 94th Cong., 1st sess., March 18, 1975, p. 7082.

25. Robert David Johnson, *Congress and the Cold War* (Cambridge: Cambridge University Press, 2006), 112–13, 186, 190; Bruce W. Jentleson, *American Foreign Policy: The Dynamics of Choice in the 21st Century* (New York: Norton, 2004), 154–55; Gibbons, "Vietnam and the Breakdown of Consensus," 97–122; and Philip J. Briggs, *Making American Foreign Policy: President-Congress Relations from the Second World War to Vietnam* (Lanham, Md: University Press of America, 1991), 176–88.

26. Foreign Assistance Act of 1973, Public Law 93–189, U.S. Statutes at Large, December 17, 1973, 93rd Cong., 2nd sess.; and Study Mission Report, Subcommittee to Investigate Problems Connected with Refugees and Escapees, Committee on the Judiciary, U.S. Senate, *Relief and Rehabilitation of War Victims in Indochina: One Year After the Ceasefire*, 93rd Cong., 2nd sess., January 27, 1974, 46.

27. Senate Committee on Foreign Relations, *Hearing Vietnam Children's Care Agency*, S. 2497, April 5, 1972, 92nd Cong., 2nd sess., 16.

28. Josiah Bennett to William Dale, October 1, 1971, Box 16, Folder: SOC-Vietnamese-American Orphans, January–June 1971, State Department records. Also see *Hearing Relief and Rehabilitation of War Victims in Indochina, Part II: Orphans and Child Welfare*, May 11, 1973, 36; and Senate Committee, *Hearing Vietnam Children's Care Agency*.

29. Excerpt from *Congressional Record*, Senate, December 14, 1973, "Children of Vietnam: Orphans of War and Neglect," in Senate Subcommittee, *Relief and Rehabilitation of War Victims in Indochina: One Year After the Ceasefire*, January 27, 1974, 156.

30. Senate Subcommittee, *Relief and Rehabilitation of War Victims in Indochina: One Year After the Ceasefire*, January 27, 1974, 144–45.

31. Senate Subcommittee, *Relief and Rehabilitation of War Victims in Indochina*, May 11, 1973, 23.

32. Rhonda Butterfield to International Social Service, May 4, 1971, Box 39, Folder: Vietnam ISS, 1971, ISS papers.

33. Senate Subcommittee, *Relief and Rehabilitation of War Victims in Indochina*, May 11, 1973, 2.

34. Senate Subcommittee, *Hearing Vietnam Children's Care Agency*, April 5, 1972, 1–2.

35. Ibid., 39–40, 125–26.

36. Letter to the Editor from Winburn Thomas, *Christian Century*, October 6, 1971, 1181–82; and Senate Committee on Labor and Public Welfare to Wells Klein, November 12, 1971, Box 39, Folder: Vietnam: Legislation, ISS papers.

37. Wells Klein to John Negroponte, October 8, 1971, Box 39, Folder: Vietnam: Legislation, ISS papers; and Senate Subcommittee, *Hearing Vietnam Children's Care Agency*, April 5, 1972, 53.

38. Richard Nixon, "Statement on Signing the Foreign Assistance Act of 1971," February 7, 1972, *The American Presidency Project*.

39. Senate Subcommittee, *Vietnam Children's Care Agency*, April 5, 1972, 16; and *Congressional Record-Senate*, 92nd Cong., 2nd sess., April 20, July 17, July 24, 1972, 14700, 23947–48, 25100–25102.

40. Wells Klein to Etta Deutsch, American Council of Voluntary Agencies for Foreign Service, July 20, 1972, Box 39, Folder: Vietnam: Legislation, ISS papers; *Congressional Record-Senate*, April 25, 1972, 6599 6600, clipping in Box 39, Folder: Vietnam: Legislation, ISS papers; and Eugenie Hochfield to Wells Klein, April 11, 1972, Box 39, Folder: Vietnam: Legislation, ISS papers.

41. House Subcommittee, *Hearings on Refugees from Indochina*, April 8, 1975, 12–13.

42. Marvin Samuel Gross, "Refugee-Parolee: The Dilemma of the Indochina Refugee," *San Diego Law Review* 13 (1975–76): 175.

43. House Subcommittee, *Hearings on Refugees from Indochina*, April 8, 1975, 32–33; and Edward M. Kennedy, "Refugee Act of 1960," *International Migration Review* 15, no. 1–2 (Spring–Summer, 1981): 146.

44. House Subcommittee, *Hearings on Refugees from Indochina*, April 8, 1975, 2.

45. Ibid., 7, 10, 11, 14, 21, 34, 46.

46. Klein to Negroponte, October 8, 1971, p. 2, Box 39, Folder: Vietnam: Legislation, ISS papers.

47. Klein to Pat Nye, November 24, 1971, Folder: Vietnam ISS, 1971, Box 39, ISS papers.

48. Hinrichs to Taylor, September 11, 1975, p. 2, Box 3, Folder: Intercountry Program Committee, ISS papers.

49. WRS to Cherney, October 29, 1965, Box 38, Folder: ISS International, Vietnam Administrative Files, January 1965-December 1965, ISS papers.

50. Klein to Nye, November 24, 1971, Box 39, Folder: Vietnam ISS, 1971, ISS papers.

51. Appendix VI: Selected Press Reports and Commentary on the Problems of Orphans and Children in *Relief and Rehabilitation of War Victims in Indochina*, May 11, 1973, 95–108.

52. Taylor, *Orphans of War*, 25, 71; and Senate Subcommittee, *Vietnam Children's Care Agency*, 112–13.

53. Senate Subcommittee, *Vietnam Children's Care Agency*, 112.

54. Taylor, *Orphans of War*, 25, 28.

55. Ibid., 71, 102, 104.

56. Wendy Grant to WAIF Adoption Division, April 22, 1966, Box 38, Folder: Vietnam Adoptions, ISS papers. Later, Grant spells her first name "Wende."

57. Clark, *After Sorrow Comes Joy*, 136–39.

58. Taylor, *Orphans of War*, 102.

59. Dr. Alex Stalcup to Dr. Marrs, May 1975, Box 10, Folder: Indochina Refugees-Orphan Airlift, Theodore C. Marrs files, 1974–76, Ford Library.

60. John E. Adams, "Evacuation of Children from Indochina," January 1976, clipping in NCOCY Newsletter Monthly Focus, Box 38, Folder: Claim Returns-Vietnam Babylift, April 1975, ISS papers.

61. Patricia Nye to All ISS Units, April 11, 1975, 2, Box 38, Folder: Vietnam-Adoptions-sec. folder, ISS papers.

62. DOMS Watch Team Memo, FORSCOM AOC (Major Walsch) to DAMO-MS (Colonel Dunne), April 29, 1975, Box 2, Records of the Army Staff.

63. Nye to All ISS Units, April 11, 1975.

64. Adams, "Evacuation of Children from Indochina," April 1975.

65. Clark, *After Sorrow Comes Joy*, 155.

66. Minutes of Meeting of Subcommittee on Intercountry Program, February 9, 1976, Box 3, Folder: Intercountry Program Committee, ISS papers.

67. Point Paper for the Special Assistant to the Secretary and Deputy Secretary of Defense, April 16, 1975, Box 10, Folder: Indochina Refugees-Orphan Airlift, Theodore Marrs files.

68. This happened with a flight sponsored by Holt Adoption Services. AOC to ROMS, DOMS Watch Team Journal Form, April 4, 1975, Box 2, Folder: Orphan Evacuation AOC Journal Entries, 1975. 8–25 April, Records of the Army Staff.

69. Telegram from U.S. Embassy in Vietnam to State Dept., March 27, 1975, Box 10, Folder: Indochina Refugees-Orphan Airlift, Theodore Marrs files.

70. Edward Daly to Gerald Ford, April 14, 1975, Box 750, Folder: Daly, Edward J. (Ed), White House Central Files, Name File, Ford Library; and Sachs, *The Life We Were Given*, 28–29.

71. AP, *Oakland Tribune*, April 5, 1975.

72. Paul Ehrlich to the President, April 8, 1975; Adeline Smith to the President, April 25, 1975; Internal Memo from Russ Rourke to Jack Marsh, April 16, 1975; Internal Memo from Russ Rourke to Jack Marsh, May 23, 1975; and Roland Elliot to Paul Ehrlich, May 21, 1975, all in Box 750, Folder: Daly, Edward J. (Ed), White House Central Files, Name File, Ford Library.

73. Timothy Wirth to Attorney General William Smith, May 21, 1984, Box 101, Folder: C-5A Orphans Aircraft, Department of Justice records.

74. Internal memo from Dick Cheney to Ted Marrs, April 12, 1975; Communication log from Theodore Marrs to Dick Cheney, April 14, 1975; and Parker to Theodore Marrs, April 3, 1975, all in Box 10, Folder: Indochina Refugees-Orphan Airlift, Theodore C. Marrs files.

75. Edward C. Schmults, Deputy Attorney General, to Fred F. Fielding, Counsel to the President, April 10, 1982, Folder: C-5A (Orphan's Crash), Box 73, Department of Justice records; and Wirth to Smith, May 21, 1984.

76. Offer in Compromise, Action Memorandum, May 13, 1976; and Memorandum for the Deputy Attorney General, J. Paul McGrath, Assistant Attorney General Civil Division, August 18, 1982, both in Folder: C-5A (Orphan's Crash), Box 73, Department of Justice records.

77. Taylor, *Orphans of War*, 245–50.

78. *Nguyen Da Yen et al. v. Kissinger*, Center for Constitutional Rights, accessed January 4, 2012, http://ccrjustice.org/ourcases/past-cases/nguyen-da-yen%2C-et-al.-v.-kissinger; and "People & Events: Operation Babylift (1975)," American Experience, accessed January 4, 2012, http://www.pbs.org/wgbh/amex/daughter/peopleevents/e_babylift.html.

79. "Findings of Fact and Conclusions of Law and Order," *Nguyen Da Yen et al. v. Kissinger et al.*, 528 F.2d 1194 (1975), 3.

80. Brief of Appellee/Cross-Appellant, *Nguyen Da Yen et al. v. Kissinger et al.*, 528 F.2d 1194 (1975), 11, 19, 22.

81. Alona E. Evans, "*Nguyen Da Yen et al. v. Kissinger et al.* 528 F.2d 1194," *American Journal of International Law* 70, no. 4 (October 1976): 843.

82. Operation Babylift Lawsuit summary, 4, Box 38, Folder: TAISSA-Adoption-Babylift, ISS papers.

83. Transcript, December 17, 1975, as cited in *Nguyen Da Yen et al. v. Kissinger et al.*, 70 F.R.D. 656 (1976) opinion, 19–20.

84. *Nguyen Da Yen et al. v. Kissinger*, 528 F.2d 1194 (1975); Evans, "*Nguyen Da Yen v. Kissinger* 528 F.2d 1194," 843; *Nguyen Da Yen et al. v. Kissinger*, Center for Constitutional Rights website; and *Daughter from Danang*, DVD, dir. Gail Dolgin and Vicente Franco (USA: Balcony Releasing, 2002).

85. Jeremy Roche, "Children: Rights, Participation, and Citizenship," *Childhood* 6, no. 4 (November 1999): 484.

86. Taylor, *Orphans of War*, 222.

87. Roche, "Children: Rights, Participation, and Citizenship," 479.

88. House Subcommittee, *Hearings on Refugees from Indochina*, April 8, 1975, 91.

89. Military Press Summaries, April 3–13, 1975.

90. Ingram, Military Press Summaries, April 5, 1975.

91. Tom Cockburn, "Children and Citizenship in Britain: A Case for a Socially Interdependent Model of Citizenship," *Childhood* 5, no. 1 (February 1998): 109. For more on the changing legal status of children in early America, see Holly Brewer, *By Birth or Consent: Children, Law, and the Anglo-American Revolution in Authority* (Chapel Hill: Omohundro Institute of Early American History and Culture and University of North Carolina Press, 2005).

92. Roche, "Children: Rights, Participation, and Citizenship," 477; and Ollie Stewart, "Fruits of War," *Baltimore Afro-American*, April 19, 1975, 4.

93. Military Press Summaries, April 5, 1975.

94. John Balaban, "Doing Good," *Hudson Review* 29, no. 4 (Winter 1976–1977): 567.

95. Johnny Adger to ISS, December 22, 1975, Box 39, Folder: Vietnam, ISS papers.

96. Sachs, *The Life We Were Given*, 12–16; and Clark, *After Sorrow Comes Joy*, 182–83. Also see James Michael Hoffman, "Operation Babylift Lawsuit Hearing: Observer's Report," January 20, 1976, Box 38, Folder: TAISSA-Adoption-Babylift, ISS papers.

97. House Subcommittee, *Hearings on Refugees from Indochina*, April 8, 1975, 38–40, 88.

98. T. H. Marshall, *Citizenship and Social Class* (London: Cambridge University Press, 1950).

99. Cockburn, "Children and Citizenship in Britain," 102. The theory of interdependence comes from works on gendered citizenship such as Leena Alanen, "Gender and Generation: Feminism and the 'Child Question'," in *Childhood Matters: Social Theory, Practice, and Politics*, ed. Jens Qvortrup et al. (Aldershot: Avebury, 1994). Also see Nira Yuval-Davis and Pnina Werbner, *Women, Citizenship and Difference* (London: Zed, 1999), Introduction.

100. Immigration and Nationality Act, October 3, 1965, Public Law 89–236, U.S. Statutes at Large 911.

101. Lori Askeland, *Children and Youth in Adoption, Orphanages, and Foster Care: A Historical Handbook and Guide* (Westport, Conn.: Greenwood, 2006).

102. Joseph Goldstein, Anna Freud, and Albert J. Solnit, *Beyond the Best Interests of the Child* (New York: Free Press, 1973), 17–20.

103. "Summary of Developments in the Hearing of December 17, 1975," Box 38, Folder: ISS International, Vietnamese Administrative Files, January–December 1965, ISS papers.

104. "Indo-China: The Orphans: Saved or Lost?"

105. Commentary in South Vietnamese newspaper *Trang Den*, translated in *Saigon Post*, April 12, 1975 as cited in Sachs, *The Life We Were Given*, 81.

106. House Subcommittee, *Hearings on Refugees from Indochina*, April 8, 1975, 24; and "Indo-China: The Orphans: Saved or Lost?"

107. Taylor, *Orphans of War*, 222.

108. Bill Paul, "Vietnam Refugees Find Starting Anew Is a Frustrating Ordeal," *Wall Street Journal*, May 22, 1975.

109. Cockburn, "Children and Citizenship in Britain," 107.

110. Deptartment of State, "Special Report: Indochina Refugee Resettlement," August 1975, 5, Box 32, Folder 10, Douglas Pike Collection.

111. Shirley Peck-Barnes, *"The War Cradle": The Untold Story of "Operation Babylift"* (Denver: Vintage Pressworks, 2000), 34.

112. Gross, "Refugee-Parolee," 175, 183, 189.

113. Jimmy Carter, "Status of Indochina Refugees: Letter to Senate and House Committee Chairmen Transmitting a Report," June 23, 1977, *American Presidency Project*, http://www.presidency.ucsb.edu/ws/?pid = 7715.

114. 1977 Amendment to the Indochina Migration and Refugee Assistance Act, Public Law 95–145, 91 U.S. Statutes at Large, 1223, October 28, 1977.

115. Eugenie Hochfield to Miss Phan Ngoc Quoi, re: Status of Vietnamese Children Born out of Wedlock, July 29, 1969, Box 38, Folder: Vietnam-Adoptions, ISS papers.

116. Internal Memo, Dept. of State: AID, May 1971, Box 38, Folder: Vietnam-Conference on the Special Needs of Children in Vietnam-July 19, 1971, ISS papers; *Congressional Record-House*, 94th Cong., 1st sess., March 12, 1975, 6349; and March 18, 1975, 7082; and quoted in Don Luce, "Amer-Asian Children in Vietnam," *Christian Century*, August 25, 1971, 996–97.

117. Josiah Bennett to William Dale, October 1, 1971, Box 16, Folder: SOC-Vietnamese-American Orphans, July–December 1971, State Department Records.

118. Moses to Grant, December 7, 1973, as cited in Taylor, *Orphans of War*, 99–100, emphasis mine.

119. John Adams to Klein, January 13, 1976, Box 38, Folder: Claim Returns-Vietnam Babylift, April 1975, ISS papers.

120. Burke to Mondale, n.d.; Mondale to Winston, June 29, 1965; and Winston to Mondale, July 12, 1965, Box 1033, Folder: Non-Resident Problems (Includes Juvenile Immigration, Transient Boys), July 1965, 1963–1968, USCB papers.

121. Paul Brinkley-Rogers, "A New Family for Duong Muoi," *Newsweek*, as cited in *Relief and Rehabilitation of War Victims in Indochina*, May 11, 1973, 98.

122. Shana Alexander, "A Sentimental Binge," *Newsweek*, April 28, 1975.

123. Erica Lee, *At America's Gates: Chinese Immigration During the Exclusion Era, 1882–1943* (Chapel Hill: University of North Carolina Press, 2003).

124. John Pascal, "Love Just Wasn't Enough," *Newsday*, May 23, 1975; "The Babylift Babies: Byron and Lana Noone and Their Adopted Children," *VVA Veteran*, January–February 2004; David V. Pyle, "Of the Nurses Who Took Part in Operation Babylift . . . ," *Vietnam*, April 1995; and Bob Shane, "Courage Revisited—World Airways Returns to Vietnam," *Airport Journals*, August 2005, all in Box 1, Folder 5, Byron and Lana Noone Collection.

125. See Henry Jessup, "Babylift Mother Delivers Hope for Vietnamese-American Reconciliation," clipping from Box 1, Folder 5, Byron & Lana Noone Collection, Vietnam Archive. See also Noone interview by author, October 2009.

126. Nye to All ISS Units, April 11, 1975, 2, Box 38, Folder: Vietnam-Adoptions-sec. folder, ISS papers.

Epilogue. The Legacy of Voluntarism: International Adoption in the Twenty-First Century

1. Intercountry Adoption Statistics, Bureau of Consular Affairs, U.S. Department of State, accessed June 11, 2012, https://travel.state.gov/content/adoptionsabroad/en/about-us/statistics .htmll; and Tobias Hübinette, *Comforting an Orphaned Nation* (Seoul: Jimoondang, 2006).

2. Karen Balcom, *The Traffic in Babies: Cross-Border Adoption, Baby-Selling and the Development of Child Welfare Systems in the United States and Canada, 1930–1960* (Toronto: University of Toronto Press, 2011), 237.

3. UN General Assembly, Declaration on the Rights of the Child (1959).

4. Committee on International Social Development, January 19, 1973, Box 17, Folder: UN Reports on International Adoption Law, ISS papers.

5. UN General Assembly, Convention on the Rights of the Child (1989).

6. "Conventions on the Rights of the Child," UNICEF.

7. Hague Conference on Private International Law, Convention on Protection of Children and Co-operation in Respect of Intercountry Adoption, May 29, 1993, accessed June 11, 2012, and U.S. Department of State, Understanding the Hague Convention, Bureau of Consular Affairs, The Intercountry Adoption Act of 2000 designated the State Department as the central authority for adoption compliance and regulation. See Public Law 106–279, 114 Stat. 825, October 6, 2000.

8. Melissa Gray, "Orphanage: Adoption Plan Needed for Haitian Children," *CNN World*, January 15, 2010; David Gauthier-Villars, Miriam Jordan, and Joel Millman, "Earthquake Exposes Haiti's Faulty Adoption System," *Wall Street Journal*, February 27, 2010; Judy Peet, "After Haiti Earthquake, Spike in Adoption Requests Benefits Other Countries in Need," *New Jersey Star-Ledger*, April 3, 2010; "Americans Rush to Adopt Orphaned Haitian Kids," *NBC Today Show*, January 20, 2010.

9. Barack Obama: "Statement by the Press Secretary: United States Government Haiti Earthquake Disaster Response Update," January 20, 2010, *The American Presidency Project*, http://www.presidency.ucsb.edu/ws/?pid=89892, accessed June 11, 2012.

10. Ginger Thompson, "After Haiti Quake, the Chaos of U.S. Adoptions," *New York Times*, August 4, 2010, A1.

11. Ginger Thompson, "Case Stokes Haiti's Fear for Children, and Itself," *New York Times*, February 2, 2010, A1; and James C. McKinley, Jr., "53 Haitian Orphans Are Airlifted to U.S," *New*

York Times, January 20, 2010, A9. Also see John Seabrook, "'The Last Babylift': Adopting a Child in Haiti," *New Yorker*, May 10, 2010, 49.

12. John M. Simmons, "Why the Decline in International Adoptions," *Huffington Post*, April 8, 2014.

13. Kathryn Joyce, "The Evangelical Adoption Crusade," *The Nation*, April 21, 2011; and Burning Both Ends website, http://bothendsburning.org/about-us/history/, accessed June 17, 2015.

14. *Stuck*, dir. Thaddeus Scheel (2013; Los Angeles: Samuel Goldwyn Films, 2013); and *Relief and Rehabilitation of War Victims in Indochina*, January 27, 1974, 160.

15. "Haitian Kids Await Adoption in Pittsburgh," *CBS News*, January 20, 2010.

16. Susan Saulny, "Girls' Rescue from Haiti Expands Family by Two," *New York Times*, January 26, 2010, A12.

17. Ibid.

18. Jeff Katz, "Haitian Adoption: What It Says About America," *Huffington Post*, January 27; and Cathy Chermol, "American Mom Brings Two Haitian Orphans Home," *Essence*, January 22, 2010.

19. Damien Cave, "At a Family's Home in Tennessee, Reminders of a Boy Sent to Russia," *New York Times*, April 11, 2010, A16. This incident, in part, led to a Russian law that, beginning in 2013, banned U.S. families from adopting Russian children.

20. Maggie Jones, "Why a Generation of Adoptees Is Returning to South Korea," *New York Times Magazine*, January 14, 2015, 36.

21. Saulny, "Girls' Rescue from Haiti Expands Family by Two."

22. *Stuck* (2013); and Jonathan Wander, "Love and Haiti," *Pittsburgh Magazine*, January 2009. The media coverage never explicitly mentioned whether Dieunette's birth mother was there when the orphanage staff arrived.

23. Zach Pluhacek, "Haitian Orphans Come Home to Nebraska," *Lincoln Journal Star*, January 22, 2012.

24. David Smolin, "A False Dilemma," *New York Times Online*, February 1, 2010.

25. Nick Cullather, *The Hungry World: America's Cold War Battle Against Poverty in Asia* (Cambridge, Mass.: Harvard University Press, 2010), 229.

26. Kathryn Close, *Transplanted Children: A History* (New York: U.S. Committee for the Care of European Children, 1953), 69.

SELECT BIBLIOGRAPHY

Archives/Papers

Child Welfare League of America papers, Social Welfare History Archives, University of Minnesota.

Douglas Pike Collection, Byron and Lana Noone Collection, Vietnam Center and Archive, Texas Tech University.

Florence Wyckoff papers, Bancroft Library, University of California, Berkeley.

Gus Edson papers, Irwin Hasen cartoons, and Belfer Audio Archive, Special Collections Research Center, Syracuse University Library.

International Social Service-American Branch papers, Social Welfare History Archives, University of Minnesota.

Margaret Herrick Library, Special Collections, Academy of Motion Picture Arts and Sciences.

National Association of Black Social Workers papers, SUNY Albany Special Collections.

National Urban League papers and NAACP papers, Manuscript Division, Library of Congress.

Public Welfare Law Section, Department of Justice, California State Archives.

Theodore C. Marrs Files and White House Central Files, Gerald R. Ford Library.

U.S. Children's Bureau papers; Department of Defense records; Senate Judiciary Committee records; Department of Justice records; Records of the Army Staff; State Department records; Displaced Persons records; and U.S. Foreign Assistance Agency records, all at the National Archives.

Books/Articles/Reports

Aeby, John. *A Home for Every Child*. Eugene, Ore.: Holt International Children's Services, 1986.

American Experience. "People & Events: Operation Babylift (1975)." http://www.pbs.org/wgbh/amex/daughter/peopleevents/e_babylift.html. Accessed August 17, 2016.

Bell, Harry. *We Adopted a Daughter*. Boston: Houghton Mifflin, 1954.

Bernard, Viola. *Adoption*. New York: Child Welfare League of America, 1964.

Bradley, Trudy. *An Exploration of Caseworkers' Perceptions of Adoptive Applicants: Final Report No. R-4, U.S. Children's Bureau and Department of Health, Education, and Welfare*. New York: Child Welfare League of America, 1967.

Brown, Florence G. *Adoption of Children with Special Needs: Older Children, Children of Minority Groups*. New York: Child Welfare League of America, March 1958.

Cady, Ernest. *We Adopted Three*. New York: William Sloane Associates, 1952.

Carson, Ruth. *So You Want to Adopt a Baby*. New York: Public Affairs Committee, 1951.

Center for Constitutional Rights. Historic Case, *Nguyen Da Yen et al. v. Kissinger*. Accessed January 4, 2012. http://ccrjustice.org/ourcases/past-cases/nguyen-da-yen%2C-et-al.-v.-kissinger.

Charnley, Jean. *The Art of Child Placement*. Minneapolis: University of Minnesota Press, 1955.

Child Welfare League of America. *Child Welfare League of America Standards for Adoption Service*. New York: Child Welfare League, 1958.

———. *Quantitative Approaches to Parent Selection*. New York: Child Welfare League, 1962.

———. *Standards for Adoption Service*. New York: Child Welfare League, 1959.

Clark, Cherie. *After Sorrow Comes Joy: One Woman's Struggle to Bring Hope to Thousands of Children in Vietnam and India*. Westminster, Colo.: Lawrence & Thomas, 2000.

Close, Kathryn. *Transplanted Children: A History*. New York: U.S. Committee for the Care of European Children, 1953.

Consumers Union. *The Consumers Union Report on Family Planning: A Guide to Contraceptive Methods and Materials, With a Special Section on Infertility and What to Do About It*. Mount Vernon, N.Y.: Consumers Union, 1962.

———. *The Consumers Union Report on Family Planning: A Guide to Contraceptive Methods and Materials for Use in Child Spacing, Techniques for Improving Fertility, and Recognized Adoption Procedures*. Mount Vernon, N.Y.: Consumers Union of U.S., 1966.

Dorow, Sara. *I Wish for You a Beautiful Life: Letters from the Korean Birth Mothers of Ae Ran Won to Their Children*. St. Paul, Minn.: Yeong & Yeong, 1999.

Doss, Carl and Helen Doss. *If You Adopt a Child*. New York: Henry Holt, 1957.

Doss, Helen. *The Family Nobody Wanted*. Chicago: Peoples Book, 1954.

Dumpson, Dr. James. Career Highlights. Accessed March 30, 2016. http://legacy.fordham.edu/campus_resources/enewsroom/archives/archive_2600.asp.

Dunker, Marilee Pierce. *Man of Vision, Woman of Prayer*. Nashville, Tenn.: Thomas Nelson, 1980.

Fradkin, Helen. *The Adoption Home Study*. Trenton: State of New Jersey; Department of Institutions and Agencies; Department of Public Welfare; Bureau of Children's Services, 1963.

Goldstein, Joseph, Anna Freud, and Albert J. Solnit. *Beyond the Best Interests of the Child*. New York: Free Press, 1973.

Gordon, Henrietta L. *Adoption Practices, Procedures and Problems: Report of Workshop Material and Proceedings of the Adoption Conference, Held May 19–21, 1948 in New York City*. New York: Child Welfare League of America, 1949.

———. *Adoption Practice, Procedures and Problems: A Report of the Second Workshop Held in New York City Under the Auspices of the Child Welfare League of America, May 10–12, 1951*. New York: Child Welfare League of America, 1952.

Hague Conference on Private International Law. Convention on Protection of Children and Co-operation in Respect of Intercountry Adoption, May 29, 1993. Accessed June 11, 2012. http://www.hcch.net/upload/conventions/txt33en.pdf;

Hill, Patricia Ruth. *The World Their Household: The American Women's Foreign Mission Movement and Cultural Transformation, 1870–1920*. Ann Arbor: University of Michigan Press, 1985.

Hilliard, David and Lewis Cole. *This Side of Glory: The Autobiography of David Hilliard and the Story of the Black Panther Party*. New York: Lawrence Hill, 1993.

Hochfield, Eugenie. "Problems of Intercountry Adoptions." *Children* 1, no. 4 (1954): 143–47.

Holt, Bertha. *Bring My Sons from Afar: The Unfolding of Harry Holt's Dream*. Eugene, Ore.: Holt International Children's Services, 1986.

Holt, Bertha and David Wisner. *The Seed from the East.* Los Angeles: Oxford Press, 1956.

Hyde, Robert. *Six More at Sixty.* Garden City, N.Y.: Doubleday, 1960.

Kirk, H. David. *Shared Fate: A Theory and Method of Adoptive Relationships.* Rev. ed. Port Angeles, Wash.: Ben-Simon, 1984.

Kornitzer, Margaret. *Child Adoption in the Modern World.* New York: Philosophical Library, 1952.

Ladner, Joyce. *Mixed Families: Adopting Across Racial Boundaries.* Garden City, N.Y.: Anchor/Doubleday, 1977.

Lazarsfeld, Paul and Robert Merton, "Mass Communication, Popular Taste, and Organized Social Action." In *The Communication of Ideas,* ed. Lyman Bryson. Cambridge, Mass.: MIT Press, 1948.

Leber, George J. *The History of the Order of AHEPA (The American Hellenic Educational Progressive Association) 1922–1972; Including the Greeks in the New World, and Immigration to the United States.* Washington, D.C.: Order of AHEPA, 1972.

Mall, E. Jane. *P.S. I Love You.* St. Louis: Concordia, 1961.

Thayer, Stuart. "Moppets on the Market: The Problem of Unregulated Adoption." *Yale Law Journal* 59, 4 (March 1950): 715–36.

Moynihan, Daniel Patrick. "The Negro Family: The Case for National Action." March 1965, Office of Policy Planning and Research, U.S. Department of Labor.

National Council of the Churches of Christ in the U.S.A., Commission on Social Welfare. *Religious Factors in Child Adoption, a Study Document.* New York: National Council of Churches of Christ in the U.S.A., 1965.

Nutt, Thomas E. and John A. Snyder. *Transracial Adoption.* Cambridge, Mass.: MIT, 1973.

Office of Armed Forces Information and Education, Department of Defense. *Manual on Intercountry Adoption: For Use in Guidance of U.S. Service Couples Seeking to Adopt a Foreign Child.* Washington, D.C.: GPO, January 1959.

———. *Manual on Intercountry Adoption: For Use in Guidance of U.S. Service Couples Seeking to Adopt a Foreign Child.* Washington, D.C.: GPO, February 1963.

Palmer, Frances. *And Four to Grow On.* New York: Holt, Rinehart, 1958.

Poling, Lillian D. *Mothers of Men: A Twenty-Five Year History of the American Mothers of the Year, 1935–1959.* Bridgeport, Conn.: Kurt H. Volk, 1959.

Schapiro, Michael. *A Study of Adoption Practice: Adoption Agencies and the Children They Serve.* New York: Child Welfare League of America, 1956.

Spock, Benjamin. *Baby and Child Care,* Cardinal ed. New York: Pocket Books, 1957.

Stride, Edna Violet. *Led by His Hand.* Upland, CA: Amko News, 1963.

Taylor, Rosemary and Wende Grant. *Orphans of War: Work with the Abandoned Children of Vietnam.* London: Collins, 1988.

UN Department of Economic and Social Affairs. *Comparative Analysis of Adoption Laws.* New York: UN Department of Economic and Social Affairs, 1956.

———. *Study on Adoption of Children: A Study on the Practice and Procedures Related to the Adoption of Children.* New York: UN Department of Social Affairs, 1953.

U.S. Children's Bureau. *The Social Worker's Part in Adoption.* Washington, D.C.: U.S. Health, Education, and Welfare, 1958.

U.S. Office of Armed Forced Information & Education, Department of Defense. *Manual on Intercountry Adoption: For Use in Guidance of U.S. Service Couples Seeking to Adopt a Foreign Child (DOD Pam 6–11).* Washington, D.C.: GPO, January 26, 1959. West, Helen Louise. *Adopted Four and Had One More.* St. Louis: Bethany, 1968.

Winter, Marjorie M. *For Love of Martha*. New York: Julian Messner, 1956.

Witmer, Helen L., Elizabeth Herzog, Eugene A. Weinstein, and Mary E. Sullivan. *Independent Adoptions: A Follow-Up Study*. New York: Russell Sage Foundation, 1963.

Wittenborn, John Richard and Barbara Myers. *The Placement of Adoptive Children*. Springfield, Ill.: Charles Thomas, 1957.

World Health Organization. "Joint UN/WHO Meeting of Experts on the Mental-Health Aspects of Adoption: Final Report." *WHO Technical Report Series* 70 (September 1953): 1–19.

Magazines

Airport Journals
America: The National Catholic Review
American Mercury
Childhood Magazine
Children Today
Christian Century
Coronet
Ebony
Good Housekeeping
Harper's
Independent
Life
Look
McCall's
The Nation
Newsday
Newsweek
Parents Magazine
Pittsburgh Magazine
Reader's Digest
Redbook
Saturday Evening Post
Time
VVA Veteran
Vietnam
Woman's Home Companion

Newspapers

Albuquerque Journal
Atlanta Daily World
Baltimore Sun
Baltimore Afro-American
Boston Globe

Chicago Defender
Chicago Tribune
Lincoln Journal Star
Los Angeles Sentinel
Los Angeles Times
New Jersey Star-Ledger
New York Times
Pittsburgh Courier
Oakland Tribune
Oregonian
Register-Guard (Eugene, Ore.)
San Francisco Examiner
San Mateo Times
Seattle Times
Sun Reporter (San Francisco)
Vidette Messenger (Valparaiso, Ind.)
Vietnam Courier
Wall Street Journal
Washington Post

Government Documents

Congressional Record
House Judiciary Committee and Subcommittee Hearings, Published and Unpublished
Immigration and Refugee Statutes-at-Large.
Senate Judiciary Committee and Subcommittee Hearings, Published and Unpublished

INDEX

ACKNOWLEDGMENTS

I OFTEN TELL MY STUDENTS that what seems like a burst of individual creativity is actually the result of steady collaboration, big-hearted peers, and lots of work. Nothing could demonstrate this adage more than *The Best Possible Immigrants*. My interest in learning more about international adoption's history came when I worked as a program director for an adoption agency in the mid-2000s. In addition to offering a strategic vantage point from which to understand the system's many jurisdictional complexities, I grew to admire the colleagues and clients who graciously brought me alongside as they taught me about the multiple ways of forming families. It was because of their stories that I wanted to understand how international adoption "came to be." To express my gratitude for their inspiration and friendship, this book is dedicated to them.

This project has benefited from the support of many key institutions. I am grateful to the University of California, Santa Barbara Graduate Division for research and writing funding. Westmont College, UC Santa Barbara History Department, UC Santa Barbara History Associates, and the University of Minnesota's Social Welfare History Archives also provided research and travel support. Without the expansive knowledge and efficient work of Dave Klaassen and Linnea Anderson at the Social Welfare History Archives, this project would have suffered. I also thank archivists at the National Archives in Washington, D.C., and College Park, Library of Congress, Ford Library, Vietnam Archive at Texas Tech University, Syracuse University Library Special Collections, California State Archives, California State Library, Bancroft Library, and Margaret Herrick Film Library. The InterLibrary Loan Departments at Westmont College and the University of California, Santa Barbara responded competently to my frequent requests. I garnered useful feedback from presentations on early versions of chapters at the American Historical Association, Berkshire Conference on the History of Women, the Society for the History of Childhood and Youth, the

Western Association of Women Historians, and the Cold War Studies Conference. A revised version of Chapter 3 was originally published in the *Journal of Policy History*. My thanks to the editors for allowing me to reprint portions of my article, "Immigration Law and Improvised Policy in the Making of International Adoption."

This book found the right home at the University of Pennsylvania Press under the supervision of Bob Lockhart. From the start, Bob advocated for this project with determination and spirit. His editorial acumen, along with Stephen Pitti and two anonymous reviewers, also refined my ideas and prose. Penn Press staff Alison Anderson and Amanda Ruffner efficiently guided the manuscript through the publication process and Sister Mary Jean's sharp copyediting caught many errors. Thanks go to John Hubbard for the cover design. I am indebted to Lisa Jacobson for her thoughtful comments, keen editing, and patience. She never failed to be both demanding and kind—proving to be just what I needed. Much of what I have learned about policy history and the welfare state comes from Alice O'Connor. Her insights sustained my focus and significantly improved the quality of this book. This project began over a decade ago under the supervision of Becky Kluchin and Joseph Pitti. Both offered invaluable counsel and friendship. As an undergraduate student, I completed an honors research project supervised by the generous and indefatigable Joan Shelley Rubin. Her coaching made the pursuit of graduate school in history a possibility.

Throughout the process, a host of mentors, colleagues, and friends read chapter drafts, commented on arguments, and asked the right questions. Thanks to Todd Holmes, Salim Yaqub, Mary Hancock, Jane De Hart, Paul Baltimore, Paul Hirsch, Roger Eardley-Pryor, Nicole Pacino, Tim Daniels, Jill Briggs, Sarah Skripsky, Karen Balcom, Laura Kalman, Ellen Herman, Chris Endy, E. Wayne Carp, Allison Varzally, Andrea Thabet Waldman, Leandra Zarnow, Beth Cruz, Mike Hernberg, Malina Dunk Walker, Patricia Schechter, Dan Ribbens, Margaret Chapman, and Jason Stohler. Special thanks to Ken Hough for directing me to *Dondi*. Terina and Joey Chen and Pat and Kendra Conley hosted me during research trips and made the weeks away from home enjoyable. Westmont College has been a supportive academic home to me. I especially thank Alister Chapman, Heather Keaney, Chandra Mallampali, Rick Pointer, Marianne Robins, Felicia Song, Judy Alexandre, Sarah Skripsky, Holly Beers, Jamie Friedman, Helen Rhee, Michelle Hughes, Omedi Ochieng, Ruben Tito Paredes, Andrea Gurney, Cynthia Toms, Alexandra Lillenberg, Paige Clenney, Angela D'Amour,

Ruby Jeanne Shelton, Jim Wright, Savannah Kelly, Chris Milner, and Mark Sargent.

My family has endured many years of a preoccupied daughter and sister during holidays and vacations. In spite of this, they have consistently provided housing, transportation, and comforting food during research trips and conferences. I am thankful for Penelope and Michael Rains, Josh and Rebecca Rains, Allison Rains, Spencer and Meggan Rains, Edwin and Jo-Ann Winslow, Keith and Amber Winslow, and Andrew and Liz Winslow for their support. My deepest gratitude goes to the two forces of nature who share everyday life with me. James selflessly shouldered extra household and childcare responsibilities so that I could squeeze in necessary hours of writing. And Logan reminded me that breaks to play with animals, dinosaurs, and Legos were necessary for my well being. Their love is the best kind of collaboration.